THEOLOGICAL
INVESTIGATIONS

Volume IV

THEOLOGICAL INVESTIGATIONS

VOLUME IV
More Recent Writings

by

KARL RAHNER

Translated by

KEVIN SMYTH

LONDON
DARTON, LONGMAN & TODD
NEW YORK
THE SEABURY PRESS

1974
DARTON, LONGMAN & TODD LTD
85 Gloucester Road, London, S.W.7
ISBN 0 232 48213 6

A Crossroad Book
THE SEABURY PRESS
815 Second Avenue, New York, N.Y. 10017
Library of Congress Catalog Card No.: 61-8189

A Translation of
SCHRIFTEN ZUR THEOLOGIE, IV
published by Verlagsanstalt Benziger & Co. AG., Einsiedeln

© Darton, Longman & Todd Ltd. 1966 and 1974
First published 1966

Reproduced and printed by photolithography and bound in
Great Britain at The Pitman Press, Bath
Nihil obstat: Lionel Swain, S.T.D., L.S.S., Censor Deputatus.
Imprimatur: Patritius Casey, Vic. Gen. Westmonasterii, die 10a Octobris, 1971.

CONTENTS

LIST OF ABBREVIATIONS

ASS	Acta Apostolicae Sedis
Am. Eccl. Rev.	American Ecclesiastical Review
Arch. T. Gran.	Archivo Teologico Granadino
Bijdr.	Bijdragen
Blätter f. d. Philos.	Blätter für die Philosophie
Bull. Thom.	Bulletin Thomiste
CIC	Codex Iuris Canonici
Coll. Theol.	Collectanea Theologica
CSEL	Corpus Scriptorum Ecclesiasticorum Latinorum
Denz.	Denzinger-Rahner, Enchiridion Symbolorum (1953)
DSAM	Dictionnaire de Spiritualité Ascétique et Mystique
DTC	Dictionnaire de Théologie Catholique
D. Th.	Divus Thomas
Estud. Eccl.	Estudios Ecclesiasticos
ETL	Ephemerides Theologicae Lovanienses
Franz. Stud.	Franziskaner Studien
GCS	Griechische Christliche Schriftsteller
Greg.	Gregorianum
GuL	Geist und Leben
LTK	Lexicon für Theologie und Kirche (2nd ed.)
Mar.	Marianum. Ephemerides Mariologicae
Münch. Theol. Z.	Münchener Theologische Zeitschrift
NRT	Nouvelle Revue Théologique
PG	Patrologiae graecae, ed. J. P. Migne (Paris 1844-)
Phil. Jahrb. d. Görresges.	Philologisches Jahrbuch der Görresgesellschaft

PL	Patrologiae latinae, ed. J.P. Migne (Paris 1857–)
RAM	Revue d'Ascétique et Mystique
Rev. Dioc. Nam.	Revue Diocésaine de Namur
Rev. M. A. Lat.	Revue du Moyen Age Latin
Rev. Univ. Ottawa	Revue de l'Université d'Ottawa
RSPT	Revue des Sciences Philosophiques et Théologiques
RSR	Recherches de Science Religieuse
RT	Revue Thomiste
Sc. Eccl.	Sciences Ecclésiastiques
Schol.	Scholastik
Stud. Cath.	Studia Catholica
Stud. Gen.	Studia Generalia
Theol. Lit. Z.	Theologische Literaturzeitung
Th. Gl.	Theologie und Glaube
Th. Rv.	Theologische Revue
TQ	Theologische Quartalschrift
TS	Theological Studies
TU	Texte und Untersuchungen
Tüb. Th. Quartalschrift	Tübinge Theologische Quartalschrift
TWNT	Theologisches Wörterbuch zum Neuen Testament (Kittel)
Wi. Wei.	Wissenschaft und Weisheit
ZKG	Zeitschrift für Kirchengeschichte
ZKT	Zeitschrift für Katholische Theologie
Z. Phil. Forsch.	Zeitschrift der Philosophischen Forschung

PREFACE

This new volume of my 'Theological Writings' (*Schriften zur Theologie*) brings together the essays on dogmatic theology which I have written since the first three volumes appeared, that is, since 1956. The attention which was accorded to the three similar volumes which preceded it may be taken as sufficient justification for this new collection. It is given the sub-title 'More Recent Essays' to indicate that they cover the same general field of theology as the first three volumes, and that the present essays, as far as the contents are concerned, should be inserted *between* the essays of the earlier volumes. Since this could not be done, for technical reasons, and out of consideration for the owners of the first three volumes of 'Writings', these essays simply follow the earlier ones and appear as 'more recent' in time. Given the objective connexion which exists between dogmatic investigations and considerations on pastoral theology based on dogma, it is not surprising that some of the essays which I collected in my book *Sendung und Gnade, Beiträge zur Pastoraltheologie* (2nd edn., Innsbruck 1959) would have fitted just as well into this volume—and vice versa ('Mission and Grace: Contributions to Pastoral Theology'). The relevant pieces there are chiefly: 'Redemptive reality in created reality', 'The meaning of the individual Christian in the history of salvation', 'Thanksgiving after Mass', 'On Visits to the Blessed Sacrament', 'Primacy and Episcopacy', 'Dogmatic preliminaries for a proper discussion of the reform of the diaconate', 'On the theology of secular institutes'. Since it may help in judging the essays presented here, we give the list of the publications in which they first appeared, following the order of the present volume: 'Considerations on the development of Dogma', *Zeitschrift für katholische Theologie*, 80 (1958), 1–16; 'On the Concept of Mystery in Catholic Theology', in Siegfried Behn, *Beständiger Aufbruch* (Przywara-Festschrift, Nuremberg 1959), 181–216; 'Remarks on the dogmatic Treatise on the Trinity', *Universitas* (Festschrift für Bischof A. Stohr), 1 (Mainz 1960), 130–150; 'On the theology of the Incarnation', *Catholica*, 12 (1958), 1–16; 'Dogmatic questions on Easter', in B. Fischer and J. Wagner, *Paschatis Solemnia* (Jungmann-Festschrift, Freiburg 1959), 1–12; '*Virginitas in partu*: a contribution to the problem of the development of Dogma and Tradition', in J. Betz and H. Fries, *Kirche und Überlieferung* (Geiselmann-Festschrift, Freiburg 1960), 52–80; 'Nature and grace according to the doctrine of the Catholic Church', *Theologie heute*, ed. L. Reinisch (Munich 1960), 89–102; 'Questions of Controversial theology on justification', *Tüb. Theol. Quartalschr.*, 138 (1958), 40–77; 'On the theology of the Symbol', in A. Bea, H. Rahner, H. Rondet and F. Schwendimann, *Cor Jesu*, I (Rome 1959), 461–505; 'Word and Eucharist', *Aktuelle Fragen zur Eucharistie*, ed. M. Schmaus (Munich 1960), 7–52; 'The presence of Christ in the sacrament of the Lord's Supper', *Catholica*, 12 (1958), 109–128; 'On the Presence of Christ in Communion', *Geist und Leben*, 32 (1959), 442–448; 'Theological principles of the hermeneutics of eschatological assertions', *Zeitschr. für kath. Theologie*, 82 (1960), 137–158; 'The life of the dead', *Trier. Theol. Zeitschr.*, 68 (1959), 1–7; 'Theological remarks on the problem of leisure', *Oberrhein. Pastoralblatt*, 60 (1959), 210–218, 233–243; 'The theology of power', Männerwerk Köln, polycopied (1960), 16 pp.

Innsbruck, October 1960   Karl Rahner, S.J.

PART ONE

Fundamental Theology

I

CONSIDERATIONS ON THE DEVELOPMENT OF DOGMA

IF we are to address ourselves to the problem of the development of dogma,[1] the difficulty and importance of the question will be clear at once to all of us who are engaged with dogmatic theology. Our vocation is to treat of the dogmas of the Church. We have not merely to propound and explain them, to bring them within the range of the understanding of modern man; we have also the task of showing, as well as we can, that these dogmas of the Church are contained in the original revelation. For the Church and its magisterium recognize that they are not the mediators of a revelation which is now being granted for the first time. They do not look on their office as prophetic, but as one that has only to guard, transmit and explain the divine revelation which came in Jesus Christ at a given point of past history. Thus the function of the Church and the magisterium differs in quality from the process of the original revelation, though the task of the Church is not to be conceived as merely that of repeating the original revelation, and presenting it as something *once* uttered long ago. The Church presents revelation as something that takes place 'now' as it is uttered by the living voice and offers itself to be appropriated this day in the hearing of believers. Thus the Church and the magisterium distinguish their function—by differentiation, not separation—from the process of revelation itself, and see their function as that of teaching men authoritatively in each age. It is true that the very fact of the Church and the magisterium, once it has been recognized by faith, is the immediate guarantee of a legitimate connexion between the original

[1] This essay is the reproduction of a lecture given at Innsbruck, 3rd October, 1957, at a congress of German professors of dogmatic theology. The essay is presented in the form in which it was given. Hence no effort has been made to turn it into a learned piece of scientific research by the addition of references to other relevant literature, monographs, etc.

revelation and the pronouncement of the magisterium. But this does not render superfluous the efforts of theologians who are trying to demonstrate such a connexion. First of all, this connexion, according to the doctrine of Scripture and the Church is not absolutely transcendent with regard to history. It is found, at least to some extent, on the plane of the historical transmission of the original message and hence is still accessible to the historian, even though a comprehensive view of it, like that of all supernatural salvific acts of God, may be reserved for the believer alone. We could undoubtedly say: the connexion between the later dogmas of the Church and the original revelation is, on principle, a necessary subject in any comprehensive fundamental theology; but since it is concerned with the individual mysteries of faith, it must also be investigated by the dogmatic theologian and its study will be his contribution, so to speak, to fundamental theology. Secondly, this task has a special significance within theology. If the theologian must explain the doctrine of the Church as such and try to make it accessible to his contemporaries, so that they can assimilate it conceptually and existentially, one of his ways of explaining the dogmas of the Church will be to show exactly how they derive from the original revelation. For the meaning, implications and limitations of the derivative dogma can only be clearly seen when one constantly returns to its source, especially as the official magisterium of the Church always makes such an effort when propounding its doctrines, at least by having recourse to Scripture. But if one of the tasks of the theologian is to demonstrate analytically and synthetically the relation between Church dogma and the original revelation, then he has a further task which he cannot avoid. It is to reflect on the *formal* structure of such connexions in general; he must consider the development of dogma as a whole, and not merely the question of the derivation of any individual dogma from its original utterance.

We are likewise well aware of the difficulty of the task thus described. The question was indeed never totally absent from Church history. Theology was never completely without the theme of the legitimate mode of tradition, nor did systematic reflexion in scientific form on the nature of theology and the connexions between the articles of faith and the individual truths of faith ever die out altogether, especially when apologetics on behalf of Church dogma against the *sola Scriptura* doctrine of Protestantism made this question more urgent in itself. But in the form in which we have to take up the question today, it is still very recent and hence to a great extent still lacks clarification. In its present form and urgency it can only have existed since the 19th century. For it is only since the rise of modern historical science and of historicism that we can measure really clearly the difference and the distance between the forms adopted by the history of the spirit in general and the history of religious assertions in particular. The heresies of liberal Protestantism and modernism on the one hand, with their denial of the identity throughout the ages of Church dogma, by an appeal to the results of the history of the human spirit and of dogma; the insufficiency of much current apologetics on behalf of this identity, on the other hand, conceding only a minor change in verbal formulas—both show how difficult and how little mastered the question still is. If one is honest one will hardly say that 'Humani Generis' did more than accomplish one task, a primary one indeed, of the magisterium, namely to warn negatively against a historicist relativization of Church dogma. A really positive and progressive doctrine on the positive legitimacy of such development and its positive modes and possibilities, will undoubtedly be sought in vain in 'Humani Generis'. The question is all the more difficult today, because we have experienced a remarkable change of fronts in recent years. In the 19th century, Protestant liberal theology reproached the Catholic Church with an unreal and fatal petrifaction of ancient dogma. Now neo-Protestant orthodoxy, with a renovated doctrine of *sola Scriptura*, charges the Catholic magisterium with an arbitrary search for novelty, which creates new dogmas without any foundation in Scripture. Hence while we formerly had to defend our maintenance of ancient Christian dogma, in fact and on principle, and our right to understand it today as it has been understood for fifteen hundred years, now on the contrary we have to uphold positively the right of dogma to undergo development. The question is therefore controverted on two sides: how namely authentic identity on the one hand and really genuine development on the other can be reconciled. The problem is undoubtedly very difficult, because it ultimately reaches down to the obscure depths of a general ontology of being and becoming, of the persistence of identity in change—and also comprises the general metaphysics of knowledge and mind, which frames the same questions in searching for truth, with regard to its identity and real historical involvement. On all these questions therefore we must confine ourselves to a few remarks, rather loosely put together, which are only meant as a basis for discussion.

For apologetics, and for the understanding of the history and development of dogma in the Church it is of supreme importance to reflect on the fact that such a development can be already observed within the New Testament. As Catholic theology is normally studied, we are accustomed, apart from a very few particular problems (perhaps especially in Christology and—naturally—in fundamental theology), to accept unquestioningly the Scriptures, especially the New Testament, as an absolutely homogeneous and undifferentiated quantity, a sort of Summa of revealed statements all laid down at once, like a code of law or a catechism composed in one piece under the same enterprise. We have of course to some extent an indisputable right to this method, which then goes on to prove individual dogmatic assertions of Church doctrine by means of *dicta probantia* chosen more or less at random from the Scriptures. Scripture, the inspired word of God, is for us as a whole and in all its parts an unquestionable authority; we see each of its assertions as dogma and not merely theology, and take each of its assertions as a legitimate starting-point for our own theology. True as this may be, and correct as may be therefore the method in question in its positive bearings, it is none the less a one-sided view of Scripture and gives a one-sided method in our dogmatic work. Modern exegesis has taught us that we can no longer reasonably overlook the fact that within what we call one Sacred Scripture, and within the New as well as the Old Testament, the assertions undergo a history and a development. No doubt the contents of Scripture are all dogma, *quoad nos*, and not just debatable theology. But it is equally certain that we must affirm that much of this scriptural dogma, which has for us the quality of inerrant assertions of revelation, is itself derivative theology with regard to a more primordial utterance of revelation. We must not naively imagine that because of inspiration (which for that very reason is not to be confused with new revelation), each sentence of Scripture as such stems from a new original revelation, tributary only to an act of divine revelation which takes place here and now. Not every single sentence of Scripture was heard as it were on its own by a sort of direct telephone connexion to heaven. We may leave aside the difficult question, too little debated from fear of modernist ideas, of how an original revelation of God to the first recipients is to be conceived. But it is imperative to say that not every sentence in Scripture is this type of original revelation. Many assertions, guaranteed as inerrant at once by the Church of apostolic times and by the inspiration of Scripture, are theology derived *from* the original revelation. Since this is so, and since this derivative theology within the Scriptures still makes the just claim on us to be accepted as obligatory doctrine of faith, while it is itself a stage of development with regard to its own origin, there is therefore in Scripture itself a real development of dogma, and not merely of theology. Thus the development of dogma within Scripture is the authenticated exemplary instance for the development of dogma in general, an example which is in itself obligatory for all who accept Scripture as a whole as authentic testimony of faith. St Paul's doctrine, for instance, of the sacrificial character of the cross of Christ, of Christ as the second Adam, of original sin, many sayings about eschatology etc., much of the Johannine theology etc., are theological developments from a few very simple assertions of Jesus about the mystery of his person, and from the experience of his resurrection. One could be tempted therefore, simply because such assertions are the obligatory norm of faith for us, to regard them as having fallen straight from heaven, even as they stand. One could be tempted therefore to spare oneself the labour of reaching an exact understanding of them by referring them back to the original source of revelation distinct from them. But in the long run one would run the risk either of misunderstanding them, or of accepting them as a Summa of positively ordained truths of faith without any real internal connexions, and thus endangering their credibility to those who are without. Since however for the most part we are still unable to manipulate this multi-dimensional disposition of the truths of faith in our theology, these facts can scarcely yet be the exemplary instance which we can use to study the laws of the development of dogma.

II. *A PRIORI* RULES FOR THE FRAMEWORK OF DEVELOPMENT OF DOGMA

(a) In the last resort, the development of dogma is not a single process which can be adequately comprehended by formal laws. This first statement that we make may sound obvious. But it is important. The unfolding of the final divine revelation is a process. As a process through which the divine revelation passes it is unique. Therefore it has no *a priori* categories, distinct from itself and superior to itself and likewise adequately determining it. Unlike the processes of natural science, it cannot be comprised under such formal laws as would enable us to predict properly any later phase. This follows from the nature of the case. If therefore the history of dogmas is constantly full of surprises, if no case is like another and each phase and the development of the different dogmas takes a different course, this is to be expected *a priori*. We cannot therefore demand that the development of one dogma will conform adequately to the laws of another and so for instance challenge the legitimacy of a given development by appealing to the contrast in another. This follows not merely from the nature of revelation and of its history, a unique history which runs only once between Christ and the end. It follows from the historical nature of the knowledge of truth in general. If man has a history, not only as a physical, biological living thing, but even as spirit, indeed, if it is only as spirit that he possesses a true history, it must be clear at once that this history takes in fact a unique course and is not the constant repetition of the same law. This must be true above all of the sublimest portion of the history of the human spirit, the history of divine revelation in the human spirit and the unfolding of this revelation. It would indeed be strange if there were a history of divine revelation—which no Christian can deny—and yet no history of the unfolding of this revelation and hence no development of dogma, with the uniqueness and unpredictability of such history. For revelation itself has a history, and necessarily so, not just because the speaker, God, can in his freedom act historically, but because the hearer, man, is a historical being. As long then as his history goes on, there must be a history of dogma, although revelation is closed, and in a very strict sense and for a very strict reason can be closed, though the history of man is not yet at an end. There is then no adequate formal theory of the development of dogma which would be in itself sufficient to permit a prognosis for the future. But in saying this we do not of course deny that there are certain formal principles with regard to this development, which follow from the nature of a historical and final revelation, just as much as does the principle enunciated above. Such principles may give rise to justifiable objections to possibly wrong developments in theology.

(b) The revelation in Christ is the final, unsurpassable revelation, which was closed with the end of the apostolic generation. This statement, so obvious in many ways, needs some further explanations, if the important consequences of this statement are to be grasped. The closing of revelation must be properly understood in two regards:

1. It is a closure, which in the last resort causes revelation to be closed, because this revelation is the dis-closure and openness for the absolute and unsurpassable self-communication of God to the created spirit. Revelation in Jesus Christ is not just the finite sum of finite single sentences, though the subject of these may be infinite. It implies the real, eschatological self-communication of God by incarnation, and by grace as glory already begun, to the created spirit. As we shall have to say more precisely later, grace and the light of faith are constitutive moments of the process of revelation even in so far as it is communication of truth, and so also in so far as it is *locutio Dei attestans*. This does not mean that revelation only becomes actuality as such in the individual believing hearers, in so far as they are such individuals. But it means that if the totality of the hearers and believers were to cease to be, revelation too, as final and eschatological, would cease to be. Where revelation is to be final and has to a certain extent no longer any future before it, it has to be accepted, that is, to be really believed. Otherwise the final judgment of God upon unbelief is come. A final and closed revelation, and a revelation whose destiny on the part of man is still in the balance, are irreconcilable concepts. A final revelation which is closed implies therefore in its concept Church, in contradistinction to synagogue, that is, the community of those who through a pre-defining grace of God have arrived at faith and are inescapably but freely comprehended in this salvific will of God. Such a revelation implies a believing Church which as a whole cannot fall away from the faith, though nothing can be said about individuals as such. (Here, by the way, is also the theological reason why the Church as the hearing Church, and hence also as the authoritatively teaching Church, is and must be infallible, though this cannot be said of the synagogue, which was however also a foundation of God's.) To have been closed is the property of the final, absolute and unsurpassable self-communication of God, as *such*, which provides for itself its believing acceptance. The closing of revelation is not the arbitrary ending of God's speaking, which could have gone on and only as a matter of fact fell silent after some chosen utterance. This must always be noted when we speak of revelation's being closed. It is man's being opened up for and into the real and not merely conceptual self-communication of God. And therein it has within itself, precisely because of this closure, which is dis-closure, its dynamism of inner development, and hence a dynamism of the development of dogma. A divine revelation which was not real self-communication

of revealed reality to the spirit of man himself, could neither be a true *self*-communication of God, nor be really conceived in earnest as closed. This is because a divine dispensation which was the pure decree, 'now he speaks no more', is basically an anthropomorphic representation of God. This is all the more true, because the concept of a personal utterance of God, though perhaps only recognizable to us after the event, cannot be in any way seriously and intelligently thought of, except where God wills to disclose *himself*. Everything else that God could otherwise say could come by way of the real creation of this communicated finite entity. Anything supernatural that could also be attained *per se* by natural means if God only willed it otherwise, would be an anthropomorphic non-concept. Hence this would also be true of a communication of truth which comes as a *locutio Dei attestans* though it could also have come otherwise.

2. On the other hand we must not overlook the fact that this revelation, which closes and discloses the infinite, has the human word as a constitutive element of its essence, as long as we are still on pilgrimage in time far from the Lord, and do not see God face to face. And we must also remember that even this immediacy which we await as the consummation will be an immediacy mediated by the Word of God become flesh. But since the human word and the finite concept remain a constitutive moment of the closed revelation, it is clear that this revelation would either not be closed, or not be constituted essentially in part by the human word, if the development which unfolds the original dogma were to ignore such earlier human concepts, if it did not also (though not only) come about by means of the human concepts in which the earlier form of revelation was uttered. What this signifies, and what are its consequences, can only become clear when we reflect later on the constitutive elements of revelation and dogma and are thus enabled to survey the causes and impulses which carry along together, and in the last resort indivisibly, the one development of dogma.

(c) The development of dogma is necessarily carried along, in an ultimately indissoluble unity, by all the elements which are constitutive of revelation and of the self-developing dogma. This statement can hardly be contested seriously in its formal generality. Dogma, or a dogma, is a unified entity which is constructed of various elements (to be mentioned at once more precisely). If dogma or a dogma develops, all the elements which go to build up such a dogma necessarily develop also. This is only possible however if a dynamic tendency to development is innate in *each* of these constitutive elements themselves. We recognize of course also at the same time that the dynamic tendencies of each of these single elements can only be effective in the totality and must remain dependent on the unfolding of the whole. Hence any effort to explain the development of a dogma one single element of the dogma and its dynamism, any effort to reduce it to one such single dynamism of development, must be rejected out of hand as false and futile, like the opinion that one can succeed in explaining a *de facto* development of dogma without recourse to all these elements.

It may be that in the various instances, as we see them, the dynamism of development in this or that element of a dogma may stand out more clearly and be grasped more consciously; but it cannot be that any of these elements be missing. Any theory of the development of dogma which disregards or denies this simple fact, and would for instance try to attribute the development of dogma as such merely to the magisterium *or* to the inspiration of the Spirit *or* to the logical explication of the virtualities implied in the human assertion, is to be discarded at once as false. This likewise eliminates the attempt to suppose different vehicles of development in the individual instances, as if the various historical cases of a *de facto* dogmatic development could be thereby more easily described and justified.

III. THE CONSTITUTIVE ELEMENTS OF THE DYNAMISM OF DOGMATIC DEVELOPMENT

We have already said that the elements of dogma are also the constitutive elements of dogmatic development, in their variety and indissoluble unity. We must now mention individually these elements of dogma and dogmatic development—taking of course a selective view of such developments—and see what follows for a correct concept of the development of dogma.

(a) *The Spirit and grace*

God's self-disclosure in the human word of revelation would nullify itself if it were not bound up with the inner light of grace and strictly supernatural faith. If God were to speak of himself in so far as he is not revealed through his creation, which is distinct from himself, and use human words without the supernatural elevation of the hearer, his utterance would come only under the subjective *a priori* of the finite spirit as such. And his utterance, if not simply nullified, would be necessarily degraded to an element of the self-understanding and the possibility of self-understanding of the mere creature. It would no longer be a real self-disclosure of God. For here too it is true that whatever is received is received according to the manner and nature of the recipient. It is also true here that knowledge is essentially a process of coming to awareness of self in him who knows. It is enlightened self-possession, so that everything that is received is grasped as an element of this self-accomplishment. Though man is undoubtedly, even as spirit in the natural order, absolute openness to being in general, and hence to God who is cause and principle of this spirit, still, if God's communication about himself were received without grace, it would only be grasped as a moment of this self-accomplishment of man within the world (even if it came as something infinitely open). Only where the act of hearing in what we call grace is really the co-accomplishment of an act of God in a strictly supernatural participation of God himself, and not merely of a quality *created* by him, can the divine utterance be strictly supernatural, that is, qualitatively supernatural in itself and not merely distinguished as regards the mode of communication from any communication made through merely created things. A divine utterance which is divine by reason of its own nature has no meaning unless it is directed towards a divine hearing. Part therefore of the expression of divine revelation is the Holy Spirit, as the strictly supernatural self-communication of God. He does not enter in merely as the guarantee of its correctness or as the originator of a process of efficient causality on the part of God which takes place *per se* in the region of the finite. He is there as the thing uttered itself and only with this can the human utterance be self-utterance of God. Here we have at once that infinite openness in the closed revelation, and the dynamism of self-development, whose only limits are in the *visio beatifica* itself. It is also true (and this is part of the fundamental dogma of a Christianity of the Incarnation) that this self-communication of God really takes place in the human word, and not merely on the occasion of it. Human words are not merely the external occasion for a pneumatic or mystic experience of transcendence directed towards the God who is nameless. Spirit and word can only be possessed in their indissoluble unity, undivided and inconfused. Hence the human word is open from the start to the infinitude of God. (This it is, in so far as it is natural, by virtue of its *potentia oboedientialis*, and so far as it is supernatural, by virtue of its being uttered by the

Spirit and by virtue of its elevation by the Spirit.) And the divine Spirit is given in and through this word, assumed by himself, in his own infinity and concrete reality.

Here we have a very special and unique conjuncture which is usually overlooked in theology. There are two modes of knowledge in the region of natural knowledge. In the first, we have an actual experience of the reality in question, in itself or in its effects, and on this basis and in view of this we form our concepts and judgments in its regard. We then constantly start out from these concepts and judgments, to return constantly to the experience of the thing itself, whence we are enabled to form anew our concepts and judgments and subject the previous ones to a critical investigation, because we can have the thing itself without any assertion about it. In the second, there exists a type of knowledge which does not possess the thing itself but relies on the assertion of another and so is unable to make direct experimental contact with the thing itself and make itself independent of the judgments communicated to it. The second is what happens in all that is called *testimonium*. Now, the Catholic, antignostic and anti-mystical view of the reality and truth of divine revelation makes the first mode impossible. That is, we cannot make ourselves independent, in our pilgrim state, of the assertions made in the testimony to revelation. Further, we cannot—like the modernists—set up a wordless state of experience with regard to what is meant in faith, to derive thence new and original statements of revelation in the form of intellectual assertions. From all this the average theology of the schools concludes (without really thinking much about it) that revelation is to be conceived of in accordance with the second of the two modes of human knowledge mentioned above and will be mere verbal testimony, which only indicates something not truly possessed and does not impart the thing itself. That is precisely what is incorrect. In the word of revelation which comes through grace we have something intermediate and higher, between the two modes of knowledge named above: in the word the thing itself is given. Behind the verbal testimony of God in human concepts we cannot go, to reach a wordless possession and experience of the divine reality itself. That will only happen when the Word utters itself in the immediacy of the final fulfilment. All the same, we now have not only the utterance, but the thing itself: God's self-communication to the spirit in his own proper reality—which is already the homogeneous beginning of the vision itself.

This of course can only be said if the Spirit who activates the super-natural hearing of the word of God is not merely a heavenly element of consciousness in the act of faith but really enters in as the light of faith. This does not necessarily mean that this light of faith must be present to the believing mind as a conscious datum and object, distinguishable from the other objects of consciousness. But there must be a genuine presence of the light of faith to consciousness, even though as a datum it is not in the state of an object or the object of reflection. If this is so—and against Molina and his followers, this will be maintained as obvious by the Thomistic school along with Suarez, following Scripture and tradition as yet unclouded by nominalistic thinking—then the Spirit cannot be imagined simply as the transcendent steersman of dogmatic development. He will be an intrinsic element of it, by means of the believing conscious-ness of the Church, the bearer of this development. In this pregnant sense, dogmatic development takes place 'in the Holy Spirit'. Where in explaining dogmatic development precisely as a process in the conscious-ness of faith in the Church, this element is not also considered and reckoned with, any explanation which claims to be adequate must neces-sarily go astray. No doubt in the explanation of dogmatic development this Spirit cannot be pointed to as an isolated element, perceptible of itself, any more than the light of faith can be objectivated in the *analysis fidei*. But just as little as in the case of the *analysis fidei*, the impossibility of mastering consciously and checking such an element in a spiritual process does not mean that this element, integral to dogmatic development, is not present as a process of consciousness. With regard to the manner in which the Spirit is a datum in the development of dogma, everything could be said that also applies to the Spirit, grace, and the light of faith with regard to human consciousness. Hence we need not go into the matter more deeply here. It need not surprise us, if we take account of a formal meta-physic of knowledge in the finite spirit. For it would be a senseless rationalism (easily refuted by a transcendental deduction) to maintain that the finite spirit, while still in the stage of becoming and incompleteness, could or should only have the objects presented to its conscious reflexion as the elements of its knowledge, the logical grounds of its judgments and the motives of its action. Even in the region of natural knowledge, the unobjectivated and unattainable datum—thus however truly a datum—is the inviolable source, the broader horizon and the underlying principle of everything that we represent to our minds on the basis of any object of which we make assertions—partly to admit the presence of that which disposes of us while being itself beyond all control, partly to hide it from ourselves and to hide ourselves from it behind the object.

(b) The magisterium of the Church

The word of God is always the word delivered by the authorized bearer of doctrine and tradition in the hierarchically-constituted Church. The element of being officially delivered, the reference back to an authorized teacher, the hearing of the word *from* this authoritative teaching person, belongs to the constitutive moments of dogma and hence also of dogmatic development. This is because dogma as such must be proclaimed by the magisterium, the teaching authority, in order that it can be believed *fide ecclesiastica* along with the Church, as a constitutive moment of the faith of this Church. Thus dogmatic development does not depend merely on the office, *in facto esse*. It also depends on the magisterium in its *fieri*. The development itself takes place in a constant dialogue of debate with the office. The unofficial elements of development (the charisma of the Spirit and the labour of theology) always anticipate the thought of the office and direct their thinking towards it. Since their thinking-out of dogma is always done *within* the hierarchically constituted Church, they always offer their thought to the authoritative teaching office. Even if it is ostensibly a matter of an individual stand-point in theology, they learn whether the authoritative office of the Church and the common consciousness of faith in the hearing Church as a whole can, in the fullness of its spirit, participate in the thinking-through of the individual line of theology, or rejects it as contradictory to its spirit. This is not the place to expound more precisely this 'ecclesiality' of the preaching of revelation and hence of dogmatic development. We should have to go back to the character of dialogue primordial to human knowledge in general. We should have to show further that—if one may say so—the *fides implicita* which gratefully and lovingly refers back its own belief to the faith of the Church, as to an element of its own critical self-transcendence, is a necessary moment of all faith, even if a *fides explicita*, without which moment faith's confident knowledge of its own blessedness would not strictly speaking be at all possible. For a real critique of the subjective limitations and impotence of all knowledge, even of the knowledge of faith, is only possible in this outward-looking self-renunciation. This is a critique which—at least when implicitly reckoned with and present as an attitude—alone allows any knowledge to be really quite true, because it abandons itself to the greater truth and the more comprehensive reality, whose adequate subject can only be God and the salvific nearness of God to us, that is, the Church. Other questions could be answered with regard to this ecclesiality of dogma and dogmatic development, where it would be seen that concrete ecclesiality always necessarily includes reference back to the teaching office of the Church.

The magisterium therefore belongs, in the manner just outlined, to the indispensable elements of the vehicle of dogmatic development. But it is just as true that it is not in itself alone the adequate cause. It has essentially the function of preserving and distinguishing. Further, as history shows, it only promotes the development of dogma when the movement has already been launched by other factors. It is dependent—not for the authority of its decisions, but for the presence of an object on which it passes judgment—on charismatic movements in the Church and the reflexions of theology. In spite of all its authority, assistance of the Holy Spirit and even—in certain cases—infallibility, it comes, and must come, to its decisions in a deliberate, free, rational and hence morally responsible act. Hence, previous to the act which is its own justification because it relies on the assistance of the Holy Spirit, it is so much in need of conscious and rationally comprehensible justification that the assistance of the Holy Spirit will always be directed to seeing that this—let us say— human conscientiousness and justifiability of the official decision will not in fact be wanting. Therefore the magisterium cannot make the work of theology and the rational justification of a new dogma superfluous; it cannot replace them, nor does it desire to do so. It is true that for individual theologians, as for the simple faithful, an official decision of the Church is a fact so founded on the assistance of the Holy Spirit in the Church that it cannot be adequately resolved into other previous data, and so to a certain extent be rendered superfluous. But it is equally true that a decision of the magisterium cannot by itself be the adequate cause of dogmatic development, or the justification demanded of theologians for its legitimacy. If one were to say simply and solely: a legitimate development of dogma has taken place here, because the Church has given a definition, one would indeed have given the individual theologian an adequate reason *that* he should accept the fact of the legitimacy of this development and presuppose it in his reflexions. But one would not have given an adequate answer to the question *why* this undoubtedly legitimate dogmatic development is in fact now legitimate. With such an authoritative answer, one would have failed to describe the actual process of such a development as it really happened historically, and one task of theology would be left undone. One would have also failed to render explicit the intrinsic and unquestionably possible grounds for the legitimacy of this development. Nor would one have brought these grounds to that degree of perceptible objectivity which is quite possibly superior to that which was immediately and clearly attainable in the pre-history of the definition. For a definition does not need to have brought its motives and justifications to the highest possible degree of explicit consciousness, at the very moment that it is given, any more than this is necessary elsewhere in human decisions which can be quite reasonably upheld.

One might be inclined to say of certain definitions (e.g. the Assumption of the B.V.M.), that here in fact nothing can be done in the line of rational argumentation or historical proof for explicit conscious faith in the event dating from apostolic times, on close examination, and that basically only reasons of congruity can be adduced which when looked at in the light of day and judged honestly, prove nothing. One might be inclined to say that the magisterium alone brought forth from the *depositum fidei* the newly defined truth, in a manner absolutely unamenable to all rational understanding, and that a sober theologian, averse to all pious enthusiasm, could not see at all how this truth was contained and implied in the ancient truths. But if one said so, one would be ascribing to the magisterium a role in dogmatic development which cannot belong to it and which it never claimed for itself. One would, basically, atomize the faith into a sum of individual statements, with no unity except in the formal authority of the magisterium. One would thereby make these atomized sentences even more faceless and unintelligible, even less assimilable, because in fact they can only have their true meaning in the totality of faith and of the reality which is the object of faith. One would reduce faith to a formal obedience, though it is more than that, since it is a contact in grace with the very reality believed by faith. One would reduce in fact the historically attainable continuity of *traditio*—which is also a continuity of content and has always been held to be such—to a continuity of the formal authority of the magisterium. One would in fact be denying that revelation was closed in Christ and that the function of the magisterium is restricted to the preservation and unfolding of this revelation. The magisterium, so understood, would be proclaiming new revelations with each new definition.

However, it is not the wish of the magisterium to see instead of us what we do not see. It does not fetch for us out of the *depositum fidei* what we would be quite unable to bring out along with it. Rather, we see along with it and explicitate along with it. It always has recourse to theology and theology has recourse to it. One is never the substitute for the other, and the importance of the one is never increased by lessening the importance of the other.

(c) *Concept and word*

It is one of the constitutive elements of divine revelation that it is given in human word and concept. In so far as this human word is spoken by the Spirit and listened to in Him, it is necessarily referred and intrinsically open to the infinite mystery of that truth which is identical with the reality of God and can only be communicated along with the communication of this reality in itself. In so far as this word is spoken by the magisterium of the Church, it always has a validity greater than the inner intelligibility of this individual word when taken by itself, though less than that authority and validity, comprehensive because open to infinity, proper to the word in so far as it is the flesh of the Spirit of God himself, who imparts himself to the hearer in the word. In so far as this word is the word of the Church (in its magisterium), it points on to the general understanding of the Church and has also therein a dignity and validity which surpasses the inner light of the individual word in itself and in the merely human understanding of the individual hearers.

All this, however, cannot hide the fact that this word itself is purely a genuine human word and is only competent to make God's word present to us, as long as the human word remains such, with all the elements and consequences of coming from the human mind. It is as in Christology: the divinity grows in equal, not inverse, proportion to the humanity. The adoption of human reality for the manifestation of God is what really redeems and frees the human element and brings it to its highest actuality —to which it is orientated by its nature, even though only as *potentia oboedientialis*. Hence too it follows that development of dogma must also take place essentially in the dimensions of human concepts and words. Of necessity, dogmatic development corresponds to what usually takes place in the explicitation of human thought and knowledge, though it is not confined to such processes. We can say at once that on the level of the human words and concepts of revelation, dogmatic development can and must make use of all the modes and means by which human know-ledge unfolds itself elsewhere. Once we have designated human know-ledge which is aware of its justification as a process of man's *ratio*—a terminology which best fits Church usage, since for very basic reasons the magisterium rejects a fundamental plurality of faculties of knowledge —we cannot but say that dogmatic development always and necessarily possesses a rational dimension. Hence, if one takes theology as the rational reflexion of faith on itself and its objects, one must also say: dogmatic development necessarily takes place in the form of the develop-ment of theology. Indeed, we have already said that the magisterium is in fact always dependent on theology, as one of its sources, for its decisions. In saying this, we reject as inadequate both a mystical and an authoritarian theory of development. Even in dogmatic development, neither charis-matic inspiration nor authoritative decision makes the rational effort of theology superfluous. Rather, they work through this theology and per-vade it. One had of course always been aware that a new dogma must be in accord with the ancient *depositum fidei* on the conceptual level. Theories that see in dogmatic development the conceptual explicitation of something already implicitly contained in another assertion; questions as to what explicitation of the formally or merely virtually implicit can be defined as *fides divina* or *fides ecclesiastica*—all presuppose the conviction that dogmatic development cannot take place without clarification of human concepts apropos of the dogma. It is however necessary to stress this obvious point. True, what has been said up to now does not define in any way the *exact mode* of such conceptual explicitation in dogmatic development. It is still an open question whether we can be content with the usual explanations given in scholastic theology, which tries to justify this explicitation on the basis of a formal logic of concepts and syllogisms. But we must not lose sight of the fact that there must be an objective connexion between the ancient *depositum* and a newly defined dogma, on principle, and that this connexion must be demonstrable. To renounce this would be to postulate in fact, even though one avoided saying so, new official revelations in the Church which would go beyond the apostolic *depositum*.

Here and there one gets the impression that the search for such rational explanations has been abandoned, wordlessly, and that theologians are ready to renounce such connexions in the theory of dogmatic develop-ment. There are various reasons for such defeatism within a rational theology. One proceeds perhaps from the false supposition that such a rationally demonstrable connexion must be able to explain and justify all and everything in dogmatic development. In doing so, one wrongly makes the rational process of explicitation the only element in dogmatic development, which of course it is not. Or one exaggerates the certainty that can be asked of such examples of explicitation. But suppose someone only admitted a theological argument from the implicit to the explicit as certain when it is in fact understood by everyone and when its stringency is denied by no one. By only accepting such an argument, he would be using a terminology which is completely alien to the Church, because the Church designates as rationally intelligible and certain a number of proofs which are contested, not accepted, by numberless people. Further, he would logically be denying that there can be any certain rational knowledge at all, because there is practically no item of knowledge which is contested by nobody, and hence he would have to say that certain knowledge does not exist. The mere fact therefore, that explicitation-arguments for a new dogma are contested by some or many theologians as not being stringent or certain, is far from being a proof that no one has succeeded in demonstrating in fact, with sufficient certainty, the connexion between the ancient *depositum fidei* and a truth to be newly defined or indeed already defined. A theologian can have the right, and indeed in certain circumstances even the duty, of declaring his arguments to be clear and certain, even when his colleagues refuse to applaud. For in such cases one may not suddenly demand more stringency and certainty than can be achieved, according to Church doctrine, in other theological or philosophical considerations which the Church qualifies as certain. No more certainty then is demanded for the processes of explicitation that can for instance be attained for the proof of the existence of God, the freedom of man, the necessity of confession or for transubstantiation—which last truth can indeed be known, according to the doctrine of the Church, *from* other data of Scripture. Hence one will at least warn people to be careful, if they are tempted, for instance with regard to the Immaculate Conception, the Assumption and so on, to deny to theological arguments the sort of certainty which alone—but really—must be demanded on this level.

All these problems have perhaps been unnecessarily aggravated by the effort to base the rational stringency of such processes of explicitation too quickly and too one-sidedly on the formal syllogistic logic of the

Scholastics. For 'rational', in our world of concepts, does not merely mean an intelligibility and certainty founded on insight into the validity of a syllogism or on the purely intellectual analysis of a concept. As we have already said, to restrict rationality to these matters would be at the very least contrary to the usual language of the Church. If, in other words, one only allowed rational certainty to be present where a new truth of faith is deduced by a simple syllogism from two revealed premisses, there will of course be hardly a single instance of a dogma's being unfolded on the level of concepts and judgments. But then one ought to be honest and cease to claim that dogmas defined in ancient times have a greater evidence and certainty with regard to their derivation from the assertions of Scripture than the newer dogmas. For instance, the sacramental nature of marriage has been a dogma for seven hundred years, but is no more stringently deducible from Scripture on these terms than, say, the dogmas of 1854 and 1950. Further, even in the region of natural knowledge it is wrong to confine certainty only to places where the stringency of a syllogism is invoked. I know, and I know with certainty, that my mother will not poison me, as long as her mind is in any way sound. And this certainty is undoubtedly rational, because according to ecclesiastical, scholastic and a just and preferable terminology no faculty gives more certain knowledge than precisely this rational one. This certainty as to my mother's behaviour can be called rational, and this massive rational certainty can be explained very subtly and circumstantially for the whole length of a dissertation. No doubt such a commentary is intelligent and indeed to some extent necessary, but it will never exhaust, never quite catch up with, the massive original and thoroughly rational certainty. Indeed, its very point will be to enable man to achieve unhesitatingly and intensively this primordial, unreflective and massive but none the less rationally certain knowledge. It will make this knowledge easier for him and give him the courage not to remain prisoner of rationalistic inhibitions and scrupulosity, but to dare boldly to achieve a genuine certainty and a rational insight. For free decision and insight are precisely not in con-tradiction with each other but are complementary moments of spiritual knowledge and certainty.

There is then in any case a rational certainty which is not properly syllogistic and which cannot be comprised under that head except imperfectly, though no doubt a transposition into such terms is useful and indeed to a certain extent necessary. Why then should not this rational certainty, in its primordial form, not be found also in theology? Why may we not consider the work of reflective theology as the necessary though always inadequate reflection of the mind of the believing Church on a primordial rational certainty by which it knows the connexion between an old and new utterance of dogma? Given such theological labour, and supposing it has been carried out with the utmost strictness and honesty, but also in an inner, sympathetic contact with the object and the primordial truth, why should it not be qualified as certain knowledge? for we may not forget that this certainty lives by reference to that more primordial certainty and is always sustained by it. Rational reflexion does not really create that certainty for the first time, since it rather lives by that certainty. But it can help it to mature, just as the flower lives by the root, and yet the root still depends on the flower.

In this connexion it is perhaps in order to say a word about the notion of the argument from congruity. The theologian's task with regard to revelation is to expound and clarify the inner meaning and the mutual connexions of revealed truths whose revelation is already established. Considerations which serve this task may be designated as arguments of congruity. Such considerations can of course rely from the very start on assured knowledge of the revealed nature of the truths whose meaning and harmony are taken as themes of study. Medieval theology had no doubt such considerations in mind for the most part, when it put the question: *utrum conveniens est . . .?*—Is it congruous? Here in consequence the question of the stringency of such considerations plays only a subordinate role. It is different with considerations which are meant to lead to conclusions not yet guaranteed as revealed by the magisterium. Here the notion of the 'argument from congruity' can only lead to difficulties which could easily be avoided. For if in such cases one designates such considerations as arguments of congruity it means strictly speaking that the argument shows that *if* God had in fact done this or that, he would have acted *reasonably*. But the expression also implies that the fact of his having so acted is not established and is not made any more certain by the argument. In other words, by using such an expression one qualifies the argument as completely insufficient for the actual end in view, and thus one rules out from the start all theological effort at such an unfolding of the dogma. But in doing so, one creates difficulties which in reality do not exist at all. For what is the true state of affairs? Such considerations, if made seriously, precisely and with all desirable rational conscientiousness, are always in the nature of a proposition—if one may say so—put before the magisterium and the understanding of faith in the Church as a whole. The question of what rational certainty is attached to such theological considerations apart from this essential element, the orientation of the thought *to the Church as a whole*, is undoubtedly a subordinate one. For it arises only from the abstract isolation of one element, the rational one, from the totality of theological thought. The only meaning of such a subordinate question would be to sharpen one's own private theological conscience and to prevent one's being superficial and easy-going with one's own theological work, that is, with what is laid before the general consciousness of the Church. But if this process of isolation and the questions arising from it are disallowed, there is no correct sense in which the argument in question can be qualified as 'of congruity'. For such a qualification evaluates the thing in question before it has reached the full perfection of its own being. But the argument, by the nature of things, is only complete when it is accepted by the universal consciousness of faith in the Church, which alone is competent to pronounce the true verdict on it. It is not from individual theologians but from the universal faith of the Church that the qualification is to come, in a process that may last for centuries, either through a definition, or through disregard of these considerations, so that the question raised by these considerations of theologians is left open. It is quite possible that such theological considerations contain elements of certainty and stringency which cannot be made clearly objective by the syllogisms and conceptual analyses of the individual theologian alone, but only in connexion with the sense of faith of the Church. Hence if one starts by qualifying a certain theological consideration as merely an argument from congruity, the books are closed before they ought to be. Or at least one gives the impression that the act of the magisterium and of the sense of faith, consequent to these theological considerations, has basically nothing to do with those considerations but produces something quite new, in a sort of *generatio aequivoca*, on the *occasion*, at most, of these considerations. But in fact, what the magisterium and the Church's sense of faith do is to give objective clarity to a stringency which resided in these considerations themselves, though this *immanent* stringency in the process of theological development is first brought to conscious objectivity through the qualification granted by the Church—which however is not a substitute for such stringency. In other words, to qualify a theological argument as merely congruous, simply because its stringency can only be recognized, fully reflectively, by the Church as a whole, would be to mistake the true nature of theological thought and to split up something which must indeed be composed of different elements but at the same time is always one in this plurality.

(d) Tradition

As the fourth element of a truth of faith and hence of dogmatic development we must expressly underline the process of 'being handed on'. A divinely revealed utterance is essentially something that takes place when person speaks to person, since divine revelation, being strictly supernatural, is essentially the self-disclosure of God. From the very start therefore, and by their very nature, revealed truths are truths which are spoken to someone. This handing on of revealed truths is therefore also valid for the dogma of the Church. This element of being handed on, constitutive in the *traditio*, which is the handing on to truth and reality together, brings with it basically at once the development of dogma. For such a *traditio* takes place at a given moment of space and time, is necessarily historical, and absorbs the recipient and his historical uniqueness, which is also a property of his knowledge, into the process of *traditio* itself. In other words, anything said to anybody, if it is really to communicate, also of necessity implies that what is said undergoes a history in the utterance; it is not a mere repetition of the same thing. This is not of course to maintain that the assertion does not remain the same, in the sense of an evolutionist theory of dogmatic development contrary to the doctrine of the first Vatican Council. But if we start from this consideration we can make it clear—just as from the *a posteriori* data of Scripture— that every kerygma, by the very fact of its being proclaimed, undergoes development, and therefore, since it must remain revealed kerygma which calls for faith, gives rise not merely to theology in history but to dogma in history and hence to dogmatic developement.

One might then ask oneself what direction must necessarily be taken by this development, which is already contained in the initial stage of the dogma. Such a question could only be answered by taking into account all the other elements which we discover in dogma. We have said above, under (*a*), that the Spirit, grace and the light of faith are one of the essential elements of dogma and therefore of its development. If one could enquire, more closely than is possible here, into the way in which this element affects the whole grasp of dogma, we should have to deduce that the light of faith, brought by the Spirit and ultimately identical with him, is the *a priori* within which the individual objects of revelation are grasped. This is comparable to natural knowledge, where being in general is the *a priori* horizon in relation to which the spirit in its transcendence grasps each object and first makes it truly intelligible. From this we are to expect *a priori* a two-fold movement within the development of dogma. The infinite breadth and intensity of the supernatural *a priori* must necessarily lead to a constantly increasing articulateness in the *unfolding* of the objects comprised within its horizon. In the confrontation and synthesis between the formal *a priori* and the *a posteriori* object of faith, the object is necessarily displayed ever more fully in its virtualities. For each *a posteriori* object of faith is grasped *as* a moment of the movement of the spirit towards the one self-communication of God, which is not merely grasped in the act of faith as a statement *about* a future thing, but actually takes place in that act. But since each truth of faith is in this way a moment of this movement towards the unifying self-communication of God, which is absolutely unified and utterly intensive, the assertion can only function when it is open to more than it contains, to the whole, in fact. But it is only open—unless it is to fulfil this demand by the mere extinction of itself in the mystic darkness of the silent mystery in general—if it unfolds itself in a greater fulness of assertions, through which it is referred ever more fully to revelation as a whole.

The theology of the increasingly lucid *analogia fidei* is therefore not just the result of an ingenious formal logic which constantly produces new combinations, constantly finds new cross-references and connexions and deduces consequences from them. The theology in question is rather legitimated by the connexion that exists between the comprehension of an individual truth of faith and the enveloping *a priori* (given in its own reality in grace) of its comprehension in true faith. This divine *a priori* of faith inaugurates the unfolding of the ancient *depositum fidei* from its virtualities. Thus the dynamism of dogmatic development aims at an ever fuller expression of the individual dogma. It is expansive. But we must likewise expect, by virtue of the same origin, a dynamism that runs counter to this. For the formal *a priori* of faith, in contrast to the natural transcendence of the spirit and its *a priori* relationship, is not a formal abstract *a priori*, founded on the potentiality of the developing spirit and its openness; it is not merely an *a priori* of possibility. It is in fact the real intensive fulness of what is meant in each individual object of faith, and that not merely in notion or idea, but in the reality itself, which is none other than the triune God in his real self-communication.

In the act of faith therefore, in the utterance and the hearing of revelation, a synthesis takes place between this *a priori* and each individual object of faith. But then such a synthesis must also launch the dynamism in the direction of a constantly progressive concentration of the variety of the contents of revelation upon this *a priori* unity which is intended in all this variety. Dogmatic development must also contain a dynamism of compression and simplification, tending towards the blessed darkness of the one mystery of God. It is not at all as if dogmatic development must always move in the direction of multiplying individual assertions. Just as important, indeed, strictly speaking still more important, is the development in the line of simplification, towards an ever clearer view of what is really intended, towards the single mystery, an intensification of the experience in faith of what is infinitely simple and in a very essential sense obvious. The more clearly the ultimate themes are disentangled from the variety of the assertions of faith, the more clearly they are grasped through acceptance of the individual assertions, the more 'dogmatic development' do we have. In practice, the former of these dynamisms will be sustained more by popular piety and by the magisterium, which is responsible to it on justifiable pastoral grounds. The latter contrary, dynamism, will be sustained in practice primarily, though not solely, by the esoteric studies of theology itself. Theology at present however, in our non-authoritative opinion, should not be confined to the service, however justifiable, of popular piety, which strives inevitably and justifiably after the greatest possible diversity, and necessarily explains to itself the fulness of divine reality by a constantly increasing number of particulars. Theology today might well take up more intensively the other charge that falls to it, and in practice, to it alone: the reduction of the multiplicity of faith's assertions to their ultimate structures, in the intelligence of which under certain circumstances the all-embracing and overwhelming mystery of God is more powerfully present for us today than where the spirit only enlarges upon the variety of the individual assertions and further distinctions among them. To use a comparison and meet the facts at the same time one might say: there is a theology of the commonplace in the supernatural by which one tries to find God in a constant multiplication of newer and more distinct particulars. But there is also a theology of the 'mystical' or the silent mystery, in which as in mysticism proper, the particulars are lost to sight as though at night, so that the one totality may become more powerful. One might well think that the second, which demands of theology just as much precision and discernment as the first, is too little practised today. It exists however in the form of a need, mostly not quite conscious of itself, even in the theology of de-mythization.

(e) The acknowledged presence of dogma, AS dogma, AS revealed by God

Where a dogma is present to the full extent of its being, it implies that the conscious faith of the Church, definitively instructed by the magisterium of the Church, holds it *as* revealed by God. This further element of dogma is now to be considered in relation to the development of dogma. The special quality of this element is that dogmatic development precisely consists of the fact that this element becomes a datum of consciousness: the Church becomes aware that it enunciates a given truth as something revealed by God. But this datum *of consciousness*—and this is what ultimately constitutes the whole difficulty of the development of dogma— was not always present. It is probably better to formulate it in this manner than to put the matter more crudely and to say that the Church once did not believe a certain truth and only grasped it later. For, looking more closely and deeply into the matter, and distinguishing between an explicitly articulate and a more undifferentiated presence of a divine revelation, one would say more correctly: the Church was not always *consciously* aware that it possessed something as a divine truth in its sense of faith, while it was in fact always present to the Church. However that may be, we have in any case to reflect on the fact that such a conscious datum, which was not always present, does enter into the development of dogma. We come now to the really problematical point. The question is; how does this entry take place? How does the Church suddenly notice, as we may say, that the assertion on which it had been brooding in its consciousness perhaps for centuries is held by it with the unconditional assent of faith? If one simply answered the question by saying: it does so because the Pope or the Council defines this truth, the question would merely be transposed. It would then be: in what circumstances and on what evidence has the Pope the right to define something? The question remains even on the unquestionable supposition that the Pope, *when* he defines something, defines correctly. The formal legitimacy of the act whereby he defines is the guarantee of the correctness of his definition *quoad nos*. But it is not the objective or the conscientious justification of the papal definition for the Pope himself. But suppose one answers the question as follows: the Pope recurs to tradition to assure himself of the justification of his definition, the old question arises once more. How can the justification be found in tradition since by hypothesis this tradition, coming *before* the definition, does not contain the element of conscious knowledge of the revealed nature of the proposition to be defined? One might say: yes, this element was already there, because—as was established in fact before the definition by the Pope's questioning the episcopate—this truth was already believed in the Church *as* something revealed by God, though not of course on the basis of a decision of the extra-ordinary magisterium. But then the question has been changed back once more into its earlier form: how then did the transition take place from a state of belief in the Church, in which a certain proposition was already held, but *not yet* consciously grasped *as* something revealed by God, to a state of belief in which this is the case? In other words, the problem remains the same in any case: how and on what grounds and with what right does the believing mind of the Church take the step from a stage in which it possessed a truth without having *consciously* recognized it as revealed by God, to the stage of making such an assertion? One might think to answer this question adequately by the sole reference to the rational validity of the arguments dealing with the connexion between the ancient *depositum fidei* and the new proposition, no matter how one conceived of this rational recognition in detail. But then logically one would have to admit that the certainty of the conclusion of this rational argument is itself dependent on the certainty of the argumentation. Therefore it can never lead to the certainty of faith itself, and the Church cannot rest adequately its absolute, irrevocable decision on such a certainty. One could of course reply by saying: this rational argumentation (in the broad sense of which we have spoken earlier and which has not been expounded more precisely here) is not meant to justify in any way the absolute nature of the definition or of the faith, but only the right of the Church to such a definition or an act of faith in which a proposition is really grasped *as* something revealed by God. But then we should have to ask again: first, how can one recognize a 'right' to such an assent, when the recognition of this right is still not the adequate justification of what really takes place in such an assent? Secondly: how does this assent come about if it contains something more definitive and absolute, and to some extent at least, something more in the line of contents than can simply be derived from the process of explicitation alone?

To put this more concretely and so to repeat once more the two questions: first, explicitation cannot prove the new doctrine, which is only now to be held *as* revealed, *as* definable, with the stringency and certainty which are contained in the act of explicit faith and the definition. Explicitation cannot in fact make this claim nor indeed *may* it make it, because otherwise the remaining motives of faith and its responsible causes would be rendered superfluous. Faith would not be the work of the Spirit and the definition would not come about under the assistance of the Spirit. How then does the Church which believes or the Pope who defines know that they can believe and define? Where do they get the right to do so? The question is not to be over-simplified or made too easy. There are of course certain definitions, or at least there seem to be, where it is clear that the extra-ordinary magisterium only laid down once more, by a definition, something that had already been taught as revealed by the ordinary magisterium and had been believed expressly by the Church. In such cases the novelty is justified by the fact that it is basically only a repetition of the old, the defence of what was already present. But in putting our questions, we are thinking of all the cases where by hypothesis the matter is otherwise, where namely the definition or the faith of the Church intervenes for *the first time* and does not merely confirm or defend what was already acquired. By what *right*, consciously known and demonstrable, does the transition take place from the stage in which a proposition is not yet held as certainly revealed by God to the stage where it is accepted as certainly revealed by God? With this the second question becomes clear: *how* is the transition made from one stage to the other? And it is clear that this passage is the decisive problem of dogmatic development, much more than the question of the content, when the implications of an ancient dogma are unfolded.

But when we look closely at the matter, the question is seen to be an ancient one, a problem known to every theologian, though it has un-doubtedly special modifications by reason of the fact that here it is a matter not of the faith of the individual but of the whole Church. We are all aware of the question of the transition, and the justification of it, from a qualitatively lower to a qualitatively higher level of knowledge in the birth of faith in general, in the case of the individual. When someone begins to believe, we have to ask: what exactly happens, and by what right does the former non-believer begin to believe? The first answer that the traditional theology of the schools will give is that he has grasped the *praeambula fidei*, the rational foundations of faith, in one way or another, and to a degree which is sufficient in his regard. Thus he knows that he has the right and the duty to believe: he has seen the credibility and the *credentitas* of the faith. Hence he believes, hence he freely decides to believe. But here a theology which goes somewhat deeper will have to say that while accepting this answer we must not overlook the qualitative difference between a rational proof of credibility, with all its problems, doubts and obscurities (no matter how much absolute or relative 'certainty' is and must be ascribed to it), and the total, absolute commitment of faith. The same problem is posed us as we discovered in the Church's development of dogma: the problem of the passage from the stage of not believing or not yet believing to that of belief. We can therefore assert that dogmatic development brings us back to all the problems, theories, differences of opinion and open questions which we meet in the *analysis fidei* when treating of the origin of faith in the individual. And everything said there can be repeated here. The leap to faith from its necessary presuppositions is the very same there as here, fundamentally. There are two aspects in official Catholic doctrine on faith with regard to its origin. On the one hand, it teaches the necessity of rational presuppositions which can be consciously grasped, and that there is a connexion between these and the faith. It defends them against theories that make the faith irrational by denying such presuppositions and leaving the faith to rest entirely on itself. On the other hand the same Catholic doctrine maintains that there is a qualitative difference between faith, which is an act of God-given grace, even in the zone of consciousness, and its presuppositions, which are rational. The same two aspects recur in our present question. We are also entitled therefore to break off the discussion of the problems posed by dogmatic development and to content ourselves here with having reduced our present question to the more general one. It is indeed enough, because the more general question is in fact a recognized subject of theological study and is clearly envisaged by it, while the question as posed by dogmatic development is probably not so clearly seen. Still less has its identity with the more general question been fully worked out.

Two things only must be remarked in conclusion. The first concerns a still more general case, which does not indeed solve the problem, but shows how real it is, since the occurrence in question is so real and unavoidable. Wherever a decision is freely taken the following case arises. On the one hand, the decision must be preceded and justified by an insight into its meaning, its rights and its duties. On the other hand the decision itself, once it is made, possesses its own evidence, which is intrinsic to it and is only attainable in the decision. In other words, no decision is merely the execution of the judgment. It is also the coming of the light which alone can justify it in the measure in which it feels it must be justified in its own eyes. There is a mental clarity which does not precede the decision but can only be attained in the decision itself, though it does not follow at all that the process is 'irrational' or that it renders superfluous the previous rational considerations which should lead to a correct decision. A metaphysic of freedom and of love would be needed to propound and clarify the matter. This would give us an element of a general existentialist ontology which could be applied to the special question we are dealing with—one which has a great need of such an existentialist ontology.

The second is this: there is a two-fold reason by which it can be shown that in our particular question we have a less acute form of the general problem of how faith arises from rational pre-suppositions without being in homogeneous continuity with them. It is because we are dealing with the *whole* Church and with a faith that grows *out of faith*. We are dealing with the faith of the whole Church. First of all, it may be affirmed *a posteriori* that up to this a papal definition has never been given where the object of the definition was not already in fact believed by the Church as a truth of faith. We will not now go into the question of whether that must be so on principle. The '*ex se infallibilis*' of the doctrinal authority of the Pope has not yet settled the matter definitely. For this doctrine only means that the papal decision does not need the subsequent assent of the Church for its validity and that the fulfilment of the conditions necessary for the decision—there are such things!—is not the subject of an examination by others, as if the validity of the papal decision depended on their varifying the conditions. If then one were to say: the Pope defines on principle only what is already believed *as* a revealed truth in the Church, one would not offend, given the distinctions just made, against the doctrine in question. However, we leave this question aside for the moment. In point of fact, at any rate, the actual faith of the Church as a whole was ascertained before, for instance, the Assumption was defined, by the questionnaire sent to the bishops by the Pope before his definition.

Hence this definition at least could be given in view of the faith already there, which recognized the truth to be defined as a revealed one. And it will undoubtedly be difficult to find a clear and convincing example of a different procedure, in point of fact.

Thus, in many cases at least, the faith of the Church with regard to a revealed truth as such intervenes prior to the act of the extra-ordinary magisterium, and hence (in connexion with the ordinary magisterium) in the form of an almost imperceptible growth and ripening of this specified consciousness of the faith, as it 'comes to itself'. The Church as a whole considers a thought which grows out of the whole content of its faith: it ripens, it merges ever more fully with the whole, while the Church lives it and perfects it. And so the Church of a certain day, if we may say so, finds itself simply there, believing in this special manner. This is not surprising. As we have already indicated, all decisions are preceded by preliminary decisions, attitudes and so on; in all decisions there are motives and urges at work, which are not themselves the object of a conscious choice. No wonder then that the same thing should happen with the Church. The interesting thing is that this passage in the development of dogma from groping to grasping, from thinking to the assent of faith, is attributed first and foremost—at least in the cases accessible at once to us—to the Church as a whole. This is easily understood. For the Church is what is ultimately intended by God by the hierarchy and its authority. It is the totality of all the God-given guidance, impulses and tendencies in historical development—whereby it would be against the doctrine of the Church to suppose that all these divine movements were always primarily introduced into the Church by means of the hierarchical office. The whole Church is therefore also the easiest place to imagine the quiet transition from one stage to another, of which we have spoken. All we have to do is think of the opposite case. Certain moral and theological pre-suppositions must be available to the Pope when he defines—and it is morally certain that he has them, because the opposite is no doubt excluded by divine providence, along with the possibility of error. How is he to have them in practice, unless he can have before his eyes a truth already present in fact to the faith of the Church, in conjunction with the *magisterium ordinarium*? It other words, how else is he to have sufficient human certainty that what he is about to define is contained in the *depositum fidei*? One might say that some other sufficiently certain theological judgment would be enough, for instance, that on various grounds, something was implicitly contained in the heritage of faith. But in point of fact it is unthinkable that this would be discovered for the first time at this precise moment by the Pope. And so the theological reason which the Pope has must also be known and active elsewhere in the Church. Who is to prove that it has not already in fact enabled the whole Church to see the implicit truth as something revealed by God, without any papal definition? Anyone who feels that the importance of the doctrinal authority of the Pope is threatened by such considerations is not thinking correctly. Before all paper definitions, the whole Church probably already believes clearly enough the doctrine about to be defined. And this fact, which has impressed itself slowly and without flourish of trumpets on the believing consciousness of the Church, is probably even the justification of the contents of the definition, though not of course the formal juridical legitimation of the moral right of the Pope to define the doctrine. But such assertions do not restrict the importance of the doctrinal authority of the Pope. For it is undeniable that such acts of the extra-ordinary magisterium also retain their sense and importance where a truth is already *de facto* explicitly believed in the Church, as revealed by God, under the influence of the ordinary magisterium, including that of the Pope. We do not maintain that the faith of the Church prior to a papal definition has no connexion with the ordinary magisterium. On the contrary, it is precisely when this faith grows and ripens under the guidance of the ordinary magisterium, even where this does not make itself heard clearly by exercising its supreme authority, that the importance of the magisterium, working in harmony with the faith of the listening Church, is all the clearer and greater. The ordinary magisterium, in papal encyclicals, addresses etc, makes a decisive contribution to the ripening and the self-awareness of the believing consciousness of the whole Church. But this process of ripening, as history shows, is more manifold, multi-storied, organic and harmonious than it would be if reduced, as some might imagine, to what survives in a methodical, juridical formalizing of the process: namely the authoritative decree and its obedient acceptance. Further, the faith of the whole Church, existing prior to the definition, does not by any means imply that every individual member already explicitly believes the proposition in question as something revealed by God. It only means that this faith exists in the Church as an attribute of this moral person which is the Church as a whole. The function of the papal decision is precisely to ascertain this faith and so to impart this general faith of the whole Church to those who do not yet believe. The Pope is the point at which the collective consciousness of the whole Church attains effective self-awareness, in a manner which is authoritative for the individual members of the Church. This does not of course mean that the individual is only bound to obedience when he has positively verified the fact that the Pope actually exercised this function as he gave his definition. The mere fact that a legitimate Pope has made a formal definition in the legal way is enough to tell the individual that the Pope has in fact exercised this function. But he does exercise it. He does so, because it is as member of the Church that he is Pope, and it is as member of the Church, on behalf of the Church, that God confers upon him his authority, and because it is the Church ultimately that must be indefectible. Hence the exercise of this authority—especially where it takes place in the service of dogmatic development—rests upon a clarification of the believing consciousness of the whole Church: just as much as it calls for such a development and brings it to its definitive self-understanding.

All that we have just said in this context comes down to this: because, and in so far as, the *whole* Church is the bearer of dogmatic development, the problem of the transition is somewhat easier than in the case of an individual coming to believe, though the fundamental difficulty remains. In addition, there is a second reason for the easing of the problem, which we shall only indicate here. In the Church, it is a matter of reaching certainty about the revealed nature of a given proposition, on the basis of revelation already believed, starting from other propositions already held by faith. It is not a matter of the complete transition from unbelief to faith, as in the case of the individual which is usually analysed in the *analysis fidei*. I am well aware that what I have said leave many questions of dogmatic development untouched. Above all, we seem to be now once more at a time when we should look more closely into the questions which were central to previous investigations into this theme, the questions namely about how precisely development takes place on the level of human concepts and propositions. One should have to ask what is the true process of the logic of invention (in contrast to the logic of syllogistic verification) both in general and in the field of theology and reflexion on the faith in particular. One should have to ask what are its laws, what are the influences to which it is subject, etc. We shall not be able to make ends meet, if we are confined there to such primitive concepts as are usually applied (formally or virtually implicit etc.). However, we cannot go into this now. All I wished to do here was to show that prior to the usual questions, there are certain questions that need to be better clarified: the question of dogmatic development within Sacred Scripture; the question of a really adequate grasp of all the elements of propulsion and guidance which are to be considered in dogmatic development, none of which is to be overlooked if a theory of development is not to be one-sided or to lead us into straits; the question of the inner connexion between the problems of the *analysis fidei* and the development of dogma; the question of the necessary rational connexion between the ancient *depositum fidei* and a new dogma; the question of the indisputable import-ance of theology within the development of dogma; the question of the course of development taking a two-fold direction. These and similar questions, which we have touched upon, would have to be solved, if we are to come to a concept of dogmatic development which corresponds to the historical facts as well as to the consciousness of the Church. For we know that in such development the faith of the Church remains the same, at one with what it received as the assertion about the absolute revelation of God, which is Jesus Christ our Lord, he who was crucified and rose again.

2

THE CONCEPT OF MYSTERY IN CATHOLIC THEOLOGY

WE shall try to indicate in these three lectures the fundamental role played by the concept of mystery in dogmatic theology. The first lecture will be an introduction to the set of problems here envisaged; the second will discuss the notion of mystery to which these problems point; the third will apply this notion to the Christian mysteries as they are presented in Catholic theology and show that these mysteries, though spoken of in the plural, are really only so many facets of the one mystery with which the Christian revelation confronts mankind.

The question is of importance in apologetics. The world in which man lives today seems to him a closed system, sealed off to a certain extent from God, a universe of unthinkable extent and variety, largely impenetrable and fully determined by its own laws. If God is not actually depersonalized, his government of the world is less easily thought of than hitherto on the analogy of the action of someone in this world. God has become more transcendent, and his name simply stands for the unfathomable mystery which lies behind all accessible and definable reality. The world has become less divine, and, by the same token, less important. Its processes are no doubt felt to be inevitable, but not as numinous—much rather as contingent and changeable. But if God is thus nameless and remote, and the world and everything within it profane, provisional, and replaceable, only at an immense remove the work of God's hand and the reflexion of his being: then man's sense of his own existence sets him a strange and oppressive problem. It is no longer so easy for him to see a definitely constituted religion, with its thousand and one truths, customs, prescriptions, and rules, as the concrete obligation of God's will and the necessary institution for his salvation. He finds all this so anthropomorphic and concrete that it is hard for him to realize that this multiplicity of details constitute God's way, and indeed the necessary way, of communicating himself to man for man's salvation.

Dogmatic theology poses the same problems, and perhaps most acutely. As long as men find it a highly complicated collection of arbitrarily linked assertions, their readiness to believe will be inhibited. And this is not because they abhor the incomprehensible. They may be rationalists with regard to a world in which they see nothing numinous, but merely the raw material for science and technology. But that does not mean that they are nothing but rationalists. They are much less so than their forefathers of the 18th and 19th centuries. They sense and revere the nameless and inexpressible. And for that very reason, they find a complicated dogmatic system too knowledgeable by far, too clever, rationalistic and positivist, too ready to lay down the law. They are not much impressed when the theologian appeals to a positive decree of God at every point where his dogmatic theology seems to be at a loss, and goes on from there to construct a world of faith held together only by such decrees, which are now christened mysteries. Men find the mystery of God so all-embracing that they cannot easily bring themselves to accept a multitude of mysteries which look very much like the complications of human reasoning which has tied itself up in knots.

It is therefore a very existential problem, when we ask how *the* mystery stands to the many mysteries of Catholic faith and doctrine and whether the whole field of mysteries can be understood as a real unity, without of course trying to reduce all mysteries to one, rationalistically. Is Christian doctrine, where it covers real mysteries, really a highly complicated system of orderly statements? Or is it rather a mysteriously simple thing of infinite fulness, which can be propounded in an immense variety of statements while its mysterious and simple unity remains unchanged? So that man, faced with this multiplicity of assertions, need not be the victim of modernistic simplifications of religion if he finds himself as he really is, the being in face of the nameless mystery which he adores: *Adoro te devote, latens Deitas.*

We start with the conventional notion of mystery as given in the current manuals of dogmatic and fundamental theology. It cannot be our task here to outline the history of the notion, and hence we do not deny that it may once have been richer and more profound than it now appears in the theology of the schools. But when we are trying to see all the problems which the notion presents today we may restrict ourselves without injustice to the average concept as proposed in the schools. There is all the less reason for quarrelling with this procedure because it can be shown that the notion of mystery as now proposed in fundamental and dogmatic theology, is more or less that of the first Vatican Council, which did not go beyond the usual problems of the schools, at least consciously and expressly.

How is the notion of mystery understood in the schools? We begin by noting three remarkable points. First, mystery is regarded from the start as the property of a statement. Then, there are mysteries—in the plural. Finally, this multiplicity of mysteries is comprised of truths which are *provisionally* incomprehensible. Of course, in the language of the Church and of theology, the object expressed by the truth, the thing to which the statement refers, is also called a mystery. This is obvious, and we do not doubt it in the least. But in the ordinary terminology, it is the truths or statements that have the quality of mystery, even though this stems from the object to which they refer. It is the *truths* that are mysterious. This is clear at once from the fact the notion of mystery is orientated from the very start to the '*ratio*'. It is something mysterious *to reason*. No one asks whether the relationship which is thus used to clarify the notion is not too narrow and superficial. Without bowing the knee to irrationalism, and without restricting in any way the essential role of *ratio* in religion and theology, we can still ask whether the precise nature of '*ratio*' itself is quite so clear and obvious, and if not, whether such a concept may be used to determine the notion of mystery. And may there not be a more primordial unity of the spirit, whatever its name, prior to the division into the 'faculties' of *ratio* and *voluntas*?—an authentically scholastic question. (cf. St Thomas, S. th., I, q. 16, a. 4)—and may not this primordial unity be the reality to which the mystery is directed and related? In other words, perhaps the will and its freedom have the same essential relation to the mystery as the *ratio*, and the mystery to them, when they are considered in their original state of unity with the *ratio*. Would it be then correct to assume that mystery and mysterious truth are one and the same thing?

Now in the terminology of the schools, mysteries are affirmations whose truth can be guaranteed only by a divine communication and which do not become perspicuous even when communicated by divine revelation but remain essentially the object of faith. This notion of mystery corresponds exactly to the standard notion of revelation, which, in contrast to the biblical theology accepted by Catholics and Protestants, is taken to be the communication of truths, that is, true statements. Revelation is of course and involves essentially the communication of truths. But if we take our concepts from the history of revelation and biblical theology, we shall have to add that it is by his *action* upon us that God imparts truths to us. The wider concept is that of a revelation which is action and event. This follows at once from the fact that in the actual order of things revelation, even as the communication of truth, only comes to us as the salvific action of God's grace in which he must first bestow on us the capacity of hearing his word of revelation and in which he imparts to us the reality of which the word of revelation speaks. The reality is spoken of only in the grace by which the reality itself is communicated, and revelation only expounds it and makes it the object of consciousness. Revelation is not a preliminary substitute for the thing, as if for the moment we had only a message 'about' the thing and not the thing itself.

Revelation, however, as ordinarily discussed in the schools, is purely a verbal communication and the concept of mystery is likewise referred from the start to statement and assertion, which are then distinguished from the truths of natural reason which can be 'seen', 'comprehended' and 'demonstrated'. Thus the special nature of these truths is measured not by the *'intellectus'* which forms a primordial unity with the will, but by the *'ratio'*, which in Vatican I and in theology is taken to be something well known and easily understood, and as the self-explanatory criterion by which these truths are to be measured. Hence it is said that these truths are not accessible to reason, that they surpass the created intellect (D 1796) and that they remain obscure 'as long as in this mortal life we are on pilgrimage far from the Lord' (cf. D 1676, 1796). The silent presupposition throughout is that we are dealing with truths which should strictly speaking have come within the scope of reason with its power to see and *comprehend*, but in this case do not meet its demands.

The pronouncements of the magisterium in the nineteenth century, and the ordinary theology of mystery, do not go any closer into the notion of this *'ratio'* to which certain doctrinal statements appear mysterious. But its meaning may be gathered from the pronouncements of Pius IX and the Vatican on mystery. It is the faculty which of its very nature is orientated to 'evidence', insight, perspicuousness and strict proof, and seeks a very definite relationship between the mind and its object: the sort of knowledge which was the ideal of the 18th and 19th centuries and stems basically from the ideal of modern science. Now Vatican I and the theologians of the time and after it, do not say that this concept of *ratio* is a relative one, which needs itself to be critically examined, or is too restricted for the character of personal communication which is proper to revelation. They take the concept for granted and go on to affirm that mysteries exist and to define them as well as they can in terms of this problematical norm. In the same way, they take it for granted from the start that if there can be any one such truth which falls within the scope of conceptual assertions, that is, of clear-sighted reason, and yet does not quite meet the demands of reason, there can be *many* such truths or mysteries.

And so the mystery is likewise regarded as, strictly speaking, merely provisional. It is a matter, or so it would seem, of truths obscure and impenetrable for the moment but which will be clarified later on and so finally be adequate to the demands made by human reason for insight and perspicuousness. Both Pius IX and Vatican I state without qualification that these mysteries exist for us 'as long as in this mortal life we are on pilgrimage far from the Lord'. The nature of the mystery as well as its duration are limited to some extent by the *visio beatifica*. With these elementary indications we have not of course exhausted the theology of the schools on the notion of mystery. Much more could be said even on these problematical points, but this is enough for the moment to arouse our astonishment.

So far we have seen that in Vatican I and current theology the criterion of mystery is the *ratio*. Since this criterion is applied to mystery and its nature defined by it, mystery is understood as a statement and therefore as something that can obviously occur in the plural. In the light of this criterion it is also understandable that mystery is given a purely negative definition. It is a truth which cannot for the moment be raised to the level of perspicuous insight which is proper to the *ratio*. It is a truth obscure and veiled, accessible only to faith but not to reason. Theologians are of course prepared to admit that a mysterious truth of faith concerning an important reality is better and more significant than a perspicuous truth of reason concerning some unimportant earthly matter. But the (negative) act by which the more important truth is attained is less highly esteemed than the other.

But what happens when just doubts arise as to the adequacy of the notion of *ratio* presupposed by the theology of the 19th century in its definition of mystery? What if we must take *ratio* itself as basically a spiritual entity of absolute transcendence and therefore as the very faculty by which the presence of the mystery is assured? What if we must take the mystery not as the provisional but as the primordial and permanent, so much so that the absence or disregard of mystery, preoccupation with the seemingly known and perspicuous proves to be the provisional, which dissolves before the gradual revelation of the abiding mystery, as such, to the finite reason? What if there be an 'unknowing', centred on itself and the unknown, which when compared with knowledge, that is, with any knowledge not really aware of itself, is not a pure negation, not simply an empty absence, but a positive characteristic of a relationship between one subject and another? What if it be essential and constitutive of true knowledge, of its growth, self-awareness and lucidity, to include precisely the unknown, to know itself orientated from the start to the incomprehensible and inexpressible, to recognize more and more that only in this way can it truly be itself and not be halted at a regrettable limit? What becomes then of the standard notion of mystery? Can it be evolved *primarily* with reference to reason, the faculty of seeing the evidence of individual truths? Can it be regarded as a merely provisional *deficiency* in a truth? And can there be many mysteries?

It is in fact remarkable that in general the theology of the schools does not confront the notion of mystery with the doctrine of God's abiding incomprehensibility even in the *visio beatifica*, a doctrine obvious in itself and dogmatically assured. God remains incomprehensible, and the object of vision is precisely this incomprehensibility, which we may not therefore think of as a sort of regrettably permanent limitation of our blessed comprehension of God. It must rather be thought of as the very substance of our vision and the very object of our blissful love. In other words, if God is directly seen as the infinite and incomprehensible, and if the *visio beatifica* must then be the permanent presence of the inexpressible and nameless: then, since to possess the absolutely simple in its immediate presence makes it impossible to distinguish between what one comprehends of it and what one does not comprehend, vision must mean grasping and being grasped by the mystery, and the supreme act of knowledge is not the abolition or diminution of the mystery but its final assertion, its eternal and total immediacy. And the concept of mystery receives a new content, which does not contradict the standard notion but becomes for the first time authentic and primordial. It is no longer the limitation of a knowledge which should by right be perspicuous. It is an intrinsic constituent of the very notion of knowledge, and the old, traditional criterion of mystery is basically reduced to a defective mode of a knowledge which is essentially orientated to the mystery as such.

We meet the same type of problem if we take the nature of spirit as our starting-point. Spirit is transcendence. Spirit grasps at the incomprehensible, in as much as it presses on beyond the actual object of comprehension to an anticipatory grasp of the absolute. The 'whither' of this anticipatory grasp—which in the act of grasping the individual and tangible attains the all-embracing incomprehensible—may be called obscure or lucid. Its reality, indescribable because non-objectivated, may be experienced as a divine darkness, or greeted as the light which illuminates all else, since the individual object of knowledge is only present and definable in relation to it. But in any case, this nameless region beyond all categories, on which the transcendence of the spirit lays hold without comprehending, is not an accessory or a preliminary sphere of darkness which is to be gradually lit up. It is the primordial and fundamental which is the ultimate transcendental condition of possibility of knowledge. It alone makes categorical clarity possible in the distinct knowledge of contours.

If then the reason which gives shape and contour to the object lives by the indefinable; if the lucidity of the spirit comes from its being open to the divine and truly super-luminous darkness—what are we to think of mystery? Can it be regarded as a defective type of another and better knowledge which is still to come? Is *ratio*, understood in the standard sense, just incidentally and secondarily the faculty of mystery, precisely because of its almost too taut tension? Or is it, in spite of the obscurity cast by the standard terminology, the very faculty which is originally and basically the faculty of mystery, and only derivatively *ratio* in the ordinary sense of the word, as supposed by Vatican I and the theology of the schools?

We are met by the same challenge when we consider the nature of spirit as being *one* in the '*perichoresis*' (circumincession) of knowledge and love. The positivism which places knowledge and love merely *de facto* beside one another in an unreconciled dualism must be excluded. For one thing —no one knows why—the same existent thing is both knowing and loving. Hence, in spite of a real multiplicity of faculties and acts, this one being must have a primordial and total relationship to itself and absolute being: a basic act, whose components are the interrelated and interdependent acts of knowing and willing, of insight and love, as we call them empirically. But this must ultimately mean that while guarding the distinction between knowing and willing, we must understand the act of knowing in such a way that it will explain why knowledge can only exist in a being when and in so far as that one being realizes itself by an act of love. In other words, the self-transcendence of knowledge, the fact that it comes to be only *in so far* as it passes over into something else, must be understood in this way: knowledge, though prior to love and freedom, can only be realized in its *true* sense when and in so far as the subject is more than knowledge, when in fact it is a freely given love. This is only possible if knowledge is ultimately a faculty ordained to an object attainable only because the object is greater than the faculty. And what but the incomprehensibility of mystery can be such an object of knowledge, since it forces knowledge to surpass itself and both preserve and transform itself in a more comprehensive act, that of love?

It is the mystery that forces knowledge either to be more than itself or to despair. For as distinct from love it is the faculty which grasps the object to submit it to its *a priori* laws, the faculty of weighing and judging, of seizing and comprehending. But in so far as the reason is more than reason, when it is understood as a potentiality only to be actuated in love, then it must indeed be the faculty which welcomes the greater sight unseen, the faculty of simple rapture, of submissive dedication, of loving ecstasy. But this it can only be if its most proper object is that sovereign and all-embracing exigence which cannot be mastered, comprehended or challenged: in a word, the mystery. And mystery is not merely a way of saying that reason has not yet completed its victory. It is the goal where reason arrives when it attains its perfection by becoming love.

This consideration is not an attack upon a well thought out Thomistic intellectualism which is also Christian. For such intellectualism cannot deny that man as spirit is ultimately *one*, and that its plurality is therefore only intelligible by reason of a prior unity: *non enim plura secundum se uniuntur*—the multiple is not one by virtue of that by which it is multiple. So there must be one last key-word which conjures up the essence of man, not two or three. And this Thomist intellectualism cannot deny that in Christianity the last word is with love and not knowledge. For we are not saved by knowledge but by love, and this can only mean that the act of loving can be the entrance-fee to a life whose essential perfection is centred on something else than that by which it was attained. If one really wishes to be true to Thomist intellectualism, one must understand the intellect in such a way that love is the perfection of knowledge itself. If so, the object, even initially, must contain something which constrains knowledge to become love, under pain of betraying its own nature. Merely to say that love is aroused when the intellect discloses the goodness and appetibility of the object, would be to fail to establish a true peri-choresis and to leave the two faculties without any fundamental unity. For, to use the language of St Thomas, either the truth would then be the good of the intellect, or the intellect's function would merely be to propose an object to be loved by the will, the intellect as such being unable to function further on the object. But then of course the question would arise as to how the intellect could even know the good as such, if it cannot as such be comprised by the formal object of the intellect. The mystery, being essential to the 'object' to which the intellect is primarily ordained, forces it either to consume itself in protest or to transform itself in the self-surrender by which it accepts the mystery as such, that is, in love, and so to attain its proper perfection. Thus the nature of spirit also shows that mystery is not just a provisional limit of thought, as it usually appears in the theology of the schools.

These are merely the most general and formal aspects under which the problems posed by the standard concept of mystery may be envisaged. Much more could be said on particular points, but we restrict ourselves to the following brief remarks. There is nothing in the concept of mystery as usually put forward in theology which assigns it essentially to the *religious* sphere, which seems however to be its proper place. Mystery is usually defined as a truth which one could only hear from God, that is, from another, and as a truth in which the inner compatibility of the terms is not perspicuous either before or after revelation. But it makes no difference to the truth of a statement and my acceptance of it, whether the truth is presented to me by an encounter with the thing itself or by a communication from another. To learn certain truths, it may be necessary that they be communicated to me by another; and it may be impossible to deduce the truth of an affirmation by inspection of its contents. But this does not really prove that the truths in question are of such a nature that they are entitled to the name of mystery. We do not hold that two terms are certainly and finally non-contradictory simply because we do not see any trace of an eventual contradiction, that is, we do not hold the rationalistic view that a mere lack of contradiction in concepts is proof of a real ontological compossibility. There are therefore many items of purely positive knowledge where the *de facto* compossibility of the terms is known directly or indirectly, but without any really clear insight into the ontological compossibility and without any note of mystery being attached to them. Neither lack of insight into the compatibility of the terms nor the circumstance that they must be communicated by another makes a truth a mystery, nor does a combination of these factors.

This can hardly be gainsaid. For otherwise, to take an example, the statement that there was a river XY in Australia would be a mystery, because not being an Australian, I can only know about it if I am told. Or again, the statement 'It is possible to have a mountain of gold as big as the Matterhorn' would be a mystery, because I might well deny that the ontological possibility of this affirmation is really known and evident. Or at least the statement, 'In Australia there is a mountain of gold as big as the Matterhorn' would be a mystery for me. But this does not really make sense. Such concepts miss the actual phenomenon of 'mystery'.

And the distinction between natural and supernatural mysteries does not take us any further. For the so-called natural mysteries, when regarded clearly, are either not real mysteries at all, or they raise again the question of what makes them mysterious. Is the note of mystery sufficiently justified by the fact that they need to be communicated by another or that the compossibility of their terms is not apparent or by both together? But in any case there are many assertions which on close inspection fulfil exactly the conditions laid down by the standard definition of mystery and which still do not necessarily have that character of the *numinous* which is ascribed to the mysteries of faith in the strict sense. We are not therefore bound to say that the ordinary definition of mystery is positively wrong. But we can say that it does not work out clearly the difference between such statements as are normally termed 'natural mysteries' and the 'mysteries strictly so-called', which must obviously be kept well apart from 'natural mysteries'. The difference cannot originally be constituted by the simple fact that they derive from different sources. The nature of the truth and our relationship to it need some other foundation than the fact that the real mysteries must either be revealed by God or remain entirely unknown. We should at least be told why some truths can be known only by revelation and why this confers on the truths *themselves* a character which does not belong to the 'natural mysteries', explaining why the *mysteria stricte dicta* are not constituted as such by the mere lack of positive insight into the compossibility of the terms. For, as we have said, the same impossibility of insight exists also in a whole field of statements which derive either from experience or from a communication which is not a divine revelation.

And the case is not really advanced if we say that the *mysteria stricte dicta* surpass even the angelic reason. Even if we prescind from the fact that we should be told expressly and clearly why this is true even of the loftiest created intellect imaginable–and so given a definition of mystery based on the special nature of the truth itself and not on its *de facto* relationship to various sorts of intelligences—my own relationship to a truth said to be a mystery is in no way altered by the fact that it remains a mystery even for another and perhaps higher intelligence. We have not explained why and in what sense something is a mystery to me, simply by saying that it is also incomprehensible to others.

Further, the ordinary concept of mystery, starting as it does always with mystery as a statement, gives no idea of why the communication of the mystery must always be a *grace*. But obviously there must be some relationship between the mystery and its communication to a subject elevated by divine grace, who responds to the mystery under the inspiration of grace. One relationship, as Vatican I says, is that the revelation of mysteries in the form of truths is necessary if man is called ontologically to a supernatural goal: grace demands the communication of mysteries. But we must go on to affirm that the relationship also exists the other way round. The communication of mystery can only take place in grace; mystery demands, as the condition of possibility of its being heard, a hearer divinized by grace. But this relationship is obscured in the ordinary definition, which does not make it clear why a truth in which the actual objective connexion of the terms and the compatibility of the concepts involved can be known only from revelation, while remaining otherwise inaccessible to man, can and may be imparted only in grace. To say that this holds good only for the divine mysteries, and not for other such statements would be to admit implicity that by demarcating the *mysteria stricte dicta* from so-called perspicuous truths nothing has been said about the real nature of the mysteries.

The problems raised by the ordinary concept of mystery, which starts with the proposition and so with propositions in the plural, can be seen still more clearly when we reflect on the silent pre-supposition that there can be *many* propositions in the nature of *mysteria stricte dicta*. From the ordinary standpoint there seems to be no possible doubt about it: if there can be any mystery at all—which may be granted for the moment—why could there not be many such? Why can there not be many propositions whose correctness can be known only by revelation and which remain obscure even after revelation?

However: a multiplicity of mysteries presupposes that each proposition has its own distinct content. They cannot all affirm the same thing, if they are really to constitute a number of propositions, each existing in its own right and different from the others. But if they are to have a really different content by which they are distinguished from one another *as* mysteries, then their sphere of reference can only exist where such primordially distinct contents, that is, distinct realities, occur: in the non-divine sphere. Even if we admit that man cannot express the absolutely simple reality of God except in plural terms, the basis of the mysteriousness of such a plurality of affirmations about God would still remain the same. It would still be the essentially mysterious Godhead of God. And the question would still be, whether the one and the same godhead of these many mysteries could really be the objective basis for *so* primordial a plurality and differentiation as is pre-supposed in the ordinary concept of mystery: a concept which more or less silently assumes that God could reveal as many mysterious propositions as he liked.

Let us suppose on the other hand that the multiplicity of mysteries was based on the multiplicity of really distinct and therefore created realities. The question then arises whether there can ever be a reality among created beings which by virtue of its natural constitution strictly as such can supply a proposition which is really a mystery. This question must be answered with a decided negative in any truly Thomistic metaphysic of being and spirit. By its very nature, any created reality must be such that some ontologically comparable intellect could be ordained to it: and for such an intellect, it would not be an absolute mystery. In other words, if being and consciousness, as Thomistic epistemology holds, grow in the same measure, there can be absolutely no created reality which would not be all the more conscious, all the more intelligible to itself, all the less a mystery to itself, the higher the level of its being. Mystery can therefore only exist where it is a matter of the relationship of God, strictly as such, to the created intellect. The multiplicity of divine mysteries, such as is silently presupposed, cannot therefore rely on the multiplicity of created realities. But then the real question is whether a plurality of mysteries is possible in the naive form of the concept as taken for granted in the conventional treatment of mystery. Must not a multiplicity of mysteries, if it is to be shown to be *possible* with its essential *limitation*, be derived from the notion of the one single absolute mystery, which is the one God as related to created knowledge?

II.   SECOND LECTURE

Our first lecture has not taken us very far. All we have achieved is the conviction that the question of mystery is more obscure than is suggested in the ordinary treatises of fundamental and dogmatic theology. And some relevant questions have been posed. In the present lecture we shall call on the philosophy of religion and then cast further afield into theology, our primary aim being to work out a notion of mystery which may indeed raise new problems for the theology of mystery but at the same time offer a starting-point from which its own questions may be answered. Our aim will be to clarify the notion of mystery in its essence, and in its capacity of including the mysteries. The second lecture therefore simply inquires into mystery.

The first stage of our undertaking will be concerned not with the mystery in itself, understood either as a thing or a proposition, but with the subject who is confronted with the mystery. This we are justified in doing because mystery is always understood as something relative, something which is mysterious *to* a given finite intellect: the silent presupposition being that God cannot be 'mysterious' to himself since he is noesis noeseos, thought of thought, the absolutely clear self-awareness of the absolutely 'illuminated' being. We could indeed ask whether it is totally acceptable and correct to understand God's knowledge simply as the absolute perspicuousness of absolute being. We could ask whether this does not set up, quite unintentionally of course, a flat and comprehensive knowledge as the divine ideal, a knowledge which is really almost a grasping at the void, because it would take place without any anticipatory grasp of an incomprehensible infinity. We could ask, in other words, whether 'mystery' as such, which suggests of course primarily some created condition, may not also imply something positive which does not appertain to the perspicuous intellect but to the mystery in contradistinction to such an intellect, and so as such must belong *eminenter* to God. We might therefore ask whether the character of mystery does not appertain to God's knowledge, essentially, in a pre-eminent and analogous sense, and how we are to conceive of this character. However, we leave this question aside, and simply suppose, as we have said above, that a mystery always regards a finite subject, from which we deduce that it is right and possible to begin the explanation of mystery with the subject *to* whom some reality or the truth expressive of it is a mystery. We inquire therefore into man, as the being who is orientated to the mystery as such, this orientation being a constitutive element of his being both in his natural state and in his supernatural elevation. This is probably the only way to show that the mystery is of itself no merely provisional element of obscurity in a reality or proposition, to be dissipated in time, but always and essentially determinative of the necessary relationship intervening between the created spirit and God. Man, made for mystery, must be such that this mystery constitutes the relationship between God and man, and hence the fulfilment of human nature is the consummation of its orientation towards the abiding mystery.

To reach an understanding of these statements, which already point to the conclusion, we begin—proceeding for brevity's sake on a number of assumptions—with the finite spirit's transcendence, which is directed to absolute being. We may fittingly suppose that man in his knowing and willing is a being of absolute and unlimited transcendence. All his spiritual acts, no matter what their object, are founded on this transcendence, which is a reaching forward of knowledge and will. We have only to ask now what this means for our present question. Obviously, this transcendence can only be described by an assertion—also obliged to express itself in objectivating categories—about the 'Whither' of this anticipatory grasp which exceeds all determinate objectivations. And again, this 'Whither' of transcendence can only be spoken of in terms of experience of transcendence as the limitless openness of the subject itself. Act and its finality, in this basic transcendent act, can only be and be understood as a unity. It is also obvious that the activation of this transcendence as such is always something other than its objectivated description, which is always a matter of subsequent reflexion and never really comes abreast of it. Finally, it is also obvious that the most primordial, underivative knowledge of God, which is the basis of all other knowledge of God, is given in the experience of transcendence, in so far as it contains, implicitly and unobjectivated, but irrecusably and inevitably, the 'Whither' of transcendence, which we call God.

With this very primitive outline of our presuppositions we now ask how precisely this transcendent experience is accorded its 'Whither', meaning always the totality of such experience, in love as well as knowledge. We speak of a 'Whither' of transcendence not to be as devious and circumstantial as possible but for two reasons. One: if we simply said 'God' we should always have to fear a misunderstanding, namely that we meant God as he is spoken of in an objectivating set of concepts, whereas the whole point here is that 'God' is known through and in this transcendence previous to such concepts, even where the object of knowledge is something finite. In other words, since we mean God as he is implicitly known in everything (in quolibet, as St Thomas says), and not as he is explicitly known and subsequently described, we cannot simply say God. Two: if we called the 'Whither' of transcendence 'object', we should conjure up the misunderstanding that it was an object such as is present elsewhere in the act of knowledge, and that we were dealing with the Whither of transcendence as if it were expressly objectivated by secondary reflexion upon this immediate transcendence. But we are speaking of the Whither of the original act of transcendence itself. We may now take up the central point of our discussion.

The Whither of transcendental experience is always there as the nameless, the indefinable, the unattainable. For a name distinguishes and demarcates, pins down something by giving it a name chosen among many other names. But the infinite horizon, the Whither of transcendence cannot be so defined. We may reflect upon it, objectivate it, conceive of it so to speak as one object among others, delimit it conceptually: but this set of concepts is only true, and a correct and intelligible expression of the content, when this expression and description is once more conditioned by a transcendent act directed to the Whither of this transcendence. One can only speak correctly of God when he is conceived of as the infinite. But he can only be grasped as such when we return to the transcendent illimitation of every act, since merely to remove the limits of the finite as such is not enough to bring about an understanding of what the absolutely and positively infinite means. All conceptual expressions about God, necessary though they are, always stem from the unobjectivated experience of transcendence as such: the concept from the pre-conception, the name from the experience of the nameless. The pre-conception given in transcendence is directed to the nameless: the condition which makes the names of God possible must itself be essentially unnamed. We could call him (if we wished to give such a title to what is meant) the nameless, that which is other than all finite things, the infinite: but we should not have thereby given him a name, merely said that he has none. We have understood the designation 'nameless' only when we have recognized it as radically and primordially different in its uniqueness from all other designations. Thus the pre-conception is also directed towards the indefinable. The horizon of the transcendent, since it is of immeasurable extent and thus provides the situation for the individual objects of knowledge and love, does indeed always differentiate itself essentially from all that comes within it as conceptual object. And so the distinction between God and all finite beings is not only clearly called for: it is even the condition of possibility for any distinction at all, both between objects in general and the horizon of transcendence, and between object and object. Human knowledge, as it forms its concepts and so makes distinctions, always presupposes, unwittingly or not, the primordial distinction between the absolute Whither of transcendence, absolute being, and all beings— otherwise there could be no distinction between beings. But it is precisely here that absolute being appears as the indefinable. For since it is the condition of possibility for all categorized distinctions and divisions, it cannot itself be distinguished from other things by the same modes of distinction. The horizon cannot be comprised within the horizon, the whither of transcendence cannot really, as such, be brought within the range of trancendence itself to be distinguished from other things. The ultimate measure cannot be measured; the boundary which delimits all things cannot itself be bounded by a still more distant limit. The infinite and immense which comprises and *can* comprise all things, because it exists only as infinite distance behind which there is nothing, and in relation to which it is indeed meaningless to talk of 'nothingness': such an all-embracing immensity cannot itself be encompassed. So this nameless and indefinable being, distinguishing itself only by itself from all else, and thus holding all else at a distance, the norm of all complying with no norm distinct from itself, this Whither of transcendence is seen as absolutely beyond determination. It is only there in so far as it determines all, and is not only physically but logically beyond any determination on the part of the finite subject. For at the very moment that the subject uses its formal logic and ontology to specify this nameless, indefinable, all-defining Whither of transcendence, to try to catch it as it were in the net of concepts, this never quite successful capture takes place once more by means of the pre-conception of what is to be determined. The measure is therefore measured by the self-same measure that is to be measured. The measure is there, it offers itself to be used, it is there as the obvious and unquestionable measure. We can hardly avoid the impression of being able to judge this measure like any other object. We feel we can use the general norms of logic and ontology which we have at our disposal to determine the special individual object of a specific science (called of course theology)—the object being 'God'. But this is false. Ontology is not a science distinct from natural theology. Ontology with its corresponding logic is not a science in which an object is defined by *a priori* norms, axioms, co-ordinates and so on, as if its only proper scope were to provide this object with a place within its systematic *a priori* where it show itself as it it is in itself. On the contrary, ontology is that mysterious event in which the primary measures or principles show themselves as immeasurable, and in which man *knows* himself to be measured. The Whither of transcendence is at no one's disposal, it is that which disposes of us silently and ceaselessly at the very moment when we begin to dispose of anything, when we make a judgment on something and try to submit it to the *a priori* laws of our understanding. So the Whither of transcendence is there in its own proper way of aloofness and absence. It bestows itself upon us by refusing itself, by keeping silence, by staying afar. To make this clearer, we must of course reflect upon the fact that in our normal experience we possess the Whither of our pre-conception only in the form of the condition of possibility of the grasp of the finite: in our normal experience at any rate we are never granted a direct view of it. It is itself present only as the Whither of the transcendence itself, which is enough to eliminate all forms of Ontologism. The Whither is not experienced in itself, but only in the subjective transcendence and it is known only unobjectivatedly. And its presence in transcendence is the presence of a transcendence which is there merely as a condition of possibility for a categorized knowledge and not of itself and by itself alone. Thus the Whither of transcendence is only there in the form of a distant aloofness. It can never be approached directly or experienced immediately. It is there only by referring us to something else, something finite, which is the object of direct regard.

The Whither of transcendence can further be designated as the holy, when the transcendence is regarded as that of freedom and love. For the Whither of an absolute transcendence of freedom, the nameless being which is at the disposal of none and disposes of all, which rules over transcendence by being loving freedom, is uniquely and precisely that which we can call 'holy' in the strict and original sense. For how should one name the nameless, sovereign beloved, which relegates us to our finitude, except as 'holy', and what could we call holy if not this? Or to what does the name 'holy' belong more primordially than to the infinite Whither of receptive love which before this incomprehensible and inexpressible being becomes trembling adoration? In transcendence therefore is found, in the form of the aloof and distant which rules unruled, the nameless being which is infinitely holy. This we call mystery, or rather, the *holy mystery*, to recall more expressly that freedom is transcendent with regard to knowledge. Every experience of transcendence is primary, non-derivative: and this same quality of the non-derivative, the non-deducible, holds good for all that is met with in it. For the transcendence and its content has nothing prior to itself: it is there in all other experiences as the condition of their possibility. The determination of its Whither imports no concepts from elsewhere from outside, to the object, but derives from the original object itself. With this experience of transcendence and its Whither one must either reject a given determination as completely unfitting and a misinterpretation of this experience: or one must concede that it is the original site and source for the intelligibility of this determination. There can be no doubt that the designation 'mystery' is called for here, and if so, this is the key to the primordial understanding of the word. We must experience here what mystery is, or we shall never understand it in its true and perfect sense.

If we have thus arrived at the primordial concept of mystery, it cannot of course have brought us to a definition of the nature of mystery. The mystery is as undefinable as every other transcendental concept, which only really display themselves in the original transcendental experience. But it is no doubt clear that in the experience of this transcendence, its Whither, absolute being, shows itself in such a way that it is the mystery pure and simple, because of its namelessness, sovereignty, illimitation, its unchallengeable mastery and direction of all knowledge and freedom. In other words, we have here the primordial experience of what we call mystery. Man is therefore, because his real being, as spirit, is transcendence, the being of the holy mystery. Man is he who is always confronted with the holy mystery, even where he is dealing with what is within hand's reach, comprehensible and amenable to a conceptual framework. So the holy mystery is not something upon which man may 'also' stumble, if he is lucky and takes an interest in something else besides the definable objects within the horizon of his consciousness. Man always lives by the holy mystery, even where he is not conscious of it. The lucidity of his consciousness derives from the incomprehensibility of this mystery. The proximity of his environment is constituted by the distant aloofness of the mystery: the freedom of his mastery of things comes from his being mastered by the Holy which is itself unmastered.

If man himself is therefore to be understood as the being of the holy mystery, it also follows that *God* is present to man *as* the holy mystery. The attribute of holy mystery does not belong accidentally to God like a qualification which could just as well be applied to any other reality. We only grasp what is meant by God when the attribute of holy mystery is seen to belong to God solely and primarily, according to which he is there as the Whither of transcendence. He would not be God if he ceased to be this holy mystery.

The nature of the mystery is therefore somehow involved in the question of the subject to whom the mystery is given. But before we inquire further into the mystery, we shall take man once more as the subject of our considerations, this time considering him as the spiritual subject deriving from the mystery, but in so far as this subject is seen as elevated by grace. Since our time is so short, we shall endeavour to make our point as briefly as possible, and simply take for granted here certain theological truths, which could of themselves be derived from a more basic and transcendental procedure.

Man, elevated by grace, is the spiritual being which is ontologically directed to the beatific vision. Grace, being strictly supernatural, is ultimately the beatific vision or its ontological presupposition. If then grace orientates its spiritual subject towards an immediate grasp of God, where knowledge of God no longer comes through objects and categories derived from created things, this essential quality of grace cannot mean that this immediacy eliminates the transcendental necessity whereby God is essentially the holy mystery. We already pointed out in our first lecture that God remains incomprehensible in the beatific vision, and that this incomprehensibility, because of the absolute simplicity of God and the relationship between knowledge and love in the creature, cannot be just a marginal negative phenomenon of the intuitive knowledge of God. The knowledge of the incomprehensibility of God must rather be one of the positive attributes of such intuitive knowledge. The beatific vision is not contrasted with pilgrim knowledge of God in the way that knowledge of the revealed and hence perspicuous is contrasted with that of the concealed and hence only vaguely suspected. The contrast is between immediate sight of the mystery itself and the merely indirect presence of the mystery after the manner of the distant and aloof. Grace does not imply the promise and the beginning of the elimination of the mystery, but the radical possibility of the absolute proximity of the mystery, which is not eliminated by its proximity, but really presented as mystery. Pilgrim man, still a stranger to the vision of God, can be deceived about the character of absolute mystery in God, because he knows the holy mystery only as the distant and aloof. When he sees God, God's incomprehensibility is the content of his vision and so the bliss of his love. It would be a foolish and anthropomorphic misunderstanding to think that the proper object of vision and bliss was something perspicuous, comprehensible and perfectly well understood, merely surrounded as it were by an obscure margin and a limit set by the finitude of the creature who must resign himself to this. What is comprehended and what is incomprehensible are in reality one and the same thing. The incomprehensible has of course its positive side. It has a blessed content which can be known even though it cannot really be expressed. Otherwise the incomprehensibility of God would be only a blank unintelligibility, the mere absence of a reality. But the knowledge in question would not bear on God if he were not grasped precisely as the incomprehensible. Knowledge as clarity, sight and perception, and knowledge as possession of the incomprehensible mystery must be taken as the two facets of the same process: both grow in like and not in inverse proportion. Grace and the beatific vision can only be understood as the possibility and the reality respectively of the immediate presence of the holy mystery as such.

When we described the nature of the holy mystery, as present to our transcendence, we said that this presence of the mystery has the nature of the distant and aloof. The holy mystery is accessible only in our experience of subjective transcendence, and only in so far as this transcendence acts as the condition of possibility of an objectivated knowledge according to categories. If these two elements of the distant aloofness of the holy mystery are eliminated: if therefore the Whither of our transcendence is no longer known merely as an overtone as it were of our subjective transcendence but experienced in itself; and if the experience no longer takes place as the condition of possibility of knowledge of categorized objects; and if such experience is possible—which we do not prove *a priori* but presuppose as guaranteed by revelation: then the holy mystery no longer manifests itself as a distant aloofness. But that does not mean that it no longer is a mystery. On the contrary, the mystery is there and most truly itself, radically nameless, indefinable and inviolable. Grace is therefore the grace of the *nearness* of the *abiding* mystery: it makes God accessible in the form of the holy mystery and presents him thus as the incomprehensible. In the vision of God face to face which grace makes possible many mysteries are indeed removed. But this only means that what they express is manifested in its own being and substance, is experienced therefore in itself and must no longer rely for its manifestation on the word that does duty for it and the authority of the recognized spokesman and prophet. Nonetheless, these mysteries remain mysterious and incomprehensible. They do not lose their mystery and become perspicuous. They can still not be resolved into something distinct from their content from which the content could be deduced and so made 'intelligible'. The Trinity for instance is not 'clearly understood' in the vision—it is contemplated as the divine incomprehensibility; otherwise it would not be identical with God who is identical with his incomprehensibility. If the incomprehensibility of God is the definitive blessing, the alpha and omega of reality, behind which there is nothing, and before which there can be nothing—precisely for him who has before him this incomprehensible God—then grace is also the grace of no longer being able to be deceived about the incomprehensibility of God, of no longer being misled into thinking it only provisional. It is the grace of loving the divine darkness without reserves, the divinely-given courage to enter this bliss which is authentic and unique, and to enjoy it as the nourishment of the strong. As long as we measure the loftiness of knowledge by its perspicuity, and think that we know what clarity and insight are, though we do not really know them as they truly are; as long as we imagine that analytical, co-ordinating, deductive and masterful reason is more and not less than experience of the divine incomprehensibility; as long as we think that comprehension is greater than being overwhelmed by light inaccessible, which shows itself as inaccessible in the very moment of giving itself: we have understood nothing of the mystery and of the true nature of grace and glory.

In the course of these considerations, which began with the recipient of the mysteries in his natural and supernaturally elevated transcendence, we have had to mention most of what can be said of the mystery in itself, as far as it can be dealt with in this our second lecture. We need not come back to them again. We shall only make a few complementary remarks about the subject of the mystery in itself. If what has been said hitherto has been rightly understood, and if the following statement is taken up correctly, then we can and must say that the mystery is, in its incomprehensibility, the obvious thing. If the Whither of transcendence is that which by disclosing itself gives transcendence its reality; if transcendence is the condition of possibility of all spiritual understanding and insight; and if the Whither of transcendence is the holy mystery: then the holy mystery is the one thing that is self-explanatory, the one thing that is its own self-sufficient reason, even in our eyes. For all insight is based on this transcendence, all light on this orientation towards the inexpressible darkness—if this is how one wishes to term the bright incomprehensibility of God. Looked at more closely therefore, the mysteriousness of this Whither is not just the contrary of the self-evident. An object of knowledge can only be *self*-evident to us if it stands on its own. But whatever is 'conceived of' only becomes understandable—though not really self-evident—when it is reduced to something else, resolved on the one hand into the laws of thought and on the other, into the elementary data of the senses. But in this process it is thrown back for its explanation and intelligibility either on the mute opacity of the purely sensible, or on the chiaroscuro of ontology—and so on the mystery. The understanding arrived at is therefore based on the unique self-evidence of the mystery. Hence it has always been familiar to us, and we have always loved it. Nothing is more familiar and obvious to the alerted spirit than the silent question which hovers over all that it has attained and mastered—the challenging question, humbly and lovingly accepted, which alone makes it wise. In his heart of hearts, there is nothing man knows better than that his knowledge, ordinarily so-called, is only a tiny island in the immense ocean of the unexplored. He knows better than anything else that the existential question facing him in knowledge is whether he loves the little island of his so-called knowledge better than the ocean of the infinite mystery; whether or not he will concede that the mystery alone is self-evident; whether he thinks that the little light with which he illuminates this little island—we call it science—should be the eternal light which shines on him for ever (which would be hell). And here we must say at once, since the opportunity may not occur again later, that if the mysteries of Christianity (in the plural) are to be really mysteries, or better, are to be correctly grasped as mysteries, their explanation must carry with it the self-evidence of the mystery, for which men today have undoubtedly an inward understanding. They have been badly explained if they only give the impression of far-fetched concepts and hair-splitting. The mystery is self-evident. That it is unattainable has already been said. Existentially, and for a theory of knowledge, it is at once a menace to man and his blessed peace. It can make him chafe and protest, because it compels him to leave the tiny house of his ostensibly clear self-possession, to advance into the trackless spaces, even in the night. It seems to ask too much of him, to overburden him with monstrous claims. It forces upon him the dilemma of either throwing himself into the uncharted, unending adventure where he commits himself to the infinite, or—despairing at the thought and so embittered—of taking shelter in the suffocating den of his own finite perspicacity.

But the mystery is the sole peace of him who trusts himself to it, loves it humbly, and surrenders himself to it fearlessly in knowledge and love. The mystery is eternal light and eternal peace. The Greek Fathers did not under-estimate the glory and the light of the beatific vision, and they did not really adhere to Platonism (an intellectualism which could only think of the incomprehensible as something provisional) when they praised the abiding mystery as blessedness. According to the Areopagite, when we reach the highest stage of life and knowledge, we enter into the darkness in which God is; according to Maximus the Confessor, not to know is the supra-rational knowledge; according to St Gregory of Nyssa, to enter the holy of holies is to be encompassed by the divine darkness. This way of understanding man and his happiness is on the contrary truly Christian, since it reconciles radical creaturehood with absolute immediacy to God, making God's incomprehensibility the blessedness of man and not the limit of his happiness, and seeing man as made for the one abiding mystery. So too we read in St Thomas (de Pot., q. 7, a. 5): *ex quo intellectus noster divinam substantiam non adaequat, hoc ipsum quod est Dei substantia remanet nostrum intellectum excedens et ita a nobis ignoratur et propter hoc illud est ultimum cognitionis humanae de Deo, quod sciat se Deum nescire, inquantum cognoscit illud quod Deus est omne ipsum quod de eo intelligimus excedere.* ('Since our mind is not proportionate to the divine substance, that which is the substance of God remains beyond our intellect and so is unknown to us. Hence the supreme knowledge which man has of God is to know that he does not know God, in so far as he knows that what God is surpasses all that we can understand of him.') Since the reason for saying that the climax of our knowledge of God is knowledge of our ignorance also holds good for the beatific vision, there is no reason for not applying this principle to the knowledge of God in the beatific vision. If St Thomas is not misread as though he said that with regard to God, the object of knowledge is different from the object of lack of knowledge—making as it were two distinct objects—the quotation speaks profoundly—and dialectically. It affirms that even in the beatific vision that which is known of God is known as the incomprehensible. The ultimate of human knowledge of God is attained only when its character of mysteriousness is most forcibly displayed: supreme knowledge is knowledge of the supreme mystery as such.

But a new type of problem now arises from the nature of the mystery as so delineated. Mystery is already there with the very essence of the natural and supernaturally elevated being of man. The primordial mystery is already there. This one mystery dominates the first effort of the spirit as well as its final fulfilment. It seems then that the Christian mysteries (in the plural) cannot be essentially new and higher mysteries, compared to the primordial mystery, but at most, secondary derivatives of it. Their very multiplicity seems to imply that they must be mysteries in the form of determinate assertions which are clearly distinct from one another. If so, if they have the character of mystery at all, it seems as though they possess it at best only in a secondary and derivative way. For the mystery which is the vehicle of all distinct and articulate truths must possess the character of mystery in a more primordial sense than the truths of which it is the vehicle and which are only intelligible within its horizon. Single truths, even if they contain mysteries, enter as such, and as differentiated from one another, into a system of co-ordinates which alone makes possible such a localization and differentiation. But the system of co-ordinates itself is, as we have shown, only a norm because it is based on the one original and immeasurable mystery, from which it seems to follow that no individual mystery can represent a heightening of our relationship to the original, comprehensive and immeasurable mystery. Thus the basic difficulty of such concepts comes to light. It is brought up by Goethe and modernism and every mystical 'night of the soul' religion, against a doctrinal and institutional religion with truths and special rites: that a silent reverence for the nameless seems to have left behind any relationship in terms of individual truths, even if these truths contain mysteries. Individual mysteries no longer appear mysterious in the original sense of the word, because they do not seem to leave the mystery to subsist as it is, but claim to know something definite about it which will satisfy curiosity. In any case, the self-transcendence of the many mysteries by which they merge in the mystery, remains so unclear, and is so little stressed in the theology of the schools, that one is inclined to think that where they are eliminated, they disappear in comprehension, and not in adoration of the abiding mystery. And hence it comes about, be it said incidentally, that contrary to the biblical data in St Paul, faith is never considered as something that abides (in its inmost kernel), but only as something transitory: '*donec peregrinamur a Domino*'. How then do the mysteries of Christianity, in the plural, stand to the mystery of which we have spoken up to this? This is the question which remains for the third lecture.

III. THIRD LECTURE

The second lecture yielded us a concept of mystery which, as we should like to believe, is more primordial than the concept usually used in the ordinary dogmatic and fundamental theology. Not in the sense that it contradicts it. But the mystery envisaged by both sets of definitions has a more original and fundamental relationship to man as a whole, in the unity of his faculties that is, to knowledge and the freedom of love, than the standard concept presents. Our notion further says that God himself is holy mystery, so essentially and perpetually, that this mysterious Whither of transcendence, mastering, unmastered and holding sovereign sway, can be given the name of God—as indeed the name of God is the nameless infinity. We may have given the impression that so far all that has been achieved is a merely natural concept of mystery derived from a philosophy of religion. It could be objected that as a purely philosophical concept it was not at all apt to describe the true nature of mystery in the strict theological sense. And on the other hand, the question already came up in the second lecture as to whether in this concept of mystery—which may be called 'absolute' in the most radical sense, because whether far or near it can never be eliminated—the theological notion of a multiplicity of mysteries was not already excluded. The question was whether there could be mysteries in the plural at all in face of the one unresolvable mystery, and whether, if there could be many mysteries, these could have real relevance for the fundamental act of religion, the adoring acceptance of the sway of the mystery in dedicated love.

However, the last lecture has already provided us with some means of transposing our philosophical concept of mystery into the region of the theological. For we considered the recipient of the mystery in so far as he was ordained by grace to the beatific vision. With regard to this subject, and hence theologically, we have shown that as such, in so far as it is ordained to the beatific vision, it is the subject made for the absolute proximity of the mystery and so is the being made for mystery, because grace and vision do not remove the absolute mystery. On the contrary, it is in the immediate present vision of God that the incomprehensible mystery of God is most forcibly evident. God is no longer simply and solely the God of the aloof and distant mystery. But as the God of the absolute proximity of self-communication he is indeed the God whose name is the holy mystery. It cannot therefore be said that our concept, taken initially from the philosophy of religion, bars the way to transposing the notion of mystery into theology. The philosophy of religion, conceiving of God as essentially and perpetually the holy mystery, can of course offer no grounds for a philosophical proof of the possibility of the beatific vision and hence of grace and the supernatural order in general. Need the holy mystery remain always the unattainable Whither of transcendence, given only in the experience of finite categories, that is, always mediated by the finite? Or can it communicate itself, as such, immediately to the creature, while still of course remaining essentially a mystery? These are questions which the creature can never answer and which the philosophical concept of mystery cannot solve. The answer can be given only by revelation, and this revelation cannot be confined to words, but must be also the giving of grace, as an inner, objectless though conscious dynamism directed to the beatific vision. This could lead us to a further consideration, if we took up the point conceded in the discussion that there exists another mystery besides the one already spoken of: the possibility of an absolute *self-communication* of the mystery, by which it enters into a radical proximity. Starting from the mystery of the absolute self-communication of the holy mystery, one could then try to reach directly the mysteries which the Christian faith as such believes in. And in fact this way is undoubtedly practicable. One could try to show, in spite of all the deadly dangers seemingly involved, that all other mysteries are already implicitly given, if it can once be supposed that the possibility of the absolute proximity of the holy mystery in a direct way had been revealed. And even if this effort could only be effective by presupposing the truth of the mysteries so explicitated; if therefore it offered and could offer no Christian theology based uniquely on the one revealed truth of the possibility of the beatific vision—still such an effort would have its point. For it is *a priori* quite conceivable that essential connexions can be recognized as strictly necessary, even if we do not succeed in deducing one element from another. And even if it were impossible to deduce the other mysteries from the radically immediate proximity of the holy mystery, a process which we shall not investigate here, still, the delineation of the connexions in question would be of fundamental significance.

But in keeping with the type of problem to which the second lecture led up, we take here a rather different starting-point for the considerations which follow. Let us remind ourselves once more of the problems in which we became involved in the second lecture. We have already pointed out that creation strictly as such can contain no absolute mysteries. It is true that all beings, and above all the created spirit in its transcendence towards absolute being, partake of the mysterious character of God, in so far as all beings are referred to God, and cannot be adequately understood without this relationship and hence without the term of this relationship. Thus J. Pieper is perfectly correct when he sums up the doctrine of St Thomas on this point by saying that all beings are inscrutable and unfathomable, because they are creatures. Since they are the *result* of the creative knowledge of God their reality and objective truth has such infinite ramifications, essential to an adequate knowledge of them, that comprehensive knowledge of even the tiniest of them is possible only to God himself. Thus all understanding of any reality whatsoever is in the last resort always a '*reductio in mysterium*', and any comprehension which is or seems to be devoid of the character of mystery, is only arrived at through the unspoken convention that this '*reductio in mysterium Dei*' should be excluded from the start. However, this silent disregard of the '*reductio in mysterium*' can be objectively justified, since the proper object of categorized knowledge on the one hand, and the Whither of transcendence on the other, give rise to two essentially different types of data for the spirit. And once this 'abstraction' is presupposed, it is absolutely true that in the region of the finite as such, there can be no absolute mysteries among the objects of categorized knowledge. Only God as such can be truly a mystery for the created spirit. Here arose the question of whether and in what sense the Christian faith can speak of mysteries in the plural, and how we are to think of the necessary unity which these mysteries form with each other and with *the* mystery, the notion of which we have been developing.

If we then begin, not with the notion of mystery which we have arrived at, but with the Christian mysteries in the plural, the first question will naturally be what mysteries of this nature are actually envisaged when revelation in Jesus Christ is understood as the revelation of *mysteria stricte dicta*—in other words, how many such mysteries are there and what they are. It is permissible to think that current theological teaching is not particularly concerned with these questions, which are nonetheless important. This lack of interest is due to something which makes it to some extent understandable. For when we ask what and how many are these *mysteria stricte dicta*, we really do not mean to deny that everything real and true in the Christian faith partakes in some way of the mysterious character of the mysteries of which we speak. To deny it would be to maintain that there was no intrinsic connexion between the various Christian truths and realities. So if there are any mysteries, the *whole* Christian message will be determined to some extent in all its elements by the character of mystery, and it becomes understandable that no particular attention is paid to the question of what truths are really '*mysteria stricte dicta*' and how many of them there are. But the question still has its importance, especially if it is understood as the search for a given number of mysteries, which can be neither greater or smaller. A faith which believes in the absolute self-disclosure of God face to face cannot imagine that God, if he wished, could constantly bring forth from the treasury, so to speak, of his truths and realities, new mysteries which surpass the understanding of man. It is impossible that the vision should reveal God under aspects which were hitherto completely unknown, just as it is impossible that God, when seen face to face, should still keep concealed within himself definite truths and realities which he absolutely refused to reveal and impart. For this reason alone the notion of an unlimited series of different mysteries is unthinkable. Each mystery is indeed of unfathomable depth and infinite extent. But *because* each of them signifies the infinity of God, which is contemplated as such in the beatific vision, their number cannot be indefinite. The question of the number of the mysteries has nothing at all to do with mathematical enumeration, any more than the question of the number of persons in the Trinity opens up a series of numbers which is then extrinsically and arbitrarily terminated.

Let us begin by trying to answer our question rather from the *a posteriori* point of view, that is, by considering the general and traditional doctrine of the mystery. We can certainly affirm that according to the general teaching of theology the mystery of the Trinity and that of the hypostatic union certainly belong to the *mysteria stricte dicta*. We are also certainly entitled to say (and it also follows from what was said above) that the mystery of the *visio beatifica* and hence that of strictly supernatural grace are also among the *mysteria stricte dicta*. The reason for this statement will at once be apparent. We need not give here a categorical answer to the question as to whether ordinary theological teaching admits other mysteries besides the three named, when the usual concept of *mysterium stricte dictum* is taken as the starting-point of this question. We can leave this question open to a certain extent, because there are in fact— apart perhaps from the mystery of the Eucharistic transubstantiation and presence of Christ, hardly any truths of which it is affirmed that they are *mysteria stricte dicta*, and (what is of course important here) cannot be understood as the necessary and intelligible consequence, as we see it, of the three already named. If we take for instance the mystery of original sin, it is comparatively easy to reduce this 'mystery' to the mystery of the supernatural sanctification of man by grace prior to his personal decision. Hence such a 'mystery' does not extend the provisional canon of the three mysteries. If one considers the mystery of transubstantiation, one would have to ask whether such a change of being is conceivable or not apart from the case of Christ, that is, independently of a *unio hypostatica*. If the question were answered in the affirmative, one could ask in turn how it could be proved that the transubstantiation of one purely natural reality into another was certainly a *mysterium stricte dictum*. It is probably impossible to give a positive answer to this question. According to our earlier considerations, which went to prove that there could be no *mysteria stricte dicta* in the region of created things as such, the possibility of transubstantiation in the purely natural order being a strict mystery must be denied. But if transubstantiation is only conceivable at all on the basis of the hypostatic union (which seems theologically more reasonable, just as the contrary seems devoid of theological proof) it follows at once that even if transubstantiation were a strict mystery, it would be so as a necessary consequence of the hypostatic union. Thus once more our canon of the *mysteria stricte dicta* would not need to be enlarged. Obviously, all positive institutions and decrees of God with regard to Church offices, sacraments and history of salvation can only be called mysteries of faith in so far as they come from a free personal disposition of God: they cannot be deduced *a priori*, but must be received as facts from the word of divine revelation and left as such. Thus they are not *mysteria stricte dicta*. The mysteries of soteriology can undoubtedly be reduced to the mystery of the Incarnation; all we have to do is to suppose something which again is not strictly a mystery: that the Word of God took on a nature from among the human race which, by the creative will of God, shared in solidarity one common history of salvation and disaster; and that this human nature of Christ was willed (as is obvious) as something to be actualized, and hence as freely accomplishing the human destiny of life and death. With these presuppositions, which are not strict mysteries, the whole doctrine of the redemption follows from the mystery of the Incarnation. We have thus listed *a posteriori* all the truths of faith which come in question as *mysteria stricte dicta*. And there are only three which can seriously be considered as such according to the teaching of theologians: the Trinity, the Incarnation and the divinization of man in grace and glory.

If we then ask *why* these mysteries are to be called *mysteria stricte dicta*, we must begin by dividing them into two groups: the trinitarian mystery of God in itself, and the mysteries of the Incarnation, grace and glory, in so far as these last deal with a relationship of God to the non-divine. It is not necessary to dwell on the proof that the mystery of the Trinity is a *mysterium stricte dictum* in the ordinary sense of the term. For if any real mysteries are possible at all, they must exist in the immanent life of God himself. If God himself were not a mystery, he could not give rise to any and hence there could be no mysteries at all. When we then examine theologically the two other mysteries (or three, if we distinguish grace from glory) we note at once that they have a common element, which links them together, marks them off sharply and clearly from all other relationships of God to the non-divine, and also makes them intelligible as a closed duality. For both mysteries involve what we call in scholastic theology a quasi-formal causality on the part of God, in contradistinction to his efficient causality. By means of his creative *efficient* causality (which is of course of an absolutely unique and divine type) God brings into existence that which is absolutely other than he. In what we call incarnation, grace and glory, God does not create *ex nihilo sui et subjecti* something different from himself, but imparts himself to the created nature. What is given in grace and incarnation is not something distinct from God, but God himself. He does not use the creature to impart himself, as when it points to God by its created reality: God imparts himself immediately of himself to the creature. This can be seen at once with regard to the incarnation, on which there is no need to insist here, but it can also be proved with regard to grace and glory. It is true that medieval theology concentrated on created grace when treating of the doctrine of grace, and that this approach still influences—through the Council of Trent—the modern theology of grace, whose positive utterances are rightly tributary to it. However, in its ontology of the beatific vision, medieval theology developed very clearly the doctrine that the vision can only come about by a self-communication of the divine essence, strictly as such, to the creature, and that this self-communication of God by means of a type of *formal* causality is the ontological presupposition for the proximity and immediacy which the *visio beatifica* implies, as a conscious process. But if this is true of the *visio beatifica*, it must be also true of grace, according to the teaching of Leo XIII and Pius XII: grace is the supernatural elevation of man and the formal beginning and ontological prerequisite of the vision. Hence in the doctrine of grace also, the central element is the 'uncreated grace', which is the immediate self-communication of God in quasi-formal causality in contrast to an efficient causality. This distinction between efficient and quasi-formal causality in God is the clear basis of the essential and radical distinction between the natural and the supernatural. And this is not difficult to understand. A reality which is not God himself, and does not exist as consequence of such a self-communication (as created actuation by uncreated act), which is therefore simply a created entity, cannot be supernatural in the strictest sense. For such a reality can as such not be a created substance: the question of its gratuitousness could have absolutely no meaning, since there would be no recipient of the gift distinct from the gratuitous gift. And an additional accidental determination which would also be a purely created one cannot be absolutely supernatural. For it is ontologically quite arbitrary to postulate the logical repugnance and impossibility of a created substance which would not be naturally on the same level of being as the supernatural accidental determination in question. A possible determination of a subject, where the determination is finite and created, can always be ordained to a possible substantial subject, *from* which it flows as its normal determination. And again, where this ordination of such a subject to such an 'act' is basically impossible, this must be taken as proving that this 'act' is uncreated. It is simply contradictory that something should belong completely to the order of creation, by being created, and still belong to the strictly divine order, by being strictly supernatural. Supernatural reality and reality brought about by a divine self-communication of quasi-formal, not efficient type, are identical concepts. Hence the *possibility* of such self-communication of God to the creature is what constitutes the theological mystery in these two mysteries. They are *mysteria stricte dicta*, because it is only through revelation (understood as salvific event and word in an indissoluble unity) that we can know that such a thing is actual and possible. The possibility of the finite being endowed with the infinite—which is not imparted and represented by a finite gift, through the possession of which alone one 'partakes' of God—constitutes the incomprehensibility of incarnation and of grace. One can leave the question of whether the *finitum* is *capax infiniti* in the obscurity of a separate discussion about the communication of God through a created gift and a communication through an uncreated gift. And then it is easy to answer the question in the affirmative. But when we really take up the question of the self-communication of God, strictly as such, which must take place by means of quasi-formal causality, we find ourselves faced with the absolute mystery, since then God as his own very self must penetrate into the non-divine region of the finite.

Here God communicates himself in his own person to the creature, as absolute proximity and as the absolute holy mystery. We can therefore affirm at once with certainty that the two mysteries of incarnation and grace are simply the mysteriously radical form of the mystery which we have shown to be the primordial one, from the point of view of philosophy of religion and also of theology: God as the holy and abiding mystery for the creature, and in both these cases, not in the guise of distant aloofness but in that of radical proximity. After all that has been said, there is no need to dwell on this, with regard to grace and glory. But we must still say a word on the hypostatic union. We must omit here the question of a more than formal parallelism between the incarnation and grace and glory; we do not enquire into the intrinsic connexion between the two mysteries. Does the vocation of all men to supernatural fellowship with God in grace and glory follow from the hypostatic union of a human nature and the Word of God, on account of its belonging to the same humanity? And again, is this elevation to grace and glory only really possible on the basis of the hypostatic union? Are these two *mysteria stricte dicta* not merely formally alike, but basically once more a unity: the one self-communication of God to the creature, which is essentially the act whereby God goes out of himself into 'the other' in such a way that he bestows himself upon the other by becoming the other? These are questions of the reduction of the two mysteries to their original onto-logical unity which we shall not further develop here. If any one is in-clined to reject the whole idea out of hand, he need only be asked how he then conceives of the permanent significance of the humanity of Christ, eternally united with the Word, with regard to salvation and glory; or again, can he seriously think that the humanity of Jesus is now only the private concern of the Word of God himself, once satisfaction for sin has been made on the cross by means of it.

On the other hand, we must still say a word about the fact that the hypostatic union too is the self-communication of God to the creature, precisely in so far *as* he is the holy mystery. We must go beyond a merely ontic understanding of the hypostatic union to try to reach an ontological one. And then we must say at once that the substantial unity of the Word of God with his human nature is such that the human nature in question is primarily constituted by God's giving himself to that which is other than himself: he constitutes this created being by taking it up *as a spiritual* one. Hence the union itself essentially comes about, as fully itself, in the human knowledge of the created spirit about its unity with the Word. Hence the presence of the Logos to the human soul in the beatific vision should not really be taken as a mere supplement to the hypostatic union: it is essentially an ontological element of the union. No objection to this statement can be drawn from the fact that we too, who are not hypo-statically united with the Logos, will also have the beatific vision. All that follows in fact is that we can only have this vision in its immediacy, in so far as it is mediated by the hypostatic union of the human nature of Jesus with the Logos of God. Hence the hypostatic union necessarily fulfils its own being in what we call (in neo-Chalcedonian terminology, if you like) the inner divinization of the human nature of Christ in grace and glory. But then it follows that the self-communication of God even in the hypostatic union is essentially the self-communication of God to the creature, *in so far as* he is the holy mystery and is the holy mystery in radical proximity. For it is in this way that he is present even in the *visio beatifica* of the created spirit of the Logos.

This truth could of course be arrived at in another way, and one more in keeping with the nature of the matter in question. One could start from the self-transcendence of the created spirit and show that its supreme culmination, even if never attainable by human effort, is to be found in what we call hypostatic union. Since we cannot develop this line of thought here, we must at least refer to the work of Bernhard Welte in the third volume of H. Bacht and A. Grillmeier on the Council of Chalcedon. There the considerations which we cannot go into here are developed boldly, but in a completely orthodox manner. Let us suppose then that the hypostatic union can be shown to be the most radical form of such created self-transcendence, unattainable from below, but fulfilling preeminently the nature of transcendence. It follows at once that the hypostatic union is not a mystery *beside* the mystery of the absolute proximity of God as holy mystery: it is this mystery itself in an unsurpassable form. It is the absolute ontological and existential self-surrender to the holy mystery which God is. And this self-surrender is the proper reality of God himself, in which the Word of God, as the *out*-spoken mystery, is itself the answer.

We may now take up once again the first of the *mysteria stricte dicta* which we mentioned. We can only give the briefest outline of what should be said on this point, and more in the form of a thesis than in that of a proof. When we consider the *de facto* development of the doctrine of the Trinity at the stage of its gradual revelation and at the stage of theological reflection on this revealed mystery, and when we reflect above all on the unsurpassable moment of this revelation given in the New Testament itself, we can certainly affirm: God has given himself so fully in his absolute self-communication to the creature, that the 'immanent' Trinity becomes the Trinity of the 'economy of salvation', and hence in turn the Trinity of salvation which we experience *is* the immanent Trinity. This means that the Trinity of God's relationship to us *is* the reality of God as he is *in* himself: a trinity of persons. Would this be Sabellianism and Modalism? Only if we ignored completely the radical character of disclosure in the hypostatic union and in grace; only if we do not regard the 'modality' of God's relationship to the supernaturally elevated creature as the way God is 'in himself'; only if we suppose God to be so untouched by this relationship to the creature that its manifold nature—as in creation and the natural relationship of God to the world—would constitute no distinction in God, but leave the distinction entirely on the side of the creature. It follows that in thinking of the Trinity we may start without misgivings from the experience of Jesus and his Spirit in us in the history of salvation and faith: the immanent Trinity is already contained therein. It is not a reality confined so to speak to its purely doctrinal expression. The immanent Trinity as such confronts us in the experience of faith—a constitutive component of which is indeed the concrete word of Scripture itself. The absolute self-communication of God to the world, as the mystery which has drawn nigh, is Father as the absolutely primordial and underivative; it is Son, as the principle which itself acts and necessarily must act in history in view of this free self-communication; it is Holy Spirit, as that which is given, and accepted by us. Since this 'as' which is used in relation to us really speaks of the self-communication of God *in himself,* this trinity appertains to God in himself—it signifies a distinction in God himself. And since in both these cases of the communication of God it is a matter of God himself and not of two created things produced by efficient causality, it must always be a matter of the one and the same God. God as the unoriginated origin of the supernatural self-communication, God as the principle itself acting and expressing itself in the world, God as the God who has come to us, been imparted to us and accepted by us, possess the one and the same nature. And they are distinct from one another, since otherwise the difference in the absolute self-communication to the creature would be found *only* in the creature, and there would be no question of a difference in the self-communication of God.

But this identification of immanent and salvific Trinity has of course a two-fold presupposition. Firstly, the relations of the three divine persons to man in grace are not simply appropriations. Each divine person has his own proper relationship to man in grace, even though each of these relations presupposes and includes the others. But this first presupposition is today no longer unusual in theology, and is in fact gaining ground. It is closer to the assertions of Scripture, if indeed it is not their only objective interpretation; it is favoured by the doctrine of the Greek Fathers; and above all, the immediate vision of the divine persons as such in the *visio beatifica* cannot be really explained ontologically without it. For the vision of God, and hence of the three divine persons as distinct, is determined by the ontological quasi-causality of *what* is to be seen, which forms a sort of '*species impressa*'. Hence there must be an ontological relationship of man to the three divine persons as distinct (and vice versa), which is not the consequence but the presupposition of knowing them. But that which is common to the three divine persons cannot be the onto-logical presupposition of their being known as distinct by the subject who knows and contemplates. The second presupposition for the identifica-tion of the immanent and the salvific Trinity is this. *Only* the Logos has such an immanent relationship to the other divine persons that he can be the one who can assume hypostatically a created reality and hence be the essential and irreplaceable revealer of the Father. For if each divine person could become incarnate, the Logos precisely could not appear as himself, as this particular person of the Trinity, in the personal manifestation of God in the economy of salvation. This second presupposition has indeed been rather abandoned and unknown since St Augustine. But it was taken for granted in theology before St Augustine and is accorded at least great sympathy, by St Bonaventure for instance. It is perfectly biblical. For the Logos is called Logos in Scripture in such a way that it can only cause great difficulties if we try to detach the immanent character of Word from the salvific. But in any case, the opposite of this second presupposition has never been proved. Every possible proof relies on the supposition that what *one* divine hypostasis can do must also be possible to each of the others. But this apparently obvious consideration is in fact a major fallacy. It proceeds entirely from the basically false supposition that what we call 'hypostasis' in God, three times, represents a *general* concept. The truth is however that what we call hypostasis in God is precisely that by which each of the divine persons is uniquely distinct from the other two, and is absolutely nothing else. It is therefore completely impossible to conclude from what one hypostasis in God can do, to what another must be able to do. We are therefore perfectly entitled to identify the immanent and the salvific Trinity. And this is the only way to prevent the doctrine of the immanent Trinity from appearing as a mere piece of subtle dialectic in a purely formal reconciliation of one and three.

Thus the first of the three mysteries which we have named, the Trinity, appears—if we may say so—as the God-ward aspect of the two absolute self-communications of God in the hypostatic union and in the grace which grows into glory. The truly immanent 'in itself' is identically the two-fold 'for us' which, because it is really self-communication of God in formal causality and not natural efficient causality, must be something of God himself.

If what we have just said, giving indeed only the briefest of indications, is really true, we may draw the following conclusions with regard to the main theme. The three mysteries, the Trinity with its two processions, and the two self-communications of God *ad extra* in a real formal causality corresponding to the two processions, are not 'intermediate mysteries'. They are not something provisional and deficient in the line of mystery which comes *between* the perspicuous truths of our natural knowledge and the absolute mystery of God, in so far as he remains incomprehensible even in the beatific vision. Nor are they as it were mysteries of the beyond, which lie or lay still further on behind the God who is for us the holy mystery. But they signify the articulation of the one single mystery of God, being the radical form of his one comprehensive mysteriousness, since it has been revealed in Jesus Christ that this absolute and abiding mystery can exist not only in the guise of distant aloofness, but also as absolute proximity to us, through the divine self-communication. The mysteries of Christianity, in the plural, can be then understood as the concrete form of the one mystery, once the presupposition is made—which can however be known only by revelation—that this holy mystery also exists, and can exist, as the mystery in absolute proximity. This of course we only know in so far as this absolute proximity has already always been granted us in the concreteness of the incarnation and grace. To this extent, the thesis here put forward does not necessarily include the affirmation that we could start with the abstract notion of the absolute proximity and self-presentation of the holy mystery, and deduce from it the incarnation and the possibility of a divinization of man by grace. The abstract notion of the absolute proximity and self-communication of God, if it is to be ontologically valid and not merely a logical and notional possibility, is and can only be attained in the experience of the incarnation and grace. But in this way it is still possible to recognize that these mysteries are really intrinsically connected, in their character of communication of the absolute proximity of the primordial mystery. And thence it can be shown (though we cannot go into it now) that the canon of the three absolute mysteries, first arrived at by an *a posteriori* listing, is on principle incapable of further extension. There are these three mysteries in Christianity, no more and no fewer, and the three mysteries affirm the same thing: that God has imparted himself to us through Jesus Christ in his Spirit as he is in himself, so that the inexpressible nameless mystery which reigns in us and over us should be in itself the immediate blessedness of the spirit which knows, and transforms itself into love.

PART TWO

'De Deo'

3

REMARKS ON THE DOGMATIC TREATISE 'DE TRINITATE'[1]

I

IN a collective volume, produced in honour of a former professor of dogmatic theology who is now the occupant of the see of St Boniface in Mainz, there is one theme at least that should not be omitted, the doctrine of the Trinity. Bishop Stohr himself has written several studies on the theme, which are still of the highest value today.[2] This is a consideration which suggests the theme, though the theme itself is rather terrifying: for the supreme mystery is also the most obscure. And the history of the theme could give the impression that the formal explanation of the formulation has reached a point which might seem almost unsurpassable, signalling something like the end of the story: since the Council of Florence there has been no official doctrinal declaration by the Church in which the magisterium might seem to sanction a real progress in the understanding of this mystery.

Much has been done no doubt since then in the line of research into the history of this dogma, from Petavius and de Regnon to Lebreton and Schmaus—to name only a few of the distinguished names in this chapter of the history of dogma. Still, one has to admit, with astonishment perhaps and a little resignedly—or is this being too pessimistic?—that research into the ancient history of the dogma has, at least for the moment,

---

[1] Some points in this essay coincide even in their formulation with the article 'Dreifaltigkeit' by Henri de Lavalette in the *LTK* III², 543–548. The friendly exchanges of ideas which preceded this article of the *Lexikon* justifies the similarities.

[2] Cf. A. Stohr, *Die Trinitätslehre des Hl. Bonaventura* (Münster 1923); 'Die Hauptrichtungen der spekulativen Trinitätslehre in der Theologie des 13 Jahrhunderts', *TQ* 106 (1925) 113–135; 'Des Gottfried von Fontaines Stellung in der Trinitätslehre', *ZKT* 50 (1926) 177–195; *Die Trinitätslehre Ulrichs von Strassburg* (Münster 1928); 'Der heilige Albertus über den Ausgang des Heiligen Geistes', *DTh* 10(1932) 109–123.

not stimulated many impulses which would carry the history itself any further. Here and there in religious literature one may undoubtedly see that efforts have been made to link Christian piety more expressly and more vitally with this mystery.[3] Theology too[4] has shown instances of writers who are more consciously and keenly aware of the obligation of presenting the doctrine of the Trinity in such a way that it can become a reality in the concrete religious life of Christians—one thinks of the dogmatic theology of M. Schmaus and of the writings of G. Philips. One notes also in the history of devotion[5] that in spite of a mystical cult of the

[3] We give as examples: V. Bernadot, *Durch die Eucharistie zur Dreifaltigkeit* (from the French) (Munich 1927); E. Vandeur, 'O mein Gott, Dreifaltiger, den ich anbete', *Gebet der Schwester Elisabeth von der Heiligen Dreifaltigkeit* (from the French) (Regensburg 1933); C. Marmion, *De H. Drieëenheid in ons geestelijk leven* (Bruges 1952); Gabriel a S. Maria Magdalena, *Geheimnis der Gottesfreundschaft*, 3 vols. (Freiburg 1957/58).

[4] Cf. P. Laborde, *Dévotion à la Sainte Trinité* (Paris–Tournai 1922); M. Retaillau, *La Sainte Trinité dans les justes* (Paris 1923); R. Garrigou–Lagrange, 'L'habitation de la Sainte Trinité et expérience mystique' *RT* 33(1928) 449–474; M. Philipon, 'La Sainte Trinité et la vie surnaturelle' *RT* 44 (1938) 675–698; F. Taymans d'Eypernon, *Le mystère primordial. La Trinité dans sa vivante image* (Brussels 1946); A. Minon, 'M. Blondel et le mystère de la Sainte Trinité', *ETL* 23(1947) 472–498; J. Havet, 'Mystère de la Sainte Trinité et vie chrétienne' *Rev. Dioc. Nam.* 2(1947) 161–176; F. Guimet, 'Caritas ordinata et amor discretus dans la théologie trinitaire de Richard de Saint Victor', *Rev. M. A. Lat.* 4(1948) 225–236; B. Aperribay, 'Influjo causal de la divinas personas en la experiencia mistica', *Verdad y vita* 7(1949) 53–74; G. Philips, *La Sainte Trinité dans la vie du chrétien* (Liège 1949); H. Rondet, 'La divinisation du chrétien', *NRT* 71(1949) 449–476, 561–588; K. Rahner, 'Dreifaltigkeitsmystik', *LTK*[2] III, 563f.

[5] In St Bonaventure, for instance, on account of his exemplarism, where his metaphysical revaluation of the *causa exemplaris* which put it on the same footing as the *causa efficiens* and *causa finalis*, helped him to overcome to a great extent the notion that the world itself could contain nothing trinitarian, strictly speaking, because it was created by efficient causality in an action belonging to God as one. Cf. also: L. Reypens, 'Le Sommet de la contemplation mystique chez le B. Jean de Ruusbroec', *RAM* 3(1922) 250–272; 4(1923) 256–271; A. Ampe, *De grondlijnen van Ruusbroec's Drieëenheidsleer als onderbouw van den zieleopgang* (Tielt 1950); idem, *Kernproblemen uit de leer van Ruusbroec* II–III (Tielt 1950/51); idem, *De mystieke leer van Ruusbroec over de zieleopgang* (Tielt 1957); St Axters, *Geschiedenis van de vroomheid in de Nederlanden* II (Antwerp 1953); L. Reypens, 'Dieu (Connaissance mystique)', *DSAM* III, 883–929; P. Henry, 'La Mystique trinitaire du B. Jean Ruusbroec', *RSR* 40(1951/52) 335–368; H. Rahner, 'Die Vision des hl. Ignatius in der Kapelle von La Storta' *ZAM* 10(1935) 17–34, 124–139, 202–220, 265–282; J. Iparraguirre, 'Vision ignaciana de Dios', *Greg.* 37(1956) 366–390; Efrén de la Madre de Dios, *San Juan de la Cruz y el misterio de la Santissima Trinidad en la vida espiritual* (Saragossa 1947); P. Blanchard, 'Expérience trinitaire et vision béatifique d'après S. Jean de la Croix',

supremely one, undifferentiated and nameless God of this mystery, the mystery has not remained the preserve of abstract theology. There has also been, no matter how rare and diffident, a true mysticism of the Trinity. We may mention in this matter St Bonaventure, Ruysbroek, St Ignatius of Loyola. St John of the Cross, Mary of the Incarnation, perhaps Bérulle and some moderns such as Bl. Elisabeth of the Holy Trinity and Anton Jans.

But this does not hide the fact that Christians, for all their orthodox profession of faith in the Trinity, are almost just 'monotheist' in their actual religious existence. One might almost dare to affirm that if the doctrine of the Trinity were to be erased as false, most religious literature could be preserved almost unchanged throughout the process. And it cannot be objected that the *Incarnation* is such a theologically and *religiously* central element in Christian life that on that account the Trinity is always and everywhere irremovably present. For when the Incarnation of God is spoken of, theological and religious intention is today concentrated on the fact that 'God' has become man, that 'a' person of the Trinity has assumed flesh—but not on the fact that this person is precisely that of the Word, Logos. One could suspect that as regards the catechism of the head and the heart, in contrast to the catechism in books, the Christian idea of the Incarnation would not have to change at all, if there were no Trinity. God, as one person, would have become man, and the average Christian who professes faith in the Incarnation does not go any farther in his express understanding of the doctrine. There are probably several modern, scientific and extensive Christologies which pay no particular attention to *which* precisely of the divine hypostases has taken on human nature. The average theological text-book today operates in fact with the abstract concept of a divine hypostasis—a concept which is however a

---

Année théol. 1948, 293–310; J. Klein, *L'itinéraire mystique de la Vénérable Mère Marie de l'Incarnation* (Rome 1937); M. Philipon, *The Spiritual Doctrine of Sister Elizabeth of the Trinity* (Westminster, Md. 1947); H. Urs von Balthasar, *Elisabeth von Dijon* (Cologne 1952); T. Mandrini, 'Una nuova mistica Carmelitana', *Scuola Catt.* 69(1941) 425–432; A. Jans, *Ein Mystikerleben der Gegenwart*, ed. M. Grabmann (Munich 1934). We cannot discuss here the relevance of the ancient *devotion* to the Logos, as distinct from speculation about the Logos (beginning with Origen), or of the cult of 'divine wisdom', as found for instance in H. Suso, L. Blosius and C. Druzbicki. Cf. W. Völker, *Das Vollkommenheitsideal des Origenes* (Tübingen 1931); A. Lieske, *Die theologische Logosmystik bei Origenes* (Münster 1938); B. Krivocheine, 'The Holy Trinity in Greek Patristic Mystical Theology', *Sobornost* (winter 1947/48) 529–537.

very analogous and precarious unity. It does not operate with the concept of exactly the second person in God as such. It asks what it means that God became man, but not what it means in particular that the Logos, precisely as himself in contradistinction to the other divine persons became man. And this state of affairs is not at all surprising. For since St Augustine, contrary to the tradition preceding him, it has been more or less agreed that each of the divine persons could become man. From which it follows that the Incarnation of the second person in particular throws no light on the special character of *this* person within the divine nature.[6]

It is not surprising therefore that piety draws no more in fact from the doctrine of the Incarnation than that 'God' became man and finds therein no clear assertion about the Trinity. And hence the existence of a clear and conscious faith in the Incarnation is far from being a proof of the fact that the Trinity means something in the normal piety of Christians. And there are other consequences, which show once more how popular piety is reflected in dogmatic theology, and how little the contrast is felt to the fixed, sacral formulas of the ancient liturgy. Theology for instance almost takes it for granted that the 'Our Father' is directed in the same way to the Holy Trinity, to all three divine persons, without any basic distinction whatsoever; that the sacrifice of the Mass is offered to all three divine persons in the same way;[7] that the ordinary contemporary doctrine of satisfaction (and therefore redemption), with its theory of a double moral person in Christ, conceives of an act of redemption which is directed essentially in the same way to all three divine persons; that this doctrine need pay no express attention to the fact that the satisfaction was given precisely by the Word incarnate, and not simply by the *Deus-homo*; that therefore one could imagine another divine person as man offering a *satis-*

---

[6] There is something strange here. All discussion of the Trinity must stress the fact that in God the hypostasis is that by which Father, Son and Spirit differ, and that wherever there is unity in the three, there is absolute numerical identity, and hence that the concept of hypostasis, when applied to God, is not a general and univocal concept which is predicated of all three persons in the same way. But then this concept is used in Christology as if it could be taken for granted that another divine hypostasis could also exercise a *functio hypostatica*, with regard to a human nature. One should at least *ask* whether the particular relative subsistence, in which Father and Spirit are distinct from and not identical with the Son, might not prevent the exercise of such a *functio hypostatica* (though it does not, in the case of the Son).

[7] The author recalls with some remorse that he felt twenty years ago that he had to take M. Schmaus to task for not accepting this assertion as obvious in his dogmatic theology.

factio condigna to the triune God; and that indeed, we could conceive of such satisfaction even if there were no question of the Trinity as the condition or presupposition at all.[8]

In the same way, the treatise called '*De gratia Christi*' gives a doctrine of grace which is in fact monotheistic and not trinitarian, from the *consortium divinae naturae* to the *visio beata essentiae divinae*. It is affirmed, of course, that the grace was 'merited' by Christ. But as this grace is explained at best as the grace of the '*Dei-hominis*', not as the grace of the Word incarnate as Logos, and as this grace appears only as the restoration of a grace which in its supralapsarian condition is mostly treated merely as *gratia Dei*, not of the Word, and still less of the Word to be made flesh: the treatise on grace is only very vaguely a theological and religious introduction to the mystery of the Trinity.[9]

The same anti-trinitarian timidity affects theologians when treating of the relationship between man and the three divine persons which is set up by grace. Exceptions like Petavius and Thomassinus, Scheeben, Schauf and so on merely confirm the rule. It is always taken to be a relation founded on 'created grace', a grace brought about by efficient causality, and the relationship is merely 'appropriated' in a different manner by each of the three divine persons. The sacraments and eschatology are naturally treated in the same way. In the doctrine of creation also, as treated today, the Trinity is hardly mentioned—in contrast to the way it was handled by the great theologians of former times like St Bonaventure. This silence is supposed to be justified by the doctrine that the works of God *ad extra* are performed so much in common by the divine nature that the created world can bear in itself no real sign of the divine inner-trinitarian life. Without of course saying so expressly, theologians consider the ancient classical doctrine of the *vestigia* or *imago Trinitatis* in the world more or less as a pious speculation, to be indulged in when the essential doctrine about the Trinity has been learnt elsewhere. Such speculations are not considered to add anything important to what is already known independently of the Trinity or of created reality.

[8] In the hypothesis of a two-fold moral person in a substantial personal unity, if there were only one person in God he could still enter upon a hypostatic union with a human nature and so make satisfaction to himself.

[9] The Trinity is not considered at all in the famous constitution of Benedict XII on the *Visio Beatifica* (*Denz.* 530). It speaks only of the 'divine essence', to which the most intimate personal act, that of self-disclosure, is attributed. But is this sufficiently explained by the themes of the immediate context?

II

As a result of all this, the treatise on the Holy Trinity remains rather isolated in the structure of dogmatic theology as a whole. To put it crudely (and of course with some exaggeration and generalization): once this treatise has been dealt with, it does not recur again in dogmatic theology. Its general function with regard to the whole is only vaguely seen. The mystery appears to have been revealed merely for its own sake. Even after the revelation, the *reality* of the mystery remains entirely centred on itself. Statements are made about it, but the reality itself has really nothing or almost nothing to do with us ourselves. We might summarize the average theological opinion as follows, without fear of being charged with exaggerating: in Christology, only one hypostatic function of 'one' divine person is considered and it could just as well be exercised by any other divine person; the only thing considered important in the concrete for us is that Christ is 'a' divine person, and which he is does not matter; in *De Gratia*, only strictly appropriated relationships are considered between man and the divine persons; objectively, only the efficient causality of the One God is considered; and this is as much as to say soberly but expressly that we ourselves have really nothing to do with the mystery of the Trinity, beyond receiving some revelation 'about' it.[10]

The only objection to be considered is that it will be our blessedness later on to see this triune God face to face, which means being 'absorbed' into the inner divine life itself, and so attaining our most real perfection, and that this is the reason why the mystery is already revealed to us. But then we must ask how can all this be true if one denies any ontologically real relationship between man and each of the divine persons, and confines it all to appropriations. We must ask whether the vision even of the supreme reality can really make us blessed when, as in the supposition which we are criticizing, it is considered to be absolutely *unrelated* to us

---

[10] We prescind here (because the opinion which we are attacking also does so) from the fact that real 'knowing', understood in the radical metaphysical sense, implies the most real relationship possible to the object known, and vice versa. But if the full logic of the axiom were applied to the question at issue, it would be seen that the revelatory communication of the mystery of the Trinity ultimately implies and presupposes a real ontological communication of the revealed reality *as such* to man. It cannot therefore be envisaged in the way that the opinion in question sees it: as a purely verbal communication, which does not change the real relationship between the giver (*as* triune) and the hearer.

in the real ontological order.[11] The appeal to the beatific vision therefore must be answered either with the challenge to draw the full and final conclusions from the position, or with the question as to whether we are not dealing with something more than mere knowledge about something absolutely unrelated. For if it were something absolutely unrelated, it would remain as isolated from our existential knowledge of ourselves as the treatise on the Trinity does, in today's theology of our pilgrimage, from the other dogmatic treatises in which we learn something about ourselves, to the real benefit of our salvation.

These considerations will help us to understand some other features of modern theology. It is now generally taken for granted that the treatise *De Deo Uno* must be divided from and placed before *De Deo Trino*. This approach, which has been in use for a long time, was recently defended as obligatory by J. M. Delmau (PSJ, II², 15f.) and others. There are only a few honourable exceptions, such as M. Schmaus and A. Stolz. One cannot however appeal to tradition for the now standard division and order of the two treatises. It only came into general use since the *Sententiae* of Peter Lombard were replaced by the *Summa* of St Thomas. One could however follow Scripture and the Greek Fathers and understand ὁ θεός primarily of the Father, without letting the word stand exclusively for the Father. Then the trinitarian structure of the Apostles' Creed, seen in the light of the Greek theology of the Trinity, would rather suggest that we begin with the Father and use this first chapter of theology to treat also of the 'essence' of God, the Godhead of this Father. It is worth noting that the Master of the Sentences, for instance, subsumes the general doctrine about God into a doctrine of the Trinity—a point which Grabmann counts as one of the 'main errors' of the Lombard. And the Summa of Alexander Halensis likewise makes no clear distinction between the two treatises. This is only done by St Thomas, for reasons which have not yet been clearly explained. St Thomas does not begin with God the Father as the unengendered origin in the Godhead, the origin of all reality in the world, but with the nature common to all three persons. And the procedure became well-nigh universal. Thus the treatise on the Trinity

[11] This formulation does not touch on the question of whether God has any 'real' relationships *ad extra*. We can prescind from this question here. 'Real and ontological', as predicated of each of the divine persons with regard to man, need be understood here only in the analogous sense (with regard to the 'reality', not the special nature of the relationship)—just as the Logos, for instance, has himself a real relationship to his human nature.

comes to stand still more in a splendid isolation, which brings it into a still greater danger than that of being found without interest for religious existence: it looks as though everything important about God which touches ourselves has already been said in the treatise *De Deo Uno*.

Possibly this division and order of the two treatises goes back ultimately to the Augustinian and western conception of the Trinity, even though this Augustinian concept had not the same predominance in the high Middle Ages which it was later to gain. Here, in contrast to the Greeks, one begins with the one single nature of God as a totality, and only considers him *after that* as constituted by three persons—though this involves a constant (and necessary) effort to avoid posing the '*essentia*' as a 'fourth element' previous to the three persons. It would be more biblical and Greek to start from the one absolutely unoriginated God, who is still the Father, even when it is not yet known that he is the Begetter and Spirator, because he is known as the unoriginated hypostasis, who may not be thought of *positively* as 'absolute', even when he is not yet known expressly as relative. But the starting-point of the Latins in the Middle Ages was different. And so it is possible to think that the Christian treatise *De Deo Uno* can and should be placed *before De Deo Trino*. But then one really writes, or could merely write, a treatise '*De divinitate una*', since the unicity of the divine being justifies this procedure, and make it very philosophical and abstract in development—which is of course what happens—with very little concrete reference to the history of salvation. It deals with the necessary metaphysical attributes of God, and not very explicitly with the experiences of the history of salvation which have come from God's freely adopted relations to creation. But if one referred to the history of salvation, one could scarcely avoid noticing that one was constantly speaking of him whom Scripture and Jesus himself calls Father, the Father of Jesus, who sends the Son and gives us himself in the Spirit, his Spirit. But if one begins with the basic notions of the Augustinian and western approach, a non-trinitarian treatise *De Deo Uno* comes apparently automatically before *De Deo Trino*. But then the theology of the Trinity cannot but give the impression of being able to make merely formal assertions about the divine persons, with the help of the notions of the two processions and the relations. And even these assertions seem to deal with a reality entirely centred on itself, a Trinity which is not opened to anything outside, and of which we, the outsiders, only know something through a strange paradox.

Efforts are undoubtedly made, in an Augustinian 'psychological' theology of the Trinity, to fill out the contents of the formal concepts[12] of *processio, communicatio divinae essentiae, relatio, subsistentia relativa*. But one must admit in all honesty that this way does not take us very far. This is not to say that such a psychological doctrine of the Trinity is only sheer —and not even successful—theological speculation. We can certainly say that the two divine processions, whose existence is guaranteed by revelation, have something to do with the two basic acts which we know belong to the spirit: knowledge and love. For this there is a foundation in Scripture. But though the basic starting-point of the Augustinian psychological doctrine of the Trinity is certainly valid, we must also point out its limitations. If one avoids artificial '*eis-egesis*', reading things into biblical theology, a frequent fault of scholastic theology in this matter, one finds that the biblical foundation is restricted to the fact that in the dispensation of redemption the divine knowledge is displayed as revealing itself and the divine love as giving itself in personal communication. When theology loses sight of this scriptural connexion, the Augustinian speculation on the Trinity is inevitably brought up against the well-known difficulty which always seems to render futile this marvellously profound type of speculation. One begins with a concept of knowledge and love taken from natural philosophy and uses it to develop a notion of the word and of the 'weight' of love; but after applying these speculative concepts to the Trinity one has to admit that they do not work: for the good reason

[12] It must however be conceded here that when Greek theology was most flourishing, among the Cappadocian Fathers, it seems to have been almost more formalistic than the theology of the Trinity in St Augustine—in spite of a starting-point for the doctrine of the Trinity which was taken from the economy of salvation and was directed towards the world. How is this to be explained? Was it not because the Greek Fathers thought of the Trinity as so clearly 'salvific' that they rightly felt that the *whole* of their theology was a treatise on the Trinity? Their treatise on the Trinity was not meant to portray the whole doctrine, but simply its formal, abstract side. And this was not really intended to be a discussion of each of the three divine persons. It was merely the solution of a problem secondary in the mind of the Greeks, that of the unity of the three persons, who appeared as distinct in theology *and* redemption. Should we not therefore say that the West took over the formal portion of the theology of the Trinity from the Greeks and made it *the* (whole) doctrine of the Trinity—since its soteriology retains only the dogmatically unavoidable minimum of the theology of the Trinity? Is not this why western theologians were forced —in contrast to the Greeks—to fill out this almost mathematical and formalistic theology by giving it more substance and content from the 'psychological' doctrine of the Trinity as developed by St Augustine?

that knowledge and love remain 'essential' concepts. One cannot and may not evolve a 'personal', 'notional' concept of the word and of the 'weight' of love on the basis of human experience. For then the Word of knowledge and the Spirit of love would demand that a Word and a Spirit should proceed from them, again as persons.

All this does not indeed imply that it is always a mistake to divide the treatises *De Deo Uno* and *De Deo Trino* and discuss them in the usual sequence. Even if it is done on the unjustifiable grounds that the division and order in question follows the process of the history of revelation itself, because it progressed from the revelation of the nature to that of the persons,[13] the treatment can simply be regarded as a pedagogical one and not a matter of principle. The important thing after all is *what* is said in the two treatises and what connexion is made between them in the usual division. The point of our present remarks was simply to note that in the present division and order of the treatises, their unity and interconnexion is not well enough worked out. This is clear at once from the totally unquestioning way in which it is supposed that this division and order is obvious and necessary.

There is another phenomenon which is no doubt connected with this way of sealing off the doctrine of the Trinity and leaving it in the air, so to speak. It is the general anxiety to eliminate all efforts at demonstrating analogies, presentiments and preparations for the doctrine outside Christianity, even in the old Testament. It would not be much of an exaggeration or simplification to say that the main interest of ancient apologetics against pagans and Jews was to find as many traces of the Trinity as possible before the New Testament and outside Christianity, at least in the elementary stage and in privileged spirits. The faith of the patriarchs of the Old Testament knew something of it, and St Augustine admitted, with a magnanimity which would cause scandal nowadays, that the great philosophers had some such knowledge. In recent Catholic apologetics, the normal thing is to reject sharply any effort at discovering presentiments of this mystery outside the New Testament. And this is unquestionably logical. For if this theology does not admit the Trinity, as a reality, into this world and the history of salvation, then it is to say the

---

[13] It would be at least equally true to say that the history of revelation first shows God as an unoriginated person in his relation to the world, and then progresses to the revelation of this person as the origin of an immanent vital process from which persons proceed.

least unlikely that even the slightest knowledge of it should be found there. Hence before the question is asked *a posteriori* whether such traces exist or not (a question which of course cannot be answered affirmatively *a priori*), it is tacitly assumed, more or less, that there *can* be no such traces. There is at any rate very little inclination to give *positive* value to hints and analogies in the history of religion or in the Old Testament. Practically all the emphasis is placed on the difference between the doctrines inside and outside of Christianity.

III

The very isolation of the treatise on the Trinity proves at once that something is wrong: the thing is impossible! For the Trinity is a mystery of *salvation*. Otherwise it would never have been revealed. But then it must be possible to see why it is a mystery of salvation. And then it must be possible to show in *all* dogmatic treatises that the realities of salvation with which they deal cannot be made comprehensible without recurring to this primordial mystery of Christianity. If the intrinsic connexion between the various treatises does not constantly appear, this can only be a sign that in the treatise on the Trinity or in the other treatises attention has not been paid to the points which show that the Trinity is a mystery of salvation in our regard and hence confronts us wherever our salvation is spoken of—that is, in the other dogmatic treatises.

The basic thesis which constitutes the link between the treatises and shows the reality and not just the doctrine of the Trinity as a mystery of salvation for us may be formulated as follows: the Trinity of the economy of salvation *is* the immanent Trinity and vice versa. This assertion must be explained, proved as far as possible and applied to Christology, so that its importance for the latter may be clearly seen. These tasks are so much interwoven and condition each other so thoroughly that they must be undertaken together and not one after another.

The Trinity of the economy of salvation *is* the immanent Trinity: this assertion is a defined truth of faith at one point, in one case,[14] for Jesus is not simply God in general, but the Son; the second divine Person, the Logos of God is man, and he alone. So there is at least one 'sending', one presence in the world, one reality in the economy of salvation which is

---

[14] At only one point, however, in one single case, which is therefore not enough to justify our calling the whole thesis simply a truth of faith.

not merely appropriated to a certain divine person, but is proper to him. Thus it is not a matter of saying something 'about' this particular divine person in the world. Here something takes place in the world itself, outside the immanent divine life, which is not simply the result of the efficient causality of the triune God working as one nature in the world. It is an event proper to the Logos alone, the history of one divine person in contrast to the others. (This is not changed by saying that the causation of this hypostatic union is the work of the whole Trinity.) There is an assertion with regard to the history of salvation which can only be made of one divine person. But if this is true *once*, then it is always *false* to say that there is nothing in the history or 'economy' of salvation which cannot be predicated in the same way of the triune God as a whole and of *each* person in particular. And the converse is also false: that in the doctrine of the Trinity, meaning what is said of the divine persons in general and particular, there can only be assertions which describe the immanent divine life. And it is certainly correct to say that the doctrine of the Trinity cannot be adequately distinguished from the doctrine of the economy of salvation.[15]

The importance of this consideration for the question in hand is often diminished or obscured in theology by three different lines of thought, which must first be examined, before the significance of the sure starting-point in dogma can be expounded in relation to the more general thesis.

We begin with the best known, most comprehensive and most radical difficulty. It is that the appeal to the hypostatic union, though based on a reality dogmatically certain, must be disallowed, because it does not and *cannot* deal with a case or instance which falls under a general principle and relationship. The statement about the hypostatic union gives absolutely no right even to consider that it may be used as a paradigm for

---

[15] One cannot escape this conclusion by the would-be clever scholastic reference to the fact that the hypostatic union does not bring about any 'real relation' in the Logos himself, and hence that nothing in the order of salvation can be predicated of the Logos as such, as touching the Logos himself. Whatever is the exact meaning of the axiom of scholastic metaphysics, that God has no 'real relations' *ad extra*, the truth remains—and it must be taken as the decisive norm for this axiom, and not vice versa—that the Logos himself is really and truly man, he and only he and not the Father and not the Spirit. And hence it remains eternally true that if everything that is to be affirmed truly and permanently of the Logos himself is to be included in a doctrine of the divine persons, then this doctrine itself implies an assertion dealing with the order of salvation.

similar assertions which would as it were open up the Trinity *ad extra* and allow the conclusion to be finally drawn that the 'economic' and immanent Trinity is identical. The reason for rejecting the Incarnation as an 'instance' of a wider relationship is said to be simple and stringent: that everything is strictly identical in God, except the opposition in the relationship of origin which forms the persons. Consequently, any one divine person can have a special relationship to the world, in contrast to the other divine persons, only by means of a *hypostatic* union as such— because only in such a union can what is strictly proper to him, his being a person, the hypostatic function, be actualized '*ad extra*'. But since there is only one hypostatic union, that of the Logos, and since any *special* relationship of any divine person can only be hypostatic the truth of the Incarnation cannot give rise to any more general principle—even with regard to possibilities, the possibilities of hypostatic union in other divine persons.

It is not our task or intention here to give a strict analysis of this basic difficulty, in the form in which it has been urged in recent years, especially by Paul Galtier,[16] against the acceptance of other than appropriated relationships between man and the divine persons through grace. This subject has been treated so thoroughly that nothing new and nothing better can be said about it in the framework of this short essay. Suffice it to say that we think the refutation of the objection as given for instance by H. Schauf,[17] is adequate enough. To say the least, it has not been strictly proved by Galtier and the theologians who share his theory that a special hypostatic relation must be strictly a hypostatic union. Positive arguments

---

[16] P. Galtier, *L'habitation en nous des trois personnes* (édn revue et augmentée: Rome 1950).

[17] H. Schauf, *Die Einwohnung des Heiligen Geistes* (Freiburg 1941); cf. also Ph. J. Donnelly, 'The Inhabitation of the Holy Spirit. A solution according to de la Taille', *TS* 8 (1947) 445–470; J. Trütsch, *SS. Trinitatis inhabitatio apud theologos recentiores* (Trent 1949); S. J. Dockx, *Fils de Dieu par grâce* (Paris 1948); C. Sträter, 'Het begrip "appropriatie" bij S. Thomas', *Bijdr.* 9 (1948) 1–48, 144–186; J. H. Nicolas, 'Présence trinitaire et présence de la Trinité', *RT* 50 (1950) 183–191; Th. J. Fitzgerald, *De inhabitatione Spiritus Sancti in doctrina S. Thomae Aquinatis* (Mundelein 1950); P. de Letter, 'Sanctifying grace and our union with the Holy Trinity', *TS* 13 (1952) 33–58; F. Bourassa, 'Adoptive Sonship. Our union with the divine persons', *TS* 13 (1952) 309–335; P. de Letter, 'Current Theology. Sanctifying grace and the divine indwelling', *TS* 14 (1953) 242–272; Ph. J. Donnelly, 'Sanctifying grace and our union with the Holy Trinity: A Reply', *TS* 13 (1952) 190–204; F. Bourassa, 'Présence de Dieu et union aux divines personnes', *Sc. Eccl.* 6 (1954) 3–23.

against such an identification will occur later in our considerations.[18]
Hence we maintain: in principle, the Incarnation can undoubtedly be
taken as a dogmatically certain 'case' of a special relationship of a divine
person to the world in the order of salvation. With this at least not
radically impossible relationship we have the possibility of a real communication of the whole Trinity as such to the world in the process of
salvation. Thus we have the identity of the immanent Trinity with the
Trinity of the economy of salvation.

The second difficulty, which is to some extent opposed to the first, has
already been touched on. It is that if one admits that each divine person
can enter into hypostatic union with a created being, then the fact of the
incarnation of the Logos really reveals nothing about the Logos himself,
that is, about his proper immanent divine being. Basically the Incarnation
only means for us, in this view, the experience of God as a person in
general—something already known anyway—but not that of a personal
God differentiated according to the proper nature of the Trinity. We
know (from communications made about it in the form of truths) that it
is precisely the *second* divine person who exercises a hypostatic function
with regard to the human reality which can be met with in Jesus. But
everything there met with and experienced would be exactly the same as
it is at present, if another divine person formed the subsistence of this
human reality. The tangible reality of salvation undoubtedly gives a
glimpse of the Trinity in the words used in the process, where Jesus
speaks of the Father, and of himself precisely as 'Son': but the reality is
not attainable in itself, because what happens in the order of salvation
could have happened just as well to any other divine person. The event
itself, being only the neutral vehicle of a revelation given in words and
not a trinitarian revelation in actions, tells nothing of the inner-trinitarian
divine life.

[18] The procedure should be carefully noted: the argument is purely *negative* to
begin with, namely that the argument of Galtier, etc., is not clearly convincing. We
do not therefore *positively* affirm that it can be deduced from the fact of the incarnation as such *alone* that there could be other similar cases where the really immanent
Trinity could enter into such an economy of salvation. (Otherwise we should be
contradicting ourselves. For we shall have to say at once that the incarnation of the
Logos does not allow us to conclude to the possibility of the incarnation of other
divine persons.) Only when the theological reasons have been given to show that
there are other cases of such a compenetration of immanent and salvific Trinity, can
it be shown that the incarnation is a 'case' of such identity.

We have already indicated how this supposedly obvious principle affects the development of Christology. But is it correct to affirm that *each* divine person can become man? Our answer is that this pre-supposition is both not proved and false. It is not proved: the most ancient tradition, before St Augustine, never thought of the possibility and really pre-supposed the contrary in its theological reflexions. The Father is by definition the unoriginated who is essentially invisible and who shows and reveals himself only by uttering his Word to the world. And the Word, by definition, is both immanently and in the economy of salvation the revelation of the Father, so that a revelation of the Father without the Logos and his incarnation would be the same as a wordless utterance. But the pre-supposition is also false: one cannot deduce from the mere fact that one divine person became man that this 'possibility' exists for another. Such a deduction supposes: 1. that in God, '*hypostasis*' is a univocal conception with regard to the three divine persons; and 2. that the unbridgeable difference between the way each divine person is a person—which is indeed so great that it is only the loosest of analogies that allows us to apply the same notion of person to all three—does not stand in the way of the other two persons entering into a hypostatic union with a created reality, by virtue of their own special and unique way of being a person, in the same way as the second person did. But what is supposed in 1. is false and what is supposed in 2. is not simply proved.[19] The thesis which we here oppose is false. For if it were true, and if it occurred anywhere except on the fringes of theological thought and were really taken seriously, it would throw the whole of theology into confusion.[20] There would be no longer any real and intrinsic connexion between the mission of a divine person and the immanent life of the Trinity. Our sonship in

[19] To deny that the Father or the Spirit could become man would be to deny a 'perfection' in them only if it were certain that such a possibility really exists for the Father or the Spirit and *hence* is a 'perfection'. But this is precisely what is not established. To proceed from the Father is for instance a perfection for the Son as Son. But to conclude from this that the Father as such must also possess this perfection would be sheer nonsense. But since the hypostatic function *ad extra is* the divine hypostasis in question, nothing can be deduced from the function of *this* hypostasis with regard to another hypostasis—even though our abstract general concept of subsistence points to no contradiction in the notion of the Father's giving subsistence to a human nature.

[20] We have already indicated at the beginning of this essay that it is taken for granted almost without a word and has considerable influence, so that it may be said to be an anonymous but very effective factor.

grace would have absolutely nothing to do with the sonship of the Son, since it would have been absolutely the same if it could have been based on any other incarnate person of the Godhead. There would be no way of finding out, from what God is to us, what he is in himself as the Trinity. These and many other similar conclusions which would follow from the thesis in question are quite contrary to the inner movement of Sacred Scripture. This can only be denied if one does not submit one's theology to the norm of Scripture but only allows it to say what is already known from one's scholastic theology and dissolves the rest away in clever and cold-blooded distinctions.

All this could and should be proved in detail. Here we must confine ourselves to affirming the contrary thesis. But since the thesis we reject cannot claim to be obligatory in dogma or theology, it is legitimate in the context of a short essay simply to state that we reject it. In doing so, one is surer of remaining within the framework of what has really been re-vealed than with the opposite thesis. One has a theology which neither expressly nor silently—which is far more dangerous—counts on an ostensible possibility of which revelation says nothing. One abides by the truth that the Logos is such as he appears to be in revelation: as *the* re-vealer of the triune God by virtue of the personal being which is proper to him alone, as Logos of the Father and not as *one* of the possible bearers of revelation.

The third difficulty,[21] which gives the second its full force, is as follows: if the human nature of the Logos is seen only as something self-con-tained, something constituted by its own rounded-off being, created according to a plan or 'idea' which of itself has nothing to do with the Logos, or at least nothing more than other possible created beings: then this nature subsists in the Logos, of whom this natural reality and its acts may be truly predicated as his own; it can be formally—but only very

[21] This difficulty is mostly present 'anonymously' in theology. It is difficult to formulate it clearly, though it is probably behind all the Christological debates which still exist today in Catholic Christology—as for instance in the difference between Chalcedonism and neo-Chalcedonism. The question is the following: is the humanity of the Logos simply an alien element which has been assumed, or is it precisely that which comes about when the Logos ex-presses himself in the region of the non-divine? Is the content of the incarnation (that is, *what* the Logos becomes) to be explained on the basis of human nature as already known—which therefore does not become any better known by the incarnation—or is human nature, to be *ultimately* explained on the basis of the self-exteriorizing self-expression of the Logos himself?

formally—said that the Logos is 'present' and 'active' in the world and its history by means of this human reality. But this whole reality really 'betrays' nothing of the Logos himself as such. He displays only the universal traits, those which are 'human' in any case, or at the very most he displays *through* this reality something miraculous and superhuman, by means of preternatural traits which can be observed in him but which do not belong otherwise to human nature. But universal human nature as such would not display the Logos as such. All he would do would be to show himself therein formally as a subject of action. And thus an immanent trinitarian reality would have gone out of itself, in the real economy of salvation, only as an empty formality. Something already known but non-trinitarian would have been created and assumed *in this form*, as something already pre-supposed, logically and objectively, if not in time. But under such circumstances one could not really say that the Logos has gone out of his immanent divine unrelatedness and has shown *himself* through his humanity and *in* his humanity. Likewise, it would not be really possible to say: he who *sees* me, sees *me*. The most one could have seen of the Logos as subject, when one met the humanity of Christ as such, would have been the formal, abstract truth of his role as subject.

Here then is the question: how are we to take the non-confusion ἀσυγχύτως of natures which is affirmed by the Council of Chalcedon? Does it mean that the human nature of the Logos has no other relationship to him than that of any creature to its creator, apart from the fact that it formally subsists by the Logos? The human nature is indeed 'affirmed' by its subject, but this subject does not really affirm *itself* in it! Possibly the difficulty has never been fully brought to light in the reflective consciousness, but it remains vaguely and therefore all the more effectively and disturbingly at the basis of every Christology. It is still more impossible to give here a proper account of the correct answer, as we see it, to the question here proposed. All we can say is, no, it is not like that: the basic relationship between the Logos and the human nature assumed in Christ is not what the difficulty in question says. The relationship between the two is more essential and intrinsic. Human nature in general is a possible object of the creative knowledge and power of God, because and in so far as the Word is essentially the expressible, he who can be expressed even in the non-divine, being the Word of the Father, in whom the Father can express himself and—freely—exteriorize himself, and because, when this takes place, that which we call human nature comes into being.

In other words, human nature is not an outward mask that is assumed (the πρόσωπον), a dress uniform concealing the Logos while he makes gestures in the world. It is, by virtue of its origin, the constitutive real symbol[22] of the Logos himself, so that we can and must say of its ultimate ontological origin that man is possible because exteriorization of the Logos is possible. We cannot discuss the thesis more closely here, and still less prove it. We must refer to recent works which consider this question either explicitly or in substance.[23] But if the answer to the question is as we have suggested, we can affirm vigorously and without any silent reserves: What Jesus is and does as man, *is* the self-revealing existence of the Logos as our salvation among us. But then we can really say, in the full sense of the words; here the Logos with God and the Logos with us, the Logos of the immanent Trinity and the Logos of the economy of salvation, *is* strictly one and the same.[24]

The Trinity of the economy of salvation *is* the immanent Trinity— that is the statement which we have undertaken to explain here. We have now shown that this axiom is verified in at least one case which is dogmatically incontrovertible. But that this case is really a precedent or instance can only be proved when we reflect on the doctrine of grace. This is a case of non-appropriated relationships of the divine persons to the justified. The problem and the different opinions to which it has given rise among theologians are well known and need not be expounded again

[22] On this concept, see my essay, 'On the Theology of the Symbol', pp. 221–252 of this volume.

[23] The following works call for particular attention here: B. Welte, 'Homoousios hemin' in *Chalcedon heute* III (Würzburg 1954) 51–80; K. Rahner, 'Current Problems in Christology' in *Theological Investigations* I (London & Baltimore Md. 1961) 149– 200; K. Rahner, 'On the Theology of the Symbol' (see note 22); K. Rahner, 'On the Theology of the Incarnation' in this volume, pp. 105–120; F. Malmberg, 'Der Gottmensch', *Quaestiones disputatae* 8 (London).

[24] This sameness—since we are not dealing here with the formal subject of the Logos in the abstract but with the concrete, incarnate Logos—is that which Ephesus and Chalcedon express as at once 'inconfused and unseparated', and hence not the sameness of a lifeless identity, where nothing can be distinguished because everything is always the same. It is the sameness in which the one and the same Logos is *himself* in the human reality, because nothing alien (human nature) has been attached to him as an addition—if it were, this 'union' could not really be thought of as a union, but merely as the juxtaposition of two realities. The Logos constitutes the other as the other, *because* he thus constitutes and expresses himself. The difference must be thought of as an inner modality of the unity itself. And hence we are to understand that within and 'without' the Trinity, the sameness is direct and immediate, not resulting from the denial of another reality, but the supreme form of true sameness.

here. But in any case, and to say the least, the thesis of proper, non-appropriated relationships is a free theological opinion and not in conflict with dogma. We pre-suppose it here,[25] and merely try to develop the well-known and widespread—though not undisputed—doctrine in the line of our thesis.

The thesis, which we pre-suppose as justified here,[26] is, when understood rightly and taken seriously, not a piece of scholastic subtlety but a simple and straightforward statement. It is that each of the three divine persons communicates himself as such to man, each in his own special and different way of personal being, in the free gift of grace. This trinitarian communication (the 'indwelling' of God, the 'uncreated grace', to be understood not merely as the communication of the divine 'nature' but also and indeed primarily as communication of the 'persons', since it takes place in a free spiritual personal act and so from person to person) is the real ontological foundation of the life of grace in man and (under the requisite conditions) of the immediate vision of the divine persons at the moment of fulfilment. This self-communication of the divine persons obviously takes place according to their personal proprieties and that means also according to and by virtue of their relation to one another. If a divine person were to communicate himself otherwise than in and through his relationship to the others, to set up his own special relationship to the justified (a reciprocal one), this would mean and pre-suppose that each single person (precisely as such, in so far as he is distinguished by reason from the one and the same nature) would be something absolute and not merely relative. The true foundation of the doctrine of the

[25] Here we note one point only. If one applies the medieval theology and its classic ontology of the beatific vision to the incontestable truth of the vision of the divine persons as such, this thesis cannot be logically denied with regard to the vision. And then it must also hold good for the grace of justification, which is the ontological basis and formal beginning of the immediate vision of God. We have therefore an immediate vision of the divine persons, which cannot be thought of as mediated by a created 'species impressa', but only by the actual reality of the object contemplated itself, which imparts itself in real quasi-formal causality to the subject, as the ontological condition of possibility of formal knowledge. But this implies necessarily a real and ontological relationship of the subject to each of the persons as such in their real proprieties. This point was perhaps not considered attentively enough by medieval theologians, but it is certainly a consequence of their theological principles with regard to the vision.

[26] Further support for the thesis will be adduced later, even if only in outline, when we consider the actual history of the revelation of the Trinity.

Trinity would be abandoned. But this means further: these three self-communications are the self-communication of the one God in the three-fold relative way in which God subsists. Hence the Father gives himself to us as *Father*, that is, in and by the very fact that being essentially himself he expresses himself and *thus* imparts the Son as his own personal self-disclosure:[27] and also in and by the very fact that the Father, and the Son who receives all from the Father, affirming themselves in *love*, inclining to themselves, coming to themselves, impart themselves in loving acceptation, that is, as Holy Spirit. God's relationship to us is three-fold. And this three-fold (free and unmerited) relationship to us is not merely an image or analogy of the immanent Trinity: it *is* this Trinity itself, even though communicated as free grace. For what is communicated is precisely the triune personal God. And the free communication in grace to the creature, *if* it takes place, can only come about after the manner of the two immanent communications of the divine essence, from the Father to the Son and the Spirit. Any other communication could not impart that which is here imparted, namely the divine persons, since they are absolutely indistinguishable from their own proper mode of communication.

We can now consider the relationship between immanent and salvific Trinity the other way round. The one God imparts himself as absolute self-utterance and absolute gift of love. This communication—the absolute mystery, which is only revealed in Christ—is however *self*-communication. God does not merely give his creature a 'share' 'in himself' (indirectly) by creating and donating finite realities through his all-powerful *efficient* causality: but he gives *himself*, really and in the strictest sense of the word, in a *quasi-formal* causality.[28] But this *self*-communication of

[27] The self-communication of the Father as he 'speaks out' the Word into the world means the reciprocal unity of the incarnation and the bestowal (*in grace*) of this Word on (believing) men. That this is so and how it is so, we cannot show further here.

[28] It follows as a formal axiom that if the difference present in something imparted by God, as such, is *only* on the side of the creature, there can be no question of a self-communication, in which there is a real difference in that which is imparted as such, therefore 'for us', God must then be differentiated 'in himself', without prejudice to his unity (which is then characterized as that of the absolute 'essence'), and this differentiation is characterized as the relative mode of the relationship of himself to himself. We may therefore affirm: if revelation (*a*) attests a real *self*-communication, and (*b*) declares that this self-communication contains differences for us (appears as mediated, but not by a mediation of a purely created type, which would destroy its character of real self-communication), then distinction and mediation is *eo ipso* affirmed of God as he is in himself and of himself.

God to us has, according to the testimony of revelation in the Scripture, a three-fold aspect. It is a self-communication in which that which is imparted remains the sovereign and incomprehensible, and which even as something received continues to be unoriginated and not at the disposal or within the grasp of anyone. It is a self-communication in which the God who reveals himself 'is there',[29] as self-expressive truth and as free directive power acting in history. And it is a self-communication in which the God who imparts himself brings about the acceptance of his gift, in such a way that the acceptance does not reduce the communication to the level of merely created things. But this three-fold aspect of the self-communication must not be considered, in the dimension of the communication, as a merely *verbal* development of a communication which is of itself undifferentiated. In the dimension of the economy of salvation, the distinction is truly 'real': the origin of the self-communication of God, his radically self-revealing and self-expressing 'existence', the acceptance, which he himself brings about, of the self-communication, are not simply one and the same thing which is merely described by different words. In other words, according to the self-understanding of the experience of faith, as attested in Scripture, the Father, the Word (Son) and the Spirit—no matter how infinitely inadequate all these words are and must be—indicate a true difference, a double mediation within this self-communication.

But again, this two-fold mediation by Word and Spirit (as shown ever more clearly and irrecusably in the history of the self-revealing self-comunication) is not a mediation on the plane of the created, where God would not be imparted really as himself. According to the testimony of faith, the salvific self-communication of God is really three-fold, and a Sabellian view of the economy of salvation is false. And again, the modes of being whereby God comes to us are not created intermediaries or powers of this world. Such a basically Arian view of God's gift would eliminate all real self-communication and reduce the eschatological event of salvation in Christ to the level of a series of provisional and incomplete mediations, such as prophets and servants of the Lord, angelic powers or

[29] It must not be forgotten that the concept of the 'Word' is to be taken in its fullest Old Testament sense, i.e. as the powerful and creative word of God expressing itself in action and decision; the word by which God declares himself, through which he is present and active—so that there is never any question of a merely self-contained and theoretical discourse. Looked at in this way, the unity of God's 'Word' is far easier to comprehend when it has become flesh and is exercising its power and judgment over the hearts of men.

descending emanations of the Gnostic or Neoplatonic type. Thus the real communication, divine in nature, which takes place in the dimension of salvation must also *be* a real communication in God's own immanent life. The 'trinity' of the relationship of God to us in the order of the grace of Christ is nothing else than the reality of God as it is in itself: a 'Trinity of persons'. This would be Sabellianism or modalism only if the character of *self*-communication were ignored in the 'modality' of the relationship of God to the supernaturally elevated creature who shares by grace in God's own reality. But in uncreated grace and the hypostatic union, this modality is the very way in which God is 'in himself', and we do not consider that God is so little involved in this relationship that the 'difference'—as in creation and the natural relationship of God to the world—implies no distinction in God himself but leaves it rather on the side of the creature.

What then does it mean for the treatise *De Trinitate* if the identity of the salvific and the immanent Trinity is pre-supposed, or confirmed in the course of the treatise?

When entering upon the doctrine of the Trinity, we need not hesitate to appeal to our own experience of Jesus and his Spirit in us as given in the history of salvation and faith. For here the immanent Trinity itself *is* already present. The Trinity is not merely a reality to be expressed in purely doctrinal terms: it takes place in us, and does not first reach us in the form of statements communicated by revelation. On the contrary, these statements have been made to us because the reality of which they speak has been accorded to *us*. They are not made to be the touchstone of faith in something to which we have no real relationship, but because our grace and our glory cannot be disclosed to us except in the statement of this mystery. Both mysteries, that of our grace and that of God in himself are the same fathomless mystery. The treatise on the Trinity should never lose sight of this. It is the existential interest of the mystery for salvation that gives the treatise life and driving force, as it also provides the true key to its understanding. If our basic thesis is rejected, the Trinity can *only* be something to be revealed in purely conceptual statements, by a revelation given in words in contrast to a revelation given in God's salvific action towards us: and it will remain such as long as we do not have immediate vision of it as it is in itself absolutely.[30] And the treatise becomes as abstract and remote from life as it is in many books.

[30] Presupposing that the vision, when so understood, implies no intrinsic contradiction or that none is apparent.

And the proof from Scripture inevitably becomes a method of subtle dialectics which draws conclusions from individual texts and builds them into a system which makes one ask whether God has really revealed us such far-fetched things in so obscure a way that it needs such complicated explanation.

If on the other hand we recognize that the Trinity itself as such is really possessed by us in the historic experience of salvation and grace which is given in Jesus and the Spirit of God working in us, we can always envisage the doctrine by having recourse to this experience. And there should be no treatise on the Trinity in which the most that is done for the doctrine of the 'sendings' is to put them into a relatively incidental or supplementary scholion at the end. Every treatise should be built up from the start from the 'sendings', even if for didactic reasons they are only treated explicitly at the end or perhaps even reserved for other sections of dogmatic theology. Indeed, the more boldly the treatise is aligned with the economy of salvation, the more likely it is to say the needful about the immanent Trinity, and make the truth really part of an understanding of the faith which is at once theoretical and existential.

The treatise can then trace the history of the revelation of this mystery. Whether this is done expressly or implicitly is a secondary question belonging to pedagogy, which we can omit here. It has been the custom of theologians in recent years to be very downright and uncompromising in their rejection of the older ideas that some sort of belief in the Trinity existed even before Christ. A more qualified judgment should now be possible, and if applied to the treatise on the Trinity, should allow of a better understanding on the ancient tradition and the history of the revelation of this mystery.[31] The whole of the Old Testament is pervaded by the basic theme that God is the absolute mystery which no one can see without dying. Yet it is this very God *himself* who acts in history and converses with the Fathers. But this revelation and self-presentation in the Old Testament is done above all by the 'Word', though it appears also as the Angel of Yahweh, etc. This 'Word' at once makes God present in power and also merely represents him, as does the 'Spirit' which enables the word to be understood and proclaimed. Where Word and Spirit do not exercise their sway, Yahweh has withdrawn from his people; and when he renews his mercy towards the 'holy remnant', he sends the

[31] Especially in the actual history of the *concepts* which underwent a real historical process as they gradually and correctly took on a trinitarian meaning.

prophets with his word in the fullness of the spirit. (The sapiential literature merely applies the same basic concept to law and wisdom, though in a more individualistic way, which is less impregnated with the dynamism of history.) God is present in the unity of Word and Spirit.

In principal, there is no precise and permanent difference between the three elements. God's presence by the Word in the Spirit must be different from himself, the eternal mystery: and yet it cannot be other than himself, something that would stand before him and veil him. If the *absolute* nearness of the God 'who comes' is to be realized with regard to the covenant in which he really and truly imparts himself to his partner, then the dynamism of this historical process leaves only two courses open. Either the Word of God and the Spirit just disappear as created things, like the many prophets and their many words, in face of the unsurpassable and overwhelming presence of God himself, which is now revealed as the secret object of all partnership with God at all times. Or these two 'communications' remain, and are then at once revealed as being themselves truly divine, that is, as God himself, one with and distinct from the God who is to be revealed, in a unity and distinction which therefore belong to God himself. On this basis, the Old Testament must be understood to contain a genuine secret pre-history of the revelation of the Trinity. And this pre-history—which no one can totally deny—no longer gives the impression of dealing with antique concepts which are suddenly used in the New Testament, and still more in early Church history, to make assertions utterly remote from their genuine contents. When the unity of the salvific and immanent Trinity is thus invoked, another danger may be banished which, when all is said and done, remains the real danger of the doctrine, not so much in the abstract theology of the schools as in the average understanding of the normal Christian. It is that of a crude tritheism,[32] not of course explicit but nonetheless very deeply embedded,

[32] There is in fact a dilemma which we must make constant efforts to avoid. The ordinary religious consciousness may ignore the Trinity, as we remarked at the beginning of this essay, and replace it by a pure, undifferentiated and lifeless monotheism. Or again, it may try hard to grasp the doctrine of the Trinity and then fall into a tritheism, which is only verbally avoided by a profession of faith in the oneness of God (which is of course never denied). It suffers from the lack of a mediating principle, which allows us to think of the intrinsic unity of the one and triune God, not merely in the formal, static abstract, or as 'God in himself', but also in the concrete and as 'for us': that is, as a reality which allows itself constantly to be vitally realized in us (that is, as the mystery, which bestows itself on us through the Word in the Spirit and as Word and Spirit).

which is a much greater danger than a Sabellian modalism. It is undeniable that the doctrine of the three persons in God evokes the almost unavoidable danger, which is usually countered far too late by express correctives, of thinking of three different consciousnesses. The danger is increased in the usual scholarly approach to the doctrine of the Trinity. It begins with a concept of 'person' taken from experience and philosophy and develops it independently of the revealed doctrine of the Trinity and the history of its revelation. The resulting notion is then applied to God and used in the proof that three *such* persons exist in God. The treatise then generally goes on to reflect on the relationship between unity and triune 'personality' in God, during which no doubt the needful is said about the more exact and correct understanding of these three 'persons'. The process is a sort of after-thought, in which—without, to be sure, admitting it—one makes the necessary modifications and restrictions with regard to the concept of person with which one began this spiritual Odyssey in the ocean of the mystery of God. But in all honesty, one must ask oneself with some embarrassment at the end what right one has to call the surviving remnant of the triune 'personality' in God a person, if one has had to eliminate from these three persons precisely what one began by thinking of as person. And then, when the more subtle distinctions of theology have been returned to oblivion, one notices that one is probably back with the false and basically tritheistic position, in which the three persons are thought of as three personalities with different centres of action.

But why not operate from the very start with a concept and a word— call it 'person' or anything else that seems fitting—which can be more easily adapted to the matter in hand and can render it with less risk of misunderstanding? This is not to affirm with Karl Barth that the word 'person' is not apt when speaking of the reality in question and that it should be replaced by some less ambiguous word in Church terminology. We may however concede that the development of the word 'person' outside the theology of the Trinity, after the definitions of the fourth century, took a very different direction from its originally near-Sabellian tone. It developed the existential meaning (as in Hermes) of the ego which is opposed to every other person in independent, proper and distinctive freedom. The ambiguity of the word was thereby increased. However, there it is, sanctioned by the usage of more than fifteen hundred years, and there is no other word which would be really better, more generally understandable and less exposed to misconceptions. We must therefore continue to use the word, even though we know there is a history behind it and that strictly speaking it is not altogether suitable to express what is meant and has no great advantages. But if one is definite and systematic in approaching the mystery of the Trinity from the stand-point of the economy of salvation, there is as little need to operate with the notion of 'person' from the beginning as in the history of revelation itself.[33] Starting from the presence of God the Father himself, communicated in the economy of salvation through the Word in the Spirit, one could show that the differentiation in the 'God for us' is also that of the 'God in himself', and go on simply to explain that this three-fold quality of God in himself may be called triune 'personality'. Thus we shall on principle confine the notion of 'person' in this context to what may be affirmed of it from this starting-point, which is that offered by the testimony of Scripture. All difficulties would not disappear, because in non-theological contexts the concept of person today has in fact another meaning. But the difficulties could be rendered less acute and the danger of a tritheistic misunder-standing lessened.

Finally, this approach to the mystery would allow us to re-state the question of the relationship, connexion and difference between the two treatises *De Deo Uno* and *De Deo Trino*. It is not so easy to distinguish them as it has been supposed to be since St Thomas set the example. For if the title *De Deo Uno* is taken seriously, we are not dealing merely with the essence and attributes of God, but with the unity of the three divine persons. It is the unity of Father, Son and Spirit and not merely the unicity of the godhead, the mediated unity, of which the Trinity is the proper fulfilment, and not the immediate unicity of the divine nature which if considered as one numerically is of itself far from providing the foundation of the three-fold *unity* in God. But if one begins with the treatise *De Deo Uno* and not with *De Divinitate Una*, one is concerned at once with the Father, the unoriginated origin of the Son and the Spirit. And it is then strictly speaking impossible to place one treatise after the other in the disjointed fashion which is still so common today.

[33] The concept of person in this connexion is sanctioned by the magisterium. But this does not necessarily mean that it must be the *starting-point* of all theological considerations. It can also be the point at which one arrives after re-tracing in theolo-gical thought the development of revelation and of the doctrine of the *Church*. And precisely because one re-traces *this* development, one never emancipates oneself for a moment from the doctrine and magisterium of the Church.

PART THREE

Christology

4

ON THE THEOLOGY OF THE INCARNATION

THIS is an effort to meditate a little on the mystery which we call the mystery of the incarnation of the Word of God. It is the very centre of the reality from which we Christians live, of the reality which we believe. For the mystery of the divine Trinity is open to us only here; only here is the mystery of our participation in the divine nature accorded us; and the mystery of the Church is only the extension of the mystery of Christ. Since our faith is contained in this conjunction of mysteries, we should meditate on this centre of theology and of Christian life, and often speak less of a thousand other things. For this mystery is inexhaustible and in comparison with it most of the other things of which we speak are unimportant. It is a gloomy sign in theology and Church preaching that when we speak of the all-embracing mystery we do little more than repeat, somewhat tediously, what has already been said. But the truth of faith can only be retained by continuous new efforts in its regard. Here too it is true to say that one can only possess the past by making the present one's own. The only consolation for this deficiency in theology is the fact that there are men who in life and death are united with the Lord in faith—hope and love.

Let us put the simple question: what do we Christians mean when we profess our faith in the incarnation of the Word of God? That is what we must try to say in ever new ways. It is the whole task of Christology, which will never be completed. We put this beginner's question, knowing well that it alone is more than enough to engage us for the brief period of an hour. And we put it in this way, because we reserve the right to be a little arbitrary in selecting this or that fraction from the whole answer which we cannot give. And we shall rather pre-suppose throughout the answer of the magisterium than repeat it in express terms. This does not mean that the ancient formulas which answer the question are eliminated or discarded as antiquated or even false. God forbid! The Church and its faith are always the same throughout their history, otherwise we should have an atomized history of religion composed of event after event, but no one history of the one Church and the abiding self-same faith. But since this one identical Church had and still has a history, the ancient formula is not merely the end. It is also the starting-point of a spiritual movement of departure and return which is our only guarantee—or better, hope—of having *understood* the *ancient* formula. For no understanding is possible anywhere if what is understood remains fixed and frozen and is not launched into the movement of that nameless mystery which is the vehicle of all understanding. If this is true in general, that is, if all our insight means being open to the incomprehensible mystery—which is not just the provisional remainder of what is to be grasped, but the condition of possibility of grasping and comprehending anything, the all-encompassing incomprehensibility of the Whole, no matter how it is named—then it is not surprising that it should be true above all when we are attempting to understand the tangible destiny of the incomprehensible Word.

The Word of God became man. To understand this statement, we must, in the brief time at our disposal, deny ourselves all consideration of the subject of the statement, the Word of God as he is in himself, about whom this statement is made. The procedure, though here unavoidable, is very dangerous. For one could well miss the meaning of the incarnation if one's ideas about the 'Word of God', who became man, are very vague. Since the time of St Augustine it has undoubtedly been customary in the schools to take it for granted that any one of that non-numerical three, whom we call the persons of the one God, could become man, presuming he willed to. On this supposition, the Word of God in the statement made above does not mean much more than any divine subject, a divine *hypostasis*: 'one of the Trinity became man'. On this supposition therefore one needs to know only what is proper to the divine 'Word' himself. Nothing more is needed to understand the sentence. But if one follows the pre-Augustinian tradition and has doubts about the pre-supposition in question, it will no longer be so easy to give up trying to understand the predicate in the light of the subject of the sentence. For if it is of the essence and meaning of the Word of God that he and he alone is the one who begins and can begin a human history; if indeed God's way of owning the world is that the world is not only his work, a work distinct from him, but becomes his own reality (as the 'nature' which he has assumed or the '*milieu*' necessarily adjoined to that nature): then it could well be that one only understands incarnation when one knows what precisely *Word* of God is. And perhaps one only understands well enough what Word of God is, when one knows what incarnation is. But we lay aside—at least for the moment—this consideration. As the starting-point in our endeavour we take the predicate of the statement which we are going to consider.

I

The Word of God became *man*. What does it mean: 'became *man*'? We are here omitting entirely the question of what it means when we say that this Word 'became' something. We are considering only *what* it became: man. Do we understand that? It could indeed be affirmed that 'man' is easily the most intelligible element of this assertion. Man is what *we* are, what we experience every day, what has been tried out and interpreted a billion times already in the history to which we belong, what each of us knows inside himself and outside himself in his environment. One could go further and say: This is so well known that we can recognize its basic constituents and distinguish its essential contents from accidental modifications on the one hand and from an ultimate self-hood on the other. We can then give the name of 'nature' to the ultimate constituent and content and say that that is 'what' it is. Thus our assertion will mean: the Word of God has assumed an individual human nature and so has become man. But do we really know from what has been said what man is and so what 'human nature' is? Of course we know a lot about man. Every day the most diverse sciences make assertions about him, and all arts speak, each in their own way, about this inexhaustible theme. But has man been yet 'defined' by all this? To define something, to give a delimiting formula which will sum up adequately all the elements, is only possible when we are dealing with an object composed of elements which are themselves ultimates and understandable in themselves, that is, which are now and by their nature limited.

We omit the question as to whether a definition in the strict sense is ever possible on these terms. At any rate, it is impossible for man. Man is, one might say in way of definition, an indefinability come to consciousness of itself. Much *about* him can be defined, at least to some extent. He can also be called ξῷον λογικόν, *animal rationale*. But before one rejoices at the simple clarity of this 'definition', one should ask oneself what λογικόν really means. But then one launches into an ocean which is literally boundless: for one can only say what man is by expressing what he is concerned with and what is concerned with him. But that is the boundless, the nameless. Man is therefore mystery in his essence, his nature. He is not in himself the infinite fullness of the mystery which concerns him, for that fullness is inexhaustible, and the primordial form of all that is mystery to us. But he is mystery in his real being and its ultimate reason, in his nature, which is the humble, conscious state of being referred to the fullness, the form of the mystery which we ourselves are. When we have said everything about ourselves that can be described and defined, we have still said nothing about ourselves, unless we have included or implied the fact that we are beings who are referred to the incomprehensible God. But this reference, which is our nature, can only be conceived and understood when we allow ourselves freely to be grasped by the incomprehensible, ratifying the act which while remaining inexpressible is the condition of possibility of all intelligent expression.

Our whole existence is the acceptance or rejection of the mystery which we are, as we find our poverty referred to the mystery of the fullness. The pre-existent object of our acceptance or refusal, of the decision which is the deed of our life, is the mystery which we are. And this mystery is our nature, because the transcendence which we are and which we accomplish brings our existence and God's existence together: and both as mystery. And here we must always remember that a mystery is not something still undisclosed, which is a second element along with what is grasped and understood. This would be to confuse mystery with the still undiscovered unknown. Mystery on the contrary is the impenetrable which is already present and does not need to be fetched: it is not a second element unmastered only provisionally. It is the indomitable dominant horizon of all understanding, that which makes it possible to understand other things by the fact that it is silently there as the incomprehensible. Mystery is therefore not something provisional which is one day to be done away with or which could in fact be non-mysterious. It is the propriety which always and necessarily characterizes God—and through him, us—so much so, that the immediate vision of God which is promised to us as our fulfilment, is the immediacy of the incomprehensible. It is precisely the removal of the illusion that our lack of total comprehension is only provisional. For in this vision we shall see by God himself and not merely by the infinite poverty of our transcendence that he is incomprehensible. But the vision of the mystery in itself, accepted in *love*, is the bliss of the creature and really makes what is known as mystery the burning bush of the eternally unquenchable flame of love.

What point have we reached now? We have come closer to our theme. If this is human nature, we begin to understand more clearly—always of course within the framework of the basic mystery which is God and we —what it means to say: God takes on a human nature as his own. The indefinable nature, whose limits—'definition'—are the unlimited reference to the infinite fullness of the mystery, has, when assumed by God as *his* reality, simply arrived at the point to which it always strives by virtue of its essence. It is its *meaning*, and not an incidental activity which could perhaps be left aside, to be that which is delivered up and abandoned, to be that which fulfils itself and finds itself by perpetually disappearing into the incomprehensible. This is done in the strictest sense and reaches an unsurpassable pitch of achievement, when the nature which surrenders[1] itself to the mystery of the fullness belongs so little to itself that it becomes

---

[1] This 'act' of self-surrender is of course primarily the 'act' of the Creator in making human nature, and not something done 'accidentally' by man as a creature in his *actus secondus* deriving from his own decision. In the relationship however which exists between man's being as constituted by God and man's own action which derives from this being, we recognize the former through the latter. The action is consequent upon the nature, in such a way that (unlike that of sub-spiritual beings) man is called in his action to confront his nature, cause it to 'come to' itself and realize itself. Thus between the nature and its spiritual self-realization there ensues a unity, which (though not simply an identity) is not brought out well enough by the formal ontological 'unity' of substance and accident alone. To understand this properly, it must always be borne in mind that what God produces as the source of the proper activity of the spiritual creature (the 'physis' in the original Aristotelian sense) is precisely not a 'thing' with static 'qualities' which are 'just there' passively. It is a substance in action, an 'actus', which for this very reason, expands in the activity proper to itself and in which this divinely-created basic act realizes itself. Hence there is no other way to express this fact than to say that the spiritual being 'gives itself, away from itself', primarily in the act as which God creates it. The abysmal perdition of the creature which refuses to give itself to God can only be truly seen under this aspect. Otherwise there would only be an 'accidental' change '*in it*', which would leave its nature basically intact, so that it would be really surprising that it perishes, and not merely the evil '*in it*'. The 'existential' self-dedication which is accomplished in the human spiritual nature of Christ corresponds in intensity to the basic act as which the nature assumed by the Logos was created by God as assumed: from the point of view of the nature, this substantial acceptance is substantial self-dedication.

the nature of God himself. The incarnation of God is therefore the unique, *supreme*, case of the total actualization of human reality, which consists of the fact that man *is* in so far as he gives up himself. For what does the *potentia oboedientialis* mean for the hypostatic union? What does it mean when we say that human nature has the possibility of being assumed by the person of the Word of God? Correctly understood, it means that this *potentia* is not one potentiality along with other possibilities in the constituent elements of human nature: it is objectively identical with the essence of man. But once this is understood, it is impossible to contest on grounds of scholastic theology that one is justified in describing this essence in such a way that it appears precisely *as* this potentiality. And that is precisely what we have tried to indicate in the simplest possible outline.

This effort does not mean, 1. that the possibility of the hypostatic union can be strictly perspicuous as such *a priori*, that is, independently of the revelation of its *de facto* existence. And it does not mean, 2. that such a possibility must be realized in every man who possesses this nature.

1. The transcendence of man makes it clear that it would be wrong to define him, to delimit and put bounds to his possibilities. At least a hypothetical extension and culmination of the possibilities given with his trancendence are justified. But any type of fulfilment whatever remains within the bounds of the hypothetical as long as (and it will undoubtedly be impossible here) it is not proved that the transcendence would lose all meaning if it did not find precisely this fulfilment. And this transcendence means being immeasurably open with regard to the *freedom* of the mystery, and being utterly abandoned to the necessity of allowing oneself to be disposed of. We can therefore deduce from the transcendence no exigency of such fulfilment. And hence a strict knowledge of its possibility, including aspects which perhaps remain hidden to us, is not possible.

Hence it follows, 2. that the potentiality need not be realized in every man. And the fact of our being simply creatures, the fact of our sinfulness and of our radical peril, shows us, when our situation is brought to light in the word of God, that the possibility has not in fact been actualized in us. And yet we can say: God has taken on a human nature, because it is essentially ready and adoptable, because it alone, in contrast to what is definable without transcendence can exist in total dispossession of itself, and comes therein to the fulfilment of its own incomprehensible meaning.

Man has ultimately no choice. He understands himself as a mere void, which one can encompass only to note with the cynical laughter of the damned, that there is nothing behind it. Or—since he is *not* the fullness which can repose contentedly in itself—he is found by the infinite and so becomes what he is: one who never succeeds in encompassing himself because the finite can only be surpassed by moving out into the unfathomable fullness of God.

But if this is the essence of man, he attains his supreme fulfilment, the gratuitous fulfilment of his essence to which through his own ways of perfection he is always tending, only when he adoringly believes that somewhere there is a being whose existence steps so much out of itself into God, that it *is* just the question about the mystery utterly given over to the mystery. He must believe that there is a being who is the question which has become unquestioning, because it has been accepted as his own answer by him who answers. And then we may perhaps say that it is not so strange, since this strange element already floats before the mind of man in the pure mystery of his primordial understanding, along with the perfected whole. The more difficult question is *how* and *where* and *when* one may give an earthly name to him who is such a being. But if one seeks *him*, to whom one can bring the eternal mystery of the pure fullness of one's own being for fulfilment, one can see very simply, if one seeks 'quietly', that is, in meekness and with the eyes of innocence, that it is only in Jesus of Nazareth that one can dare to believe such a thing has happened and happens eternally. The rest of us are all farther from God, because we always have to think that we are the only one to understand ourselves. But he *knew* that only the Father knows his mystery, and so he knew that only he knows the Father.

To avoid misunderstanding, we must note that the Christology outlined above is not a 'Christology of consciousness' in contrast to an ontological Christology affirming the substantial unity of the Logos with his uhman nature. It is based on the metaphysical insight, derived from a strict ontology, that true being is the spirit as such itself. It tries to formulate the necessary ontological counterpart to the ontic statements of tradition, so that we may reach a better understanding of what is meant, and in order that the true traditional affirmations do not give the impression that God has wrapped himself in the disguise of a human nature which only clings to him exteriorly and has come to his earth to set things right because they could not be managed from heaven. And there is another remark to make. It might be imagined that this God-becoming-man takes place as often as men come into existence and that the incarnation is not a unique miracle. This would imply that the historicity and personality in question was reduced to the level of the nature which is everywhere and always the same: and this would be nothing short of mythologizing the truth. It would also ignore the fact the humanity of God—in which he is there as an individual for each individual man, not having come to divinize nature—can be and is *in itself*[2] favoured with nothing essentially more or less in the line of closeness to and encounter with God, than that which is in fact provided for *each* man in grace: the beatific vision.

II

The Word of God has *become* man: this is the assertion which we are trying to understand better. We take the word 'become'. Can God 'become' anything? This question has always been answered in the affirmative by pantheism and all other philosophies in which God exists 'historically'. But it leaves the Christian and all really theistic philosophers in a difficult situation. They proclaim God as the 'Unchangeable', he who simply *is*—*actuus purus*—who in blessed security, in the self-sufficiency of infinite reality, possesses from enternity to eternity the absolute, unwavering, glad fullness of what he is. He has not first to become, he has not first to acquire what he is. And precisely because we have received for our part the burden of history and change, as a grace and a distinction, we necessarily proclaim *such* a God, because it is only because he is the infinite fullness that the processes of spirit and nature can be more than the pointless self-awareness of absolute emptiness which collapses into its own void. And hence the acknowledgement of the unchanging and unchangeable God in his eternally perfect fullness is not merely a postulate of philosophy, it is also a dogma of faith. Nonetheless, it remains true: the Word *became* flesh.

[2] The words 'in itself' should be noted. All Catholic theologians are familiar with the view that the hypostatic union of the humanity of Christ with the Logos has as a necessary consequence the *intrinsic* divinization of this human nature. Though it is a consequence of the hypostatic union which is morally and indeed ontologically necessary, it is distinct from the union, and through it alone is the humanity of Christ sanctified and divinized 'in itself'—and (though in a unique measure of intrinsic holiness) is precisely that which is to be bestowed on all men as grace of justification.

And we are only truly Christians when we have accepted this. It will hardly be denied that here the traditional philosophy and theology of the schools begins to blink and stutter. It affirms that the change and transition takes place in the created reality which is assumed, and not in the Logos. And so everything is clear: the Logos remains unchanged when it takes on something which, as a created reality, is subject to change, including the fact of its being assumed. Hence all change and history, with all their tribulation, remain on this side of the absolute gulf which necessarily sunders the unchangeable God from the world of change and prevents them from mingling. But it still remains true that the Logos *became* man, that the changing history of this human reality is *his* own history: our time became the time of the eternal, our death the death of the immortal God himself. And no matter how we distribute the predicates which seem to contradict one another and some of which seem incompatible with God, dividing them up between two realities, the divine Word and created human nature, we still may not forget that one of these, the created reality, is that of the Logos of God himself. And thus, when this attempt at solving the question by the division and distribution of predicates has been made, the whole question begins again. It is the question of how to understand the truth that the immutability of God may not distort our view of the fact that what happened to Jesus on earth is precisely the history of the Word of God himself, and a process which *he* underwent.

If we face squarely the fact of the incarnation, which our faith testifies to be the fundamental dogma of Christianity, we must simply say: God can become something, he who is unchangeable in himself can *himself* become subject to change *in something else*.[3] This brings us to an

---

[3] One can confine oneself to saying that the created thing is the humanity of the Word in itself, and that therefore something has happened, a change has taken place. But if one sees the event as taking place only on this side of the boundary which separates God and the creature, one has seen and said something which is true, but missed by a hairsbreadth and omitted what is really the point of the whole statement: that this event is that of God himself. This has not yet been expressed if one speaks for instance merely of the 'inconfused' human nature! To call it then a 'change' does not really matter: it is a reality (namely, that God *himself* has become flesh, through the fact that something has taken place in this human dimension), even though one fights shy of the term 'change'. If we do call it a change, then, since God is unchangeable, we must say that God who is unchangeable in himself can change in another (can in fact become man). But this 'changing *in* another' must neither be taken as denying the immutability of God in himself nor simply be reduced to a

ontological ultimate, which a purely rational ontology might perhaps never suspect and find it difficult to take cognizance of and insert as a primordial truth into its most basic and seminal utterances: the Absolute, or more correctly, he who is the absolute, has, in the pure freedom of his infinite and abiding unrelatedness, the possibility of himself becoming that other thing, the finite; God, in and by the fact that he empties *himself* gives away *himself, poses* the other as his own reality. The basic element to begin with is not the concept of an assumption, which pre-supposes what is to be assumed as something obvious, and has nothing more to do than to assign it to the taker—a term, however, which it never really reaches, since it is rejected by his immutability and may never affect him, since he is unchangeable, when his immutability is considered undialectically and in isolation—in static concepts. On the contrary, the basic element, according to our faith, is the *self*-emptying, the coming to be, the κένωσις and γένεσις of God himself, who can come to be by *becoming* another thing, derivative, in the act of constituting it, without having to change in his own proper reality which is the unoriginated origin. By the

---

changement *of* the other. Here ontology has to orientate itself according to the message of faith and not try to lecture it. The formal truth of the oneness of God is not denied by the doctrine of the Trinity. But this oneness, such as we can conceive it (and which is a dogma) cannot be used to determine what the nature of the Trinity may be. So too here. We must maintain methodologically the immutability of God, and yet it would be basically a denial of the incarnation if we used it alone to determine what this mystery could be. If, to expedite the mystery, one transferred it into the region of the creature alone, one would really abolish the mystery in the strict sense. For in the finite alone as such there can be no absolute mysteries at all, because one can always conceive a finite intellect proportionate to any finite thing and able to fathom it. The mystery of the incarnation must lie in God himself: in the fact that he, though unchangeable 'in himself', can become something 'in another'. The immutability of God is a dialectical truth like the unity of God. These two truths only —*de facto*—retain their validity for us when we think at once of the two other truths (of the Trinity and the incarnation). But *we* cannot and may not think of either as prior to the other. We learn from the doctrine of the Trinity that radical unity (as we might conceive it, were our thinking it out not dominated from the start by divine revelation) is not an absolute ideal. Even in the Most High it is a Trinity because he is absolute perfection. In the same way we learn from the incarnation that immutability (which is not eliminated) is not simply and uniquely a characteristic of God, but that in and in spite of his immutability *he* can truly *become* something. He himself, he, in time. And this possibility is not a sign of deficiency, but the height of his perfection, which would be less if in addition to being infinite, he could not become less than he (always) is. This we can and must affirm, without being Hegelians. And it would be a pity if Hegel had to teach Christians such things.

fact that he remains in his infinite fullness while he empties himself—because, being love, that is, the will to fill the void, he has that wherewith to fill all—the ensuing other is his own proper reality. He brings about that which is distinct from himself, in the act of retaining it as his own, and vice versa, because he truly wills to retain the other as his own, he constitutes it in its genuine reality. God himself goes out of himself, God in his quality of the fullness which gives away itself. He can do this. Indeed, his power of subjecting himself to history is primary among his free possibilities. (It is not a primal must!) And for this reason, Scripture defines him as love—whose prodigal freedom is the indefinable itself. What then is his power of being creator, his ability to keep himself aloof while constituting, bringing out of its nothingness, that which in itself is simply something else? It is only a derivative, restricted and secondary possibility, which is ultimately based on the other primal possibility—though the secondary could be realized without the primal.

It follows—and this truth is now situated on a profounder level than before—that the creature is endowed, by virtue of its inmost essence and constitution, with the possibility of being assumed, of becoming the material of a possible history of God. God's creative act always drafts the creature as the paradigm of a possible utterance of himself. And he cannot draft it otherwise, even if he remains silent. For this self-silencing always presupposes ears, which hear the muteness of God. Though we cannot go into it here, this truth might be the key to understanding why precisely the Logos of God became man and why he alone become man. The immanent self-utterance of God in his eternal fullness is the condition of the self-utterance of God outside himself, and the latter continues the former. It is true that the mere constitution of something other than God is the work of God as such, without distinction of persons. Yet the ontological possibility of creation can derive from and be based on the fact that God, the unoriginated, expresses himself in himself and for himself and so constitutes the original, divine, distinction in God himself. And when this God utters himself as himself into the *void*, this expression speaks *out* this immanent Word, and not something which could be true of another divine person.

And now we can understand better what it means to say: the Logos of God *becomes* man. There are of course men who are not the Logos himself. There could of course be men, if the Logos had not become man. The lesser can exist without the greater, though the lesser is always

founded on the possibility of the greater and not vice versa, as an unworthy, resentful and proletarian type of thinking would have it, all too
often and readily—a type of thinking which from sheer force of habit
makes everything grow out of a lower stage. But when the Word becomes man, his humanity is not prior. It is something that comes to be
and is constituted in essence and existence when and in so far as the Logos
empties himself. This man is, as such, the self-utterance of God in its
self-emptying, because God expresses *himself* when he empties himself.
He proclaims *himself* as love when he hides the majesty of this love and
shows himself in the ordinary way of men. Otherwise his humanity would
be a masquerade in borrowed plumes, a signal that tells of the existence of
something but reveals nothing of what is there. That there are other men,
who are not this self-utterance of God, not another way of being God
himself, does not affect the issue. For 'what' he is is the same in him and
us: we call it human nature. But the unbridgeable difference is that in his
case the 'what' is uttered as his self-expression, which it is not in our case.
And the fact that he pronounces as his reality precisely that which we are,
also constitutes and redeems our very being and history. He says openly
into the freedom of God what we are: the truth in which God could
express himself and expose himself to the empty nothingness which necessarily surrounds him. For he is love, and therefore necessarily the miracle
of the possibility of the free gift, or better: as love, he is the incomprehensible obvious.

We could now define man, within the framework of his supreme and
darkest mystery, as that which ensues when God's self-utterance, his
Word, is given out lovingly into the void of god-less nothing. Indeed,
the Logos made man has been called the abbreviated Word of God. This
abbreviation, this code-word for God is man, that is, the Son of Man and
men, who exist ultimately because the Son of Man was to exist. If God
wills to become non-God, man comes to be, that and nothing else, we
might say. This of course does not mean that man is to be explained in
terms of his ordinary everyday life. It means that man is brought back
home to the region of the ever incomprehensible mystery. But he is such a
mystery. And if God himself is man and remains so for ever, if all theology is therefore eternally an anthropology; if man is forbidden to belittle
himself, because to do so would be to belittle God; and if this God remains the insoluble mystery, man is for ever the articulate mystery of
God. He is a mystery which partakes for ever of the mystery on which it

is founded, and must always be accepted in blissful love as the undecipherable mystery, even in the eternity where the provisional is past and done with. For we may not think that we could completely understand God's expression of himself outside himself, which is man, so that it, and we too, could become tedious to us. We do not think that we could see what is behind man except by seeing through him into the blessed darkness of God himself and then really understanding that this finite being is the finitude of the infinite Word of God himself. Christology is the end and beginning of anthropology. And this anthropology, when most thoroughly realized in Christology, is eternally theology. It is the theology which God himself has taught, by speaking out his Word, as our flesh, into the void of the non-divine and sinful. It is also the theology which we pursue in faith, unless we think that we could find God without the man Christ, and so without man at all.

We could still say of the creator, with the Scripture of the Old Testament, that he is in heaven and we are on earth. But of the God whom we confess in Christ we must say that he is precisely where we are, and can only be found there. And though he still remains the infinite, this does not mean that he is 'also' that and different elsewhere. It means that the finite itself has been given an infinite depth and is no longer a contrast to the infinite, but that which the infinite himself has become, to open a passage into the infinite for all the finite, within which he himself has become a part—to make himself the passage and the door, through whose existence God himself became the reality of nothingness. In the incarnation, the Logos creates by taking on, and takes on by emptying himself. Hence we can verify here, in the most radical and specifically unique way the axiom of all relationship between God and creature, namely that the closeness and the distance, the submissiveness and the independence of the creature do not grow in inverse but in like proportion. Thus Christ is most radically man, and his humanity is the freest and most independent, not in spite of, but because of its being taken up, by being constituted as the self-utterance of God. And the humanity of Christ is not the form in which God appears, in the sense of a vaporous and empty apparition which has no validity of its own in comparison with and in contrast to what is manifested. Since *God* himself 'goes out of' himself, this form of his existence has the most radical validity, force and reality.

We must therefore regard as heretical any concept of the incarnation which makes the humanity of Jesus only a disguise used by God to signal his challenging presence. And it is *this* heresy, which was rejected by the Church in its struggle against docetism, Apollinarism, monophysitism and monotheletism, and not the truly orthodox Christology, which is today felt to be mythic and is rejected as mythology. It must indeed be conceded that such a mythological understanding of Christology can be implicit in the minds of many Christians, in spite of their professed orthodoxy, and inevitably calls forth the protest against mythology. The idea exists that God disguises himself as a man, or that needing to make himself visible, he makes gestures by means of a human reality which is used in such a way that it is not a real man with independence and freedom, but a puppet on strings which the player behind the scenes uses to make himself audible. But this is mythology, and not Church dogma, even though it may be a fair description of the catechism in many Christians' heads in contrast to the printed catechism. And one might go further and ask whether the would-be demythologizers of Christianity have not precisely the same idea of Christian doctrine as the pious and myth-minded Christians, though *both* know the orthodox formulas. And it may be that some non-Christians are thus led to rely on a cryptogamous heresy of Christians in their effort at demythologizing, thinking all the while that it is a dogma of Christianity.

We must on the other hand consider something which may make it more tolerable to listen to many docetic and monophysite overtones in the way some Christians speak of the incarnation. Many of those who reject the orthodox formulation because they misunderstand it, may still make a genuine existential act of faith in the incarnation of the Word of God. If one looks to Jesus, to his cross and death, and really believes that there the living God has said his last word, decisive, irrevocable and hence comprehensive; if he really believes that there God redeems him from the imprisonment and tyranny of the existentials of his blocked, guilty and doomed existence: he believes something that can only be true and real, if Jesus is what the faith of Christianity confesses. Whether he knows it consciously or not, he believes in the incarnation of the Word of God.

This is not to deny the importance of the formula which is objectively correct and which forms the ecclesio-sociological basis of the faith held and pondered in common. But only the heretic (not the Catholic)—one who identifies a genuinely heart-felt faith in the redeeming truth with the profession of the orthodox formulas of the Church—can deny *a priori* that there can be true faith in Christ even when the correct formulation of Christology is rejected. In living out one's existence, one cannot adopt existentially every position which is conceptually thinkable. And therefore: whoever accepts Jesus as the ultimate truth about his life, and confesses that in him and in his death God says the last word to him, by which he lives and dies: such a one accepts him thereby as Son of God, such as the Church confesses, no matter how unfortunate or even false may be his own theoretical and conceptual formulation of the faith whereby he directs his existence to Christ. Moreover, Christ has confronted many who did not know that they were laying hold of him and casting themselves into his life and death to find there happiness and redemption: they did not know that they were meeting him whom Christians rightly call Jesus of Nazareth. Created freedom is always the risk of the unknown which, heeded or unheeded, lies within the known object on which the will is set. That which is *absolutely* unseen and *wholly* other is not appropriated by the free act, when it aims at definite and limited objects. But that does not mean that what is not expressed and formulated is necessarily quite unseen and unsought for. And the grace of God and Christ are in everything, as the secret essence of all eligible reality: it is not so easy to grasp at anything, without having to do with God and Christ— one way or another. Anyone therefore, no matter how remote from any revelation formulated in words, who accepts his existence, that is, his humanity—no easy thing!—in quiet patience, or better, in faith, hope and love—no matter what he calls them, and accepts it *as* the mystery which hides itself in the mystery of eternal love and bears life in the womb of death: such a one says yes to something which really is such as his boundless confidence hopes it to be, because God has in fact filled it with the infinite, that is, with himself, since the Word was made flesh. He says yes to Christ, even when he does not know that he does. For he who lets go and jumps, falls into the depths such as they are, and not such as he has himself sounded. Anyone who accepts his own humanity in full—and how immeasurably hard that is, how doubtful whether we really do it!— has accepted the Son of Man, because God has accepted man in him. When we read in Scripture that he who loves his neighbour has fulfilled the law, this is the ultimate truth, because God himself has become this neighbour. He who is at once the nearest to us and the farthest from us is always the one person who is accepted and loved in our nearest and dearest.

Man is a mystery. Indeed, he is *the* mystery. For he is mystery not merely because he is open in his poverty to the mystery of the incomprehensible fullness of God, but because God uttered this mystery as his own. For supposing God wills to speak himself out into the void of nothingness, supposing he wills to call out his own Word into the mute desert of nothingness—how else could he do it than by creating the inward acceptance of this Word and by uttering his word to be accepted? And so it is all one: the self-utterance of God's Word and its acceptance. That this takes place at all is a mystery. A mystery is something that is totally unexpected and incalculable, something that is at once blissfully, mortally amazing and yet obvious—but obvious only because in the last resort the mystery makes the conceivable understandable and not vice versa. And so the incarnation of God is the absolute and yet the obvious mystery. One could almost think that what is strange, historically contingent and hard about it is not the thing in itself but the fact that the obviously absolute mystery has taken place precisely in Jesus of Nazareth, there and now. But when the longing for the absolute nearness of God, the longing, incomprehensible in itself, which alone makes anything bearable, looks for *where* this nearness came—not in the postulates of the spirit, but in the flesh and in the housings of the earth: then no resting-place can be found except in Jesus of Nazareth, over whom the star of God stands, before whom alone one has the courage to bend the knee and weeping happily to pray: 'And the Word was made flesh and dwelt amongst us'.

5

DOGMATIC QUESTIONS ON EASTER

THE title of this short essay should be taken seriously. It puts *questions* and gives few answers. And the answers themselves should really be taken as questions: it is only to avoid tediousness that they are not all put in the interrogative form. The dogmatic theologian must ask himself new questions about Easter in his present studies. For when he looks up the dogmatic text-books of today[1] and sees what the dogmatic theologian has to say as a professional on the theology of the resurrection, he has to confess somewhat regretfully that apart from some distinguished exceptions, of which there are naturally a few, at the present time very little is said about this fundamental event of the history of salvation. And that is not because there is little to be said about it. For it cannot be that dogmatic theology has nothing to say on the subject. It can only be due to an accident of history and a shortcoming in the fulfilment of the task that every text-book today offers a long treatise on Good Friday and disposes of Easter in a few lines. But if dogmatic theology is to say more about the Easter event and so help to build up faith among men, it must first be clearer about what it should speak of in this curtailed treatise. The first thing therefore that the theologian must do is to ask himself some questions. And some of these questions are presented here. They do not of course appear here for the first time. They are in fact questions which the faith and theology of the Church as a whole have

---

[1] Compare for instance the recent text-books of L. Ott and J. Solano, which are really excellent on the whole. L. Ott, *Grundriss der Dogmatik*[4] (Freiburg 1959) gives a page and a half (232f.) to this point, which are almost completely taken up with the apologetic aspects of the resurrection. Its soteriological import is given seven lines: the resurrection belongs to the perfection of the redemption and is the exemplar and pledge of our own bodily and spiritual resurrection. A few lines (234f.) on the soteriological import of the Ascension do not alter the situation. J. Solano, *Summa Sacrae Theologiae per Patres S.J. Facultatum Theol. in Hispania Professores* III[3] (Madrid 1956) offers a Scholion of less than a page to discuss the resurrection, in a Christology of 329 pages.

always been answering in chorus. It is however the task of man and of the theologian in particular to repeat the old questions in a new way, so that they may really have a new and vital understanding of the old questions.

The reasons why the theology of the resurrection as a whole has gone through such an astonishing process of shrinkage are undoubtedly very numerous. Our first task should be to ask what these reasons are, because an illness can only be cured as a rule when its causes are diagnosed. One reason is undoubtedly this: at the end of the 18th century, apologetics and fundamental theology were separated from dogmatic theology and became an independent science, whose object was to give the reasons for Christianity in general, and not just defend Catholic against non-Catholic Christianity. It followed that fundamental theology justifiably claimed the resurrection of Christ as the most important proof of the divine mission of the *legatus divinus* who founded Christianity. This makes it understandable, though not justifiable, that the dogmatic theologian should have gained the impression that everything important about the resurrection was already said by his colleague in fundamental theology. He thought then that in view of his chronic shortage of time for lectures, and the lack of space in the text-books, he could dispense himself from taking up the theme again and giving it full treatment. But in doing so, he forgot that fundamental theology cannot envisage at all the true content of the resurrection, since it views it only from the formal and hence standard viewpoint of miracle, as the attestation of a divine mission.

The dogmatic theologian could perhaps think that dogma had no more to say about the resurrection than to affirm its reality, and perhaps to add that it is the transfiguration of the body of Christ and therefore something which Christ could claim to have merited—although he was *comprehensor* from the start through his immediate vision of God. If so, he does not need to go much beyond what has been said in fundamental theology. Further, the dogmatic theologian may succumb to the view that all that is to be said specifically about the risen and glorified Lord will be presented in eschatology in general, where the resurrection and bodily glorification of all men is spoken of. But one need do no more than leaf through a work of biblical theology, such as that of Durrwell,[2] on the

---

[2] F. X. Durrwell, *The Resurrection of Jesus* (translated from the French) (London & New York 1960); cf. also J. Schmitt, *Jésus ressuscité dans la prédication apostolique* (Paris 1949); further literature on the dogmatic aspect of the resurrection is given in the *LTK*[2] I, 1035, 1041, where Protestant literature is also given.

resurrection, to realize that Scripture does not allow us to say as little about the resurrection as is usually said on account of this strange division of labour between fundamental and dogmatic theology.

But the real reasons for the shrinkage in dogmatic theology lie deeper and are older. In contrast to St Thomas, and to Suarez, for instance, in post-Tridentine theology, the modern theology of the schools has become accustomed, without much misgiving, to pass over in silence the various mysteries of the life of Christ as a whole, apart from the incarnation and the crucifixion. They are omitted from Christology and left entirely to exegesis and pious reflexion. It is no wonder then that the mystery of the resurrection knew no better fate. But if we ask why these mysteries of the life of Christ, the circumcision, the baptism, the temptation, the transfiguration and so on, hold so little interest for the dogmatic theologian, we come closer to the profound reasons for the wilting of the treatise on the resurrection. The ultimate reason for this general phenomenon is surely the fact that occidental theology adopted a purely juridical interpretation of the redemption and of the meaning of Christ for salvation, apart from his role as teacher and founder of a religion and a Church. If God only confers salvation upon us because having demanded a *satisfactio condigna* for the guilt of mankind, he prepared it for himself in the death of Christ on the cross, all other events of the life of Christ can naturally only be regarded as mere preparatives for this salvific action of God, which is formally concentrated on the cross alone. The one decisive event is Good Friday alone, as such. One can no doubt still pay tribute to the older liturgical tradition and celebrate Easter as the chief feast of Christianity, but the real 'feast-day' of Christianity is Good Friday, and the crucified, the man of sorrows, is the object of piety, love and contemplation.

This juridical theory of satisfaction starts from the silent presupposition, that God could have taken any work of satisfaction done by the God-man, no matter what, once it is dignified by the value of the person who does it, and fixed it as the work of redemption; and that in fact he decreed to choose the death of Christ on the cross. Everything then follows naturally from this silent presupposition. Easter is really only interesting with regard to the private destiny of Jesus. It can have no real significance with regard to salvation. It may be honoured at best as a confirmation of the fact that our interpretation of Good Friday is correct. When Protestant Christians make Good Friday the chief feast of the liturgy and when a Rudolf Bultmann in his work of demythologizing appears to look away from Easter, to concentrate his theology, and the faith, exclusively on the cross: these are all consequences, though perhaps of the most radical type, of the 'juridical decree' theory of redemption. It is a theology which can probably be traced back from St Anselm through St Augustine to the beginnings of a specifically western theology in Tertullian and St Cyprian. It looks on the incarnation—not of course consciously, in a rigidity which would be almost on the way to becoming heretical—as really nothing more than the setting up of the subject, who, when he wills to, and when his act is reckoned by God as man's accomplishment, can make an equivalent satisfaction for the insult offered to God by men's sin. Consequently, it is also only natural that western theology should declare that the incarnation of the Logos was only willed by God in view of the obliteration of sin. It is likewise understandable that western theology is slightly embarrassed when it has to answer the question as to what function the risen and exalted Lord still has. The happiness of his humanity in heaven seems after all to mean no more than his own personal bliss.

The Thomistic doctrine of a permanent and 'physical' mediation of grace allotted a function to the humanity of Christ after his resurrection. But the doctrine remained so obscure, and was so constantly controverted,[3] that it could exercise no really formative influence on Christian life and piety. Theological speculation on the blessedness of the individual was based entirely on the concept of the immediate vision of God—*nulla mediante creatura in ratione obiecti visi se habente*, Denzinger 530. There seemed to be no room here for the humanity of Christ, so this type of speculation also made it difficult to assign a permanent salvific function to the glorified Lord. The constant intercession of the risen Lord (cf. Jn

[3] Cf. Th. Tschipke, *Die Menschheit Christi als Heilsorgan der Gottheit unter besonderer Berücksichtigung der Lehre des hl. Thomas von Aquin* (Freiburg 1940); D. van Meegeren, *De causalitate instrumentali humanitatis Christi iuxta D. Thomae doctrinam* (Venlo 1939); L. Seiller, *L'activité humaine du Christ selon Duns Scot* (Paris 1944); J. Backes, 'Die Lehre des hl. Thomas von der Macht der Seele Christi', *Trierer Theologische Zeitschrift* 60 (1951) 153–166. A purely moral causality of the humanity of Christ after his resurrection is not a new act of his free will and hence can only be the permanent validity (morally) of the redemptive act of his earthly life. It offers therefore no solution to our problem. See further: K. Rahner, 'The eternal significance of the humanity of Jesus for our relationship with God' in *Theological Investigations* III (London & Baltimore, Md. 1967); J. Alfaro, 'Christo Glorioso, Revelador del Padre', *Greg.* 39 (1958) 222–270.

14.2f.; 14.16; 16.7; Rom 8.34; Heb 7.25; 9.24; 1 Jn 2.1), and the bliss of conversing with him in his humanity, appeared almost as an anthropomorphism. It is no wonder that the piety of the West, refusing of course to abandon Christ and not finding sufficient satisfaction in the earthly life of Jesus, concentrated on the presence of Jesus in the Blessed Sacrament. Here he was close to Christians. J. A. Jungmann has traced the disappearance of the mediatory function of Christ in salvation, which naturally obscured above all the meaning of Easter, to the struggle of the West against Arianism. It made Christ simply 'God with us', and Christ's role of mediator with the Father had necessarily to recede into the background. This would agree with what has been said above, since the decisive element in the western theory of redemption is simply the dignity of the divine person, so that the peculiar inner-trinitarian relationship of the Son to the Father plays no indispensable and necessary role.[4] This again accords well with the basic attitude of western theology, which, in contrast to the earlier tradition, has taken for granted since St Augustine that each divine person could appear hypostatically in the world, so that the mediation of the Logos within the Trinity is not really continued in the sending of the Son into the world.[5] And one could go on to ask whether this curtailment of the mediatorship of Christ since St Augustine is also connected with the anti-Arian polemics of St Augustine.

No doubt the struggle with Arianism affected all these questions, and so also contributed to the minimizing of the resurrection in theology and piety. But it is far from explaining adequately the historical phenomenon in question. A disciple of Jungmann, H. J. Schulz, has published an interesting book[6] in which he asks why in the East, according to the testimony of the liturgy, an intense devotion to Easter, with cosmic overtones, could be cultivated along with an equally emphatic stress on the divinity of Christ in the same liturgy, which however also allows the strict mediatory function of the man Christ with regard to God to recede to a great extent into the background. Schulz thinks that the answer to the question is to be found in the phenomenon of neo-Chalcedonian theology. In other

---

[4] Since western theology holds fast to the view that the redemptive sacrifice is also offered to the Logos himself, it has to suppose a double moral 'subject' in Christ, a concept which would allow any other person of the Trinity (or a merely monotheistic God, who becomes man) to make such satisfaction.

[5] Cf. e.g. M. Schmaus, *Die psychologische Trinitätslehre des hl. Augustinus* (Münster 1927).

[6] H.-J. Schulz, 'Die "Höllenfahrt" als "Anastasis"', *ZKT* 81 (1959) 1–66.

words, the Christology of St Cyril of Alexandria, while upholding of course the orthodoxy of Chalcedon with its emphasis on the non-confusion of the two natures in Christ, stresses more clearly than pure Chalcedonism the divinization of the creature by the Godhead who assumed it. It could therefore be more amenable to the notion that the cosmic process of divinization inaugurated by the incarnation could bridge the gulf between God and the creature, and attain its definitive triumph in the resurrection of Christ.

Schulz' theory is attractive. It answers a question which can in fact be only clearly formulated when one already has this key-word 'neo-Chalcedonianism' in mind, as the possible answer. But we must proceed carefully, and ask is this answer really correct, and above all, is it adequate. One could begin by putting a sceptical counter-question. Can such a subtle nuance in Christology, of which we are only now beginning to be aware, be invoked as the explanation of the important and palpable difference which exists between the piety of the East and the West with regard to Easter? And there is a further question. Was there not something objectively like neo-Chalcedonianism in the Christology of the West also, as a result of its marked anti-Arianism, and why had it not the same effect as Schulz supposes it to have had in the East? One could also ask whether neo-Chalcedonianism was not a result rather than a cause, stemming from a basic religious and theological attitude of the East which is lacking in the West. It manifests itself in the East in the strong devotion to Easter, which cannot but be absent from the West, even if a certain neo-Chalcedonianism of a conceptual and theoretical type can be found in western theology. Indeed, it is probably true that the theology of redemption was already different in the East and in the West, at a time preceding the differentiation in Christology. In other words, the West was thinking in juridical and moral terms before the 5th and 6th centuries. But in the East, while the significance of the cross was not lost sight of, the redemption was felt to be a real ontological process which began in the incarnation and ends not so much in the forgiveness of sin as in the divinization of the world and first demonstrates its victorious might, not so much in the expiation of sin on the cross as in the resurrection of Christ.

Clearly, there are already enough questions to be asked even with regard to the history of the dogmatic theology of Easter and its influence on piety. The few we have touched upon were chosen because of their bearing on the shrinkage of Easter theology and piety in the West. Nothing at all has been said about the history of the individual truths present or called for in such a theology of Easter.

We add some questions about the content of the Easter dogma to the historical questions discussed above. The correct starting-point for a genuine theology of Easter is probably a correct understanding of Good Friday and Holy Saturday, that is, a true theology of death. And this means that the theology of the West need not deny its past to win a larger future for the theology of Easter. It only needs to enquire more profoundly and intensively into a question which has always engaged its attention, the death of Christ. We shall try here to indicate some questions which tend in this direction. First of all, one should begin with the nature of the death and not merely enquire into the painful sufferings which preceded the death. It is almost automatic in the theology of the death of Christ and its soteriological significance to discuss the mortal suffering and to treat the death itself as the almost happy ending of the suffering to which attention has been confined. But then theology is discussing a subject, called the death of Christ, which is really not essentially different from any other possible work which Christ did or could have done during his life. And then its significance in the work of salvation can only be assessed in moral categories. But then one has missed the death by a hairs-breadth. And probably justifies the oversight by saying that the theology of the salvific significance of Christ's death needs an object of moral value. Such is said to be absent from the death of Christ as such, in which he only passively undergoes the separation of soul and body, but is said to be found in the 'bitter sufferings' before it, since they alone provided Christ with the opportunity of exercising obedience and love. But before one settles for this, and actually abandons objectively the theology of the death of Christ as such, though perhaps not expressly, one should ask whether one has a correct concept of death at all, such as can make room for a theology of the death of Christ and open up new horizons.

For death[7] cannot perhaps be adequately described merely as the 'separation of soul and body'. Strictly speaking, regarded in the light of the process itself, though it is the climax of the extreme weakening of man's powers and his helpless collapse under the nameless mystery of

[7] See on the following K. Rahner, *On the Theology of Death. Quaestiones Disputatae* 2 (London [5]1964).

existence, still, it is also the supreme act of man in which his whole previous life is gathered up in the final decision of his freedom and mastered,
so that he ripens for his eternity. If so, the human death of Christ is not
just one moral act among others, performed in the moments preceding his
actual death. It is of its nature the totality of the life of Christ in act, the
definitive act of his freedom, the complete integration of his time on earth
with his human eternity. All we can do here is point enquiringly to this
truth. But if it is so, then the resurrection of Christ is not another event
after his passion and death. In spite of the duration of time which intervenes, which is anyway an intrinsic component of even the most unified
and indivisible act of spatio-temporal man,[8] the resurrection is the manifestation of what happened in the death of Christ: the imposed and
enforced handing over of the whole bodily man to the mystery of the
merciful loving God, by the concentrated freedom of Christ as he disposes of his whole life and existence. In this way, Good Friday and Easter
can be seen as two aspects of a strictly unitary event of the existence of
Christ which are essentially related to one another. And one need no
longer have the impression that Good Friday could really retain it soteriological significance, as satisfaction for the insult to God's majesty, even if
no Easter followed. But once this illusion has been eliminated, the soteriological significance of Easter can be seen to go far and essentially beyond
its apologetical value and Jesus' personal blessedness. A piece of this
world, real to the core, but occupied by the pure and sovereign power of
the dispassionate freedom of Christ, is surrendered, in the total self-
mastery which can be achieved by fallen man only in the act of death, to
the disposition of God, in complete obedience and love. This is Easter,
and the redemption of the world.

   The resurrection of Christ is essentially, and not merely through being
juridically accepted by God, the event in which God irrevocably adopts
the creature as his own reality, by his own divine primordial act, as he had

---

[8] A scholastic philosopher who has pondered the nature of the (temporal and
spatial) continuum, should not find it hard to understand that a thing or process is not
at once independent and distinct because it follows another in time. These moments
can be temporal moments in a strictly unitary process, which though prolonged in
time, cannot be disjointed as a being. The moments of a being (or at least of a process)
do not need, in order to be one, to be simultaneously co-existent at any arbitrarily
chosen point of time. We may recall here that even modern physics seems to admit
ultimate atoms of time even for physical time, which are not really divisible although
they 'last' and so seem to consist of still smaller parts.

'already' done in the incarnation of the Logos. It is likewise the event in which God so divinizes and transfigures the creature that this glorification is accomplished as the total acceptance of this divine assumption by the freedom of the creature itself. But we must bear two things in mind if we are to understand this assertion. One is that this total acceptance of the divine assumption by the free creature must necessarily be death in an infralapsarian order of things, where death is the birth of life set free. The other is that the world is such a unity, physically, spiritually and morally, that the decision of the man Christ, as a real component of the physical world, as a member of the biological family of humanity (born of a woman as a child of Adam), as a member of the human community in its history of light and shadow, is ontologically, and not merely by a juridical disposition of God, the irreversible and embryonically final beginning of the glorification and divinization of the *whole* reality. This is not to deny, but rather to affirm positively, that the unity of the world in all its dimensions and Christ's real ontological participation in this world is freely constituted by God. But then he does not just assign the world a juridical status in his mind. He creates its real, intrinsic and proper structure.

The notion of sacrifice may also throw light on what has been said. It is of the essence of sacrifice, and not just a more or less certain consequence extrinsic to its being, that it is accepted by God. That is why it needs the authorization of God, the appointment of a priest. God himself creates the possibility of men offering in such a way that their offering is accepted. A sacrifice only really exists when man's gift has really left the sphere of the profane and has entered that of the sacred, has become the 'possession' of God and has passed over to his exclusive disposition. Sacrifice and accepted sacrifice are one and the same thing. And where the sacrifice is offered not just by means of cultic symbol, but 'in the spirit and the truth', that is, where the intention expressed by the cultic sign, the total dedication of human reality to the absolute disposition of God's holiness, is truly effected: the acceptation of the sacrifice, which is of its essence, cannot be a juridical friction. It must be a reality. The proffered gift, which is the man himself, in all its dimensions, in its whole concrete reality, must be at the absolute disposition of God who has graciously accepted it. To be accepted totally and definitively, without restriction or reserve, by God who reveals and communicates himself: that is nothing else than being transfigured in the whole bodily reality, that is, being raised up from death and finally exalted. Hence the sacrifice of Good

Friday is only really consummated as a sacrifice when it is the sacrifice accepted in the Easter event. During the three days of Good Friday, Holy Saturday and Easter Sunday, the one, self-same, total event of salvation is accomplished in a sacred memorial (*anamnesis*), and it remains strictly one even though it continues in order to be itself.[9]

And now theology must look backwards to the question of the essence of the incarnation, to pose it anew and more deeply, so that in its light, the life of Jesus, its salvific value and so the resurrection may be more clearly understood. And it must look onwards to the question of the fact and meaning of the permanent, consummated—not 'ended'—mediation of the exalted Lord as he exercises this function for all men and for all eternity.

The first question might be put as follows. Can we understand the incarnation, the assumption of human reality by the Word, and the essence of this reality itself, in such a way that the event of the incarnation is seen from the very start not just as the adoption of a fungible, statistical reality, but as the acquisition of a time, a history, a life-giving death by the Logos himself? So that in virtue of the inmost essence of the incarnation, seen itself as a formally salvific act, the one event composed of death and resurrection is implied and accepted? The history of man, his free action, and the absolute climax of his freedom are not to be considered as accidents attached to the unmodified substance of a nature conceived of as one thing to be registered among others. It must be regarded as the self-realization of a being which only attains its own reality in such a process of freedom, which is therefore not to be regarded so much as a 'faculty' which man 'has' as the power of free disposal which one is,[10] in order to be able to bring one's own imposed being, as itself, to its proper fulfil-

---

[9] Cf. on this point M. de la Taille, *Mysterium Fidei*[3] (Paris 1931); *Elucidatio* XII–XV, 131–180.

[10] This is of course to be understood with the reserves which are always to be made in such statements when we are speaking of a finite being and not of the absolute God. But again, once this distinction is made, we must not overlook the fact that the 'act' of a sub-personal being has essentially a more extrinsic relationship to the nature of this being than in the case of a being which is aware of itself and realizes itself in freedom. In this case, the being is entrusted to itself. Though it cannot use its freedom to 'destroy' itself or eliminate itself, the free act still affects the nature in such a way that it is not merely the subject of the act, but becomes in a certain sense the act itself. Man for instance does not merely commit evil actions: he himself becomes evil by these actions. And vice versa, where a free spiritual being is willed and accepted, the self-realization as such is willed and accepted, and not merely 'made possible' and (eventually) foreseen.

ment. From this point of view, the event of the incarnation is more closely and essentially allied to the fulfilment of the human life which is taken on, than if it is regarded as the setting up of a human subject, within whose life this or that event is afterwards added in.

With the correct interpretation of the death of Christ in mind, we can also look forward to what comes 'after' death. It is not to be regarded as an event prolonged in time and attached merely to the event of the death. It is the fully self-matured finality of this temporal life itself which has been fulfilled most really by death itself.[11] But if so, the Lord who abides must have a real salvific function which abides, otherwise no such salvific function can be ascribed to death itself. Death ends time by being its consummate validity and therefore eternity. Hence what follows 'after' death (and resurrection as essential element of *this* death) is precisely the definitive thing which took place in death. And vice versa: what now takes place is definitive and hence what is truly and eternally real and effective. The life of the exalted Lord is not the personal recompense for something which he did in his earthly life and which merely has 'consequences' which now persist in themselves after their cause is past. It is the very reality of the soteriological significance of his temporal life, accepted by God, set free to work, and actually effective.

We must of course ask ourselves how precisely this effective reality of a soteriological nature may be more adequately conceived of. How for instance is one to explain the fact that the humanity of Jesus retains its significance here and now, precisely where the infinite reality of the eternal God presents itself to the vision of the blessed to be enjoyed by them? One would have to show, in other words, that in the incarnation, and in the resurrection which is its consummation, the transfigured human reality of the Logos remains truly and perpetually the mediator to the immediacy of God. One would have to show that the essence of the supernatural grace bestowed upon creatures, given in the hypostatic union and essentially deriving from it[12] and not elsewhere, implies an immediacy which

---

[11] Cf. on this point e.g. K. Rahner, 'The Life of the Dead' in this volume pp. 347–354.

[12] There is in fact reason to think that the connexion between incarnation and uncreated grace, in which God bestows himself supernaturally on man, is not merely *de facto* but essential. As regards the hypostatic union, this statement will hardly be contradicted by theologians. All will concede—to avoid falling into an unavowed Nestorianism and contradicting the real intention of the Christology of St Cyril— that the human nature of Christ must also be intrinsically divinized by what we call

has a certain ontological presupposition, which may be indicated by the concept of a mediated immediacy. For immediacy is always immediacy to something. The need for a certain manner of being or condition, etc., in the term to which something is to be immediately related, is not a contradiction of this immediacy but its necessary pre-supposition. Hence, for instance, all theological tradition, including the Council of Vienne, postulates the *lumen gloriae* as the presupposition for the immediate vision of God, and does not feel that this concept is contradictory to the immediacy, though this *lumen* is considered to be a created reality. It admits therefore to the immediacy of God, it is sheer openness, it is that strictly supernatural created thing which in contrast to the natural order, and in *consequence* of a strictly formal and not efficient causality on the part of God, refers of itself to God as the infinitely remote ground of its being but, further, gives God himself absolutely, because it exists only through the absolute self-communication of God.

This leads to the question of how the *lumen gloriae*, which admits to the immediacy of God, is related to the glorified humanity of Christ, for which we have also claimed the function of perpetual mediation of the immediacy of the vision of God. This function must exist, if we are really to affirm a perpetual function of mediatorship in the God-man, and if it is not to be excluded by what is after all the essence of salvation and supernatural bliss, the immediate vision of God. The risen and exalted Lord must be the permanent and ever-active access to God, which is always being used anew and can never be left as something passed over and past. He must always show the Father. Only when we have under-

---

sanctifying grace. But then one must also note that this human nature is essentially part of mankind (as may be shown by a transcendental deduction from man's character as partner in a dialogue and as member of a family community) and hence cannot ultimately (as nature!) be withdrawn from its solidarity with the one human nature as a whole. We can then understand why the divinization of the human nature of the Logos by grace necessarily implies the call of all men to supernatural fellowship with God. And hence it is not too daring to suspect that there is also a necessary connexion from the other side: if there is to be grace as, a supernatural participation of man in the inner life of God through God's real self-communication to man, there must also be incarnation (where both are free because they are one consistent thing, and the necessity is the necessary consequence of something in itself free and necessary). But to make this quite clear, we should have to show that the hypostatic union is the necessary mediation of the immediacy which exists in the immediate vision of God, the supreme actuation of grace. But this demonstration cannot be attempted within the limits of this short essay.

stood this, have we understood Easter as it is: the consummation of the world which gives access to God, who is really all in all through the Easter event, which has already begun but is still reaching completion in us.

When these considerations, which have been put here in the form of questions, have been really exactly answered, a more exact insight must result into the relationship between Easter as event and the fact of Christ's being risen (to indicate briefly what we mean). The relationship between an event and its effects, between a process and its results is not always the same. The event in which something eschatologically final comes to pass is infinitely closer to the result than an event which produces something which then continues to exist in the same process of time in which it came about. In the former case, the result does not go 'on', but *is* definitively what happened there. And in such a case, the event cannot recede into the past: it cannot become merely something that has been there, because the state of having been something only ensues when what remains takes on a new and different future, which is no longer that which came about by the event in question. A closer exposition of these observations must lead to the insight that the Easter feast refers to the event of Easter in an *anamnesis*[13] or memorial which really celebrates it, since the event has remained present in an ontologically unique and unsurpassable manner. But this again determines the unique character of the celebration itself. *Anamnesis* and that which is made present by it in its celebration condition each other reciprocally. On this basis one might show how every eucharistic celebration is essentially an Easter feast, not merely because it refers back to a 'past' event, but because it is the presence of that which came to be at Easter, to be finally the validity of the event itself. And then the feast of Easter would be merely a higher degree of expressiveness of what is always celebrated in the Eucharist in veritable *anamnesis*: the one event composed of the death and resurrection of Christ, which is of course past in the physical world (cf. Rom 6.9; Denzinger 2297) and which indeed had really to pass, in order that the definitive could come and stay, but which 'remains' in what is proper to it and *hence* can be enacted in its celebration.

[13] Cf. A. Darlapp 'Anamnese', *LTK*[2] 483–48

6

VIRGINITAS IN PARTU

A contribution to the problem of the development of dogma and of tradition

IT is well known that the question of the meaning and bearings of the Mariological doctrine, which is traditionally summed up as the doctrine of the *'virginitas in partu'*, has recently been posed anew by the book written by A. Mitterer.[1] An (unprinted) Innsbruck dissertation by W. Zauner (*Untersuchungen zum Begriff der 'Virginitas in partu'*, Innsbruck 1955) expressed cautiously worded agreement with the theory of

---

[1] *Dogma und Biologie der Heiligen Familie* (Vienna 1952). For comment on Mitterer's position see H. Doms, 'Ein Kapitel aus den gegenwärtigen Beziehungen zwischen Theologie und Biologie', *Th. Rv.* 48 (1952) 201–212. W. Dettloff, 'Virgo-Mater. Kirchenväter und moderne Biologie zur jungfräulichen Mutterschaft Mariens' *Wi. Wei.* 20 (1957) 221–226; For other recent discussion of the question see (apart from text-books of theology and Mariology in general) H. Koch, *Virgo Eva–Virgo Maria. Neue Untersuchungen über die Lehre von der Jungfrauschaft und Ehe Mariens in der ältesten Kirche* (Berlin–Leipzig 1937); J. C. Plumpe, 'Some little-known early witnesses to Mary's Virginitas in Partu', *TS* 9 (1948) 567–577; H. Rahner, *Die Marienkunde in der lateinischen Patristik: Maria in der Offenbarung*, ed. by P. Sträter (Paderborn 1947) 137–182; J. Ortiz de Urbina, *Die Marienkunde in der Patristik des Ostens, ibid.* 85–118; Ch.-G. Le Jouassard, 'Marie à travers la Patristique' in H. du Manoir, *Marie. Etudes sur la Sainte Vierge* I (Paris 1959) 69–157: J. Auer 'Maria und das christliche Jungfräulichkeitsideal. Eine biblisch-dogmatische Studie', *GuL* 23 (1950) 411–425; G. Soll 'Die Mariologie der Kappadokier im Lichte der Dogmengeschichte', *TQ* 131 (1951) 288–319; 426–457; G. Miegge, *La Vergine Maria. Saggi di storia del dogma* (Torre Pellice 1950); J. Guitton, *La Virgen—Maria* (Madrid 1952); A. Garcia ' "Integritas carnis" e "virginitas mentis" in Alano da Lilla', *Mar* 16 (1954) 125–149; G. M. Roschini, *La Madonna secondo la fede e la Teologia* I (Rome 1953); M. Balagué, 'La virginidad de Maria', *Cultura biblica* 11 (Seville 1954) 281–292; Th. U. Mullaney, 'Mary Ever-Virgin', *Am. Eccl. Rev.* 131 (1954) 159–167, 256–267; Ch. Donnelly, 'The Perpetual Virginity of the Mother of God', in E. Carol, *Mariology* (Milwaukee 1954) 228–296; G. Owens 'Our Lady's Virginity in the Birth of Jesus', *Marian Studies* 7 (1954) 43–68; A.M. Sancho, *La virginidad de Maria Madre de Dios. Estudio historico-teologico del dogma* (Madrid 1955); J. Rózycki 'De Beatae Mariae Virginitate in Partu', *Coll. Theol.* 27 (Warsaw 1956) 439–467.

Mitterer, though following a quite different method, more critically speculative and more concerned with the history of dogma.

Mitterer does not take as his starting-point the traditional content of the title '*virginitas in partu*', as understood in fact in theology. He uses modern science to make a close analysis of the concepts of motherhood and virginity, in a way which must be called *a priori* from the point of view of theology and its data. On the supposition that full motherhood and full virginity are to be ascribed to Mary, according to the testimony of faith, Mitterer's analysis of the concepts leads him to the conclusion that full motherhood includes the processes which are denied it by the traditional interpretation, on the grounds that they are excluded by the '*virginitas in partu*'—the opening of the genital passages, the breach of the hymen, the birth-pangs. He holds that full virginity can be preserved, hence even '*in partu*', when these processes take place,[2] because they have nothing to do with the concept of bodily virginity. Accordingly, the miracle of the '*virginitas in partu*', according to Mitterer (who maintains both the virginity and its miraculous character in the case in question), is not concerned with the actual manner of the process of birth and its consequences;[3] the miracle consists of the fact that in this birth, which took place according to the natural processes, the natural presupposition is lacking, which it should have had in the natural order of things, and for which the normal birth is the unambiguous sign: the conception of the child from the man. Mitterer therefore holds that the '*virginitas in partu*' is not a separate process, but simply the application of the doctrine of the perpetual virginity of Mary to the birth. And this has a sense, because normally the birth is the decisive criterion which excludes full virginity. The meaning usually given to '*virginitas in partu*' is said to betray too much pre-occupation with the hymen, growing out of other times and cultures, to endanger true motherhood by having logically to deny the

[2] Mitterer is correct in saying that its absence is not an unambiguous proof of virginity. If for instance a child is conceived by means of artificial insemination and the birth takes place by means of a Caesarian operation, the mother retains the traditional signs of *virginitas in partu*, but there is in fact no question of *virginitas in partu*.

[3] For Mitterer, these constitute the signs of true motherhood for a mother who has given birth to a child, and hence must not be treated as indifferent or worthless. Mitterer also correctly emphasizes that according to Scripture (Lk 2:6) and tradition Mary is mother in the full sense of the word, and hence actively gave birth to her child in a truly human process.

mother any active part in the process of child-birth, and to eliminate all pain, though Mary did not escape suffering elsewhere.[4] As far as we know, only a few authors, apart from W. Zauner, have given unmistakable, though cautious assent to the theory of Mitterer (cf. L. Ott,[5] W. Dettloff, H. Doms). Others, like J. de Aldama,[6] expressly reject the theory.

Here we offer some observations on the problem which has thus been re-opened. They do not aim at being more than marginal notes. They do not uphold any set thesis and they do not take sides for or against other opinions. They only claim the right to be more modest in a brief essay than a dogmatic theologian is allowed to be when he has to present a definite and well-rounded thesis in a dogmatic text-book or in a complete treatise on Mariology, and to give the doctrine of the Church clearly, exhaustively and sifted out from mere theological propositions. Since we are dealing only with marginal notes, the order in which they appear is also unimportant.

I

In recent Catholic theology one can note a certain tendency, independently of Mitterer, Ott and so on, to be more reserved when giving the theological qualification of this doctrine, and above all, when determining the contents of it. J. B. Heinrich, for instance, with Th. Specht, and among recent authors L. Lercher and F. Dander maintain that the bodily integrity of the Blessed Virgin during the birth as defined doctrine, understanding this integrity in the traditional way.[7] But F. Egger, H. Hurter, M. Glossner, Ch. Pesch, J. Pohle–J. Gummersbach, F. Diekamp–

---

[4] One could point to the fact that pious meditation thinks of the new-born *child* as capable of suffering and actually suffering, just as Scripture and dogmatic theology do in general in combating Docetism as contrary to the faith. If so, how can one refuse to ascribe to the child the 'pain' of *being born*, without the risk of Docetism? And then how can one deny that there was likewise 'pain' (in the theological and biological sense) when Mary gave birth, such as is normally to be found in the process of birth in the present biological (infralapsarian) order of things?

[5] L. Ott, *Grundriss der Katholischen Dogmatik* (Freiburg ³1957) 247f.

[6] J. de Aldama, 'Mariologia', in *Sacrae Theologiae Summa* III (Madrid ³1956) 392.

[7] J. B. Heinrich, *Dogmatische Theologie* VII (Mainz 1896) 402; Th. Specht, *Lehrbuch der Dogmatik* (Regensburg ³1925) 380; L. Lercher, *Inst. Theol. Dogmat.* III (Barcelona ⁴1945) 288; F. Dander, *Summarium Tract. Dogm. De Matre-Socia Salvatoris* (Innsbruck 1952) 8.

K. Jüssen etc, qualify this *'integritas corporalis'* only as *'de fide'*.[8] J. de Aldama[9] assesses it as *'de fide divina et catholica'*, but expressly declares that he prescinds from any precise explanation of the *'integritas corporalis'* which is asserted. L. Ott uses the qualification *'de fide'*, but gives the statement the meaning already mentioned, which is *essentially* more restricted. B. Bartmann[10] likewise qualifies it as *'de fide'*, but for all practical purposes really gives up all effort to determine the exact content of the phrase. But he adjoins a warning against docetism and contests the parallel often drawn by Fathers and theologians between the processes of the resurrection and the birth—entrance or exit through 'closed doors'. M. Schmaus[11] takes the same line: the assertion is a truth of faith, it means primarily 'bodily integrity', but 'we are not in a position to decide what is the essence of bodily integrity as understood by revelation'.

Here the question arises as to which statement is more important: that one must maintain the 'bodily integrity' as a matter of faith—and that therefore the concept is bound up with a certain content, which one must know to be able to believe it—or that we do not know what constitutes bodily integrity. But the first statement undoubtedly possesses more normative force, as Schmaus too certainly holds. Hence a *certain* determination of the content of the phrase, 'bodily integrity' cannot be eliminated as radically as Schmaus thinks, though he may be correct in thinking that the delimitation of the concept can only be carried out on a restricted scale. But then the question arises, *why* this, no doubt relative, reserve in determining the content of the concept is on principle not merely justifiable, but demanded, when theological tradition on the whole gives little sign of such reserve.[12] The truth is that a certain reserve is called for both with regard to the qualification and content of the *'virginitas in partu'*, in spite of all the respect due to a theologically binding tradition in this

[8] F. Egger, *Enchiridion Theol. Dogmat. Spec.* (Brixen [9]1928) 511; H. Hurter, *Theol. Dogmat. Spec.* II (Innsbruck [7]1891) 512; M. Glossner, *Lehrbuch der Dogmatik* I (Regensburg 1874) 104; Ch. Pesch, *Compendium Theol. Dogmat.* III (Freiburg [5]1935) 101; J. Pohle–J. Gummersbach, *Lehrbuch der Dogmatik* II (Paderborn [10]1956) 390; F. Diekamp–K. Jüssen, *Kath. Dogmatik* II (Münster [10]1952) 382.

[9] J. de Aldama, *op. cit.* 394.

[10] B. Bartmann, *Lehrbuch der Dogmatik* I (Freiburg [8]1932) 425.

[11] M. Schmaus, *Kath. Dogmatik* II/2 (Munich [5]1955) 171, 176.

[12] See for instance the pages devoted by F. Suárez to the question of the after-birth at the birth of Jesus: F. Suárez, *De mysteriis vitae Christi*, disp. V, sect. 2 (Op. omn. XIX, 83ff.); disp. XIII, sect. 1 (Op. omn. XIX, 212ff.).

matter, which exists alongside of what is dated and lacking authority. One cannot seriously maintain, with Scheeben, that the doctrine is already expressed in the Apostles' Creed.[13] If it is supposed to be expressed simply in the '*semper virgo*' of tradition and of many official utterances of the magisterium,[14] we must first ask whether the magisterium, in designating Mary by this title, wishes to define also the content of the title itself. But above all, we must point out that the precise content of the '*virginitas in partu*' which is perhaps included in the title still remains an open question.[15] It is true that the Synod of Milan, under St Ambrose, also condemned Jovinian for denying the virginal birth of Christ, which St Ambrose certainly took to be 'the retention of the virginal bars in the genital parts'.[16] But this is only a local synod, and it would be difficult to prove that the condemnation of Jovinian[17] amounts to a positive sanction of everything that was in the mind of his opponent, St Ambrose, on this matter. Siricius himself does not mention the point under the heads of the accusation which he drew up against Jovinian and sent to

[13] As St Ambrose first tried to argue, quoting the '*natus ex Maria Virgine*': St Ambrose *Ep.* 42:12 (*PL* 16, 1128). Cf. M. J. Scheeben, *Handbuch der kath. Dogmatik* II (Freiburg 1933) 939. So too St Augustine, cf. Note 31, p. 142.

[14] Cf. e.g. *Denz.* 13, 201f., 214, 255f., 344, 429, 462, 735, 993; John II, *Ep.* 3 *ad Senat. Const.*, Mansi VIII 803 E ff.

[15] It is not enough to say that the expression must be understood in the general sense in which it was used in ecclesiastical terminology at the time when it was used by the magisterium. This hermeneutic principle is correct fundamentally. But it cannot be applied to this case. For a number of examples can be adduced from tradition where the *virginitas in partu* implied by *semper virgo* was in fact understood only *ratione conceptionis*; there are examples which show that the perpetual virginity was sometimes only understood as the exclusion of all sexual intercourse; it could be shown that even where a miraculous child-birth was in question, the notion of what took place in the process was far from uniform. Once a concept has come into use in tradition and the magisterium (as ἀειπαρθένος was, as for instance in the *Symbolum Epiphanii*, at a time when the exact meaning of *virginitas in partu* was far from clear or well established), its continued use to express truths of faith is not in itself enough to prove that it can or ought sanction all the precise shades of meaning that may have been attached to it later in theology and piety, even though such *de facto* meanings were very widespread.

[16] St Ambrose, *De institut. virg.* cap. VIII, 52 (*PL* 16, 320): '*Porta igitur Maria . . . genitalia virginitatis claustra non solvit*'. Cf. Ph. Friedrich, 'St Ambrosius von Mailand über die Jungfrauengeburt Marias (virginitas Mariae in partu)' in *Festgabe für A. Knöpfler* (Freiburg 1917) 89–109; J. Huhn, *Das Geheimnis der Jungfrau-Mutter Maria nach dem Kirchenvater Ambrosius* (Würzburg 1954) 110–226.

[17] W. Haller, *Jovinianus, die Fragmente seiner Schriften, die Quellen zu seiner Geschichte, sein Leben und seine Lehre* (Leipzig 1897) 127, 151–158.

St Ambrose. Hence the Roman synod of 390, which condemned Jovinian, cannot be invoked as an authority on this point.

St Leo the Great writes, in the *Epistola dogmatica ad Flavianum*, cap 2: 'Her virginity was intact when she brought him forth, just as it was intact when she conceived him'.[18] But the statement of itself has not, of course, the same dogmatic weight as the letter has when dealing with the precise point of controversy against Eutyches. Further, though the virginity at the birth is taught, nothing is said as to what precisely it implies. St Leo does not go beyond the '*semper virgo*'. In the letter of Pope Hormisdas,[19] the traditional doctrine is undoubtedly re-affirmed. But there is of course no question of a definition here. It is merely the repetition and transmission of the traditional doctrine. The Lateran synod of 649, under Martin I, which dealt with monotheletism, says in c. 5 (Denzinger 256) that the '*semper virgo*' also '*incorruptibiliter genuisse*',[20] just as she conceived without man's action, and was to remain a virgin after the birth. But here it must be said at once that this synod did not acquire the rank and importance of a general council in the mind of the Church as time went on. Though a certain tendency could be noticed, which sought to range this synod as the sixth general council after the earlier five, this place was in fact reserved for the council of 680.[21] The main reason for promulgating the canon was the fact that the monophysites and the monothelites had appealed to the '*virginitas in partu*' to establish the complete domination of the Word over his body, such as the doctrine of the one nature and the one *energeia* implied, as they saw it.[22] The orthodox declared on the contrary that Christ was really born in the body, otherwise docetism, with which the monophysites were reproached in the question, could not be avoided. It was for this reason that the '*virginitatis integritas*' had to be a miracle.[23] The Latin '*incorruptibiliter*' is meant to render the Greek ἀψθόρως. The content of this '*incorruptibilitas*' and the '*virginitatis integritas*', of which Martin I spoke in his explanatory discourse to the council, the denial of '*solvere virginitatem*', is not exactly determined. No doubt the Pope thought of the content in the terms which were then

[18] Mansi V 1370 A.

[19] Epist 79 (*PL* 63, 514C) '. . . *matris vulvam natus non aperiens* . . .'

[20] In connexion with a general summary of the faith, chs. 1–5.

[21] Cf. E. Caspar, 'Die Lateransynode von 649', *ZKG* 51 (1932) 75–137.

[22] Cf. Mansi X 961 C, 965 E (giving the opinion of the Monothelite Theodore of Pharan on the birth of Christ).

[23] Mansi X, 963ff. (the discourse of Martin I at the Synod).

already current, especially as the parallels with the risen Lord's leaving
the tomb and Christ's walking on the waters also recur at this point. On
the other hand, the Pope stresses against the monophysite Theodore of
Pharan, that the child was not born '*incorporaliter*' and not '*absque corporeo
tumore*' (ἀόγκως) and that Christ did not pass through Mary as through a
fistula, in the Apollinarist sense.[24] He even appeals to St Gregory of
Nazianzen, who held that Mary was subject to the νόμος κνήσεως.[25]

It is not easy to say how the Pope considered that these disparate elements of his thought were to be combined clearly and without tension.
But one may draw the conclusion that no strict explanation and dogmatic
determination of any more precise content was intended, and hence we
may say: a local synod repeats incidentally the doctrine of the perpetual
virginity, against the background of the interpretation then current, without wishing to give a doctrinal definition of the exact content of this interpretation. Indeed, we may note the clear consciousness of the need of
avoiding the danger of docetism in this question, and of preserving the
truth of the real motherhood and birth. It is remarkable that in 675, at
the first synod of Toledo (Denzinger 282), the '*partus Virginis*' is spoken
of in such a way that its miraculous character—in spite of the quotation
from St Augustine, who clearly takes the side of the traditional thesis in
his own special context—is based really on the virginal conception alone.
When Sixtus IV (1476) and Paul IV (1555)[26] stress the perpetual '*virginitatis integritas*', even '*in partu*', as Paul IV says, they merely re-affirm
what must be held as the dogmatic kernel of the tradition, that Mary is
ever virgin, and they avoid any more precise determination of the content
of the assertion. The same is true when Pius XII ('*Mystici Corporis*')
says: 'She brought forth Christ in a marvellous way'.[27]

In view of the magisterium therefore, the marked reserve of recent
theology, with regard to the qualification and the determination of the
content of the doctrine, is quite understandable. There is no question of
an express definition. If one wishes to qualify the doctrine as '*de fide*',
which is quite justifiable, in view of the fifteen hundred years of the doctrine and the ordinary magisterium of the present day, one will have to
emphasize at the same time that this does not solve the question of the
exact determination of the content of the doctrine. For one could use a
more precise history of the doctrine to prove that the determination of its

---

[24] Mansi X, 966D.   [25] Mansi X, 968A.
[26] *Denz.* 734 993.   [27] *AAS* 35 (1943) 247.

content is not so uniform and clear, and not always so free from misgivings that one could simply say: the careful, somewhat vague and
generalized assertion of the '*virginitas in partu*' in the ordinary magisterium, in the present state of the pronouncements of the extraordinary
magisterium and in the average preaching of the faith, means precisely
what is said more exactly and in detail in the Fathers and theologians, and
in much edifying literature.[28] The doctrine as it strictly is, and the
authority it carries, are not always presented in such a way that they are
expressly and consciously distinguished from a given set of images,
which are used to couch the doctrine which is specifically taught. Can it
be proved in detail that the tradition[29] in question lacks from many points
of view the purity, clarity, firmness and unquestionable intrinsic theological foundation, which would enable us to declare it simply, wholly
and without nuances a sheer, pure *traditio divino-apostolica?* Such a proof,
to be completely convincing, could be given only by an exact and critical
history of the doctrine,[30] which clearly cannot be attempted here.

[28] One must be very careful with such arguments, as may be seen from the doctrine
of the formation of Adam from the dust of the earth. Here too a tradition of two
thousand years' duration expressed a permanent truth in a definite, concrete imagery,
distinct from the truth implied and not a permanent form, which was not however
distinguished by tradition from the truth implied.

[29] Tradition, *historically* speaking, is simply the concrete sum of the theological
propositions to be found in the Church, along with their transmission, in so far as the
ordinary or extraordinary magisterium has not discounted such propositions as not
permissible in the Church. This tradition contains, without precise, conscious and
official distinction both the *traditio divina-apostolica* and the *traditio humana* (theological views and efforts and opinions of profane, human origin), which are propa-
gated together. It may indeed be said that whatever is preached (even without the
intervention of the extraordinary magisterium, over a long period) expressly, clearly
and universally as *certainly* part *of the faith*, does in fact belong to the *traditio divina-
apostolica*. But it cannot be said that only such things are part of it, nor that everything is proved to be *traditio divina-apostolica* simply because it has been in fact unchallenged in the (whole) universal tradition and been generally held to be correct.
There can be a *traditio mere humana* which is universal, of long standing, and universally held in the Church, and it need not be always expressly and consciously
marked off and distinguished from the *traditio divina-apostolica*. If the magisterium
does not note this difference at a given point, this does not mean that it does not exist.
Such conscious demarcations have a real history. To prove that they did not exist
earlier is not a proof that such distinctions are not objectively justified. Cf. *Die
mündliche Überlieferung. Beiträge zum Begriff der Tradition*, H. Bacht, H. Fries, J. R.
Geiselmann, ed. M. Schmaus (Munich 1957).

[30] At least when we prescind from the indirect argument which is considered
equivalently in Part II.

II

If a professor of dogmatic theology wants a clear, telling and easily managed example of the history and development of dogma, which he can use as a model by which to demonstrate to his pupils the problem of such development, he has one here, which could hardly be bettered. The example is remarkable in many ways. We first have the impression that this doctrine can be traced back explicitly and immediately to the apostolic preaching. St Augustine[31] had already presented the matter in this guise, and even referred the doctrine to an express communication of the Lord.[32] But then we see that this is historically impossible. We come inevitably to the conclusion that we are dealing with a strictly theological process of explanation, though the later doctrine is qualified as '*de fide*'. If we pursue the history of this explanatory process more closely, we see that the first beginnings of the process are more or less buried in obscurity, and that *in part* they were conditioned *de facto* by pressures which were not theologically irreproachable—though the final result is not open to doubt. It would be seen that these pressures, exactly as today, do not always come primarily from the magisterium and the learned theologians. We could use this model to study something which is not always clearly kept in mind even today in dogmatic theology as it is actually practised, namely that the so-called argument from tradition and the Fathers can have two meanings, which are essentially different:

(a) The dogmatic meaning, that is, it undertakes to prove that something was taught by the Church and believed in it at a given time *as* divine revelation, and that it is therefore binding on us today also. Here, as a matter of principle, it does not matter *what* particular period of time is involved in the proof, how near this period is to the apostolic age, and whether the conviction of faith in a given age can be proved, by *historically* clear and tangible data and testimonies, to derive immediately and explicitly from the Apostles.

(b) The meaning in the history of dogma, that is, it undertakes to prove —a task which is one of the tasks proper to dogmatic theology itself— that (and in what manner) the doctrine in question stems from the apos-

---

[31] St Augustine, *Sermo* 196, ch. 1 (*PL* 38, 999); *Sermo* 225 (*PL* 38, 1073); *Enchiridion* ch. 34 (*PL* 40, 249). Cf. Ph. Friedrich, 'Die Mariologie des hl. Augustinus' in the *Festschrift K. Adam* (Düsseldorf 1952) 213–224.

[32] St Augustine, *In Jo. evang. tract* 91, n. 3 (*PL* 35, 1862).

tolic preaching, and can be traced back to it historically. This it does by proving that the doctrine was already directly and expressly proclaimed, though perhaps in another formulation, in the apostolic teaching. Or it can prove that the doctrine, being implicitly contained therein, has grown out of the apostolic doctrine, by a legitimate historical, logical and theological process, as its authentic development.

These two points of view are not usually kept apart in text-books of dogmatic theology when dealing with the doctrine now in question. They thus give the impression that the apostolic origin of the doctrine has been proven *historically* (and not merely dogmatically) when explicit statements of the Fathers can be adduced in its favour from the 3rd century on. One often has the impression that such dogmatic text-books suppose that the gap between us and apostolic times has been bridged historically, if one can produce texts of the Fathers for this doctrine from the beginning of the 3rd century. There are of course exceptions, but most theologians pay too little attention to the background of the text in question, its spiritual *milieu* and its real bearing.[33] This typical example could provide an opportunity of practising how to use these tools of research.

And here perhaps it is permissible to make a point which can serve as an example, one which the author finds a certain satisfaction in making in this volume in honour of J. R. Geiselmann to which he contributes this modest essay. As is well known, J. R. Geiselmann has re-opened and re-kindled the old question and controversy between Catholics on the relation of Scripture and tradition.[34] It is not our intention to take up a set position of our own in this essay, with regard to the controversy. But we cannot refrain from making a few remarks. H. Lennerz[35] has written an essay on the subject in which he flatly rejects the position of Geiselmann. The main reason for the rejection seems to be, when very simply formulated: there are many truths which are to be considered revealed

[33] The average text-book of dogmatic theology does not make it at all clear that the text constantly quoted from Clement of Alexandria, which figures as one of the main witnesses in this question, is more of a difficulty than a proof. We shall have to come back to this later.

[34] J. R. Geiselmann, 'Das Konzil von Trent über das Verhältnis der Heiligen Schrift und der nicht geschriebenen Traditionen. Sein Missverständnis in der nachtridentinisch Theologie und die Überwindung dieses Missverständnis', in *Die mündliche Überlieferung. Beiträge zum Begriff der Tradition*, by H. Bacht, H. Fries, J. R. Geiselmann, ed. M. Schmaus (Munich 1957) 123–206.

[35] H. Lennerz, 'Scriptura sola?' *Gr.* 40 (1959) 38–53; 'Sine scripto traditiones' *Gr.* 40 (1959) 624–635.

truths of faith and yet are not expressed in Scripture and cannot be deduced from relevant statements in Scripture. Therefore tradition *must* be a material source of revelation *beside* Scripture, and the '*partim—partim*' in the declaration of the Council of Trent,[36] though it was omitted and replaced by '*et*', remains the obvious and unavoidable meaning of the declaration. This essay, as we have said, is not the place to investigate whether there are in fact such truths of revelation which cannot be derived from Scripture. We cannot therefore deal with the pre-supposition and the main interest of Lennerz' position.[37] But in this context we may

---

[36] *Denz.* 783 'Recipiuntur libri sacri et traditiones Apostolorum'.

[37] I have tried to explain elsewhere why the fixing of the canon by the Church cannot be considered as a 'case' of a more general law and relationship, cf. *Über die Schriftinspiration. Quaestiones Disputatae* (Freiburg ²1959) 42–45, 80–84. The other examples and cases adduced by Lennerz are at least open to reasonable doubt as to whether when correctly interpreted, with due and precise attention to the substance of the doctrine, they cannot be deduced from Scripture, that is, from the total meaning of the Christian message contained in and attested by Scripture, when truly lived and adequately interpreted. Why cannot this be true of the sacramental character and similar doctrines? And why did the Fathers always search hard for such a derivation in their theology, considering tradition rather as a proof for the correctness of this derivation than as simply an independent source of such truths? This leaves untouched, as we have said, the essential point of difference between Geiselmann and Lennerz. We may however make one remark, even if strictly speaking we do not decide here whether tradition is an independent and materially important source of revealed truth *apart* from Scripture, or not. Even if one adopted Lennerz' thesis with regard to the interpretation of Trent, one could always say that justice has been done to it by the acceptance of the canon on the basis of tradition alone, even though one might deny that this was a case capable of being applied more extensively. And one could still maintain the position (which need not be contested even by a Protestant theologian today) that tradition as such, that is, in so far as it obviously preceded Scripture, as apostolic kerygma, and continued after the coming of Scripture, did not of course cease, in its fundamental formal character, to testify to this apostolic *content*, and that such tradition is still valid today and hence must be accepted *pari reverentia*. And one can still ask whether this tradition really contains things which are not also really contained in Scripture, and whether one is forced by Trent to draw this further conclusion (which is not expressed but must be at best deduced). One may still doubt it. What is meant, for instance, when the Church declares that Scripture is also the 'ultimate foundation' for the Assumption of Mary? It is hard to conceive of any truth which is less directly and explicitly in Scripture than this. It will therefore be difficult to find cases where tradition must have a larger role to play than here. And yet even here Scripture is the ultimate foundation. But something can only be the foundation of a given truth when this truth is *contained* implicitly in this 'foundation'. For it will be hard to indicate any other sort of foundation which can be seriously called a foundation. The fact that a truth (or truths) does not contradict another set of truths, or is compatible

refer to the typical instance we are dealing with and call attention to the following points.

Lennerz' position would be attractive, because it simplifies the problem, if it were really true, as Lennerz supposes far too optimistically, that the truths whose derivation from Scripture Lennerz casts doubts on, could be traced back with ease and certainty to apostolic times, as explicit doctrine, by a procedure based on proofs from the history of dogma. But this is precisely what one may doubt, and the doctrine we are now dealing with is an instructive example. For what has been gained when one has made a 'cross-section' of dogma from the faith as firmly held in a given period, and so proved *that* the doctrine *must* be of apostolic origin? Much, no doubt. But the dogmatic theologian still has the task of making an overall survey of the history of dogma to show *how* and *why*, even historically speaking, the doctrine in question is of apostolic origin. Merely to appeal to tradition—in the dogmatic sense of a dogmatic argument— does not help him at all. He has to show that either (a) the doctrine was explicitly asserted in the apostolic age itself or (b) it must have been at least implicitly contained in the assertions of the time. It is not a sufficient proof of (a) to show for instance, as is the case of the doctrine now in question, that it is clear in the 3rd century. For simply to say that tangible proofs are lacking earlier, because the literary tradition is too fragmentary to follow, but that they *must* have existed, is to replace work on the history of dogma by a dogmatic postulate—even though it is perhaps correct.[38] But such a postulate would be quite wrong, when it could be

with them, etc., does not permit one to affirm that the former have the latter as their foundation. But what other types of connexion between Scripture and the dogma of the Assumption can we think of, except these two possibilities (implication or compatibility of a negative type)? But if one cannot call the second type 'foundation', only the first in fact remains: implication. But if it is true in this case, what truths (apart from the fixing of the canon) can be named of which one would be *obliged* to say that they are certainly not contained in Scripture? In a word: Lennerz must be asked whether in his opinion it is a truth, certainly defined, that there are truths of faith— apart from the canon—of which a theologian is obliged to say *positively* that they are *certainly not* contained in Scripture, either implicitly or explicitly. And he must further be asked, what is the point of this statement, supposing it must be made, if up to the present there has never existed a consent in the Church, as to *what particular* truths are involved, and whether he believes that agreement will ever be reached on this question.

[38] Correct however only when it is *certainly* proved that the doctrine in question could not have been present merely implicitly in former times and hence must always have been transmitted explicitly. But such a proof is scarcely possible in any concrete

shown, with more or less historical certainty, though possibly only in-directly, as in the present case, that the missing historical links with the apostolic times can never have existed at all. This can be done when it can be shown that the first actual historical testimonies are of such a nature that earlier testimonies of the same type cannot have existed before them.

But if it is then postulated, in accordance with the second procedure described above, that there were other truths in the apostolic preaching in which the doctrine in question must have been *implicitly* contained, because there are no earlier explicit testimonies available or because they cannot have existed: by what right—and with what hope—does one pos-tulate that the apostolic tradition really contained more than is still avail-able to us, when the Scripture as a whole is examined carefully and search-ingly enough? The first two centuries are too well known to us for anyone to make out a plausible case to the effect that certain truths were then *universally* presented in the *official* preaching of the Church, as matters of faith, which, through an accident of history, are no longer accessible to us. If more historical testimonies to the apostolic doctrine had come down to us, we should certainly have a more detailed and plastic image of the doctrine, but not really something which would be a new addition to our previous knowledge and not deducible from it. And in this connexion there is something else which we must not overlook. It would be no help dogmatically if in the question we are dealing with for instance, we had a statement from a Father of the Church from the middle of the 2nd cen-tury instead of from the beginning of the 3rd. If the Father did not do us the pleasure, which is more than unlikely, of declaring expressly and solemnly that the doctrine in question was of apostolic origin and of absolutely universal authority in the Church, the Father's statement would only tell us that the doctrine is contained in tradition, but not that it certainly belongs to the *traditio divino-apostolica*. And that is the impor-tant point.

But this can only be ascertained when it is proved that the truth stands

---

case, and always probably relies on theoretical presuppositions about the nature and possibilities of the development of dogma, which again can be contested (relying for instance on the assertion that *only* a metaphysically necessary deduction from two *revealed* premises can be taken as a revealed truth, and hence that where such a deduction cannot be demonstrated, the truth in question must always have been *explicitly* present, if it is to claim later to have been revealed).

in a (sufficiently) necessary relationship to those truths of faith in which we are already sure that they were authoritatively preached from the beginning as explicit elements of revelation. But all such truths are to be found in Sacred Scripture. (There is nothing in all this which allows us to under-estimate the irreplaceable function of tradition, as the objective and material aspect of the living magisterium. This should be obvious and does not need to be expounded here. It can be read up in Geiselmann himself.) Hence Lennerz' position has not in fact the dogmatic advantages which Lennerz claims for it in contrast to the thesis of Geiselmann. A dogmatic *and historical* proof from tradition, if worked out honestly and carefully, offers in fact as many difficulties as a proof from Scripture, especially with regard to those truths of faith, which do not occur in Scripture in the 'way' in which they were later formulated. This observation can be illustrated precisely by the typical case we have in mind. And this brings us back to our original theme, to examine it more closely.

How does our doctrine stand with regard to all the points of view and all the questions which have suggested that it can be used as a typical case by the dogmatic theologian when he is studying the actual history and development of dogma? We call attention to one point only, which seems to us to be decisive in the matter: it is the first visible trace we have of the explicit doctrine of the *'virginitas in partu'*. If we do not presuppose what is to be proved, and so do not read a *'virginitas in partu'* into the 'born of the virgin' (because it can be understood of a virginal birth by reason of the conception, and was so understood originally),[39] the first

---

[39] Hence St Ignatius of Antioch (*Ep. ad Smyrn.* 1, 1, in *Die Apost. Väter*, ed. J. A. Fischer [Darmstadt 1956] 204) is not a witness to our doctrine, especially as St Ignatius is here interested specifically in the reality of the birth as against Docetism. He says (*Ep. ad Eph.* 19; *op. cit.* 157) that the mystery of the birth of Christ was hidden from the devil; but he does not say why or in what regard. If St Ignatius held that the position of Jesus as κύριος remained hidden throughout all the moments of his life, and that contrary to the opinion of the Docetae, *all* the stages of the bodily existence of the κύριος were mysteries, the meaning of the passage is quite clear, without its including a special miracle *in partu*. Neither is St Justin (*Dial.* 84 [Otto 303f.]; cf. also *Dial.* 67 [Otto 237]) a witness for the *virginitas in partu* except *ratione conceptionis*, as is clearly shown by the context of the explanation of Isaiah 7:14. And neither is St Irenaeus (*c.* 190) (*Epideixis* 2, 54: TU, ed. A. von Harnack–C. Schmidt III [Leipzig 1907]59)—against Bardenhewer, Plumpe, etc.—since, though he cites Isaiah 66:7, he sees the text as fulfilled by the 'unhoped-for and unexpected' event of the birth alone, as is also shown for instance by his *Adv. haer.* IV, 33, 4 and III, 19, 3 (Harvey II, 259 and II, 90); he does not appeal to any particular circumstances of the birth. In *Adv. haer.* IV, 33, 11 (Harvey II, 266) all that can be said is that everything is

testimony, if we leave the apocrypha aside for the moment, is in Clement of Alexandria.[40] Writing towards the end of the 2nd century he affirms that 'some say' that Mary was 'found to be a virgin' after she had given birth and been safely delivered, but that 'most still' hold for a perfectly normal birth. This testimony is very precise and all its elements are to be studied carefully. Clement obviously knows that the assertion has a *history*.

(a) Clement, who is pleading *for* the '*virginitas in partu*', concedes that it was more or less unknown (explicitly) earlier on, that 'even now most people' reject it and only 'some' hold a different opinion. We may there-fore affirm that round the beginning of the 3rd century there is no ques-tion of a universal doctrine of the '*virginitas in partu*', much less of its being obligatory in the Church. But the doctrine is already known, in-deed, making progress, but it is still a minority doctrine. If it had always been present, in the state of explicit profession, since the apostolic tradi-tion was in force, the situation described by Clement would not have been possible. And when Clement appeals to the opinions of others, it is only to support his own opinion. To put it in modern terms, he knows only '*sententiae liberae et disputatae*' in the matter. His testimony is like-wise completely in accord with what we know otherwise. It accords with the fact that Tertullian[41] does not really attack the '*virginitas in partu*', but, without any misgivings,[42] takes the opposite opinion for granted,[43] and goes on, with the help of a crude description, to defend the true birth

---

obscure: who is meant (the Church or Mary or both) and what is meant (the 'pure opening of the womb' tells rather against than for virginity in the birth). We need not give here the literature on this much-discussed text (cf. N. Moholy, *St Irenaeus. The Father of Mariology. Franciscan Marian Congress* [Burlington 1952] 129–187.

[40] Clement of Alexandria, *Strom* VII, 16, 93, 7 (Stählin III, 66:20ff.):

Ἀλλ', ὡς ἔοικεν, τοῖς πολλοῖς καὶ μέχρι νῦν δοκεῖ ἡ Μαριὰμ λεχὼ εἶναι διὰ τὴν τοῦ παιδίου γέννησιν οὐκ οὖσα λεχώ· καὶ γὰρ μετὰ τὸ τεκεῖν αὐτὴν μαιωθεῖσαν, φασί τινες παρθένον εὑρεθῆναι.

[41] Tertullian, *Adv. Marc.* 3, 11; 4, 21 (*CSEL* 47, 393; 47, 488); *de carne Christi* 4; 23 (*CSEL* 69/70, 196; 69/70, 247).

[42] Though he is undoubtedly familiar with the *nove nasci* with regard to the vir-ginal conception.

[43] There is nothing to suggest that Tertullian was in the least conscious of coming into conflict with anti-Gnostic and anti-Docetic Christians, or of starting a contro-versy within the Catholic Church. All he does is to emphasize against Marcion his concept of the true, human birth of Christ, to which he adheres unquestioningly as an anti-Docetic Christian.

of Christ against Marcion, as something which is of the essence of Christianity. (Origen too, at the beginning, agrees that the womb, etc., were opened at the birth. He sees no contradiction with the perpetual virginity of Mary, which he so often stresses.)[44]

(b) What are we to think of the 'some' upholders of the '*virginitas in partu*' in the other sense, of whom Clement speaks? They are the apocryphal histories of the Infancy,[45] which must be dated before Clement, probably about the middle of the 2nd century: the Protoevangelium of James,[46] the *Ascensio Isaiae*,[47] the *Odes of Solomon*[48] and (perhaps) the eighth *Sibylline Oracle*.[49] This is not the place to analyse this literature with regard to its antiquity, tendencies and theological level, or to give a more precise exegesis of its testimonies to the virginal birth. But we may undoubtedly say that they all have an unmistakably docetic[50] tinge in this matter: the birth as such, which is asserted by St Luke, is passed over (the child is simply there), or more or less clearly replaced by another process (a luminous cloud which condenses into a child). The child takes its mother's breast, but merely so as not to be recognized.[51]

---

[44] Origen, *Hom. 14 in Lc* (*GCS* 9, 100).

[45] More exactly, the circle in which this literature arose.

[46] Translation of the Protoevangelium Jacobi, by O. Cullmann, 'Kindheitsevangelien', in E. Hennecke, *Neutestamentliche Apokryphen*, 3rd, completely revised edition by W. Schneemelcher I (Tübingen 1959) 277–290. Cf. L. M. Peretto, *La Mariologia del Protoevangelo di Giacomo* (Rome 1955).—It is quite possible that Plumpe (p. 572) is correct in thinking that the purpose of the Protoevangelium is not merely edification, but that the two women (the midwife and Salome) who quarrel about the virgin birth, represent the two parties in the debate, of which Clement tells us. 20, 4 (Hennecke 89f.) perhaps concedes that the virginal birth had been unknown up to this.

[47] J. Flemming–H. Duensing, 'Die Himmelfahrt des Jesaia', *Neutestamentliche Apokryphen*, ed. E. Hennecke (Tübingen 21924) 303–314.

[48] Translation of the Odes of Solomon by H. Gressmann in Hennecke, 455f.

[49] J. Geffcken, 'Christliche Sibyllinen', in Hennecke 475f.

[50] It may at least be suspected that the Odes of Solomon show in general Gnostic tendencies, so that the otherwise harmless text (Ode 19) at any rate belongs to the same literary genre as the other texts. It is not quite clear what is meant by παρθενικὸς τοκετός in the eighth Sibylline oracle.

[51] The content of the doctrine also varies to some extent in these first testimonies. In the Protoevangelium, Mary has birth-pangs, which is why a midwife is wanted. The most important thing is the integrity of the genital passages. The Ascension of Isaiah also mentions this, but adds, for the first time, that the birth was painless. Hence there is no midwife. The Odes of Solomon mention only the painlessness of the birth.

(c). Clement's testimony also fits in with the observation that, according to all reasonable expectations, a really apostolic *explicit* tradition is most unlikely in this matter. Is it psychologically probable that Mary herself would have given information about the intimacy of child-birth? It is probable that Mary alone, and not Jesus himself, who is the source for the history of the infancy of Jesus,[52] as recounted in Luke and Matthew, which she probably told after the death of Jesus. But it does not by any means follow that she also gave an account of the much more intimate details which did not concern Jesus directly, unlike his virginal conception. And even if she had done so, we could not say we knew the exact contents of the narrative, which, as a record of an actual experience, would of course have to have been based on actual details. For when the question of the process of the birth of Jesus is first audible, the information given is anything but uniform and does not give the impression of going back to the concrete narrative based on the experiences of an eye-witness. The infancy narratives of Matthew and Luke, in spite of the emergent interest in biography which is apparent in them, in contrast to the body of the gospels, and in spite of being based on special sources which are not simply identical with the apostolic message of salvation (which begins with the baptism when it tells of the life of Jesus, Ac 1.21f.; 10.36ff.; 13.24ff.), are genuine Christian theology of revelation and present the message of salvation. This is because they are still genuinely linked with the kernel of the Gospel message. But even if this is so, we may not overlook the fact that these narratives are already definitely marginal. It is therefore historically most improbable that there were other explicit and authoritative[53] accounts in circulation which dealt with the details of the history of the infancy.

If this supposition is correct, the starting-point of all discussion of the '*virginitas in partu*' must be as follows: the doctrine of the '*virginitas in partu*' must be considered, in theological method, as contained only implicitly at first in the apostolic deposit. If—and in so far as—the later explicit preaching of the faith does not provide a sure dogmatic proof of a more copious, detailed or definite content to the doctrine,[54] we can only

[52] Cf. P. Gaechter, *Maria im Erdenleben* (Innsbruck 193) 75.

[53] If we do not make these presuppositions, a (hypothetical) explicit testimony of apostolic times would leave us at a loss (unless it came from Mary herself): how could one know that it was true?

[54] If this were in fact the case (though we hold that the case is unreal), it would not prove that the basic principle just put forward must be false. As with other doctrines

take as dogmatically binding what can be deduced by explicitation from the explicit apostolic tradition. The testimonies must of course be carefully and methodically weighed, and as much as possible in the light of the whole heritage of faith. Anything that cannot be proved, according to the criterion of apostolic tradition, to be implicitly contained in other truths, may not be maintained as binding in faith. Once the content of the doctrine has been thus determined, anything else that occurs in the line of concrete details in the *de facto* theological tradition of the doctrine, in Fathers and theologians, must be considered as free theological propositions, or as free interpretations of what is strictly meant by the doctrine—as long as there is no *strict* dogmatic proof that the content of the doctrine, in so far as it is binding in faith, is really wider. And then the more detailed concept of the content which occurs in the Fathers and theologians would really be sanctioned. But, as we have said, we do not think that such is really the case in point of fact.

We cannot properly justify this assertion here, because the proof would demand a precise and complete history of the whole doctrine of the '*virginitas in partu*'. But we can at least give some indications. We have already mentioned the reserved attitude of the magisterium, and also the growing cautiousness of present-day theologians. We must keep clearly in mind the reality of the birth of Jesus from Mary, understanding it actively and passively. We must note that two possible human beings are concerned, and that passibility is a truth of faith, of soteriological significance. From the point of view of method, it must be noted that the reality of the birth, which is a truth of faith, is the critical norm for the doctrine of the '*virginitas in partu*', rather than vice versa. It follows from all this, that it is not so easy to give the second doctrine a content which will do justice to the first. Many elements in the de facto tradition must certainly be rejected as theologically unsound, e.g. the parellels drawn with the resurrection. There is much in the tradition which reveals problems which were not solved, but buried gradually in silence. Ratramnus

of the Church which were only made explicit later, it is quite possible that the individual theologian has simply not yet in fact managed to actualize sufficiently by theological methods the theological virtualities which are present in the *depositum fidei* of the primitive Church and were made explicit in an instinctive and general way by the sense of faith of the whole Church. Cf. K. Rahner, 'The Development of Dogma' in *Theological Investigations* I (London & Baltimore, Md. 1961) 39–77; 'Dogmenentwicklung', *LTK* III², 457–463; *Considerations on the Development of Dogma*, in this volume 1–35.

of Corby asks, for instance (PL, 121, 82), is it possible to understand virginity at the birth as the 'integrity' of the genital passages, if the reality of the birth demands that the child must pass through the normal channels to see the light of day—unlike the resurrection, which had no fixed route. The question had already been touched on by St John Damascene (PG, 94, 1161), but it can hardly be said that an intelligible answer was ever found. Many Fathers emphasize expressly that the *manner* of the birth remains a mystery; so, in the East, St Athanasius,[55] St Gregory of Nazianzen,[56] Amphilochius of Iconium,[57] St John Chrysostom,[58] Proclus[59] and St Cyril of Alexandria;[60] in the West, St Jerome[61] and St Augustine[62] among others. One may well ask how this is possible, when writers like St Ephraim,[63] St Epiphanius of Salamis[64] and Zeno of Verona[65] claimed to know the manner of the birth even in the most indiscreet details, and indeed must have known it, on the supposition of a direct and explicit tradition coming from Mary and Christ. The fact that the '*virginitas in partu*' is declared to be a miracle does not make the thing itself, that is the manner of it, very mysterious. What of the real process of birth itself, when for instance St Gregory of Nazianzen,[66] St Epiphanius[67] and Zeno,[68] and later, the theologian Paschasius Radbertus,[69] in express terms, reject an after-birth as unfitting? The exact content of the doctrine is not given quite uniformly. St Athanasius,[70] St John Chrysostom,[71] Proclus,[72]

---

[55] *Expos. fidei* 1: *PG* 25, 201.

[56] *Orat.* 40, 45: *PG* 36, 424 B.

[57] *Orat. in occ. Dom.* 2: *PG* 39, 48 B.

[58] *In nat. Christ. diem:* *PG* 56, 388.

[59] *Sermo de S. Clem.:* *PG* 65, 845 A.

[60] *In Jo. Ev.* 1: *PG* 73, 21 B.

[61] *Hom. in Jo.* 1, 1–14: G. Morin, *Anecdota* III, 2, 390, 16.

[62] *Ep.* 137, 2, 8: *PL* 33, 519.

[63] Assemani II, 266 A–C, D; II, 422 F; cf. L. Hammersberger, *Die Mariologie der ephremischen Schriften* (Innsbruck 1938) 47ff.

[64] *Adv. haer.* c. 78, 79: *PG* 42, 700–756.

[65] *Tract.* II, 8, 2f.: *PL* 11, 414 A–417 A.

[66] *Orat.* 40, 45: *PG* 36, 424 B.

[67] *Adv. haer.* II, 2 (Anaceph.): *PG* 42, 879 A. But in *Adv. haer.* III, 2, 19: *PG* 42, 730 C, Epiphanius seems to admit that the opening of the womb would not be contrary to virginity.

[68] *Tract.* II, 8: *PL* 11, 415.

[69] *De part. virg.* 2: *PL* 120, 1385.

[70] *Ep. ad Epict.* 5: *PG* 26, 1060.

[71] *In nat. Christ, diem:* *PG* 56, 388.

[72] *Orat.* I, 10: *PG* 65, 691 A (though here Proclus, like Epiphanius, does not hesitate to combine the *claustra virginitatis* with the statement: *naturae quidem portas aperuit ut homo*, connecting the virginal integrity expressly with Christ *ut deus*).

Hesychius,[73] St Cyril,[74] St Hilary,[75] Zeno,[76] St Jerome,[77] St Ambrose,[78] St Augustine,[79] Rufinus,[80] Gaudentius,[81] St Maximus[82] and St Gregory the Great[83] speak expressly of the integrity of the hymen or the genital passages. But only St Ephraim,[84] St Epiphanius,[85] St Cyril,[86] Zeno,[87] St Maximus,[88] and St Peter Chrysologus[89] mention the painlessness of the birth. And only St Gregory of Nazianzen, St Epiphanius and Zeno (see above) mention the absence of the after-birth. St Ephraim, Amphilochius, St John Chrysostom, Proclus, Hesychius, Theodotus and St Cyril do not mention the matter at all, but none of the Fathers concedes it expressly. It is interesting that St Ephraim, in the 'Parable of the Mussel'[90] is so intent on preserving the reality of the birth that he even thinks of a sort of *restitutio in integrum*, after the birth has taken place in the normal way. It is also remarkable that St Jerome is the first to reject expressly one of the oldest sources for the doctrine of the virginal birth, the apocrypha (cf. for instance, the story of the mid-wife).[91] As in the case of the Assumption, the apocrypha were in fact the first 'source', in the sense of an initial theological reflexion.

[73] *Hom. IV de S. Maria Deipara: PG* 93, 1466.

[74] *Adv. Anthropomorph.: PG* 76, 1129 A.

[75] *De Trinit.* III, 19: *PL* 10, 87 A (where some see in the controverted phrase *ipsa de suis non imminuta* the first western testimony for the *virginitas in partu*, though *De Trinit.* II, 24–26: *PL* 10, 66 A–68 seems rather to testify to a natural birth: '*Dei igitur imago invisibilis pudorem humani exordii non recusavit, et per conceptionem, partum . . . omnes naturae nostrae contumelias transcurrit . . . Quia omnia continet, humani partus lege profertur*').

[76] *Tract* II, 8, 2: *PL* 11, 415 A.

[77] *Comm. in Ez.* 44, 3: *PL* 25, 430 A; cf. J. Niessen, *Die Mariologie des hl. Hieronymus* (Münster 1913) 141–144.

[78] *De inst. virg.* 8, 53: *PL* 16, 320 A B.   [79] *Ep.* 137, 2, 8: *PL* 33, 519.

[80] *Comm. Symb.: PL* 21, 349.   [81] *Sermo* 9: *PL* 20, 900.

[82] *Sermo* 53: *PL* 57, 638.   [83] *In Evang. hom.* II, 26, 1: *PL* 76, 1197.

[84] Assemani II, 266 C.   [85] *Adv. haer.* I, 2, 20: *PG* 41, 438.

[86] *In Lc.: PG* 72, 489 C.   [87] *Tract.* II, 8, 2: *PL* 11, 417.

[88] *Hom.* 5: *PL* 57, 235 C.   [89] *Sermo* 117: *PL* 52, 520.

[90] Assemani II, 266 C; cf. P. Krüger ('Die somat. Virginität der Gottesmutter im Schrifttume Ephräms des Syrers': *Alma Socia Christi* V, 1: *Acta Congr. Mariolog.-marian.* Romae 1950 (Rome 1951) 46–86, who does not go into the statement in the parable of the mussel.

[91] *Contr. Helv.* 8: *PL* 23, 192; *Comm. in Mt* 13:50: *PL* 26, 84. On the parallel drawn between the *uterus clausus* and the 'closed gate' of Ezekiel, see A. Kassing, 'Das Verschlossene Tor, Ezk 44:1–3,' *Wi. Wei.* 16 (1953) 171–190.

III

If it is methodologically correct in the present question to treat the *'virginitas in partu'* as a truth only implicitly contained in the apostolic preaching (contrary to what might appear at first sight), then the question arises as to *where*[92] this doctrine is to be found implicitly. On this point too, where of course a clear idea of the dogmatic development of this truth is decisive, we can only offer a few observations, which do not claim to give a comprehensive answer to the question.

(a) In spite of the reserves made above, Mary is a real theological theme of the apostolic preaching, and not merely an unavoidable detail in unintentional but unavoidable biographical notes about Jesus. This is clear from the theology of St Luke and from the Apostles' Creed. This apostolic Mariology contains a basic concept, not very consciously formulated perhaps, but still real, and capable of offering matter for reflexion. This is not the place to discuss how this basic concept should be more precisely formulated.[93] At any rate, Mary is a person who as such is part of the history of salvation. Our salvation therefore depends in part on her. Her motherhood is free, completely human, not merely biological and so sub-human. And in this motherhood, by the power of the free, gracious and divinely-initiated coming of the Logos as our unique salvation, this eschatological salvation was freely accepted for Mary and for us all. Thus Mary herself became, as this final salvation became flesh 'out of Mary', the perfected prototype of the redemption and of the absolute new begin-

---

[92] For our purposes and the limited scope of our investigation we may be permitted here simply to interrogate the rest of Mariology as a whole with regard to the origin of the *virginitas in partu*. It is of course possible that by doing so we shall take as premises for our doctrine certain Mariological statements which again need to be based on the primary data of apostolic Mariology, to satisfy the demands of history of dogma. And thus it would be true to say that we are merely transposing the problem elsewhere. But when properly viewed, the problem then becomes quite naturally part of certain doctrines which cannot be made the theme of our present study, though of course they must be part of a general Mariology.

[93] Cf. e.g. B. J. Bover, 'El principio mariológico de analogía', *Alma Socia Christi* XI, 1–13 (*Acta Congr. Mariolog.-marian.* Romae 1950); K. Rahner, 'Le principe fondamental de la théologie mariale', *RSR* 42 (1954) 481–522 (Engl. tr. *Theological Digest* 4 (1956) 72f.); P. Sanchez-Cepedes, *El misterio de Maria. Mariologia biblica I: El principio fundamental* (Santander 1955); P. Mahoney, 'The Unitive Principle of Marian Theology', *Thomist* 18 (1955)443–479; C. Dillenschneider, *Le principe premier d'une théologie mariale organique* (Paris 1955); A. O. Patfoort, ' "Le" principe premier de la Mariologie?' *RSPT* 41 (1957) 445–454.

ning in flesh and spirit.[94] No matter what further precisions are given to this picture, we may be sure at least of one thing: that the active birth (the act of giving birth) is not simply a biological event which is merely a fractional happening within the sphere of a human being, and which could then be the same even in people who were inwardly different. It is much rather, and must therefore be considered, an act that involves the *whole man* and will express the totality of the human person in question in the way in which it is done, suffered and experienced.[95]

Once this concept of the active birth as something involving the whole man is presupposed,[96] the following formal, theological and anthropological proposition may clearly be formulated at once: that in Mary, the active birth corresponds to her nature. But since her whole reality is a unique and miraculous work of grace, the same holds good *eo ipso* of her act of child-bearing. This of course brings us for the moment only to a formal delimitation of the special nature of the birth. However, it brings us at once to the fundamental justification of a theological assessment of the birth. And it also allows us to ask whether we have attained a correct concept of the '*virginitas in partu*' only when the content has been expressed unambiguously in material and biologically concrete terms. And it may also suggest that whether we approach the concept from the point of view of the history of the dogma (which began as a truth merely implicit in the original revelation), or whether we approach it from the

[94] As thus radically and perfectly redeemed, she is the 'immaculate conception', as a radically new beginning in spirit and flesh she is virgin mother, in such a way that (as being perfectly redeemed) she is totally given to this function in the history salvation for all her life, so that person and office are one.

[95] And possibly also the impotence of the person to master events exterior to his person and to build them into the totality of a being which understands itself to be free, to make them part of his authentic 'existence', to 'understand' them in the light of the kernel of his being, 'know what to do with them', express himself in them and stamp them with his character. Cf. K. Rahner, 'The Theological Concept of Concupiscentia' in *Theological Investigations* I (London & Baltimore, Md. 1961) 347–382.

[96] Mitterer's mistake, formally speaking, is that he works only with a circumscribed, biological notion of birth, and so finds himself faced from the start with only two alternatives. He must indicate and admit certain material peculiarities of a miraculous nature for the birth; or he can point to no peculiarities (at least in the formal process) which would differentiate this birth from others. He is then forced to find a difference (which on account of tradition he cannot totally deny) which is totally derived '*ab extrinseco*', from the virginal conception in fact; but the birth as such—which is what tradition is thinking of after all—must be kept really distinct from the conception.

point of view of Mary's nature[97] (which certainly expresses itself in her way of giving birth), no direct statement as to its material content may be expected at all, on principle. If these misgivings are justified by the very nature of the matter, then the fact that the doctrine is only formally determined, and cannot at once be translated into sturdy propositions readily accessible to the imagination, is not an argument against our view, but rather tells in favour of it. In any case, we have not yet reached the final stage in the clarification of the formal statement.

(b) One could of course object at this stage of the proceedings that the perspectives here opened up allow us to appreciate the fact that Mary's act of giving birth is indeed *Mary's* as such, 'Marian', we may say, but do not help us to understand how it is virginal. We must ask in return whether we are clear about what virginal means when applied to the birth. The presence or absence of pain has undoubtedly nothing to do with virginity (—whether there were in fact pains or not may be left a completely open question). But no one can seriously maintain that the notion, at least, of 'bodily integrity' has anything to do with virginity, except in so far as this is connected (also) with sexual intercourse, but not as it is connected with birth.[98] Hence '*virginitas in partu*' appears as at least a highly problematical notion when the concepts are analysed. In any case, the process which the traditional doctrine takes to be the concrete *content*, cannot be derived from the (logically anterior) concept of '*virginitas in partu*', which can only be regarded as a subsequent and not very happy summary of what one knows of the process from other sources. Thus the question arises as to what is the consistent objective basis from which the details in question could eventually be determined.

A close analysis of tradition reveals very soon that the train of thought

---

[97] By 'nature' we mean of course always the whole, concrete, unique, natural and supernatural, personal and ecclesial reality of Mary (as element of the economy of redemption). But if this *nature* is essentially mystery, one reason for which is the dialectical duality of the attributes of Mary (who is of the race of sinners—and beginning of the new redeemed creation; who is under the law of suffering and everyday life—and freed from the concupiscence of the flesh, etc.), we should not expect her child-bearing to be described in the undialectically smooth and clear terms, lacking all touch of mystery, which some 'pious people' seem to think is the most pious and orthodox theology.

[98] Here Mitterer is quite right at the start. His position only becomes questionable when it presupposes, more or less silently, that if the peculiarities attached to the birth by tradition cannot be deduced from the objective notion of virginity, they are at once excluded.

is not: Mary is a virgin in the act of giving birth; but the concept of virgin obviously implies certain factors; these factors must have been characteristic of the birth. The patristic teaching may often give the impression that the argument proceeds on these lines. But that is an illusion, arising from their pedagogical methods of instruction. For one has only to ask how it could be known that Mary was, in this sense, 'virgin' at the birth. Can it be seriously maintained that the content of the doctrine (no matter how envisaged) is deduced from the logically anterior revealed abstract notion of virginity? Or is the content of the concept in fact established by arguments 'from what is fitting', that is, not from the formal concept of virginity, but from the dignity of the divine motherhood, etc? In view of all this, one can easily assert that the objection, which is apparently so clear, is really unjustified.

And with this in mind, one may also answer the difficulty by pointing out that in the statements in question 'virgin' stands simply for Mary in her whole reality. Mary is 'the virgin' during the birth: and this means precisely what we said above, that the child-bearing of the Blessed Virgin corresponds to the unique and marvellous figure of the Blessed Virgin as a whole in her God-given role in the history of salvation. We do not need to confine ourselves to this provisionally formal statement of the nature of the birth, though one could already say at this point that we have attained a certain understanding of tradition, formal though it be, and hence an 'intelligible' content for the doctrine—even though we did not succeed in completing it with more material details.[99] And hence we ask: what particular elements in the general mind of the Church can be drawn on, in order to reach a still more concrete picture of the doctrine?

One element must certainly be considered: the 'integrity' of the Blessed Virgin, that is, her freedom from concupiscence. We must proceed carefully here, for many reasons. First of all the doctrine of the integrity of Mary is no more express and tangible in the apostolic tradition as such than is the doctrine which we are discussing. Consequently, the methodological observation made above is to be kept in mind here. But though this difficulty of method and therefore of fact is to be carefully noted, one can still say: the detailed explicitation of a general concept of the nature of Mary and her place in the economy of salvation may not have reached a

[99] It seems to us that this consideration provides us with some sort of answer (if only a formal one) to the question which we did not deal with at the beginning when presenting the doctrine of M. Schmaus.

given statement by a transition which seems to us today to be the almost indispensable link.[100] But this does not prove that when we use this transition we do not interpret correctly the faith of the Church, even of the ancient Church.[101] But there is still another difficulty which must be clearly envisaged, if we are not to draw false conclusions from the notion of freedom from concupiscence. Such integrity must be understood essentially, as indeed in Jesus Christ himself, as 'infralapsarian'. This does not diminish it. It rather reinforces it, but still it must not be understood automatically in the light of paradise and Adam. It must be understood in the light of Christ. And then it appears as the power of full moral integration of the whole being (here exposed to *suffering* and *death*) into the personal decision.[102] What this warning implies will be at once clear.

Biblically, our proposed view may be stated as follows. The actual manner of child-bearing appears, according to the testimony of Scripture (Gen 3.15) as a process which combines with its positive, human, God-given structure and meaning, the stigma of sin and death, which are the usual powers of the world,[103] and affect everything in it.[104] But if Mary is

---

[100] Something of the sort is an everyday experience in profane matters; the spiritual unity of consciousness contains many objects which are more or less consciously present, and also contains the connexions between these objects, which are likewise known either expressly or in a general way. In other words, there can be a genuine discovery of the truth, where the result can appear clearly before all the objective reasons are seen with the same clearness, even though they had been subjectively at work. And the subjective efficacy of such objectively efficacious reasons cannot be denied on the grounds that a quick, spontaneous discovery of the (correct) result, which seems to omit the objectively valid process of thought, was *also* in fact stimulated and enlightened by subjective preferences and attentiveness and the spiritual attitudes of the times in question, which cannot claim permanent validity. The human aspect of the development of dogma can undoubtedly show such traits.

[101] In a comprehensive Mariology we should have to show that as understood by the ancient Church, Mariology contained the doctrine of her integrity, and why it did so. But here again, integrity must be correctly understood, not as miraculously paradisaical, but as 'infralapsarian'. And we should have to show how even if grasped only in a general and inarticulate way, it could help the doctrine in question to be expressly stated.

[102] Cf. K. Rahner, 'The Theological Concept of Concupiscentia' in *Theological Investigations* I (London & Baltimore, Md. 1961) 347–382. And then, going more deeply into the question, J. B. Metz, *Der Begriff der Concupiszenz bei Thomas von Aquin* (Munich 1961).

[103] But in the most profound and central processes (always when seen as involving the *whole* man) this law of sin and death takes on its sharpest and most challenging outlines. And this is most precisely true of the act whereby man emancipates himself

the mother of the redeeming Word of God, if her child-bearing, the act of the immaculate, is part of the new beginning of the world, then the birth cannot carry this stigma; this birth must be 'different'. Since she is not subject to concupiscence, she integrates the passive elements of her life entirely, though in an infralapsarian way, into the basic decision of her personality. She can turn what she has to submit to into the pure expression of her active decision. Thus she undergoes the passive adventure of child-bearing in a way different from other human beings, who always experience what the life-forces of the world inflict upon them as something alien and restrictive, which works upon them to the detriment of their freedom. We must not leap to the conclusion, in the light of Gen 3.15, that this birth was therefore free from pain. This formula may well suggest itself to someone who feels that he has the whole of tradition behind him, and indeed that he could arrive at this conclusion from the starting-point which has been developed here. But he still must ask himself does he knew so exactly what pain is, and when and in what measure pain is really an expression of sin and not that of a healthy nature and an exuberance of life. Does he know well enough how pain is constituted, with its purely physiological components *and* its basic spiritual attitude, so that he can be asked how he understands painlessness, in view of the complexity of the concept of pain? Has the physiological element been changed, or the personal interpretation, which is an *intrinsic* element of the pain which is experienced? He must ask himself whether for instance a pain which serves life[105] can, from the anthropological and theological point of view, be simply ranked with pain caused by hostile attack and

---

for a new and responsible life of his own, and asserts himself against the law of death, which he himself set up. Cf. K. Rahner, *On the Theology of Death. Quaestiones Disputatae* 2 (London ⁵1964).

[104] The theological meaning of the expression must be formulated in this way because if one concentrates too directly and materially on the 'birth-pangs', one could get the impression that the text of Genesis was meaningless, since such pains are not always felt and it is morally lawful to try to avoid them.

[105] St Thomas, for instance, undoubtedly gave such pains as such an interpretation which was physiologically wrong, when dealing with our question (*S. Th.* III q. 35 a. 6; III q. 28 a. 2; cf. also *S.c.G.* IV c. 45). He thought they came from a violent opening of the genital passages and a lesion of them. They are of themselves, in reality, a normal accompaniment of the mother's action, as she expels the child by compressing the womb. They are intrinsically closer to the active child-bearing, which may not be denied in the case of Mary, than was hitherto thought. Hence in former times it was easier to deny their existence, without further ado, than it is today.

moral misdeeds.[106] Has he paid enough attention to Jn 9.1ff. in *this* connexion? Has he considered well enough that painless birth need be anything but a miracle? And has he considered that Mary's integrity is infralapsarian, that is, that it works in and through the law of suffering and pain, on which the Christian doctrine of Mary as Queen of Martyrs and mother of sorrows, who passed through death to her glory, is perfectly clear?

We cannot simply conclude however from these considerations that Mitterer is right and that we should definitely attribute birth-pangs to Mary. We could even say it follows certainly from our basic principle that the subjective experiences of Mary at the birth were different from those of other human beings. It may be objected that this element of a beneficent process can only be felt as painful by a human being who is subject to concupiscence, because only such a one will feel the apt experience as contradictory to his basic attitude, and hence painfully and strangely unintegrated. But if one is thinking in these terms, it can and must be said that Mary felt no 'pain' at the birth—but nothing will have been decided thereby about the purely physiological side of the process. For no matter how this aspect is thought of, the decisive point is always how this element is integrated with her personality and attitude as a whole, where it receives its final determination. Since the whole person of Mary was essentially different, through the miracle of grace, the whole, and hence every element of her child-birth, even as such (and it was a truly human type), was different from that of sinful mortals. But if we bear this principle in mind, we can understand how prudent one must be, to say the least, if one tries to depict this 'otherness' in detail. One finds oneself forced to maintain dialectically opposed positions at one and the same time: a really new beginning, in the midst of the old, which is being truly and patiently taken over in the flesh and the spirit—this is the criterion of the salvific economy of Christ in general. It is difficult, if not impossible, to balance out both sides correctly. This is also true of Mary as she gives birth to the Lord.

And there is another difficulty which must be noted in this connexion.

---

[106] Mitterer, to my mind, overlooks this essential distinction when he appeals to the birth-pangs of Mary to make the concept of 'mother of sorrows' at once intelligible. Theologians exclude, for instance, all 'sickness' in the case of Jesus (but when is one 'sick'?), though they do not wish to deny his suffering—and this is interior, though caused by external assaults which are hostile to life and contrary to the moral order.

Hesychius of Jerusalem seems to have been the only writer in the patristic age who referred expressly to Gen 3.16 in *this* context.[107] This observation of W. Zauner may be correct. But we can safely say that wherever the Fathers speak of the pangs of birth as something that ought not to be, and hence foreign to Mary (though they do not forget that Mary had to suffer otherwise), these pains are viewed in the light of their general interpretation of human existence: all these experiences are seen as a sign of the sinfulness of human existence. For what other reason could they have for denying that Mary suffered these pains? Perhaps because they were 'unpleasant'? But then they would have had to exclude them from all other situations of her life. Or perhaps because pains were not quite fitting at a *joyful* birth? But then why did the Fathers not have recourse to Jn 16.21? And then they would have had to deny that the child suffered the pain of being born, the misery of the stable, etc—which, at least for the most part, they did not do. It is therefore safe to consider that the background of their theological propositions was their understanding of Gen 3.16, even though it is not cited expressly. Since the sinful flesh is redeemed in this birth (cf. also Jn 1.13), since a new beginning is made here, the Fathers could justifiably think that it was not the same as other births. And hence they deny the 'pain'. They may have drawn their conclusions without enough theological nuances and without all the necessary care, still, they base their considerations on the same principles as we have tried to enunciate more specifically here.

(c) What are we then to think of the other details with which tradition tried to render the difference in Mary's child-bearing? We have already remarked that one is not obliged to accept at once all such elements of tradition as definitely dogmatic and certainly binding. But leaving this consideration aside, the question arises once more: what is really included in the concept of 'bodily integrity' and what does it imply? If it is considered as a revealed concept, anterior to the individual details, it will be difficult to say what it really implies and whether the usual conclusions drawn from it really follow. Is, for instance, the normal expansion of the genital passages in a completely healthy birth to be considered a breach of 'bodily integrity'? Will anyone have the courage to maintain this categorically? Are any of the processes of normal birth to be placed under the rubric of 'injury' or 'damage' (*corruptio*)? And if so, what has been damaged? The 'virginity' or a bodily 'integrity', 'soundness'? All this is very

[107] *Hom. de S. Maria Deipara* IV: *PG* 93, 1454.

problematical, and can hardly be a pointer to the concrete details which we are looking for, as should be clear from the general trend of the discussion in Mitterer and in these pages.

Some theologians may firmly reject all these efforts, and take up the stand-point that the usual details indicated by tradition (painlessness, non-rupture of the hymen, '*sine sordibus*'—by which the Fathers meant above all the after-birth) cannot seriously be deduced from any other source, and still hold that they are data which must be accepted as a matter of faith. But then they must be consistent and say: they have been explicitly revealed in these terms, and have only been summed up subsequently in the general notion of 'integrity'—of virginity, of body, etc. But what theologian would be ready to make such an assertion today? How would he then explain the hesitations and variations of tradition when indicating such details? Can it be really true that the item usually named in the third place, the '*sordes*', was explicitly revealed? And why should this be in a less privileged position? And does one not come then to a docetic idea of the birth? Why should other physiological processes, such as the signs of pregnancy, the giving suck to the child, etc, which tradition has no hesitation in ascribing to Mary, be considered less 'unfitting'? But if the '*sordes*' are conceded, why should the other two elements be in a stronger position, either from the nature of things or from tradition? If we consider all these difficulties and unsolved problems, it is impossible to say that we are clearly faced with the necessity *either* of being able to deduce (and deducing) the concrete details from our initial principle *or* of giving up this principle as insufficient and not doing justice to tradition. Hence we by no means affirm, with Mitterer, that these particularities never existed. All we say is this: Church doctrine affirms, with the real substance of tradition, that Mary's child-birth, as regards both child and mother, like the conception, is, in its total reality, as the completely human act of this 'virgin', in itself (and not just by reason of the conception, as Mitterer says), an act corresponding to the nature of this mother, and hence it is unique, miraculous and 'virginal'. But this proposition, which is directly intelligible, does not offer us the possibility of deducing assertions about the concrete details of the process, which would be *certain* and *universally* binding.

PART FOUR

The Doctrine of Grace

7

NATURE AND GRACE[1]

THE discussion of the theme 'nature and grace' is generally left
nowadays to a very small circle of specialists. But at least they come
back to the theme again and again, and do not just talk about it
when it cannot be avoided, as in the theology of the schools. The theme
is passionately debated. There is no general agreement and the controversy
is obviously more than a scholastic exercise. We can be glad of this. For
since the controversy between Catholics and reformers grew sterile and
died away in the 18th century, and since the traditional scholastic theology
came once more into its own in the neo-Scholasticism of the 19th century
after the meagre efforts of the 'Enlightenment' period, the general impression was that the books had been closed on the theme of 'nature and
grace' by general consent, and that anything worth knowing about it was
more or less already known.

If we now try to give the average concept of nature and grace in post-
Tridentine and neo-Scholastic theology, it must be remembered that we
are always talking about the *average* approach. No one denies that the
theology of today is the heir to all the ages of theological thinking.
Nothing is ever quite forgotten in the Church. And the explicit assertions
of theology always contain inexhaustible riches of implicit meanings
which are part of the whole, even though not immediately seen. It would
therefore be easy to impute injustice and distortion to the description of
the average way of understanding a question in the current theology of
the schools. But such average concepts do exist. And sometimes they
affect the life of the Church more than the sublime insights which are the
possession of the few.

---

[1] The bibliographical notes can obviously offer only a very limited and inevitably
arbitrary choice from the theological and historical literature on the dogmatic doctrine
of grace. In general, we must confine ourselves to a choice from the literature of the
last two hundred years.

What then has been the average concept of the relationship of nature and grace in neo-Scholasticism? To see the peculiar elements of this concept, which was not strictly speaking clear to the theologians themselves, we must start by discussing a position which is apparently only a marginal one in the doctrine of supernatural grace. This grace by which man is justified, and by which he is enabled to perform salutary acts, was taken to be something totally beyond the region of consciousness. In itself, this is merely a scholastic opinion, which was always in fact disputed. For Thomistic theology always maintained that a supernatural act had a formal object which could never be attained by a purely natural act. But the opposite opinion was predominant in the schools and determined the average mentality: supernatural grace is a reality of which one knows something through the teaching of faith but which is in itself completely inaccessible and gives no sign of its presence in the conscious, personal life of man. Once taught of its existence by faith, man must of course refer to it, take care to possess it (by moral acts and the reception of the sacraments), treasure it as the divinization of his being and the pledge and presupposition of eternal life. But the space where he comes to himself, experiences himself and lives, is, as regards the data of consciousness, not filled by this grace. His experience of his spiritual and moral acts in their proper reality (in contrast to their proposed objects, which are distinct from the acts) remains exactly what it would and could be, if there were no such thing as a supernatural 'elevation' of these acts. Thus grace, of itself, according to this very common opinion, is a superstructure beyond the realm of consciousness, with regard to the mental experience of the moral being, though it is of course a conscious object of faith and acknowledged to be the most sublime and divine element in man, his only salutary possession.

This view also seems to be the only possible and the obvious one. One can know nothing of one's state of grace, or at most, one can make deductions about it, more or less probable, using certain indications. But one does not 'notice' grace at all, or at the very most, only some of the 'healing' graces which help to fulfil the natural law and are of themselves natural aids. Simple experience and the teaching of Trent[2] (Denzinger 802;

---

[2] Cf. for instance: A. Stakemeier, *Das Konzil von Trient über die Heilsgewissheit* (Heidelberg 1947); V. Heyneck, 'Das Votum des Generals der Konventualen Bonaventura Costassiaro vom 26 Nov. 1546 über die Gnadengewissheit', *Franz. Stud.* 31 (1949) 274–304, 350–395; Fr. Buuck, 'Zum Rechtfertigungsdekret. Die Unter-

805; 825; 826) seem to confirm this opinion which anyway presents itself as the obvious one. Once it is accepted, the region where we know ourselves as active spiritually and morally seems to be naturally identifiable with the dimension of 'nature'. Indeed, this state becomes the very definition of what we mean by nature: that which we know about ourselves without the word of revelation—for that is nature and *merely* nature. And vice versa; nature alone and its acts are the components of the life which we experience as our own. We use the elements of natural concepts, attitudes etc, to construct the acts in which we refer ourselves by our intention to the realities of the revealed mysteries of God, acts which we know to be 'ontologically' elevated to the supernatural plane— but only 'ontologically'. Supernatural 'enlightenment', moral 'impulse' and 'inspiration' to good acts, the 'light' of faith, the breath of the Spirit and other similar concepts from Scripture and tradition (the unction, the signing of the Spirit etc.), are reduced either to this purely entitative elevation of our natural moral acts, or to a natural influence of a psychological type—which is however considered to be providentially directed to our supernatural salvation. In a word, the relationship between nature and grace is conceived in such a way that they appear as two layers so carefully placed that they penetrate each other as little as possible.

In the same way, the orientation of 'nature' to grace is conceived of in as negative a way as possible. Grace is, it is true, an unsurpassable perfectioning of nature; God as the Lord of this nature can command man to submit to his *de facto* will and to be receptive to his grace, which direct man to a supernatural life and end. But of itself nature has only a '*potentia obedientialis*' to such an end, and this capacity is thought of as negatively as possible. It is no more than non-repugnance to such an elevation. Of itself, nature would find its perfection just as readily and harmoniously in its own proper realm, in a purely natural end, without an immediate intuition of God in the beatific vision. When it finds itself in immediate

scheidung zwischen fehlbaren und unfehlbaren Glauben in den vorbereitenden Verhandlungen', Fr. J. Schierse, 'Das Trienter Konzil und die Frage nach der christlichen Gewissheit' both in: Georg Schreiber, *Das Weltkonzil von Trient* I (Freiburg 1951) 117–167; G. M. Lachance, 'L'homme peut-il savoir, qu'il a la grâce?' *Rev. Univ. Ottawa* 24 (1954) 65–92; M. Guérard des Lauriers, 'Saint Augustin et la question de la certitude de la grâce au Concile de Trente' in *Augustinus Magister* (Congrès International Aug. 1954), *Communications* 2, 1057–1067; L. M. Poliseno, 'I Carmelitani e la certezza dello stato di grazia nel Concilio Tridentino', *Carmelus* 1 (1954) 111–145.

possession of itself—as is part of the essence of the spirit, *'reditio com-pleta in seipsum'*—it meets itself as though it were 'pure nature'. According to the well-known axiom (which is a matter of opinion), it is distinguished from pure nature only *'sicut spoliatus a nudo'*. And this 'state of being despoiled' is silently considered as a merely extrinsic element with regard to the absence of sanctifying grace: a deprivation due to a divine decree (which demands the possession of grace) and to an historical fact of the past (the guilt of Adam). But we do not usually think that the lack of grace might be different in the two cases, that of pure nature and that of fallen nature.

This popular view cannot be absolved from a certain 'extrinsicism', as it has been called, if it can be shown that all the data of official Church teaching on the relationship of nature and grace can be maintained un-touched even if the relationship is held to be closer than it is described in this current opinion. And it cannot be denied, though it is distasteful to some to admit it, that the current view is not without danger in practice. For if it is correct, the known spiritual life of man must take place within the region of his pure nature, which has two sectors: the 'purely natural' which is totally confined to its own dimensions, apart from an 'elevation' which is outside consciousness, and then a number of acts of knowledge which are (subjectively) composed of purely natural elements (in matters of the spiritual as such) and are referred to the supernatural only by their objects (by faith, by a pure intention etc.). If this is true, then it is not surprising—though not of course justifiable—that man should take very little interest in this mysterious superstructure of his being. After all, he does not not find grace where he finds himself, in the immediate activation of his spiritual being. And one could have the impression—not objec-tively justifiable—that something originally called grace had come to be considered, in the course of the medieval evolution of dogma, as an act produced by nature's own capacity (e.g. its possibility of loving God above all things); after which, to conceal the process, this same act was once more placed above nature as the 'supernatural'. And then this super-natural was displaced into a region beyond consciousness, as an uncon-scious modality of what was spiritual and moral in nature, so that it was very hard to say what use it was at all. Let us think, for instance, of the distinction (correct in a certain sense) between a natural and a super-natural 'love of God above all things'. How are these two acts to be distinguished *as acts of love, that is, spiritually*, if the supernaturalness of supernatural love *only* consists of its entitative 'elevation'? Is it *totally* misguided, to see modern naturalism as having *some* connexion with this theory? Is it quite wrong to suggest that the modern lack of interest in the supernatural can only have developed on the basis of such a view of grace, which must be to some extent nominalist?

The correctness or adequacy of the standard view is now once more the subject of theological debate, for many reasons.

One is *philosophical*. It is the contribution of a school of scholastic philosophy which is linked with the work of J. Maréchal.[3] In his intellectual and transcendental dynamism, Maréchal considers man (as spirit, i.e. in his 'nature') in the inmost heart of his being as '*desiderium naturale visionis beatificae*'—to use the words of St Thomas. This desire is conditional and so there is no necessity for the actual call to the vision by grace. But it is a real longing for the absolute being and one which is present in every spiritual act as its *raison d'être*. Without being expressly and conceptually present, it is the *a priori* condition of all knowledge where a finite object is grasped. Thus the return to the doctrine of the natural desire for the immediate vision of God in Maréchal shows at once how an apparently minor thesis in St Thomas becomes the essential and central concept for the understanding of a spiritual nature. It is understandable that the theology of the 1930's was much pre-occupied with the question of how this *desiderium naturale* in Maréchal and his followers was to be understood and whether it was compatible with the Church doctrine of the supernatural nature and gratuitousness of the immediate vision of God.[4] At any rate, there was an increasing understanding of the

---

[3] In this short theological essay, we do not give a bibliography of this philosophical trend, which has been of great importance in the confrontation of scholastic philosophy with modern philosophy. A large proportion of present-day Catholic philosophy is tributary to a greater or lesser degree to the doctrine of Maréchal. We may think of the work of A. T. G. Hayen, A. Grégoire, G. Siewerth, Max Müller, J. B. Lotz and many others.

[4] See for instance B. E. Brisboir, 'Désir naturel et vision de Dieu' *NRT* 54 (1927) 81–97; H. Lennerz, 'Kann die Vernunft die Möglichkeit der beseligenden Anschauung Gottes beweisen?' *Schol.* 5 (1930) 102–108; 'Ist die Anschauung Gottes ein Geheimnis?', *Schol.* 7 (1932) 208–232; M. Corvez, 'Est-il possible de démontrer l'existence en Dieu d'un ordre de mystères strictement surnaturels?' *RT* 37 (1932) 660–667; R. Garrigou-Lagrange, 'La possibilité de la vision béatifique peut-elle se démontrer?' *RT* 38 (1933) 669–688; further literature in *Bull. Thom.* 1932, n. 743–769; 1933, n. 896–907; *Bull. Thom.* V (1937ff.) n. 632–643; n. 728; P. Descoqs, *Le mystère de notre élévation surnaturelle* (Paris 1938). Further literature in Z. Alszeghy, *Greg.* 31

view that man's orientation, as spirit, towards God was not merely something that was 'also' present in man, but that man's ordination to God, even though an implicit and *a priori* transcendental, makes him what he experiences himself to be, something that he can deny and repress only at the cost of sin, because even then it is affirmed in every act of his spiritual existence (though only as an implicitly transcendental *a priori*).

From the point of view of *history* of theology,[5] new approaches were

(1950) 444–446. This whole complex of questions also brings up the question of whether a finality ordained to God such as Maréchal accepts, could at least demonstrate the possibility of the beatific vision. We cannot go into this question here.

[5] We can refer here only to a small selection of the literature of the last twenty-five years, omitting biblical theology, because it has had unfortunately little influence on the whole on the dogmatic theology of the schools. We list first the book of H. Rondet, which gives a survey of the whole history of the theology of grace, then some works on patristic theology, and then the history of the dogma of grace in medieval and modern times. H. Rondet, *Gratia Christi. Essai d'histoire du dogme et de théologie dogmatique* (Paris 1948); H. Rahner, Die Gottesgeburt. Die Lehre der Kirchenväter von der Geburt Christi im Herzen der Gläubigen' *ZKT* 59 (1935) 333–418; E. Mersch, *Le corps mystique du Christ* I–II² (Louvain 1936); A. Lieske, *Die Theologie der Logosmystik bei Origenes* (Münster 1938); J. Gross, *La divinisation du chrétien d'après les pères grecs* (Paris 1938); A. Lieske, 'Zur Theologie der Christusmystik Gregors von Nyssa' *Schol.* 14 (1939) 408–514; J. Loosen, *Logos und Pneuma im begnadeten Menschen bei Maximus Confessor* (Münster 1941); A. Mayer, *Das Bild Gottes im Menschen nach Clemens von Alexandrien* (Rome 1942); H. U. von Balthasar, *Présence et Pensée. Essai sur la philosophie religieuse de Grégoire de Nysse* (Paris 1942); J. B. Schoemann, 'Gregors von Nyssa theologische Anthropologie als Bildtheologie', *Schol.* 18 (1943) 31–53, 175–200; J. Daniélou *Platonisme et théologie mystique. Essai sur la doctrine spirituelle de saint Grégoire de Nysse* (Paris 1944); H. du Manoir, *Dogme et spiritualité chez S. Cyrille d'Alexandrie* (Paris 1945); P. Galtier, *Le Saint-Esprit en nous d'après les pères grecs* (Rome 1946); A. Lieske, 'Die Theologie der Christusmystik Gregors von Nyssa', *ZKT* 70 (1948) 49–93; 129–168, 315–340; J. Grabowski, 'St Augustine and the Presence of God', *TS* 13 (1952) 336–348; E. Braem, 'Augustinus' leer over de heiligmakende genade' *Augustiniana* I (1951) 7–20, 77–90; II (1952) 201–204; III (1953) 328–340; IV (1954) 196–204; H. Merki, 'Ὁμοίωσις θεῷ von der platonischen Angleichung an Gott zur Gottähnlichkeit bei Gregor von Nyssa (Freiburg/Switzerland 1952). H. Doms, *Die Gnadenlehre des seligen Albertus Magnus* (Breslau 1929); J. Schupp, *Die Gnadenlehre des Petrus Lombardus* (Freiburg 1932); F. Stegmüller, *Zur Gnadenlehre des jungen Suarez* (Freiburg 1933); F. Stegmüller, *Francisco de Vitoria y la doctrina de la gracia en la escuela salmantina* (Barcelona 1934); F. Stegmüller, *Geschichte des Molinismus I: Neue Molinaschriften* (Münster 1935); E. Köster, *Die Heilslehre des Hugo von St Viktor* (Emsdetten 1940); H. Bouillard, *Conversion et grâce chez saint Thomas d'Aquin* (Paris 1944); R. C. Dhont, *Le problème de la préparation à la grâce. Debuts de l'école franciscaine* (Paris 1946); M. Flick, *L'attimo della giustificazione secondo S. Tommaso* (Rome 1947); Z. Alszeghy,

opened up by research into the history of theological reflexion on the supernatural and how it is distinguished from the natural. Theologians came to recognize that the present theological concept of the supernatural (and so the concept of nature in contrast to the supernatural) was the result of a slow development, and that it only came very slowly to be applied to the various individual theological questions—such as the necessity of internal and strictly supernatural grace for every salutary act; the possibility and the limits of the distinction between naturally and supernaturally moral acts; the distinction between supernatural actual grace and habitual grace; the exclusion of a positive preparation for justification by moral acts not activated by strictly salutary grace; the possibility of a purely natural final happiness of man etc. It may be said on the whole that all these developments were legitimate and evolved correctly from the initial data of revelation strictly speaking. It may therefore be said that the development was not an aberration. It may also be said that it was so far advanced in St Thomas that one can see in him the direction of later evolution—which does not mean that it had reached with St Thomas the stage verified in Cajetan and after Trent. But the course of the development is now clear enough to show that we may not read into earlier theologies all the insights and concepts of a later time. And once this piece of this history of dogma has been acquired, one is once more in the situation of being able to ask oneself whether part of the price of progress was not the loss of some valuable insights of earlier times and so whether one must not try to win back some of the gains that were once the possession of theology.

It may well be that some studies of the history of dogma exaggerate the

'La teologia dell'ordine sopranaturale nella scolastica antica' *Greg.* 31 (1950) 414–450 (with wide survey of the literature of the last decades); S. Gonzalez Rivas, 'Suarez frente al misterio de la inhabitacion' *Estud. Eccl.* 24 (1950) 341–366; J. Auer, *Entwicklung der Gnadenlehre in der Hochscholastik mit besonderer Berücksichtigung des Kardinals Matteo d'Aquasparta*, I (Freiburg 1942), II (Freiburg 1951); A. M. Landgraf, *Dogmengeschichte der Frühscholastik* Part 1, vols. I–II, *Die Gnadenlehre* (Regensburg 1951–1952); H. Lais, *Die Gnadenlehre des hl. Thomas in der Summa contra Gentiles und der Kommentar des Franziskus Sylvestris von Ferrara* (Munich 1951); J. Alfaro, *Lo natural y lo sobrenatural. Estudio historico desde santo Thomas hasta Cayetano (1274–1534)*, (Madrid 1952); O. Lottin, *Psychologie et morale aux XII et XIII siècles*, I, II, III, 1–2, IV, 1–2 (Louvain 1942–1959); W. A. van Roo, *Grace and Original Justice according to St Thomas* (Rome 1955); Z. Alszeghy, *Nova creatura. La nozione della grazia nei commentari medievali di S. Paolo* (Rome 1956).

difference between the medieval theology of grace, above all that of St Thomas, and the post-Tridentine. It may well be that the 'Augustinian' theology of grace as taught in the 17th and 18th centuries contain certain elements which cannot be held today, even though Benedict XIV defended them against the charge of crypto-Jansensism. But once the nuances of a spiritual development have been noticed, once it has been understood that this history cannot simply be divided into the story of an unchangeable truth, always clear and never contested by a truly orthodox theologian, and the story of a merely wicked and heretical doctrine: then a historical survey will be more than a mere account of how we have now reached the definitive and unsurpassable results of the theology of today. It will be the re-discovery of themes which were once well-known but have today been forgotten by a conventional theology which is always liable to take the handiest and simplest form of a doctrine as the criterion of truth and sacred tradition. And then one sees—to take some examples from the question which interests us here—that the concept of the *desiderium naturale in visionem beatificam* in St Thomas is not just a piece of historically explicable atavism going back to an age when theology was not so clear about the supernatural and gratuitous quality of the vision of God (as St Thomas himself was); that the reluctance to admit a strictly supernatural actual grace (along with the habitual) is not merely due to a stubborn blockage of thought, which could only be brought slowly to see that a salutory act preceding justification, and still impossible without grace, necessarily demands such a grace;[6] that one can still learn something from St Thomas about the compenetration of sacrament and personal act, which has been either almost forgotten or over-simplified in later theology; that medieval theology had a greater and profounder idea of 'uncreated grace' than the post-Tridentine theology of the schools, which derives the 'indwelling of the Holy Spirit' more or less exclusively from 'created grace' and is too much inclined to consider the latter as *the* grace, strictly speaking, in its reaction against the Reformation.

The third impulse for re-opening the question of the relations of nature and grace comes from the revival of dialogue with Reformed

---

[6] For St Thomas, the really 'preparatory' acts before justification are essentially acts of the ' taking over ' of justification, which are already done with the grace of justification; *hence* he did not need to pay much attention to preparatory acts which also precede justification temporally; he can therefore tell *us* something new, and not just we him.

theology.[7] By the nature of things, this theology has to put itself this question, though from other viewpoints. And it has done so once more: with regard to the Bible, with regard to Luther, with regard to its debate with modern humanism and an Anglo-American optimistic view of the world. So it had to ask itself: what then is man, if he is a sinner, how far does he remain a sinner when he is justified? The ancient doctrine of the Reformers is maintained, that there is absolutely no good in man, which serves his *salvation*, without grace. But the question really only begins with this statement, which if properly understood, is also affirmed by Catholics; and this opens up new possibilities of discussion with Catholic theology, which have been to some extent exploited. And Catholic theology in turn, though only in the case of a few theologians, has felt itself impelled to ask once more what true interests the Reformers represent and how such interests may be better catered for among Catholics. It is a matter of asking how Christocentric is the whole actual world and order of salvation; of proving that the supernatural character of grace does not mean that man is in fact a closed, self-contained and finished system, which he can work out in his 'natural' existence, while grace is a sort of pure superstructure imposed on it, but leaving the lower element unaltered in itself; of considering whether and in what sense a Catholic understanding of the axiom '*simul justus et peccator*' might be found; of giving full value to the existentialist, actualist and personalist elements which are implicit also in the traditional Catholic concept of grace and are capable of clearing up the misunderstanding, that an 'entitative' and 'habitual' infused grace implies an unjustifiable distortion of the biblical concept of grace.

That the mentality of the *present day* must be an effective stimulus to theology does not need much proof. After the synthesis of the diversity of reality, a unified view of man is sought for. Thought is 'existential'. One strives to 'experience' the reality of grace precisely there where one lives one's own existence; and so one tries to see supernatural—and not just medicinal—grace as the activation and the force of concrete existence.

---

[7] We mention here only a few Catholic works on the matter: H. U. von Balthasar, 'Deux Notes sur Karl Barth', *RSR* 35 (1948) 92–111; J. Hamer, *Karl Barth. L'occasionalisme théologique de Karl Barth. Etude sur sa méthode dogmatique* (Paris 1949); H. Volk, *Emil Brunners Lehre von dem Sünder* (Münster 1950); H. U. von Balthasar, *Karl Barth, Darstellung und Deutung seiner Theologie* (Cologne 1951); A. Ebneter, *Der Mensch in der Theologie Karl Barths* (Zurich 1952); H. Küng, *Justification* (London & New York 1964).

In keeping with other tendencies in the spirit of the times, one tries to see grace as something more than the presupposition and content of individual salvation. More conscious effort is made to reflect once more on the ecclesiological aspects of the doctrine of grace, on grace in the history of salvation outside Christianity constituted as a Church, on the possibility of grace and its most sublime manifestations in the world of non-Christian religions.

If we now indicate some of the 'results' of these theological efforts, we are of course not speaking of 'results' which have already been officially recognized or become simply '*sententia communis*'. The development of Church doctrine does not go so fast, especially as today the immediately topical questions, especially of morals, and Mariology, claim more attention than such deeper questions of theology, which inevitably need a long time to mature. All we can attempt to do here is to indicate very vaguely (more is impossible here), with reference rather to the doctrine itself, what are the essential lines of development in these theological efforts.

One may well think that the question of 'uncreated grace' may be taken further.[8] In the encyclical '*Mystici Corporis*' Pius XII indicated that there

---

[8] On the whole question of uncreated grace and the appropriated or non-appropriated indwelling of the divine persons we mention a few recent works: H. Kuhaupt, *Die Formalursache der Gotteskindschaft* (Münster 1940); H. Schauf, *Die Einwohnung des Heiligen Geistes. Die Lehre von der nichtappropriierten Einwohnung des Heiligen Geistes als Beitrag zur Theologiegeschichte des neunzehnten Jahrhunderts unter besonderer Berücksichtigung der beiden Theologen Carl Passaglia und Clemens Schrader* (Freiburg 1941); Ph.J. Donnelly, 'The Inhabitation of the Holy Spirit: a solution according to de la Taille', *TS* 8 (1947) 445–470; J. Trütsch, *SS. Trinitatis inhabitatio apud theologos recentiores* (Trento 1949); S. J. Dockx, *Fils de Dieu par grâce* (Paris 1948); C. Sträter, 'Het begrip "appropriatie" bij S. Thomas', *Bijdr.* 9 (1948) 1–41, 144–186; J.-H. Nicolas, 'Présence trinitaire et présence de la Trinité', *RT* 50 (1950) 183–191; Th. J. Fitzgerald, *De inhabitatione Spiritus Sancti doctrina Sancti Thomae Aquinatis* (Mundelein 1950); R. Morency, *L'Union de grâce selon saint Thomas d'Aquin* (Montreal 1950); P. Galtier, *L'Habitation en nous des trois personnes* (Rome 1950); H. P. C. Lyons, 'The Grace of Sonship', *ETL* 27 (1951) 438–466; C. Kaliba, *Die Welt als Gleichnis des dreieinigen Gottes. Entwurf zu einer trinitarischen Ontologie* (Salzburg 1952); P. de Letter, 'Sanctifying Grace and our Union with the Holy Trinity', *TS* 13 (1952) 33–58; Ph. J. Donnelly, 'Sanctifying Grace and our Union with the Holy Trinity. A Reply', *TS* 13 (1952) 190–204; F. Bourassa, 'Adoptive Sonship. Our union with the divine persons', *TS* 13 (1952) 309–335; P. de Letter, 'Current Theology. Sanctifying Grace and the Divine Indwelling', *TS* 14 (1953) 242–272; F. Bourassa, 'Présence de Dieu et union aux divines personnes', *Sc, Eccl.* 6 (1954) 3–23; K. Rahner, 'Some Implications of the scholastic concept of Uncreated Grace' in *Theological Investigations* I (London & Baltimore Md. 1961) 319–346.

were open questions here, which were deliberately left open by the magisterium. If, as Pius XII emphasizes, grace and glory are two stages of the one divinization of man; if, as classical theology has always emphasized, glory means a self-communication of God to the created spirit which is not a created quality or entity distinct from God, produced by efficient causality, but God's imparting himself to man by means of quasi-formal causality: then this notion can be applied far more explicitly to grace than has been customary hitherto in theology. 'Uncreated grace' will then no longer appear to be merely a consequence of the creation of 'infused' habitual grace, regarded as a 'physical accident'. It will be rather seen as what is truly central in grace—which will explain much better the strictly mysterious character of grace, since a purely created entity, strictly as such, can never be an absolute mystery. God communicates himself to man in his own proper reality. That is the mystery and the fullness of grace. Starting from here, it will be much easier to find the link with the mystery of the Incarnation and that of the Trinity.

It seems indeed to be true that the opinion maintained by Petavius, Scheeben and others, each in their own way, is gaining ground: that grace founds a relationship between man and each of the three divine persons which is not an appropriation, but something proper to each divine person. If one supposes that the immediate vision of God can only be based on a quasi-formal self-communication of God in vision, and not (adequately) on a created quality in the spirit of man; and if one recalls the obvious truth, that each of the three divine persons is the object of immediate intuition in his personal propriety: then that entitative (ontic) quasiformal communication of God, which takes the place of a *species impressa* as the ontological foundation of man's possession of God in knowledge, must include a non-appropriated relationship of each of the three divine persons to man. On this basis, the relation of the 'immanent' to the 'redemptive' Trinity could be thought out anew. And the supreme mystery of the Christian faith could appear more clearly as a reality with which man has to do not merely conceptually (and through the incarnation of the Logos) but also really, in the exercise of his life of grace. It could be seen that God is not only trinitarian in himself, but also communicates himself in a trinitarian way, in grace, which means more than efficient causality on the part of God in the line of *creatio ex nihilo* outside himself—though it remains true that where God exercises *efficient* causality, the work is to be attributed to the whole Trinity as one single cause.

One may and perhaps must go still further. As a rule, the connexion between the Incarnation and grace is thought of as merely *de facto*:[9] God has in fact decreed that the order of grace should depend on the Incarnate Word. It is implicitly supposed that things could be otherwise. But is this supposition clear and certainly correct? Both the order of grace and the Incarnation derive from God's free grace. But does it follow that both these objects of God's gracious will, in both of which he communicates himself, as himself, *ad extra*, though in different ways, are really *two* different acts of his freely exercised love? Is there anything in Catholic principles to prevent us taking the Scotist point of view and considering the primal act of God, in which everything else is in fact given, as the self-exteriorization of God who is the love which gives itself in the incarnation? And then the order of grace would already be instituted, which would (probably) be unthinkable without such a decree of God with regard to his personal communication. Are there any valid arguments against the position which holds that the *possibility* of creation rests on that of the Incarnation, even though the fact of creation (as nature) does not necessarily imply the actual realization of the self-exteriorization of God in the Incarnation? Let us assume this position, which is recommended by its lofty simplicity, not to mention its more positive support in the Logos-theology of pre-Nicene and pre-Augustinian theology. Then grace has a much more radically Christological character. The Logos who has become part of the world is not merely the *de facto* mediator of grace by his merit—which only became necessary because Adam had cast this grace away—he is also the person who by his free Incarnation creates the order of grace and nature as his own presupposition (nature) and his milieu (the grace of the other spiritual creatures). This would enable us, as we have already said, to reach a deeper understanding of the immanent Trinity. The Logos would not be merely one of the divine persons who could become man if they wished: he would be *the* person in whom God communicates himself hypostatically to the world. The Incarnation would mirror the personal propriety of the second divine person, the Logos as such. The Trinity of the economy of redemption would enable us to have some insight into the immanent Trinity. This is not impossible,

---

[9] Cf. N. Sanders, 'Een bovennatuurlijke orde mogelijk zonder Christus?' *Stud. Cath.* 29 (1954) 152–158; K. Rahner, 'Thoughts on the theology of Christmas', in *Theological Investigations* III (London & Baltimore 1967); *ibid.* 'The eternal significance of the humanity of Jesus for our relationship with God'.

because the axiom that the efficient causality of God *ad extra* is common to the one God without distinction of persons cannot be applied to this quasi-formal causality. This invites us to re-consider the speculation of pre-Nicene theology and of the Greeks in general. It will appear that on this point St Augustine had too little understanding of the most ancient theology, which held that it is the Logos who appears and must appear if God wishes to show himself personally to the world.

With a more exact concept of 'uncreated grace' in mind, we can also see more clearly how the Catholic theology of grace, on its own proper principles (grace is not just pardon for the poor sinner but 'participation in the divine nature'), can go beyond the notion of a *merely* entitative, created state and the merely 'ontic' and non-existential element of a 'physical accident'.[10] Grace is God himself, the communication in which he gives himself to man as the divinizing favour which he is himself. Here his work is really *himself*, since it is he who is imparted. Such grace, from the very start, cannot be thought of independently of the personal love of God and its answer in man. This grace is not thought of as a 'thing'. It is something that is only 'put at man's disposal' in that act of 'letting oneself be disposed of' which is the proper gift of the freest grace, the miracle of love. Ontic categories are only maintained here (even by Catholics) because and in so far as a Catholic philosophy does hold that the real (and what could be more real and effective than the love of God?) must be thought of as 'real' and 'being', that the highest must be expressed in the most abstract words, and that therefore the act of divine love towards us—God's act, not ours, though enabling us to act, and not just submit—previous to our act, must be considered as that which renders possible our moral and religious decisions. It cannot therefore be expressed except in categories of being such as state, accident, habit, infusion etc. Such expressions are not confusing if properly understood, and they need not distort one's view of the fact that grace is always the free action of divine love which is only 'at the disposal' of man precisely in so far as he is at the disposal of this divine love. One must indeed always remember that God is not diminished by our becoming greater. And in the last resort, Christianity is not the religion whose basic attitude is fear of its going to our head—and not into our grateful heart—if we extol the greatness to which God has raised man in order that he might praise God. This is true of Mariology. And it is also true of

[10] J. Auer, 'Um den Begriff der Gnade', *ZKT* 70 (1948) 341-368.

grace, of which Mariology is merely the most beautiful part of the doctrine.

This grace affects our conscious life, not just our being but our existence. The Thomistic doctrine[11] of the specific object of the act entiatively elevated to the supernatural, an object which, as formal, cannot be attained by any natural act, must be fully considered once more and again be given a predominant place. For in such a context 'object' does not mean 'something present like other objects, distinguishable from them and placed beside them by reflexion'. A formal object is neither a datum of knowledge nor an abstract and merely consequent summing up of what is common to many individual objects. It is the *a priori* horizon given in consciousness, under which, in graping the individual *a posteriori* object, everything is known which is grasped as an object strictly speaking. If we understand aright the old scholastic doctrine of the formal object as the *a priori* 'light' under which and in which all single objects are grasped, no one can object to the old Thomistic doctrine of the formal supernatural object by appealing to 'experience', which is supposed to know nothing of such a formal object—meaning in fact material object! It must only be noted that the *a priori* formal object of an act is not the same thing conceptually as a formal object which is clearly *distinguishable* by reflexion from another formal object. For a metaphysics of knowledge, there is no great difficulty in recognizing that transcendence towards being in general, the natural openness for being as a whole, cannot be clearly distinguished in subsequent reflexion from the supernatural transcendence, the openness of the soul informed by grace, which is directed in all its supernaturally elevated acts towards the God of enternal life, towards the immediate experience of the (triune) absolute being. And this is true although both modes of transcendence, the formal object of the natural spirit and the formal object of the super-

---

[11] There is no point in quoting here the text-books which deal with this question. We only remark in passing that this question is also of great importance in the problem of the foundations of faith. Cf. for instance A. Lang, *Die Wege der Glaubensbegründung bei den Theologen des 14 Jahrhunderts* (Münster 1950); F. Schlagenhaufen, 'Die Glaubensgewissheit und ihre Begründung in der Neuscholastik', *ZKT* 56 (1932) 313–374, 530–595; G. Englhardt, *Die Entwicklung der dogmatischen Glaubenspsychologie in der mittelalterischen Scholastik vom Abälardstreit bis zu Philipp dem Kanzler* (Münster 1933); R. Aubert, *Le problème de l'acte de foi* (Louvain ²1950). Cf. also K. Rahner, 'Reflections on the experience of grace' in *Theological Investigations* III (London & Baltimore, Md. 1967).

naturally elevated spirit, are both given in consciousness. Such considerations, taken from a metaphysics of the spirit, though barely indicated here, show that the ancient Thomistic doctrine is perfectly defensible.

It has in its favour that it is a transposition into metaphysical and theological terms of a conviction which is voiced in the Scriptures. Let us take the doctrine of Scripture as it is, honestly and without prejudice, and without correcting it in the light of the silent presupposition that it cannot have said something, because this something is supposed to be impossible. Then we must say that for Scripture, the communication of the Spirit (the divine *pneuma*) is not just a trans-conscious entitative 'elevation' of the conscious moral acts of man, which remain existentially the same and are only changed extrinsically by the *fides ex auditu*. It is 'life', 'unction', 'consolation', 'light', the inexpressible co-intercession of the Spirit, *pneuma* which is more than *nous*, an inward attraction, testimony given by the Spirit etc. It would be well if the doctrine of Scripture were carefully examined in the light of this scholastic controversy. If this were done, one would gradually rid oneself of the unavowed opinion that in an objectively serious and religiously important question one is already certain *a priori* that no more light is to be had from Scripture if the subject is controverted in the schools, because otherwise the question would have been settled long ago. Once all the schools are of the opinion that supernatural actual graces are to be described as 'lights' and 'inspirations', this doctrine of tradition must be taken seriously. It may not be so interpreted in anti-Thomistic teaching that nothing of it in fact remains. For an entitatively elevated act which remains from the point of view of consciousness a natural act, cannot be characterized as an inward illumination and inspiration without doing violence to language. The fact that the anti-Thomistic (Molinist) thesis still holds on to this characterization and tries to do justice to it, shows how strongly tradition is convinced that the act due to supernatural grace is even spiritually different from the natural act. The difference is felt to be conscious and existential, and not confined to an entitative modality.

Here we must note something else, which should be borne more clearly in mind than is usually the case. Acts inspired supernaturally by grace are not confined to the justified. There are stirrings of grace which precede the act of accepting justification in a free act of faith and love. There is also grace outside the Church and its sacraments. The offer of grace to a man who has reached in his spiritual development the immediate possibility of an existential decision is not intermittent, restricted to some very definite occasions and 'actual' in this momentary sense. There is no stringent theological reason for thinking it should be so. 'Actual' means that grace is given prior to an existential decision, as an 'offer' and 'possibility' (of a free salutary act). In this sense, the moral freedom of man to dispose of himself always exists in the prior possibility of supernatural acts, a possibility effected by grace.[12] If this is so, then we may say that the supernatural transcendence is always present in every man who has reached the age of moral reason. That does not necessarily mean that he is justified. He may be a sinner and an unbeliever. But where and in so far as he has the concrete possibility of a morally good act, he is in fact constantly within the open horizon of transcendence towards the God of the supernatural life, whether his free act is in accord or in conflict with this prior state of his supernaturally elevated spiritual existence. *If* in every moral act he takes a positive or negative attitude to the *totality* of his *de facto* existence (a supposition whose reality we need not examine here): *then* we must say: every morally good act of man is, in the actual order of salvation, also in fact a supernaturally salutary act. We should *then* have arrived at the well-known point of view maintained by Ripalda. This conclusion need not terrify us. First of all, the thesis of Ripalda, though rarely maintained, is exposed to no theological censure. And secondly, one could still hold the basic position outlined here, even if the supposition which brought us to the thesis of Ripalda were contested, which would avoid the position of Ripalda. However that may be, the notions which we have outlined show clearly that it is quite conceivable that the whole spiritual life of man is constantly affected by grace. It is not a rare and sporadic event just because grace is unmerited. Theology has been too long and too often bedevilled by the unavowed supposition that grace would be no longer grace if it were too generously distributed by the love of God! Our whole spiritual life is lived in the realm of the salvific will of God, of his prevenient grace, of his call as it becomes efficacious: all of which is an element within the region of our consciousness, though one which remains anonymous as long as it is not interpreted from without by the message of faith. Even when he does not 'know' it and does not believe it, that is, even when he cannot make it an

[12] Under the necessary external presuppositions, hence the external possibility of faith, where however we must note that in the theory of Straub, everyone who has come to the use of moral reason can possess it, at least as *fides stricte dicta sed virtualis.*

individual object of knowledge by merely inward reflexion, man always lives consciously in the presence of the triune God of eternal life. God is the unexpressed but real 'Whither' of the dynamism of all spiritual and moral life in the realm of spiritual existence which is in fact founded, that is, supernaturally elevated by God. It is a 'purely *a priori*'. Whither, but always there, present to consciousness without being in the nature of an object, but nonetheless there.

We do not need to insist on the existence of such an *a priori* of a supernatural nature in spiritual existence, even though it can only be clearly expounded and translated into objectivated knowledge in the light of the word of revelation which comes from without. It manifests itself as the mysterious activation of individual and collective spiritual life in countless ways, which would not exist if this mysterious activation and dynamism were not at work. It follows that even outside the process of official revelation the history of religion is not merely a product of natural reason and sin. Precisely in its consciously tangible results, in its objective spirit, it is the product of the natural spirit, grace and sin. Thus when man is summoned by the message of faith given by the visible Church, it is not the first time that he comes into spiritual contact with the reality preached by the Church: such conceptual knowledge of it is not primary. The call only makes him consciously aware of—and of course forces him to make a choice about—the grace which already encompassed him inarticulately but really as an element of his spiritual existence. The preaching is the express awakening of what is already present in the depths of man's being, not by nature, but by grace. But it is a grace which always surrounds man, even the sinner and the unbeliever, as the inescapable setting of his existence.

We are now in a position to face the real problem[13] of 'nature and

[13] We can offer here only a somewhat arbitrary selection from the controversial literature which grew up, above all, around the historical and theological writings of H. de Lubac. We include some essays which deal with the doctrine of the encyclical *Humani Generis*, since it is well known that the encyclical takes up a position on this matter. Other works dealing with *Humani Generis* are listed, e.g. in the *Revista Española de Teologia* 11 (1951) 173–176; 311–339. We recall therefore: H. de Lubac, 'Remarques sur l'histoire du mot surnaturel' *NRT* 61 (1934) 225–249, 350–370; J. Martinez-Gomez, 'Notas sobre unas notas para la historia de la palabra sobrenatural', *Arch. T. Gran.* 1 (1938) 57–85; H. de Lubac, *Surnaturel. Etudes historiques* (Paris 1946); H. Rondet, 'Nature et surnaturel dans la théologie de St Thomas d'Aquin', *RSR* 33 (1946) 56–91; C. Boyer, 'Nature pure et surnatural dans le "Surnaturel" du Père de Lubac', *Greg.* 28 (1947) 379–395; G. de Broglie, *De fine ultimo humanae vitae*.

grace' in the strict sense and to pose it properly. It is clear that by living out his spiritual existence, man always attains his 'nature', even in the theological sense, where this concept is opposed to that of grace and the supernatural. For in every question which he poses about himself, in every judgment where he contrasts himself with an object and grasps it in the perspective of an unlimited transcendence, he experiences himself as something which he must necessarily be, as something that is a unity and a totality which cannot be dissolved into variables, which either is there as a whole or is not there at all. He grasps his metaphysical being: spirit in transcendence and freedom. And on the basis of this initial transcendental analysis of what is implicitly asserted about man in each of his human acts, much more could probably be affirmed as 'essential' to him: his existence in a world, his having a body, his belonging to a society of his fellows. In a word, there is such a thing as a metaphysical knowledge of man, his essence and nature, by the light of his reason, which means here primarily independently of the word of revelation; but it also means knowledge through the means (his reason) which is itself an element of the essence so grasped. But it also follows from the theological data already given that this *de facto* human nature, as it knows itself here, and in view of all its experiences (especially when this human experience

Pars prior, positiva (Paris 1948); H. Rondet, 'Le problème de la nature pure et la théologie du XVIᵉ siècle', *RSR* 56 (1949) 80–121; H. de Lubac, 'Le mystère du surnaturel', *RSR* 36 (1949) 80–121; Ph. J. Donnelly, 'The gratuity of the beatific vision and the possibility of a natural destiny', *TS* 11 (1950) 374–404 (with literature); W. Brugger, 'Das Ziel des Menschen und das Verlangen nach der Gottesschau', *Schol.* 25 (1950) 535–548; M. J. de Guillou, 'Surnaturel', *RSPT* 34 (1950) 226–243; R. Panikkar, *El concepto de naturaleza. Analisis historico y metafisico de un concepto* (Madrid 1951); G. Weigel, 'Historical Background of the Encyclical *Humani Generis*', *TS* 12 (1951) 208–230; G. Weigel, 'Gleanings from the Commentaries on *Humani Generis*', *TS* 12 (1950) 520–549; J. Simon, 'Transcendence et immanence dans la doctrine de la grâce', *Rev. Univ. Ottawa* 21 (1951) 344–369; L. Renwart, 'La "nature pure" à la lumière de l'encyclique *Humani Generis*', *NRT* 74 (1952) 337–354; E.Gutwenger, 'Natur und Übernatur', *ZKT* 75 (1953) 82–97; H. U. von Balthasar–E. Gutwenger, 'Der Begriff der Natur in der Theologie', *ZKT* 75 (1953) 452–464; J. Ternus, 'Natur-Übernatur in der vortridentinischen Theologie seit Thomas von Aquin', *Schol.* 28 (1953) 399–404; M.-R. Gagnebet, 'L'enseignement du magistère et le problème du surnaturel', *RT* 53 (1953) 5–27; L. Malevez, 'La gratuité du surnaturel', *NRT* 75 (1953) 561–586; K. Rahner, 'Concerning the Relationship between Nature and Grace' in *Theological Investigations* I (London & Baltimore, Md. 1961) 297–317. R. Bruch, 'Das Verhältnis von Natur und Übernatur nach der Auffassung der neueren Theologie', *Th. Gl.* 46 (1956) 81–102.

is viewed in the light of the whole history of mankind, where alone its development is fully realized) cannot and need not be considered as the reflexion of that 'pure' nature which is distinguished in theology from everything supernatural. Our actual nature is *never* 'pure' nature. It is a nature installed in a supernatural order which man can never leave, even as a sinner and unbeliever. It is a nature which is continually being determined (which does not mean justified) by the supernatural grace of salvation offered to it. And these 'existentials' of man's concrete, 'historical' nature are not purely states of being beyond consciousness. They make themselves felt in the experience of man. By simple reflexion on himself, in the light of natural reason, he cannot simply and clearly distinguish them from the natural spiritual activity which is the manifestation of his nature. But once he knows from revelation that there is an order of grace, not due to him and not belonging to the necessary constitutives of his being, he becomes more cautious. He must allow for the fact that much of his concrete experience which he is almost automatically tempted to attribute to his 'nature' may perhaps in fact be the effect in him of what he must recognize as unmerited grace in the light of theology.

This does not mean that he is now quite ignorant of what is natural to him. The nature of a spiritual being and its supernatural elevation are not opposed to each other like two things which lie side by side, so that they must be either kept separate or confused. The supernatural elevation of man is, though not due to him, the absolute fulfilment of his being, whose spiritual quality and transcendence towards being as such prevents its being 'defined', that is, 'delimited' in the same way that sub-human entities can. For these are 'defined' by the fact that it is their essence to be restricted to a certain realm of reality. (It is therefore impossible, for instance, for them to be 'elevated' to a supernatural fulfilment: such an elevation would destroy their being which is essentially limit.) The 'definition' of the created spirit is its 'openness' to being as such: as created, it is open to the fullness of reality; as spirit, it is open to absolute reality in general. It is not therefore suprising that the grandeur of the (varying) fulfilment of this openness (which does not of itself imply necessarily an absolute and unsurpassable fulfilment and yet, as absolute openness, still has a sense without such fulfilment) cannot be recognized at once as 'due' or 'undue'. And yet the basic essence of man, his nature as such openness (transcendence) can be perfectly well established. The initial elements of such fulfilment are already present: the experience of infinite longings, of radical optimism, of unquenchable discontent, of the torment of the insufficiency of everything attainable, of the radical protest against death, the experience of being confronted with an absolute love precisely where it is lethally incomprehensible and seems to be silent and aloof, the experience of a radical guilt and of a still abiding hope etc. These elements are in fact tributary to that divine force which impels the created spirit—by grace—to an absolute fulfilment. Hence in them grace is experienced *and* the natural being of man.

For the essence of man is such that it is experienced where grace is experienced, since grace is only experienced where the spirit naturally is. And vice versa: where spirit is experienced in the actual order of things, it is a supernaturally elevated spirit. As long as we confine our considerations of the relationship of nature and grace to the most general formalities, the question offers no particular difficulties, though the spiritual nature is only found in a supernatural order and the spirit as 'pure nature' is never met with. But let us ask more precisely what is now, in the concrete and in particular, natural to this nature, and what is real in it and expected of it, just because it is a nature elevated to the supernatural order. Let us ask, for instance, whether the resurrection of the body appertains to any form of the fulfilment of man as a spirit-person, or is it something that is only a consequence of grace. Or let us ask how we are to think of the fulfilment of pure nature in the concrete. Then we find ourselves faced with questions which could only be answered if one could make experiments on pure nature and draw up a concrete teleology on this basis.[14] But in reality all such efforts fail to go beyond an essentially formal teleology of a 'natural' type, which, as was obviously to be expected from what has been said, is merely the concrete supernatural teleology rendered in an abstract, formal way. It follows therefore from these considerations that the great theologians of the middle ages did well not to cudgel their brains too hard about natural beatitude. There is in fact no such thing, and further, the result would be basically only a formalizing abstract set of concepts derived from what theological teleology knows in fact as the supernatural end, (and which is not very helpful); and again, where it tries to be concrete or becomes so unwittingly, it borrows illegitimately from the theology.

[14] If there can be any such thing, given the endless openness of this nature—and if every such concrete end is not either a finite perfection freely decreed by God but not deducible *a priori* from the nature, *or* its absolute fulfilment.

In point of fact, such a 'pure' philosophy of the essence of natural man is also unnecessary. When one speaks to a non-believer, one has only to take care that no premises are derived from the historical word of revelation, as long as the interlocutor does not admit its existence. When in such a discussion an item of man's experience of himself is appealed to, one will simply have to note what the non-believing partner accepts of such experience. If he refuses it at a given point, it may be because he is incapable of having a certain legitimate 'natural' experience, either because it has not been properly demonstrated to him or because in spite of the demonstration he does not consciously follow it (though he has the experience). Or it may be that one has in fact appealed to an experience of grace which the other has not had clearly enough for him to understand the argument drawn from it (though he has had it to some degree, according to what has been said above). Since both cases can arise, and since even Christians find it hard to distinguish one from the other, because a 'supernatural' argument can be quite meaningful and successful even with an unbeliever (where an argument from the word of revelation is not possible): the question of whether a metaphysical (that is, pre-theological) argument starts in fact from 'pure' nature or actual nature is of little practical importance.

The concept of pure nature is legitimate. If someone affirms: I experience myself as a being which is absolutely ordained for the immediate possession of God, his statement need not be false. He will only be mistaken if he maintains that this unconditional longing is an essential element of 'pure' nature, or if he says that such pure nature, which does not exist, *could* not exist. Where man knows of the *visio beatifica* by the word of revelation, and experiences it as the marvel of the free love of God in his longing for it, he has to say that it is not due to him (by nature), even as an existing nature—so that the gratuitousness of creation, as a free act of God, and grace as a free gift to the creature, as something already existing, are not one and the same gift of God's free act. To say this is to recognize implicitly the concept of 'pure nature'. And it is not an empty concept of otiose theological speculation but a concept which, in the long run, is the necessary background against which one recognizes that the beatific vision is a gratuitous grace, not merely not due to man as a sinner, but not due to man even as a creature.

Even when the gratuitousness of grace for human nature as such has been recognized, it is still helpful to try to work out more clearly how human nature is ordained to grace, as a *potentia oboedientialis*. It is not necessary to take this *potentia oboedientialis* as more or less just a non-repugnance, which would be the extrinsicism of which we have spoken already. To be ordained to grace, and to be so constituted that there is an exigency for grace which would render the whole ordination to grace futile if grace were not actually imparted, are by no means the same thing. Spirit, that is, openness for God, freedom and conscious self-possession, is essentially impossible without a transcendence whose *absolute* fulfilment is grace. Still, a fulfilment of this sort is not owed to it, if we suppose that this conscious possession of self in freedom before God is meaningful in itself, and not just as a pure means and a mere stage on the way to the beatific vision. This supposition arises from the absolute (not 'infinite') value and validity of every personal act, in itself. If it be granted, it follows that there can be no spirit without a transcendence open to the supernatural; but spirit is meaningful, without supernatural grace. Hence its fulfilment in grace cannot be demanded by its essence, though it is open for such grace. Once this is clear there is nothing to prevent us—as for instance, an apparent danger of failing to recognize the supernatural and gratuitous character of grace—applying it clearly to the super-naturally-orientated transcendence of the spirit and working it out as rigorously as possible.

Man is only really known in his 'indefinable' essence when he is understood as *potentia oboedientialis* for the divine life and when this is his *nature*. His nature is such that it must look to grace for its *absolute* fulfilment, and hence, as regards itself, it must reckon with a *non-frustrat-ing* absence of an absolute fulfilment. One can even try to understand the hypostatic union in the line of the absolute fulfilment of what man means strictly speaking. Such considerations, which aim at the closest possible combination of the doctrine of grace with a metaphysical anthropology, and try to see the higher as the gratuitous fulfilment of the lower,[15] are not just amusements for a leisure hour. In the long run, it would be impossible without them to arouse the existential interest of man in that mysterious life which is given with supernatural grace. Further, such an exposition of the content of the concept of *potentia oboedientialis* must not

[15] Fulfilment and gratuitousness in one, in a truly differentiated world constructed hierarchically without discontinuity (and such is the construction of the world where differences derive from the One), are characteristic of the relationship between two realities.

be confined, as it too often is, to man's *knowledge*. If, according to Scripture, God is love and not 'thought of thought', no understanding of man and of the absolute fulfilment of his being (by grace) can succeed, unless man is considered as freedom and love, which again may not be considered just as a by-product of the act of knowledge.

In the light of what has been said up to this, it is no great loss if the analysis of man as *potentia oboedientialis* is not a 'chemically pure' presentation of pure nature but is mixed up with trace elements from actual nature, and hence from its state of grace. Who can say that the utterances of earthly philosophy, even of a completely non-Christian or pre-Christian type, are merely the voice of pure nature (and perhaps of its guilt)? May they not be the sighing of the creature, secretly moved by the Holy Spirit of grace, which longs for the glory of the children of God and already unwittingly feels itself to be such a child of God?

Much more could be said on the subject of grace in present-day theology and of what it ought to be. One could speak for instance of grace in its relationship to the Church,[16] on the social significance and bearings of grace, which in the current manuals of theology is considered in a perspective which is strangely narrow. One could refer to the newly-opened discussion of the relationship between grace and the personal action of man. But space forbids us here.

Tiny advances or displacements in the field of scientific theory often begin by being impossible to evaluate. Such changes may appear at first as pastimes reserved to the leisurely keen-wittedness of scholars. But when one considers that such new acquisitions then become part of the general consciousness and so become the automatic presuppositions of action, one can perhaps recognize that much may depend on them, and sometimes everything. This is also true of theology. It is very strange. But we Christians often seem to be completely unconvinced of the power of thought with regard to our Christian faith, and to be very doubtful that 'theory' can bring about very practical effects. That is why we often prefer to think over Church politics, social questions, methods of propaganda and so on. That is why living theology is so little esteemed. Many people in the Church have the impression that it merely casts useless obscurity on truths that have long been clear, that it generates unrest and distracts from more important matters. Such people miss the point,

[16] H. de Lubac, *Catholicisme. Les Aspects sociaux du dogme* (Paris 1938).

that a living, questing, questioning theology is working today for the preaching of tomorrow, so that it can reach the spirit and heart of man. Such theological work may often seem fussy and futile. It is nonetheless necessary. Even though the heart and grace remain the one thing which is irreplaceable.

8

QUESTIONS OF CONTROVERSIAL THEOLOGY ON JUSTIFICATION[1]

THE book which we shall discuss briefly here is important enough to justify further study of it. But as it is already well known in its main outlines, we may be permitted to confine ourselves to a few remarks on some questions raised by it. So we suppose that its contents are known. The remarks which we have to make should not give the reader the impression that the most important points in the book have been singled out. That is not the case at all. Thinking as we do, as we shall shortly explain, that we do not understand Barth's doctrine better than Barth, and that Küng propounds on all essential points a doctrine of justification which is in accord with Catholic doctrine, nothing very noteworthy can be said here on the actual theme of the book. Our considerations are therefore *marginal* notes with regard to the object and contents of the book, and we wish them to be understood as such.

I. BARTH'S AGREEMENT WITH THE CATHOLIC DOCTRINE OF JUSTIFICATION

Küng gives a picture of Barth's doctrine of justification (pp. 21–101; cf. also 253ff.). In the second section he also gives the Catholic doctrine of justification (pp. 105–276). In this second section he is undoubtedly interested in working out as far as possible those aspects of the Catholic doctrine which must be of primary importance for an accord with Barth. In doing so, Küng undoubtedly includes theological propositions which are not simply taken for granted in conventioned Catholic theology— which does not mean at once that they are contested. We shall have

---

[1] Remarks about the book of Hans Küng, *Justification. The Doctrine of Karl Barth and a Catholic Reflection* (London & New York 1964).

189

occasion to speak of the most important of these propositions. Küng has every right to use them. If we voice now and then a mild wish for greater clarity and less ambiguity, as can be done with regard to even the best theological works, this is no reason for doubting the orthodoxy of the general presentation of the Catholic doctrine of justification in Küng. Its orthodoxy has also been attested by Bouyer, de Broglie, Ebneter,[2] Stirnimann and many others. If Küng gives more space to truths which Barth misses in Catholic doctrine, than to those which are known to Barth, the procedure is understandable, given the object of his discussion. His point is to show that those very truths which Barth finds lacking in the Catholic position are actually held in it, the truths which he declares must never be given up if the gospel is to be maintained. Küng is not open to the reproach of having suppressed or minimized for the sake of his thesis those Catholic truths which seem at first sight unpleasant or misleading to Protestants. He tries to explain them and make them intelligible. And this is the task of controversial theology, which is not allowed to attribute either stupidity or malice to its opponent. On this basis, all that is left is to explain one's own doctrine better, more comprehensively, more fully, from new standpoints and in other contexts and another vocabulary, in the hope that the intelligent and benevolent opponent may understand one's real meaning and can agree that it is correct. If one does not take this course, one has really renounced any effort at dialogue, even though one does not admit this officially.

Küng therefore presents much of the Catholic doctrine of justification from stand-points other than the usual ones. He says some things expressly which are elsewhere skipped as being 'questions in themselves'. This is not only his right but his duty in controversial theology, provided that

[2] Cf. e.g. A. Ebneter in *Orientierung* 21 (1957) 157: 'We may say in general that Küng's presentation gives the orthodox doctrine as taught by the Church'. Similar positive verdicts (from J. Aranguren, H. Fries, N. Greitemann, R. Grosche, J. P. Michael, W. Seibel, E. Stakemeier, W. H. van de Pol) are to be found in H. Küng, 'Rechtfertigung in katholischer Besinnung', *Schweizerische Kirchenzeitung* 125 (1957) 619–621, 637–639. Stirnimann too may be taken as a friendly witness, in so far as he 'stresses very clearly' (*Freiburger Zeitschrift für Philosophie und Theologie* 4 [1957] 321f.), that 'the most important reserves' which he makes 'are concerned with questions which are dealt with "intra muros" '. It seems to me however that Küng deserves more good will, a more sympathetic understanding and a juster and more balanced consideration of all the elements in his presentation than he finds, to my mind, in Stirnimann. But Küng has already expressed himself sufficiently on this matter.

he says nothing that may not be said in the Catholic Church, and is not led by a false eirenism to pass over in silence what must be said in the Catholic Church. But Küng has fulfilled these conditions. When his business brings him to make use of theological themes which are not simply doctrines of the magisterium, he is also within his rights. He can think that they are attested in Scripture or tradition and that they could contribute helpfully to the image of the Catholic doctrine of justification which non-Catholics might find convincing. But more important still in this connexion is a reason which may be looked on as basic: may it not be that a truth (a defined one, for instance) will only appear intelligible and acceptable to a non-Catholic when it is enunciated in conjunction with a truth which is not defined, which is indeed perhaps controverted? If one starts by accepting the formal teaching authority of the Church, there will be no problems in this matter. But things are different in controversy with Protestant Christians. It is the other way round: they often have difficulties in accepting the formal authority of the magisterium, because they have difficulties with doctrines taught by the magisterium. To overcome *this* inhibition, it may be quite necessary existentially in controversial theology to have recourse to assertions and theological propositions which are *not* official teaching, in order to make defined truths more assimilable. It may be necessary to use mere theology in order to proclaim dogmatic truth.[3] How could one for instance give an intelligible account today of the Catholic doctrine on original sin, without stressing and developing the theological proposition about the analogous character of this sin in comparison with personal sin? This is actually the only way even for Catholic theologians to learn something from theological controversy. We are often too little ready to learn, and that is why we are so little successful in teaching. We have to emphasize this, in order that what follows may be understood correctly.

Now Barth declares in his accompanying letter (pp. 11–12), expressly and almost solemnly, both that Küng's presentation of the doctrine of

---

[3] It is not really unfortunate that now and again the main witness adduced is a relatively 'lone' theologian, whose authority will not tell particularly with the reader who is not already convinced of the correctness of the proposition in question. And there is likewise no strict principle which enables us to say that a view for which one can quote a Catholic theologian who has not been officially challenged, is thereby proved to be at least tolerable '*intra muros*'. But in any case, Küng mostly quotes so many good authorities, that he must be said to have proved that the propositions which have no official standing can still find a place in Catholic theology.

justification is correct, and that he could accept the presentation of the doctrine which Küng puts forward as the Catholic one.[4] On the second point Barth makes the reservation that Catholics have to decide whether what Küng puts forward as his own view is really the Catholic doctrine of justification. This reservation can be catered for. Küng's presentation is Catholic. Not in the sense that everything it says is defined or universal doctrine, but in the sense that none of it is in contradiction to any doctrine of the magisterium. More one cannot ask. Otherwise all a Catholic theologian could do would be to recite word for word the Council of Trent, which is obviously not all that can be asked of him. For it follows from the nature of things and from the history of Catholic theology that as soon as a Catholic theologian takes it upon himself, at his own risk, to explain and expound what the Church teaches, he must inevitably go beyond the doctrine to be explained and make affirmations with which not everyone will agree fully. To my mind, the most one could object to in Küng's presentation of the Catholic doctrine is that some elements of it could be 'misunderstood' and are therefore 'dangerous' and so on. In answer to this one can only ask in return whether they *must* be misunderstood—and affirm that they need not be—and whether the supposed 'danger' is really greater than that which terrifies the pure and simple 'orthodox', whose great fear is that they may not meet with agreement from the other side. Or—for heaven's sake—has contradiction from the other side become the unambiguous criterion of our having kept to the truth and of having enunciated it in the best possible way?

This two-fold agreement on the part of Barth is astonishing. It seems to me that it should have been greeted with greater surprise and joy than it has been hitherto, as far as I know. Barth is not simply *the* Protestant

---

[4] This second point, to my mind, was not given its due weight in Ebneter's article. For if we bear it in mind, it will not do to put a question-mark after Küng's presentation of Barth's doctrine by appealing to Barth's dogmatic theology—which again needs interpretation. To be able to question Küng's conclusions, one would have to explain how it was that Barth could declare himself to be in agreement with Küng's presentation of Catholic doctrine (put forward as agreeing with Barth's), though Ebneter admits that this presentation is correct. If one refuses to admit that there is agreement, as Küng aimed at proving, there is only one answer left: Barth read this presentation of Catholic doctrine with so much good will and through such strong Barthian spectacles, that he simply read his own doctrine into it—in other words, he must have completely misunderstood Küng. This is not *a priori* impossible. But it would need to be proved very exactly and seriously. And meanwhile we must presume the contrary.

doctrine of justification. Here (p. 276) Küng in fact exaggerates a little at the end of his book. Schlink, for instance, whom Küng cites (p. 275) as contesting a merely imputed righteousness, would still maintain that he could not accept the Tridentine doctrine of justification. But is not this agreement still amazing and something that can stir the heart and the spirit? Barth is not just anybody in Protestant theology. And he says: You give a hundred pages to my doctrine of justification; the presentation is excellent and completely acceptable. And I have no difficulty in accepting what you put forward as the Catholic doctrine. Is this something easily imaginable? Or is it evidence of a development which strengthens our Christian hope, which God's commandment obliges us to have, that it is *possible* to advance in matters of the unity of the Christian faith? It is simple and comfortable to remain 'sober' and 'realistic' in these matters and not to let oneself 'be excited'—because after all, everything remains the same. But it would be more Christian to allow oneself to hope, to give God thanks, that everything is not at a deadlock, and to deduce from this event that it is worth while working for a real understanding in controversial theology.

We should not be too quick to say that this consent is only 'verbal'. It is restricted, to be sure, for the moment in any case to *one* point, the doctrine of justification, and Barth is separated from us in the faith by enough other things (original sin, doctrine of election, sacraments, Church, papacy, Mariology, etc.), as Küng indeed recognizes. And undoubtedly Barth's theology has a certain 'slant' (as Küng notes (pp. 270–272) and remarks on expressly), which can lead to dissent not only in these points, but also in the doctrine of justification itself. No doubt certain statements of Barth need to be interpreted with benevolence —but what theologian or Father of the Church can do without it?—and to be considered in the light of his doctrine as a whole, if they are to be given a Catholic sense. One can certainly ask whether we (and Barth himself) are not bound to understand his doctrine of justification otherwise than Küng and Barth himself do, if they think it out with reference to certain other positions of Barth, his doctrine of predestination, for instance, and develops it consistently on such lines. However, one could just as well put the question the other way round and correct Barth's other positions in the light of his doctrine of justification; in a theology which stems from copious use of Scripture texts and tries to take all their assertions seriously, there is—happily—no systematic principle which claims to be so primary and unique that everything else is reduced to a dependent function of it.

All this is true, but it does not give us the right to speak of a merely verbal consent. It is not our intention to debate with experts in Barthian theology whether Küng's interpretation corresponds exactly and in all regards to the objective contents of Barth's Church dogmatics. That would be too difficult a task, which must be left to the experts in this field. It is enough for the non-expert and more important objectively, as we shall shortly have to show, that Barth himself considers that Küng renders his views correctly and in *both* parts of his book. And the layman has only to add finally that it is Barth who must know best what he really means. We can believe him and register the fact gladly and thankfully, even though we know that it is far from making Barth a Catholic. In contrast to this, it is in any case a secondary, if not superfluous, matter,[5] to point an accusing finger and say: yes, there and there Barth has said something which is inconsistent with that! Why should Barth not have understood better what he really meant, as he was reading Küng? Why should such a progressive piece of controversial theology not have offered him formulations in which he sees his interests clearly served, and which in the eyes of Catholics avoid the dangers which made us anxious about the previous formulations of Barth? Is an agreement arrived at in such a way merely verbal? We do not of course mean to say that those who claim to understand Barth better than he does himself are *only* seeing ghosts. They see dangers which are really present in Barth. But there is something else that we must remember here, and the fundamental importance of such considerations is so great that we are justified in dwelling on them for a moment. It is that we cannot pursue controversial theology merely in terms of objective truths, that is, we cannot confine our debate with our Protestant brethren to the subject of the Church, the papacy and the magisterium, until agreement is reached *on these points*, on the plea that any other agreement must be precarious and hedged about with reserves, as long as there is no agreement about these formal criteria of orthodoxy. For the truth is, as we have said, that the existing

[5] We still of course have the task of reading Barth critically, of noting inconsistencies, etc. The fact that he declares a certain presentation of the Catholic doctrine of justification to be acceptable, obviously does not mean that every single sentence which he wrote down previously must be beyond suspicion. But we have the right and even the duty of interpreting favourably, as far as possible, his individual statements and lines of thought.

disagreement about these formal criteria lives (to some extent), psychologically and historically, from dissent with regard to other matters. If this is so, then when conversing with Protestants, we are exactly in the position that a Thomist and a Molinist would be in during their debates, if they did not know all the time that they both owed allegiance to the one Church and its magisterium. The Molinist could always say to the Thomist: yes, you accept verbally the freedom of man under grace; but if you were really serious about it and really understood what it meant, you could not defend the *praemotio physica*. And the Thomist could always say to the Molinist: yes, you hold verbally the efficaciousness of grace even with regard to freedom, and you reject verbally the semi-Pelagian position. But with the *scientia media* you maintain positions which nullify in fact these verbal concessions. And each of the two would declare that though there were two aspects to his doctrine in each case, he refused to allow himself to be faced with the dilemma of having to choose between the two aspects of his doctrine, or to pick out one aspect as more decisive, or as more important if he had to make a choice between them. He would insist that he cannot give up either aspect of his position. To put it more generally: wherever an agreement is reached between two men, who have come to this agreement from *different* directions,[6] and when this consent is not based on a third element, that of formal authority which both have accepted prior to the debate, the consent is always and essentially precarious and threatened, and can always be called in question. Indeed, the fact of consent can never be established with absolute certainty, because every *formula concordiae* aimed at establishing that the parties have agreed in fact and not merely in words, needs in turn a *formula concordiae* for the *formula concordiae* and so *ad infinitum*. For this reason, to say that agreement is merely verbal is absurd. The *process of agreement* upon truth always takes place on common sociological ground between men, and if it is reached *there*, it is reached in fact. But it is reached *there*, when it is reached in words and statements, (verbally, if one wants to put it that way), which are employed by men who listen carefully and speak circumspectly.

[6] This coming together from *different* sides, which is still noticeable in each of those who have reached agreement, is in fact the destiny which weighs down the finite spirit in its search for truth, since it inevitably has different perspectives even when it is looking at the same truth and reality. And since this always makes itself felt, unity and truth, if it is really to be seen and made permanent, must include love, humility, mutual tolerance and patience.

We cannot ask such men to try to see into the inmost depths of the spirit of others, where only God can see and tell what they are 'really' thinking. In a controversial theology in particular the danger could arise that a too neurotic fear of not being perhaps 'really' in agreement 'in depth' could disrupt the unity which is possible. Such fears then give rise to those strange efforts (noticeable in the theology of controversy) to find new sets of ever more subtle formulae and nuances so as to prove the existence of mutual dissent. This procedure is found necessary at points where our ancestors of the sixteenth century, less subtle in their phraseology, would have registered a disagreement which everyone could recognize and express—or would have simply reached an agreement. We have now reached a point in many items of controversial theology where only the finest theological eloquence can manage to show the initiates (not the normal man) where the real difference is to be found. In such cases (there are of course many others of a different type) it would be better and more Christian to admit that one is in agreement or could perfectly well be; just as Barth has done, courageously and soberly. To have the right to live in separate Churches, one would have to be sure (to put it crudely for once) that one is clearly in disagreement about the truth. It is not enough not to be quite sure of being really in agreement, or of what the other exactly means or of having understood him quite correctly. This principle results, to my mind, from the Christian duty of unity in one Church and from the essential impossibility of an *absolute* certainty about an *ultimate* inward uniformity of conviction. Absolute certainty about *one's own inmost* orthodoxy in the sight of God (which would be the presupposition of such absolute certainty) seems to me to be as impossible and as un-Catholic as absolute certainty about one's own justice in the sight of God. And perhaps the formulas of union of ancient times, which were drawn up apparently rather artificially and as a matter of politics, were not in fact the worst. The artificiality of an apparently merely verbal unity is often the only thing possible for men who are placed before the incomprehensible mystery. They must try to find a formula which allows both sides to retain what they consider as indispensable in the controversy and in the act of union; and one which obliges both sides to see and to express the truth which each had overlooked in the position of the other, or if not overlooked, had not seen clearly enough to recognize that it had been preserved.

It would therefore be wrong to add to every formula of agreement:

keep on asking questions, and divergencies will show, which were only masked by the very general formulations. As if such suspicions could not be occasioned by every agreement among Catholics! Or would it not be said today that Galtier and Parente, for instance, conceal very important 'divergencies' under the same Chalcedonian formula? Even among us Catholics there should be a limit to cross-questioning, if one wishes to avoid discovering all sorts of differences in matters on which we wish to be and must be and *are* at one. In spite of the fact that the abiding truth is always liable to being corrupted by and *in* finite man, men can be really at one. This of course we cannot dwell on now, as an exact proof of it is a matter of the philosophy and theology of human knowledge. Not everyone who could fall has in fact fallen, even though his genuine proneness to falling could be demonstrated. In the same way, an erroneous opinion is not held by everyone of whom it could be proved that from his mentality, from his loosely formulated premises, from his placing of emphasis, that he was liable to fall into the error in question. Least of all should one use a hyper-intelligent dialectic to force him either to overcome positively at once the peril of his presuppositions, which he often cannot and is not obliged to do, *or* to acknowledge the full-blown error.

It may be thought on the other hand that without at least the formal authority of which we spoke earlier nothing more than a verbal agreement could be possible. But this would be to overlook two things. Firstly, formal authority as such and union under it can indeed promote and guarantee agreement on a given matter, but cannot replace it in essential things. Union is not possible simply on the grounds that one accepts in common the same formal authority *a priori*, if it is accepted simply as a formal authority—to some extent, simply by *fides implicita*. Secondly, we do share with Barth a common authority, Scripture. Why should we not feel at one, where, having accepted unreservedly the *same* testimony of Scripture, we permit ourselves to think that we have come to an agreement about its interpretation. The Church has a common official teaching, but there are also several different explanations of it. Only the naive who have not understood them can separate these explanations cleanly and wholly from the general doctrine binding on all, and so find it no problem but simply obvious that we should be united 'on real matters'. But if these different schools come from very different directions and even had ancestors 'tainted with original sin', called heretics, why should Barth's doctrine be only admitted to be above suspicion, when its origin could no longer be recognized?

The fact remains, as we think, that Küng's book has achieved an astonishing result: the consent of a great Protestant theologian to a presentation of a doctrine of justification which must be considered as capable of and needing improvement on certain points, but which cannot be designated as un-Catholic. One can be a Catholic and hold this doctrine of justification, which Barth has declared to be the same as his own. Barth cannot therefore affirm that it is the doctrine of justification which prevents him from being a Catholic, as long as Küng's presentation has not been condemned by the Catholic magisterium as un-Catholic on some essential point, or as long as it has not been rejected by Catholic theologians as clearly contradicting Catholic doctrine. Barth asks does Küng's presentation really render the Catholic doctrine. The answer must be the counter-declaration that an official approbation of this rendering is not to be expected but that neither is it necessary; one could be of Küng's opinion and remain in full and positive agreement with the Church and its official doctrine. For it is not at all likely that the limits set by the magisterium ('definitions') in its defensive statements of a truth, will express adequately all aspects of the truth as it exists in the mind of the Church. Nor are they meant to spare the individual Christian the trouble of trying to understand the truth and so forming his own theological opinion.

II. MINOR POINTS OF CRITICISM

We have already said that we have no doubts about the orthodoxy of Küng's presentation of the Catholic doctrine of justification. But this does not mean that there are no questions to be asked and no objections of a minor nature to be raised on some particular points. It would be foolish to take this to mean that we are half-way to withdrawing our general verdict. Orthodox theology can occasion such questions and misgivings, as is shown by the differences of opinion which exist among theologians. And often enough the unquestionable orthodoxy of a manual—where it does not simply repeat Denzinger—means no more than that although one could put critical questions, one has given up doing so either from boredom or routine. But when someone begins to do theology on his own, in a dialogue with a new and serious opponent, the reader finds that the old becomes young and that he is listening hard, putting questions and forming objections. Some of these are presented here. They are all concerned with the Catholic doctrine, not with the exposition of Barth's position.

(a) Justification and sanctification: faith and love

One may readily concede that Scripture makes a distinction between justification and sanctification: it uses distinct terms for the two and so makes the distinction in the same perspective as that in which it sees the one salvation of the sinner by grace. Küng proves this directly from Scripture and can appeal to important Catholic exegetes. We may also readily concede to Küng that it is not unjustifiable (*if* and *in so far as* the above distinction exists) to see *faith*, in contradistinction to love, as primarily ordained to justification. We can then speak in this definite sense of 'justification' by *faith* in a way in which we cannot speak of justification by love. Further, to avoid any misunderstanding of Küng, we must expressly emphasize the fact that where he attributes man's justification to faith (justification here being very pregnantly distinguished formally, not materially, from sanctification), he speaks expressly of living faith, of *fides formata* (p. 250f.; 252), of faith to which love is inwardly present, and that hence his doctrine is irreproachable. But still this chapter of Küng's book leaves something to be desired. And one fells that even if these desires were met with, one could still understand Barth and go to meet him as far as possible (even as far as consent). To begin with, it does not seem to me to remain always clear in Küng as in Barth, whether justification and sanctification are two *aspects* of one and the same process, *or* two *stages*, one after the other. It seems to me that according to Trent and its ordinary interpretation in Catholic theology and also according to the Scriptures, one must speak of two sides of one and the same process, *not* of two phases one after another—at least if we understand justification not as the 'objective' process of 'redemption', but as that real, efficacious absolution from sin, which makes the individual righteous when he believes (in the Pauline sense) and is baptized.

Justification may be understood (as in Barth) as that objective and *real* transformation of the existential situation of each (and of 'all') which is already realized by the incarnation, death and resurrection of Christ (prior to a subjective decision (faith) and a sacramental conferring (baptism) in the individual). Then of course justification may be seen as a special phase of salvation which precedes the event in which man consciously and really ratifies and makes his own this existential situation, which was created for him without his doing by Christ alone. What the second phase is to be called *in this case* (simply 'sanctification' or 'subjective' justification-sanctification) would be a further question. In any case Küng (like Barth) is quite right to avoid strange nominalistic ways of speaking, in spatial categories, and not to restrict to subjective redemption the real importance of redemption in Jesus Christ for the individual. No matter how one forms the ontological categories and concepts which may help one to grasp the matter clearly, there can be no doubt about the thing itself. Prior to any subjective attitude, man *is* really different (from what he *would* be as mere creature and mere sinner), because redemption has taken place in Christ, because God loves him in Christ as long as he is on pilgrimage: so much so, that for all eternity, even in his damnation, man remains determined by this 'is'. This 'is' which determines him for ever is not procured by faith and love. He rather 'takes cognisance' of it through faith and love, accepting it of course and ratifying it existentially, so that through this act, something happens in him which means his salvation, because if he 'took cognisance' of it with refusal or indifference, this same reality, this 'is', would mean his damnation. If we call this 'is' a supernatural existential we could say: prior to any subjective appropriation of salvation, man is inwardly determined by a supernatural existential, which consists of the fact that Christ in his death 'justified' sinful man before the all-holy God. Anyone who finds such terminology painful, need only think of the following in simple scholastic terms: if through faith bestowed by grace and through love man *can* be subjectively justified before God, and if this 'can be' obviously *precedes* the act of (subjective) justification, then this 'can', this potency, is *his* on the one hand, hence 'intrinsic' to him (no matter how much it permanently depends on the grace of God); and it is still something on the other hand which is not due to him by 'nature', but only comes to him by the death of Christ. This *intrinsic* ability, necessarily prior to the subjective appropriation of salvation of which it is the vehicle and in which it becomes one's own, can be simply called the supernatural existential of being (objectively) redeemed or of being (objectively) justified. Difficulties can really only arise where one thinks that man ceases to be at the point where his skin forms a limit, and that everything is extrinsic which cannot be localized imaginatively within this sack of skin; or when one thinks

that complicated words are being used for something obvious which
every Christian knows and which could be put more simply. There is
good reason for putting it so, because it is the only way of making it
clear in theological concepts, though it is of course always known by the
genuine Christian: the fact that the event of the subjective justification of
the individual is really and most intimately connected with Christ and his
cross. It is not simply a subjective conversion to a God who by reason of
his metaphysical goodness has to be gracious in any case, if we ourselves
are only interested in it. This is the only way to make it clear that the
death on the cross is not merely a historical matter, but that it is now the
essential vehicle of my salvation, since God has done something *to* me *in*
Christ before I do anything. All this is correct and of decisive importance.
And it may and can be said that the supernatural existential of being
justified (objectively) by Christ before God precedes the subjective
appropriation of salvation—which of course also brings about supremely
'objective' relationships.

But—to return to the actual question—if one is speaking of the
subjective justification of the individual by faith and baptism, justification
and sanctification can only be considered as two *sides* or aspects of one
and the same process. The two concepts can still be *formally* different in
content, so that one need not be able to say formally the *same* thing of
justification and sanctification. And this formal distinction need not be an
otiose matter of pure hair-splitting. And in fact it is not. For if one
distinguishes different aspects in one and the same reality, for the sake of
our necessarily manifold knowledge, though these aspects cannot be
separated in the thing itself, then and only then does one gain a full view
of this reality. One can respond to it fully by a multiplicity of attitudes,
which are distinct from one another and must be so, and can only be so
when the *difference* of the inseparable aspects are seen in the one thing.
Thus, for instance, justice and goodness are inseparable aspects in God.
But I must distinguish them to be able to respond realistically to the one
reality of God by a multiplicity of acts which correspond to each different
aspect: for instance, by fear of God and by confidence, which are not the
same thing. But if justification and sanctification are merely different
aspects—not different succeeding phases—of the same process (and are
really such!), then I can ordain a particular human act specifically to
justification, in so far as it is brought about by God, and another to
sanctification, in so far as this is also God's action on me. If one liked,

one could put it this way: justification takes place when one knows and makes one's own the efficacious absolution of sinners which is the work of God alone in Christ. It may then be rightly said to take place precisely in 'faith', because this is the terminology of Scripture and clear expression is thus given to its character of being mere acceptance of the act of God on man—this acceptance remaining of course an action brought about by God as the deed of man. It is thus distinguished from a work accomplished by man, in which man produces something (autonomously in the Pelagian sense or by grace in the Christian sense) which claims to be valuable before God (wrongly or rightly). And in view of this, there is no harm in refusing to say that justification (formally as such, i.e. in so far as it can be distinguished from sanctification) takes place through love (formally as such, in so far as it can be distinguished as one aspect of one total act of the process of justification from other aspects, faith and hope).

However: if justification and sanctification are only two aspects of the one process, love must be included in this process as much as faith. Hence it seems to us that Küng leaves himself somewhat open to misunderstanding when he speaks at times as if love, in the faith *that justifies*, is present merely in embryo or initially, or as if it is not really a presupposition for the one process, of which one aspect is in fact justification.[7] On the contrary, faith, in so far as it justifies, is a faith informed by love, where love itself must also be fully present, if the process is to be one of justification. Further, one should not try to prove the immediate relationship of justification-faith (in contrast to sanctification-love), by ranging love among (grace-inspired) 'works'. Theologically speaking love is no more a work than faith. One may, with a perfect right, not only distinguish faith from the Pharisaically autonomous works of a total or partial ('synergistic') *self*-justification before God; one may also make a justifiable distinction between faith and work[8] brought about by grace as fruit

[7] Thus Küng says (249) that as regards justification 'man has no other recourse than to place his whole trust in the Lord'. Either that is too little, because if man is to be justified, he must love, or one must make the sentence mean in fact that only he who loves puts his whole trust in the Lord.

[8] When Küng, appealing to St Thomas (238f.) says that not only are the works of the ritual law excluded from justification in faith, but also the works of the decalogue, his statement is correct but would have benefited by more precision. The works of the decalogue are of a two-fold kind which are to be sharply distinguished: the effort to accomplish such works autonomously, by one's own strength, and without grace, —and the works of the decalogue as fruit of the Holy Spirit. One cannot simply say

of the Spirit, where God favours us so that we can bring forth fruits of eternal life worthy of praise and reward. And in *this* sense we may say with St Paul and the Council of Trent that we are justified by faith and not by works, because according to the Council *nothing at all* (not even faith) which precedes justification (and sanctification) merits this justification (and sanctification), since such fruits and works can only be produced by one who has been changed from death to life, from being an evil tree to being a good tree. But even under this aspect, love, as the way in which justification and sanctification take place, belongs to the side of faith and not of works. Not only because in justification as such itself, which has no works by reason of which it is given, love is already there, whereas the supernaturally meritorious works only follow justification (and sanctification). But because love, as much as and even more than faith, is a process in which man looks away from himself, forbidden to envisage any merit (even if objectively some has been placed therein), and gives himself totally and without reserve to God for his own sake (and not for ours)—because God gives himself to us in grace and therein, by communicating to us the Spirit of his love, first makes it possible for us to leave ourselves.

'Works', even those which do not try to be self-justification before God, but which are the gift of God who grants to his beloved child the possibility and the reality of works valid before him and his judgment, are different from this love. To put it in scholastic terms: by (good) works (in so far as they can and must be distinguished from love as such), I mean the finite moral good, which is aimed at in love set free by God himself, in which I may and must love myself; by love I mean God himself (as in faith), as he has given himself to me by his act in Christ, and only so. Hence this love is precisely the truest climax of what takes place in faith. It is not something which comes after faith, like a work. It is radical, loving and total capitulation of man before God. It can only be accomplished by man when he gives up the sinful fearfulness of his self-centred autonomy to see and accept the fact that God loves him and has accepted him in Christ: which leaves him culpably stupid if he does not dare to orientate his love away from himself. Catholic dogmatic theology recognizes no love of God except where this act itself is an act of faith

that both types of works of the decalogue are excluded in the same way, though this may be said of both types with regard to the process of justification, in the sense of *Denz.* 801.

(formally or *eminenter*), because the higher and more complete activity of the one Christian existence includes the partial activity or aspect and preserves its formal nature—which cannot be said of every 'work' as such. It seems to us to follow from what has been said that the subjective attainment of salvation is justification as forgiveness of sin and sanctification as inward quickening in one act with two distinguishable formal aspects. And in the adult, this single process is so determined by faith (with hope and contrition) and love, that these two aspects of the subjective appropriation can be ordained to the two other aspects of salvation (as an act of God). But in this one process, love plays as decisive a role as faith. It is not merely required to be there 'in embryo', but has the peculiarity and uniqueness, in contrast to all other modes of behaviour, that it contains the whole in itself and is not merely a partial element of the whole. To maintain that the sanctifying process of justification embraces faith and love as *aspects* of the one process is not of course to deny that given the temporally and materially pluralistic constitution of man various acts are possible, which do not bring with them this event of justification as such and as a whole. Still, these acts are already orientated to it under the impulse of grace, and among these acts there can be found a 'faith' which has not yet transformed itself into love and so, being *fides nondum caritate formata*, does not yet justify. It may be pointed out that the doctrine of Trent on the temporal and historical plurality of preparation for justification (under the impulse of a grace already becoming efficacious) is far from proving that one should be able to indicate existentially the moment of entry into justification for the individual. It may be pointed out that the doctrine of the possibility of faith's remaining in spite of the loss of grace, as proposed by Trent, is primarily a distinction of principle with regard to the nature of things. It does not decide whether in practice in very many or in most cases mortal sin is not also a sin against faith. After all, the outward confession of faith and a certain psychological readiness to believe and to be influenced by the preaching of faith are no sure proofs that man believes in the depth of his being by a faith inspired by grace. And it is certain that for a more penetrating 'psychology', these Christian attitudes, in spite of their plurality, are more closely linked together than a happy-go-lucky everyday experience thinks. Hence most sins are committed because one does not sincerely believe, and vice versa, every sin by its very nature tends to fulfil itself in unbelief. All this is true, yet according to Trent one cannot deny on principle (nor does Küng of course) that faith can exist as the initial working of grace and yet of itself not justify. The inevitable consequence is clear: when speaking of the one process of justification—sanctification, one cannot push love so completely to one side as Küng seems to do at times.

(b) Faith as an act inspired by grace

We may here call attention to something which links up very fittingly with the question which we have just treated. Küng (like Barth) is very interested in proving that faith, which is the presupposition of (subjective) justification, is truly not a 'work' and not a 'merit' with regard to justification. To make this—quite correct—point, Küng has recourse, or so it appears to me, to the notion found in Barth that one must distinguish[9] between an act of faith which man makes as the condition of justification, and a faith which *God* brings about—which latter, (am I right?) Küng then identifies with the 'infused' habit of faith (255). Granted this distinction it is of course clear that the faith which man has in a very human way

[9] One can and must of course distinguish, with Trent to which Küng appeals (248), between the act of faith which disposes to justification and the infused virtue of faith. But this distinction does not simply mean that the former is purely human and the latter given by God. The act is as radically a gift of God as the infused virtue—which are distinguished not by their *cause* but by their *duration*, as *actus* and *habitus*. But if this is clear, I find the argument put forward (249) to explain why the act of faith can do as little as any other human act for justification, somewhat hard to follow: namely, that it cannot *cause* justification because it is itself an element of the justification which *God* works in man. We shall discuss expressly in the next pages the sense in which Trent says (*Denz.* 801) that faith does not bring about justification. We must however admit explicitly that in another context (e.g. 244) Küng speaks of 'God's justifying grace which overcomes and gives life to these human acts', or can say that human acts 'must cling to and be informed by the reality of grace given ("infused") by God in Christ' (249). But Küng goes on to say—though primarily as a rendering of Barth's position, which however is obviously accepted—'The *believer* [so he does believe!] is wholly dependent on God's action which allows a new state of existence to become real in him and only thus makes him capable of the *true* [hence obviously different from the preceding!] faith necessary for justification' (my italics). And then one has once more the ambiguous impression, that an effort is being made to construct a purely human faith (beside another which is of a divine type), to be able to say more easily that it does not justify, that it has merely a 'cognitive character'. From the point of view of the Catholic doctrine of grace, one should really say that a human 'faith', which is not itself the work of God's grace, is not even a correct 'recognition' of the objective redemption (the objective 'justification' in Barth's terminology): it would not only not be 'creative', it would not even be 'cognitive'.

and in merely a human way, cannot be a 'work' which can claim justification as its reward; even though it is active and free, it is really only man's allowing the divine action to happen to him. It seems to me however, that this is not a very happy way of speaking, and not a very good explanation of what is to be maintained, namely that the grace of justification is absolutely beyond all meriting. I even find that the ordinary Catholic text-book way of talking is better suited to Barth's purposes than the formulas given by Küng. Küng (p. 258) rightly rejects any 'synergism' in grace, which would make God and man pull at the same rope and each credit himself with half the achievement. But if one rejects such synergism —and the Catholic doctrine of grace is not a synergism of this type, in spite of the *'cooperari'* of Trent—one should also not distinguish between a divine and a human faith, as if they were two different realities. The very faith which man has as his own free human act is the faith which God gives us in his action upon us, because he can give to the creature not only its passively accepted determinations, but the free act of its 'yes' to the grace of God; not only the offer, but the acceptance of the offer is entirely the grace of God. And since the acceptance is free, the very freedom of this acceptance is once more the gift of God. And every Catholic theologian, including Küng of course, knows and confesses—the Molinists too, for that matter—that God's grace is the *natural* basic possibility of the acceptance, inasmuch as the power to accept is created by God out of his free bounty, and—as Küng would rightly add (cf. sect. III, below)—this faculty is only preserved in sinful man because he has been created in Christ and redeemed by him. The *power* to accept is God's free gift: it is the possibility of an act which really *corresponds* to the call of God's personal self-disclosure, of a supernatural salutary act, as we say. It can therefore be only fully constituted by prevenient grace, which alone makes man truly capable of believing in a way which is for his salvation. Beyond this again, the acceptance of justification is the gift of God, according to the universal doctrine of theologians, absolutely decisively—a point that Küng does not stress enough against Barth, though it seems to clinch the matter: not only the *possibility* of the acceptance, in all its components, but the free actuation itself of this possibility by man, that is, what the actual act adds to the power of acting, is again the free gift of God. He acts through what Catholic theology calls the necessarily efficacious grace of God, in contradistinction to 'sufficient' grace, which gives the full power, but not the actual free act.

Every Catholic theologian confesses that the salutary *act*, even in the extra element which distinguishes it from the God-given *power* to make a salutary act, is once more the free gift of the grace of God which cannot be merited. Hence likewise man's faith itself is the pure grace of God; in so far as it precedes justification, it is not merely not something which could merit grace (because it is 'human'): it is itself a grace bestowed by God. The question therefore cannot arise, as to whether it could merit grace, because it is itself a grace.

Here we can see once more what we may rightly concede to Küng in the previous question. The act, which following Scripture we call 'faith' consists precisely of the fact that it accepts itself directly for what it is: the free grace of God. One could almost say: the act inspired by super-natural grace, in so far as it understands itself directly and explicitly as the act *of God* which justifies man is faith (*fides caritate viva*). For *in itself,* the gracious and gratuitous character of an event or of a gift received is not diminished or weakened, if it is understood as the *effect*—and hence 'merited'—of a previous act which is itself a pure grace of God's absolute and gracious initiative alone. In the eyes of a Catholic theologian, it does not derogate from the graciousness of the order of salvation, it merely describes in juridical terms (which are also found in Scripture) what Scripture likewise depicts as growth and development and fruit-bearing of a god-given life, if an act inspired by grace is called 'meritorious', with regard to an act which stems from it or with regard to an 'increase' of grace. (From a certain point of view, every subsequent act and all 'increase' of grace are linked to some extent to grace which is absolutely gratuitous and unmerited; and furthermore, *every* salutary act and hence perseverance in 'increased', 'habitual' grace depends immediately and ever anew on each new efficacious grace. Thus all depends on something absolutely 'actual', the ever new event of God's goodness and favour, which as such cannot be merited at all.)

Yet Catholic theology affirms with the Council of Trent that even this faith which leads to justification in no way merits this justification, even though it is a gift of God's free grace: such is the anxiety to remove the notion of merit all the way from this faith right up to justification. When therefore it is kept in mind that 'human' faith itself is a work of divine grace, we have undoubtedly an even stronger assurance against the idea that the faith which leads to justification is another sort of 'work' which could merit salvation—a stronger assurance than it seems to me is given in Küng's presentation.[10] This would also make it clearer, why Catholic theology is not in danger of holding a doctrine of an apocatastasis or of reducing faith to a mere act of recognition—which is ultimately of no importance whatsoever for the decision which God has taken in Christ alone. Faith itself is the grace and act of God in Christ, not merely the 'objective' justification (redemption) by God alone as it is taken cognisance of in faith. If this faith itself has real significance for salvation, the 'triumph of grace' (to use G. C. Berkouwer's terms) is not thereby diminished. For grace itself triumphs in the same way in the 'objective' and in the 'subjective' sphere, because it supports the *whole* reality of man's salvation, which, being in the created order, is constituted by a polarity of two mutually irreducible realities: by the conditions of and the room for and the previous possibility of freedom in the creature on the one hand, and by the act of freedom itself on the other. But both components are the result of grace, each in its own way; in *both* grace triumphs. But to say that grace is deprived of its full triumph where it is not accepted—that is forbidden to man. All he could say in this case would be that *man* does not gain his only possible victory, which is to allow himself to be given gifts by the love of God. Whether in the sight of God, and for him, God's spurned love has not conquered, or whether it celebrates its most incomprehensible triumph—what creature can tell, as long as we are on pilgrimage far from the Lord?

(*c*)

There are *other themes* on which Küng stimulates us to think further and more carefully, and to which he contributes a mass of material from all corners of theology and its history, so that his book is often a useful work of reference. We mention only some of them here, without any further comment: biblical terminology and its normative character—the fact and its limits (pp. 116–118; 123; 180ff.; 195f.; 206); the nature and meaning of

---

[10] It would not then be necessary to insist so anxiously, as Küng appears to do (253, 246), that faith is merely the condition, not the cause of justification. It may be safely considered as *that through which* God works in us in his act of justification. When we have put it this way, it remains equally clear that faith does not merit justification. Küng himself speaks boldly—in his interpretation of Barth, 82f.—of the 'creative power' of faith, which faith itself receives from God. But it is precisely this faith which we mean when we speak of the faith of man who is to be justified; and the act of faith which man freely makes is precisely the faith which God brings about in us.

tradition and ecclesiastical definitions for theology[11] (pp. 116–124); the Catholic sense of '*simul justus et peccator*' (pp. 231–242); the concept of 'reward as grace' (pp. 263ff.);[12] the relationship of the Logos become man to all time (the pre-existence of the *Verbum incarnandum et incarnatum*) (127–138; 277–288); the effort to go beyond the controversy between Thomists and Scotists on the motive of the incarnation (pp. 127–150; 169–171); the exact interpretation of some canons of the Council of Orange (pp. 176–178; 186; 188); the sense in which the acts of sinners and unbelievers can still be said to be good (pp. 186–188);[13] the biblical and

[11] One must also note the explanations which Küng has added in his answer to Stirnimann, *Schweizerische Kirchenzeitung* 125 (1957) 619–621.

[12] We permit ourselves to remark here that these explanations (following J. Schmid and G. Didier) do not seem to us to be among the clearest things that Küng has written. We hold with Trent that every 'work', since it means bringing forth fruit by the action of God, is in the same dimension as the coming blessed life of the same children of God. And hence we continue to think that there is no real difficulty in calling this work a beginning and a cause, and hence objectively, 'from outside' as it were, a meritorious thing with regard to the 'reward in heaven'. This objective connexion results simply from the nature of things, which is that of sowing and harvest. A completely different question is whether this objective connexion of merit and reward may be made the first and last *motive* of the Christian life. As every Catholic schoolboy should know, this question is to be answered with an unambiguous No. Every Christian should know that no one can be saved unless he loves God first and last, and makes this the attitude which encompasses his existence and into which all others must be integrated. But when and in so far as one loves God, one cannot seek in such an act one's merit and one's reward. An act which would do so would not be an act of love. But besides love, in the wide field which it sustains and leaves free, there are and must be, on account of the plurality of man as a creature, other acts and attitudes of man; and the acceptance of this plurality can be an act of the humility of man's love, which is not of course the simplicity of God and hence is not absolutely 'love'. This is not denied when we assert the necessary primacy of love which does not seek the reward which is actually there. Is one therefore bound to say, in order to avoid being a Pharisee, if one is considering matters objectively, that is, not giving motives, that even justified man 'always falls short of the task proposed to him'? His real 'task' was always to allow himself to be surpassed by the demands of the love of God, but to be humble and loving and joyful therein; his ultimate 'duty' was to act, not from duty but from love. His merit (in the objective sense) is precisely in the act of love, which seeks for no reward. But such 'merit', bestowed on him by God's grace, is objectively and truly valuable in heaven.

[13] The statement (180) that 'the majority of Catholic theologians' now concede that there is *de facto* 'no purely natural good acts exist in fact' is undoubtedly somewhat of an exaggeration. Most theologians today would still maintain the contrary against Ripalda and Vasquez. Whether they or the few who are on the other side (Schmaus, for instance) are right is of course another question.

ecclesiastical terminology of freedom, *liberum arbitrium* etc. (pp. 181–185); sin as always an act against Christ[14] (pp. 172f.); the Catholic understanding of '*sola fide*' (pp. 243–256).

III. CREATION AND CHRIST

We come now to a further point, which is perhaps the most interesting in Küng's book. We said at the start that Küng has a perfect right, when seeking agreement with his interlocutor, to appeal to theological propositions which are not express doctrines of the magisterium, the only condition being that they do not contradict such doctrine. This procedure is now followed by Küng at one point where it is very noticeable. We devote some consideration to it here, not to dispute the theological proposition, but to look for some further light on it.

The thesis is that the actual order of creation (of man and the world) is founded even as a natural order on Christ (the *Verbum incarnandum et incarnatum*) and reposes on him, so that the world even in its natural state is in fact everywhere and always a Christian thing, even though it is possible to some extent to 'prescind' from this, and (another) world without Christ is possible. From this the conclusion is drawn, for instance, that all sin is against Christ, that the conservation of the natural state of man as something capable of salvation is already the grace of Christ. Otherwise sin by its nature would have cast man down to absolute ruin, through death to the 'second' death or through total annihilation. But it was caught up by the mercy of God because it was committed in the order of things belonging to Christ and remains involved in it. Hence too the natural and yet Christ-borne realm being the place of this sin automatically absorbs its consequences. The 'nature' of man which is still present and capable of salvation in the sinner is not 'the *remnant* which survives unharmed in sin', but the beginning of salvation constantly renewed by God's goodness in Christ, against sin and its universally destructive tendency. This new beginning stems from the unrepentant loyalty of God towards his covenant, which has ordained all creation from the start to his absolute yes' to Christ. This eternal affirmation upholds everything from the beginning and can maintain even a given temporal event eternally, as when it envisages the temporal and spatial

---

[14] But one can hardly appeal (163) to the Church's rejection of the '*peccatum philosophicum*' to prove this.

determinations of the eternal Logos in the flesh. It follows, for instance, that free will, in so far as it survives after sin according to Trent, is not merely a natural, neutral good (lacking only what it should have, its supernatural elevation) but actually a grace of Christ. It only remains because God's merciful loyalty to his covenent in Christ, which upholds everything, even the actual creation, continues to preserve it. Otherwise it would have been buried at least in the damnation of the absolute impossibility of doing otherwise.

This, we hope, is an objective summary of Küng's opinion. We need not dwell on the fact that it goes very far to meet Barth's concept of the priority of the covenant to creation and of Christology to any form of anthropology, nor on the fact that it could actually take the inability of the sinner to do anything of himself for salvation, even further than the Reformers. We have called this theory a theological proposition. But that does not mean that it is no more than an arbitrary hypothesis,[15] without hints or testimonies of it in tradition. On the contrary, Küng can adduce a very impressive body of support from Scripture and tradition. All one

[15] Stirnimann rejects this as 'pure speculation', which even reminds him 'in a way, of Gnosticism', but this verdict is quite unjust. It is not very difficult to admit that the whole 'de facto' order of things (in contrast to another possible one: Stirnimann objects at once to the expression) is not foreseen and decreed simply by the 'Deus unus' of metaphysics and of a treatise 'De Deo uno . . . et creatore' drawn up only on metaphysical lines in which the 'Deus unus' appears as the cause and the end. And it is not difficult to admit that the present order depends on the Word by which all things were made, and exists because this Logos wished to communicate himself (in incarnation and grace) to uncreated being, so that in this sense he is really the 'ground of being' of all created reality (the other expression to which Stirnimann objects). This is all that is necessary for Küng's position, and this is all that he actually affirms in his thesis. And it is enough to enable him to draw the consequences with regard to sin and soteriology against which Stirnimann protests. I hold that it is incorrect to say that sin could have as its consequence the annihilation (instead of the damnation) of man, if its effects were not arrested by the mercy of God in Christ. Küng leaves the question open in the last resort. But is it certainly false and dogmatically untenable? It is not incompatible with the natural immortality of the soul. But if one leaves the question hypothetically open, a good Thomist would not find it so bad 'to go on to the annihilation of the whole cosmos'. Without spirit, the material world would have no meaning. See also A. Grillmeier in: Fragen der Theologie heute, edited by J. Feiner, J. Trütsch, F. Böckle (Einsiedeln 1957), 270: 'The recognition of the fact that the locus classicus for the praedestinatio Christi, Col. 1:15ff., speaks of the incarnate Word (and hence that what is said there about the pre-existing Logos must not be separated from what is said of Christ as man) provides a strong biblical foundation for the concept (that our history and creation in general is absolutely Christocentric)'.

can say is that anyone who opposed the thesis would not be attacking a doctrine so clear, express and universal that he would have to expect an immediate protest from the magisterium. One can undoubtedly differ from Küng on this point without fear of contradiction from the official voice of the Church, and to this extent at least Küng's thesis is *his* opinion, and therefore a theological proposition which will be accepted by those who find his arguments convincing. Given the possibility of growth in the knowledge of the faith and in the sureness of our knowledge with regard to what belongs to divine revelation, to qualify a thesis as a theological proposition (*quoad nos*) does not imply that the statement in question is of itself and objectively to be excluded from the truths of revelation. Küng's effort to prove that the substance of his thesis is found in Scripture and is therefore part of revelation is perfectly legitimate, and is not in conflict with the qualification which we have attributed to it.

We shall not here discuss the basic position itself, that is, the fact of the actual creation in its entirety and not merely supernatural grace being based on Christ, and we shall not examine the arguments for the position and so on. We accept the position as a hypothesis. Taken in general, it is certainly not open to reproach in the name of certain truths of faith; it even appears to us—if we may say so, without offering any proof—correct on the whole and theologically demonstrable. Our purpose here is rather to ask whether the fundamental thesis gives adequate support to all that Küng deduces from it. To explain what we mean, we must take up another point.

Is it true that the statement, God could have created a world without Christ had he willed to, he could have created spiritual beings without the grace of his self-communication and divine sonship, *merely* a statement about a *possible* world which does not in fact exist, and which therefore is without importance for us and our statements about the actually existing world? Or is something significant with regard to the religious understanding of our actual situation, something important theologically, given expression in this form of statement, which seems so abstract and hypothetical? The latter is true. Why? Because it is a way of expressing the fact that we who exist, and are realized (in our 'nature') receive grace once more—as grace, as free benevolence, in our present state. It is not true, as the 'new theology' was tempted to say from time to time, that everything is grace, because everything has been given freely by God, or because everything that is or will be is eventually given in fact to *sinners.* What is called 'supernatural grace' in Catholic doctrine is something uncalled-for with regard to our present *de facto* permanent condition (our 'nature'), even prior to sin. It is not merely free with regard to our 'non-necessary existence' and God's free, uncalled-for decision to create us. If then the term of reference itself, 'nature', is totally free, in so far as nature has no 'right' to be called into existence by God and God does not owe it existence, a similar state exists once more *within* the whole of *de facto* human nature: nothing is due to it, there is a complete lack of rights and claims as regards any endowment with the divine life, any personal self-communication of the triune God, so far as existing human nature is concerned. This created being must not only say: I am something freely instituted by God, but: God disposes of me freely. This is important, because on the one hand, given the inner coherence of the various elements of the nature of an existing being, the case in question does not arise for all the elements of such a being. Many must be considered as existing in combination only as the result of the *one* disposition of the rational action of God. The personal self-communication of God on the other hand, if justice is to be done to its nature, must not appear as something inevitably instituted with the creation of man of itself. It must appear as the free gift of incalculable grace even to man in so far as he has been constituted. The mere creation of man is as it were a transcendent free act of God, the anonymous miracle which is always man's background. *Within* his life, however, another miracle is to take place, that of the historical self-communication of God, which to some extent is not anonymous but falls under categories. But if the formal gratuitousness as such of this event were to be placed on the same level as the 'grace and favour' of creation (or as a gift given to a sinner *qua* sinner) this self-communication would no longer be that miracle of unfathomable benevolence which it is felt to be in Scripture (though this cannot be demonstrated here).

This must be remembered, if Küng's theologumenon is to be correctly assessed and interpreted, according to the terms in which we have set it out, correctly, as we hope. What we have just said does not make it necessarily untrue. We can say at once, even bearing in mind what has just been said, that the creation of 'nature' takes place in Christ. There is no difficulty in thinking that the first, primal and comprehensively eternal will of God is his own self-expression, through which the Logos of God comes to exist in the emptiness of the non-divine, and that in *this* act of will God wills the humanity of Christ and hence creation in general as its setting. There is no basic difficulty in thinking that the *de facto* creation takes place as the presupposition which God creates simply because he, the eternal, decrees to have a history, that of love giving itself—a covenant: and that hence he wills, in this eternal decree, the natural creation as it actually is; and that he wills it, because once it exists by virtue of *this* will, it can never be excluded from this covenanting will of God, which also upholds it as the presupposition of this irrevocable covenant. There is no difficulty likewise in saying that sin denounces and destroys the covenant with God, so far as this lies within sin and its unnaturalness, that it does all it can to hurl creation and man into absolute destruction, since it contradicts what upholds the natural creation in the existing order of things. And this affirmation need not be complicated by the question as to whether the immortality of the human soul is 'natural', that is, resulting from its nature without a new intervention of grace, or not. For it is quite thinkable in Catholic theology that the unnaturalness of sin, in its radical monstrosity and mysterious irrationality can be directed with absolute hostility against something that is natural, and drive something destructively into its definitive unnaturalness—an unnaturalness which consists precisely of the fact that it is *definitive* in its radical self-negation. Sin would cease to be serious and would become triumphant before God, if the sinner could really escape into simple non-being.

But it must be remembered just as clearly that this original, eternal, comprehensive and all-important covenanting will of God, intent on his supernatural self-communication must bring about this distinction and this bent within the structure of the creature.[16] God can only impart himself, and will to impart himself, by creating something for whose very existence this communication is a pure grace. In view not only of the

[16] Küng (137) does indeed speak of a 'double gift' (creation and creation in Christ). But he does not seem to have made it quite clear that the first gratuitousness is not simply that of a possible order of things, but that both are found differentiated in the actual world, even though the second encompasses and sustains the first, but without eliminating the first as differentiated from the gratuitousness of the specifically supernatural order. The theme is indeed intoned (169, 170) in so far as it is affirmed that this grace of Christ, which is given with the preservation of creation, is 'grace (in the widest sense)', 'grace (in an all-encompassing sense, not in the sense of "justifying" grace)'. But it is not only barely touched on, it is also not very happily formulated by the use of 'justifying' grace as its opposite (instead of: supernatural grace of salvation).

possible but of the actual creature as such, God owes it to the sheer sovereignty of his love not to make the creature the *pre*supposition of this act of most personal love, except in such a way that even when created and instituted it must receive as free grace that for which in fact it was created. And hence one has to say that it could have been created without this communication.

If this nature exists without grace and justification, when and in so far as it is sinful, its further existence as something that can be saved from damnation is indeed a grace, since it is due to the decree of God to impart himself, to uphold his covenant, to be incarnate in Christ. In the actual order of things, this is true even with regard to continued existence as a man. But this 'grace', whereby this nature continues to exist on account of Christ, is not simply the same grace as the divine self-communication itself. Before and after sin, there is the same discrepancy between the two graces as between natural creation and God's self-communication to it, as between nature and supernatural grace, as between creation and covenant. This can perhaps be seen most clearly from the fact that the 'grace' of the conservation of natural man in and in spite of sin, remains ambiguous in itself and for us. It remains an open question, which we can never answer, even if this state of continued existence became entirely transparent to us. We can never know whether the sparing and preservation of the sinner is for judgment or for a new salvation, whether we use it aright or pervert it by sin, which one can never do with grace strictly speaking. If this split did not exist within the one concrete human being, if even 'in Christ' our nature was not still ambivalent—as real grace never is—it would be incomprehensible that creation could really *not* believe and that unbelief could be more than merely apparent—or ultimately quite harmless. A subject whose being or nature was grace in such a way as grace is just grace, would be, even as a subject, the pure affirmation of God, and could do nothing else but ratify the affirmation of God in Christ: it would have to believe. And since the subject is real and therefore very 'objective', without this objective inclination in human nature, there would be no difference at all between objective and subjective redemption, there could be no possible contrast between the two dimensions which would be more than apparent. Not only are there grades[17] of 'being in Christ' (p. 148f.), there are also

---

[17] It is also emphasized (272) that the mystery of creation is never to be placed 'on a par with' the mystery of the incarnation.

essential gradations in the gratuitousness of grace itself. An example of the first case would be the permanence of the free will in a sinner. It can be called a 'grace' in Christ, because it is willed and preserved *by reason of* the divine decree with regard to God's self-communication in Christ and with regard to the forgiveness of sins which is already predefined in that decree. But these two reasons are *different* from this free will, which in *itself*, strictly *as* such, even in the present order of things is a 'grace' of creation, but not *'in itself'* a grace of Christ. An example of the second case would be the communication of the Holy Spirit, which is *in itself* grace in the strictest sense. If the higher makes the lower its presupposition, as the condition of its own possibility, the lower does not cease to be lower than the higher. The grace of the strictly supernatural procures for itself the grace of creation as its own presupposition on a lower level, maintains and animates it by virtue of the stronger will of God with regard to the higher grace: but it still leaves it as the lower grace.

From this we can understand why ecclesiastical terminology, in spite of or in consequence of the Council of Orange, does *not* use the word grace to designate the human nature which survives in sin, free will and so on, when it speaks of justification and the like.[18] Everything exists in Christ; there are degrees in this 'everything'; Küng rightly stresses the two things. But—a point which Küng seems to me to bring out less clearly—the existence which the degrees have in Christ is of different kinds. The lower 'degree' only has its existence in Christ, the higher 'degree' consists essentially of the self-communication of God in Christ. This implies fundamentally and radically an essential difference from merely 'having existence', even though once more the mere 'existence' is given in the actual order of things because God decreed to impart himself. To work out more clearly this distinction, which has been barely indicated here, we should not begin by taking 'nature' as a fixed and obviously settled concept as mostly happens in the Catholic theology of the schools, and hence, in spite of all mutual reassurances on the part of Barth and others, gives the impression of something which remains untouched by

[18] This is even truer of the use of 'natural' and 'supernatural'. The being of man itself has, in the actual order, an inevitable orientation towards God's strictly supernatural grace (a supernatural existential); but to designate it then as in itself 'supernatural' instead of 'natural' can only lead to hopeless confusion and blur beyond recognition the objective distinction between nature and grace. Hence this seems to be more than 'a semantic and therefore a secondary question', as Küng affirms (138).

sin and the loss of grace. We must begin with man as a unity and totality, willed by God in Christ and for the sake of Christ, called to the covenant and to immediate fellowship with God and of himself sinful. And *then* we must show that the Catholic distinction between nature and grace within *this* one actual man is demanded by *this* starting-point, to the praise of the sovereign grace of God—and not because the 'natural' remains intact in any case.[19]

The notion of such gradated grace is no stranger to scholastic theology and is even quite normal as a matter of terminology. Theologians have been long accustomed to the concepts of entitatively and modally super-natural. And on the question precisely of whether fallen man as such can keep the natural moral law wholly or in part, they make use of the concept of a 'medicinal' or 'healing' grace, which is on the one hand 'entitatively natural' and on the other, since it is given by God, in spite of the un-worthiness of the sinner, in view of the supernatural end, and for the sake of Christ, is said to be *quoad fontem et finem* supernatural in its modality. This distinction may seem at first sight a little extrinsic and arbitrary, and rather in the nature of a concession to popular religious speech, which gives the name of 'grace' even to the external helps provided by God, such as good dispositions, absence of temptation etc. But this classic distinction can be given its profoundest and final justification if we use the point developed by Küng. Since everything is created in Christ and for him, and since from the start 'nature' is always and irrevocably conceived by God as the presupposed condition of possibility of grace strictly speaking, nature itself cannot be entitatively supernatural grace. But it is *always* and *necessarily* endowed with a supernatural finality in its existence, in its conservation in spite of sin, in all the helps provided by God, even on the natural level, for the conservation and development of its existence. It is modally supernatural. The unity *and* difference of nature and (entitatively supernatural) grace, precisely from the point of view of gratuitousness, result from the same principle. Hence nature is not simply and non-dialectically non-grace. It is not something which—in the actual order of things!—rests on its own foundations and is sufficient 'for itself', even without grace. It is not the substructure which could exist even without the superstructure, but the lower, which though the pre-supposition of the higher, still depends on the higher, because in the last

[19] Cf. for instance the indications given in my article 'Anthropologie' (dogmatic) in *LTK*[2] I, 618–627.

resort all depends on the highest—who freely willed to be the love that imparts itself.

We asked at the beginning of this section whether in view of the precisions which we have tried to indicate, Küng's basic thesis could be still equal to the task for which it is used in his book. His point was to show that the Catholic doctrine of the persistence of man's being and power of choice (the permanence of his God-given 'nature') by no means involved the autonomy and indifference of this nature with regard to grace and the covenant, as Barth thought. We must now sum up and answer this question. Even when we keep clearly in mind the distinction between nature and strictly supernatural grace in man as he now exists, it remains possible—even using traditional terminology—to consider the existence, conservation and activity of fallen, though redeemable, nature as grace, in the actual order of things. This is because the origin, existence and one end of *all* this, which preserves even the natural from radical damnation is to be found in God's absolute and irrevocable will that the Logos should become man as a member of the one, though sinful, humanity. This 'grace' is conceivable as the deficient mode of the grace which must presuppose this 'grace' as the condition of having anybody at all who can be endowed with grace.

PART FIVE

The Sacraments

9

THE THEOLOGY OF THE SYMBOL

FROM its beginnings to the present day,[1] the theology of devotion to the heart of Jesus, as understood by the simple faithful, by the theologians in their discussions and by the magisterium in its pronouncements, teaches that the heart of the Lord is a *symbol*[2] of the love of Christ. Whatever answer is to be given to the question as to what is the proper object of this devotion, what is the relationship of the physical heart of the Lord, as object of devotion and as symbol of the

---

[1] Here too there has been a certain change. An equally ancient tradition, which is now falling into the background (it is not mentioned for instance in '*Haurietis aquas*') takes the heart also to be the 'seat' and 'organ' of love or of the life of the soul in general. Thus the translator of Origen, Hieronymus, speaks of the *principale* (τὸ ἡγεμονικόν) *cordis Jesu*, because according to Stoic doctrine, followed by Origen, the ἡγεμονικόν has its seat in the heart. Cf. K. Rahner, *RAM* 14 (1934) 171–174. On לֵב, καρδία, as seat of physical life and of the life of the soul in general in the Old Testament, among the Greeks, and in the New Testament, see Kittel, *TWNT* III, 609–616; see also *Etudes Carmélitaines, Le Cœur* (Paris 1950). But even here we should ask how far this description of the heart as the seat and organ of the inner life of the soul is already to a great extent to be understood 'symbolically' (even though it is prompted by physical feelings in the heart during strongly emotional experiences), and hence means ultimately the same thing as we express by speaking of the heart as a 'symbol'.

[2] So for instance (if we prescind from the middle ages) in the more recent forms of devotion to the heart of Jesus: in G. I. Languet (Hamon IV, 83); in J. Croiset (1895 edition, Montreuil-sur-Mer, p. 5): '. . . *il a donc fallu trouver un symbole; et quel symbole plus propre et plus naturel de l'amour que le cœur?*', before this, however, we read (p. 4) that the heart is '*en quelque manière et la source et le siège de l'amour*', as L. Galliffet and P. Froment (Hamon III, 389; IV, 44) took it to be, about the same time; this was contradicted by Benedict XIV (*De servorum Dei beatificatione* IV, §2, c. 31 and 25); in Pius VI (*Epist. ad Scip. Ricci Episc.*, 29th June, 1781); in Leo XIII (Encycl. '*Annum Sacrum*', 25th May, 1899: '*inest Sacro Cordi symbolum atque expressa imago infinitae Jesu Christi caritatis*' *AAS* 31 [1898–99] 649); Pius XII ('*Haurietis Aquas*' *AAS* 48 [1956] 316, 317, 320, 327, 344: '*naturalis index seu symbolus caritatis; signum et index divini amoris; naturalis symbolus*' are the expressions used); among theologians, as for instance Franzelin (*Tractatus de Verbo incarnato*[5] [Rome 1902] 469–473), Lercher

object of devotion, to the love of Christ, which is certainly implicated in the object of this devotion; the word symbol cannot be avoided in the theology of the devotion. It indicates a component without which the nature and meaning of devotion to the heart of Jesus cannot be properly understood. But this calls for a more precise statement about what a symbol is in general. For it is not true, as is often thought, that the word 'symbol' has in general a clear and definite meaning in every instance and that therefore if there is any difficulty in understanding the assertion; the heart of Jesus is the symbol of the love of Christ, the difficulty does not come from the word symbol at least. An enquiry into the general sense of the word 'symbol' will show however that the concept is much more obscure, difficult and ambiguous than is usually thought, so that one of the tasks of these considerations must be to show that it is wrong to take the concept as an obvious one. This will in turn allow us to state clearly what it really means or can mean to speak of the symbol in the theology of devotion to the Sacred Heart. Such investigations, at least in this context are almost entirely lacking. If then the effort raises many problematical and unsolved points, the fair-minded reader will not be surprised.

I. THE ONTOLOGY OF SYMBOLIC REALITY IN GENERAL[3]

In the short space at our disposition, we must renounce the attempt to approach the question proper from the point of view of history of

---

(*Inst. Theol. Dogmat.* III[3] [Innsbruck 1942] 247–255) and in the other classical works on devotion to the heart of Jesus, which we need not indicate here. We should note, however, as regards the use of the word 'symbol' in this doctrine: a. on the whole, the general sense of the word symbol is hardly clarified in this context. When, for instance, '*Haurietis Aquas*' speaks of a '*naturalis symbolus*', we need understand no more than a symbol which comes to mind spontaneously and as it were, of itself. The expression gives no grounds for an exact and positive determination of the concept, such as we shall give here. There will of course be no contradiction between the two concepts. They will be related to each other as any other current concept in everyday language is to an attempt at a metaphysical explanation of it. b. Similarly, as regards *how* the heart is symbol of the love of Christ, and how these two elements are elated to each other with regard to the object of devotion to the heart of Jesus, theologians are not unanimous. We shall not discuss the point here. At the end of our considerations, we shall take up the theory of Solano and others who do their best in fact to exclude the notion of 'symbol' from the theology of devotion to the heart of Jesus.

[3] We cannot attempt to give here even an approximately exhaustive *bibliography* on the philosophy and to some extent on the theology of the symbol. We shall merely

list some works, very arbitrarily chosen indeed, which may give the uninitiated reader some idea of the variety of philosophical effort with regard to the concept of the symbol.

J. Volkelt, *Der Symbolbegriff in der neuesten Aesthetik* (Jena 1876). Fr. Th. Vischert, *Altes und Neues* (Stuttgart 1889), from which the essay 'Das Symbol' is re-printed in *Deutscher Geist, ein Lesebuch aus zwei Jahrhunderten*, 2 vols., S. Fischer Verlag (Berlin 1940) 726ff. R. Hamann, *Das Symbol* (Diss. Berlin 1902). M. Schlesinger, *Grundlagen und Geschichte des Symbols* (Berlin 1912). E. Brunner, *Das Symbolische in der religiösen Erkenntnis* (Tübingen 1914). R. Gätschenberger, *Symbola. Anfangsgründe einer Erkenntnistheorie* (Karlsruhe 1920). F. Ebner, *Das Wort und die geistigen Realitäten* (Regensburg 1921). R. Otto, *Das Heilige* (Breslau [6]1921). E. Cassirer, *Philosophie der symbolischen Formen*, 3 vols. (Berlin 1923–31; Freiburg [2]1954). H. Schreiner, *Geist und Gestalt* (Schwerin 1926). R. Guardini, *Von heiligen Zeichen* (Mainz 1927). O. Casel, 'Kath. Kultprobleme', *Jb. f. Liturgiewissensch.* 7 (1927) 105–124, O. Casel *The Mystery of Christian Worship* (London & Westminster, Md. 1962). *Blätter f. d. Philos.* 1 (1928): No. 4 as a whole treats of the symbol. E. Unger, *Wirklichkeit, Mythos, Erkenntnis* (Munich–Berlin 1930). P. Tillich, *Religiöse Verwirklichung. Aufsätze* (Berlin [2]1930) 88f., 'Das religiöse Symbol'. R. Winkler, 'Die Frage nach dem symbolischen Charakter der religiösen Erkenntnis', *Christentum und Wissenschaft* (1929) 252 ff. W. Müri, *Symbolon. Wort- und sachgeschichtliche Studie* (Bern 1931). F. Weinhandl, *Über das aufschliessende Symbol* (Berlin 1931); reviewed by M. Radacovic, 'Zur Wiedergeburt des symbolischen Denkens', *Hochland* 29 (1931–1932) 494–505. K. Plachte, *Symbol und Idol. Über die Bedeutung der symbolischen Formen im Sinnvollzug der religiöse Erfahrung* (Berlin 1931). C. G. Jung, *Archetypes and the Collective Unconscious* (London & New York 1959). C. G. Jung, *Psychological Types* (London & New York 1923). R. Scherer, 'Das Symbolische. Eine philosophishe Analyse', *Phil. Jahrb. d. Görresges.* 48 (1935) 210–257. K. Bühler, *Ausdruckstheorie* (Jena 1936). H. Noack, *Symbol und Existenz der Wissenschaft. Untersuchungen zur Grundlegung einer philosophischen Wissenschaftslehre* Halle 1936). G. Söhngen, *Symbol und Wirklichkeit im Kultmysterium* (Bonn 1937, [2]1940). G. Söhngen, *Der Wesensauf bau des Mysteriums* (Bonn 1938). J. Maritain, 'Sign and Symbol', *Journal of the Warburg Institute* 1 (1937). W. M. Urban, *Language and Reality* (London 1939), ch. 12, 'Religious Symbols and the Problem of Religious Knowledge. W. M. Urban, 'Symbolism as a Theological Principle', *Journal of Religion* 19 (1939) No. 1. G. Thomas, 'Myth and Symbol in Religion', *Journal of Bible and Religion* 7 (1939) 163–171. O. Doering–M. Hartig, *Christliche Symbole* (Freiburg [2]1940). E. Bevan, *Symbolism and Belief* (London 1938). M. D. Koster, 'Symbol und Sakrament', *Die neue Ordnung* 5 (1947) 385 ff. T. T. Segerstedt, *Die Macht des Wortes. Eine Sprachsoziologie* (from the Swedish) (Zurich 1947). K. Jaspers, *Von der Wahrheit* (Munich 1947). K. Jaspers, *Philosophie* (Heidelberg 1948). St. V. Szmanski, *Das Symbol* (Diss. Innsbruck 1947). E. Gombrich, 'Icones Symbolicae. The Visual Image in Neo-Platonic Thought', *J. Warburg and Courtauld Institute* 11 (1948) 163 ff. H. Friedmann, *Wissenschaft und Symbol* (Munich 1949); the same, *Epilegomena* (Munich 1954) 130–155 'Die symbolnahen Begriffe'. J. S. Bayne, *Secret and Symbol* (Edinburgh 1949). H. Schmalenbach, *Phénoménologie du signe: Signe et Symbole* (*op. coll.*) (Neuchâtel 1949). H. Ording 'Symbol und Wirklichkeit', *Theol. Lit. Z.* 3 (1948) 129 ff. M. Heideggar, *Holzwege* (Frankfurt a. M. 1950). E. Biser, *Das Christusgeheimnis der Sakramente* (Heidelberg 1950); 'Das religiöse philosophy and the human understanding of existence in general. There would be many points to be considered: the usage and history of the word symbol and kindred words; how its changing meanings are related to the original radical meaning which made such changes possible; the meaning and history of concepts which point linguistically and objectively in the same direction: εἶδος μορφή, sign, figure, expression, image, aspect, appearance, etc. We must omit all such historical preparatives which lead up to the actual question, though we thereby risk overlooking many relevant questions on which light could be thrown by the history of the problem. We take up the matter in hand therefore without preparing the ground beforehand.

1. Our first statement, which we put forward as the basic principle of an ontology of symbolism, is as follows: all beings are by their nature symbolic, because they necessarily 'express' themselves in order to attain their own nature.

We should already be dealing with merely derivative modes of symbolic

Symbol in Aufbau des Geisteslebens', *Münch. Theol. Z.* 5 (1954) 114–140. J. Münzhuber, 'Sinnbild und Symbol', *Z. Phil. Forsch.* 5 (1950) 62–74. J. Daniélou, 'The Problem of Symbolism', *Thought* 25 (1950) 423–440. Th. Bogler, 'Zur Theologie der Kunst', *Liturgie und Mönchtum* 7 (1950) 46–63. A. Brunner, *Glaube und Erkenntnis* (Munich 1951); the same, *Die Religion* (Freiburg 1956). M. Eliade, *Images and Symbols* (Paris 1952). M. Thiel, 'Die Symbolik als philosophisches Problem und philosophische Aufgabe', *Stud. Gen.* 6 (1953) 235–256. H. Looff, 'Symbol und Tranzendenz' *Stud. Gen.* 6 (1953) 324–332; the same, *Der Symbolbegriff in der neueren Religionsphilosophie und Theologie (Kantstudien*, Cologne 1955). H. Meyer, 'Symbolgebilde der Sprache', *Stud. Gen.* 6 (1953) 195–206. J. Pieper, *Weistum, Dichtung, Sakrament* (Munich 1954). F. Kaulbach, *Philosophische Grundlegung zu einer wissenschaftlichen Symbolik* (Meisenheim 1954). R. Boyle, 'The Nature of Metaphor', *The Modern Schoolman* 31 (1954) 257–280. L. Fremgen, *Offenbarung und Symbol* (Gütersloh 1954). G. Mensching, 'Religiöse Ursymbole der Menschheit', *Stud. Gen.* 8 (1955) 362–370. A. Rosenberg, *Die christliche Bildmeditation* (Munich 1955). E. Przywara, 'Bild, Gleichnis, Symbol, Mythos, Mysterium, Logos', *Archivio di Filosofia* 2–3 (Rome 1956) 7–38. K. Kerenyi, 'Symbolismus in der antiken Religionen', *ibid.*, 119–129. A. Grillmeier, *Der Logos am Kreuz* (Munich 1956). F. König, *Religionswissenschaftliches Wörterbuch* (Freiburg 1956) 849–851. G. van der Leeuw, *Phänomenologie der Religion* (Tübingen ²1956). K. Rahner, *Theological Investigations* III (London & Baltimore Md. 1967): 'Priest and Poet', 'Behold this heart', 'Some Theses . . .'; the same, 'Der theologische Sinn der Verehrung des Herzens-Jesu' In *Festschrift zur Hundertjahrfeier des Theol. Konvikts Innsbruck 1858–1958* (Innsbruck 1958) 102–109. M. Vereno, *Vom Mythos zum Christos* (Salzburg 1958). B. Liebrucks, 'Sprache und Mythos: Konkrete Vernunft', *Festschrift E. Rothacker* (Bonn 1958) 253–280. G. Kittel, *TWNT, eidos*, II, 371–373; *eikon*, II, 378–396; *morphe*, IV, 750–760. *Enciclopedia Filosofica*, IV, 625–627.

being if we started with the fact that two realities, each of which is supposed to be already constituted in its essence and intelligible of itself,
'agreed' with one another on a certain point, and stated that this 'agreement' made it possible for each of them (more particularly the better
known and more accessible of the two, of course) to refer to the other and
call attention to it, and hence be used by us as a symbol for the other,
precisely by reason of the 'agreement'. Symbols would then only vary,
and be distinguishable from one another, by the degree and precise mode,
of this subsequent similarity between the two realities. Since in the long
run everything agrees in some way or another with everything else, to
start the analysis of symbols this way would make it impossible to
distinguish really genuine symbols ('symbolic realities') from merely
arbitrary 'signs', 'signals' and 'codes' ('symbolic representations'). Anything could be the symbol of anything else, the orientation from the
symbol to the thing symbolized could run the other way round or be
determined merely accidentally, from a view point extrinsic to the matter
itself, by the human observer, who finds one aspect more telling than
another. Such derivative, secondary cases of symbolism do of course exist,
so that it is not easy to say where the function of being merely a sign and
indicator so predominates over the 'function of expressiveness' that a
symbol loses its 'overplus of meaning' (Fr. Th. Vischer) and sinks to the
level of a sign with little symbolism. The margins are fluid. One need only
recall that our numbers once had a religious and sacral character. Indeed
it often happens that in a vocabulary more attentive to history of art and
aesthetics 'symbol' represents a very derivative case of the symbolic. It is
a feature of such terminology that the symbol (an anchor, a fish and so on)
indicates a lower degree of the symbolic than for instance a religious
image. We shall not discuss these matters further now. Our task will be
to look for the highest and most primordial manner in which one reality
can represent another—considering the matter primarily from the formal
ontological point of view. And we call this supreme and primal representation, in which one reality renders another present (primarily 'for
itself' and only secondarily for others), a symbol: the representation which
allows the other 'to be there'.

To reach the primary concept of symbol, we must start from the fact
that all beings (each of them, in fact) are multiple,[4] and are or can be

---

[4] We choose here a method which will bring us to our goal as easily and quickly as
possible, even though it simplifies matters by presupposing ontological and theo-

essentially the expression of another in this unity of the multiple and one[5] in this plurality, by reason of its plural unity.[6] The first part of this assertion is axiomatic in an ontology of the finite. Each finite being as such bears the stigma of the finite by the very fact that it is not absolutely 'simple'. Within the permanent inclusive unity of its reality (as essence and existence) it is not simply and homogeneously the same in a deathlike collapse into identity. It has of itself a real multiplicity, which is not merely a mental distinction and division extrinsic to the reality and only due to the limited intelligence of the external and finite observer, who only explicitates for himself the absolutely simple fullness of the being in question by using several terms (presuming that it would be thinkable at all under these circumstances).

In saying this, however, we do not mean to assert that an intrinsic plurality and distinction must *always* be merely the stigma of the finiteness of a being. We know, on the contrary, from the mystery of the Trinity—we are doing theological ontology, which need not be afraid of adducing revealed data: that there is a true and real—even though 'only' relative—distinction of 'persons' in the supreme simplicity of God, and hence a plurality, at least in this sense. Let us now further consider—in keeping with a theology[7] of the 'traces' and 'reflexions' of the inner-trinitarian plurality—that it is quite thinkable that the pluralism of the finite creature is not merely a consequence and indicator of its finiteness, as a merely

---

logical principles which would have to be demonstrated, not supposed, in a properly worked out ontology of the symbol. However, in view of the reader who is primarily envisaged here, these presuppositions may be made without misgiving.

[5] We say very vaguely 'one'. This 'unity' of a moment in a being can of course again only be envisaged analogically, in comparison with the unity and totality which is predicated of the Being which is totally one and yet plural in itself.

[6] We do not wish to anticipate here the question as to whether the one moment, in relation to the other within the one plural being must necessarily have a *formally* expressive function (for instance, to use the theological formula of the Trinity, must proceed from the other moment '*in similitudinem naturae*', or is only *de facto* 'expression' and displays a 'likeness'. Even in the second case, the important point remains, that the likeness is originally constituted as an inner self-realization, and *qua* distinct, is an inner moment of the abiding unity itself.

[7] We may mention a modern effort in this direction, inspired by present-day philosophy, the book of C. Kaliba, *Die Welt als Gleichnis des dreieinigen Gottes. Entwurf zu einer trinitarischen Ontologie* (Salzburg 1952), which, in spite of the misgivings it arouses on particular points, takes up a theme which is unduly neglected today.

negative qualification, but also a consequence—even though not naturally recognizable as such—of that divine plurality which does not imply imperfection and weakness and limitation of being, but the supreme fullness of unity and concentrated force: then we may say candidly, though also cautiously, that being is plural in itself, and formulate this as a general principle without restrictions. On this supposition, we do not need to take it as merely part of the ontology of the finite as such. Even where it is applied to a plurality of the finite as such, we can take it as an assertion which understands even the plurality of the finite as an allusion —disclosed only in revelation—to a plurality which is more than an indistinguishable identity and simplicity. We should of course have to think of it so, if even our sublimest ontological ideals were not further directed by the self-revelation of the God who is still loftier than these ideals, and who by thus surpassing our always approximate metaphysical ideals comes once more, suddenly and strangely, that is, miraculously and mysteriously, close to us. It is therefore true: a being is, of itself, independently of any comparison with anything else, plural in its unity.

But these plural moments in the unity of a being must have an inner agreement among themselves on account of the unity of the being, even though the plurality of moments in a being must be constituted by the reciprocal diversity of these moments. And they cannot have this agreement as the simple juxtaposition, so to speak, of moments which are there as such originally. This would imply a denial of the unity of the being in question: unity would be the subsequent conjunction of separate elements which once stood only on their own. This would be to betray the profound principle of St Thomas: *non enim plura secundum se uniuntur*: there can be no union of things which are of themselves multiple. A plurality in an original and an originally superior unity can only be understood as follows: the 'one' develops, the plural stems from an original 'one', in a relationship of origin and consequence; the original unity, which also forms the unity which unites the plural, maintains itself while resolving itself and 'dis-closing' itself into a plurality in order to find itself precisely there. A consideration of the Trinity shows that the 'one' of unity and plurality, thus understood, is an ontological ultimate, which may not be reduced to an abstract and merely apparently 'higher' unity and simplicity: it cannot be a hollow, lifeless identity. It would be theologically a heresy, and therefore ontologically an absurdity, to think that God would be really 'simpler' and hence more perfect, if there were no real distinction of persons in God. There exists therefore a differentiation which is in itself a 'perfectio pura' and which must be taken into consideration from the very start of a theological understanding of being. It is not provisional, but something absolutely final, an ultimate of the self-communicating unity itself as such, which constitutes this unity itself: it does not half destroy, so to speak, this unity. Being *as* such, and hence *as* one (*ens* as *unum*), for the fulfilment[8] of its being and its unity, emerges into a plurality—of which the supreme mode is the Trinity. The distinct moments deriving from the 'one' which make for the perfection of its unity stem essentially, i.e. by their origin in and from another, from this most primary unity: they have therefore a more primary and basic 'agreement' with it than anything produced by efficient causality.

But this means that each being, as a unity, possesses a plurality—implying perfection—formed by the special derivativeness of the plural from the original unity: the plural is in agreement with its source in a way which corresponds to its origin, and hence is 'expression' of its origin by an agreement which it owes to its origin. Since this holds good for being in general, we may say that each being forms, in its own way, more or less perfectly according to its degree of being, something distinct from itself and yet one with itself, 'for' its own fulfilment. (Here unity and distinction are correlatives which increase in like proportions, not in inverse proportions which would reduce each to be contradictory and exclusive of the other.) And this differentiated being, which is still originally one, is in agreement because derivative, and because derivatively in agreement is expressive.

That that which is derivatively in agreement, and *hence* one with the origin while still distinct from it, must be considered as the 'expression' of the origin and of the primordial unity needs some further explanation. The agreement with its origin (by reason of its derivation) of that which is constituted as different within the unity is at once, in a certain sense, the constitution of the derivative *as* an *expression*. For there is an agreement which is explained by the relation of being originated. We may therefore prescind from the question as to whether we must always consider such a derivation as the formal constitution of the agreement as such and hence whether we must always think of it formally *as* expression.

---

[8] '*For* fulfilment' can and must be in some cases (e.g. the Trinity) understood also as '*on account of* its being perfect'. What is common to both cases is that the other which is constituted in an act of self-realization (*actus, resultatio, processio*) necessarily belongs to the perfection of the agent.

Whether and when and why this is so in certain cases may be left without misgivings to a special ontology concerned with certain spheres. We shall meet such cases in the (second) theological consideration of the matter. But prescinding from this question, we may already affirm: every being as such possesses a plurality as intrinsic element of its significant unity; this plurality constitutes itself, by virtue of its origin from an original unity, as the way to fulfil the unity (or on account of the unity already perfect), in such a way that that which is originated and different is in agreement with its origin and hence has (at least in a 'specificative', if not always in a 'reduplicative' sense) the character of expression or 'symbol' with regard to its origin. But this brings us to the full statement of our first affirmation: being is of itself symbolic, because it necessarily 'expresses' itself. This affirmation needs some further explanation in the light of what has been said, and then its applicability to some well-known themes must be demonstrated.

Being expresses itself, because it must realize itself through a plurality in unity. This plurality is often, and in many respects, an indication of finiteness and deficiency, but it can also be something positive, of which at least a 'trace' remains even in the plurality which is given formally with the finiteness of a being. The self-constitutive act whereby a being constitutes itself as a plurality which leads to its fulfilment or rather (in certain circumstances) which is a reality given with the perfection of the being, is however the condition of possibility of possession of self in knowledge and love. *In tantum est ens cognoscens et cognitum, in quantum est ens actu.* This statement also holds good of course if inverted: the degree of '*reditio completa in seipsum*' is the indication of its degree of being. 'Being present to itself' is only another way of describing the actuality, that is, the intrinsic self-realization of the being. But then it follows that a being 'comes to itself' in its expression, in the derivative agreement of the differentiated which is preserved as the perfection of the unity. For realization as plurality and as possession of self cannot be disparate elements simply juxtaposed in a being, since possession of self (in knowledge and love) is not just an element, but *the* content of that which we call being (and hence self-realization). And it comes to itself in the measure in which it realizes itself by constituting a plurality.[9] But this means that each being—in as much as it has and realizes being—is itself

[9] These considerations are not open to the objection that, if correct, they could deduce the Trinity from purely rational philosophical considerations. For their

primarily 'symbolic'. It expresses itself and possesses itself by doing so. It gives itself away from itself into the 'other', and there finds itself in knowledge and love, because it is by constituting the inward 'other' that it comes to (or: from) its self-fulfilment, which is the presupposition or the act of being present to itself in knowledge and love.

A symbol is therefore not to be primarily considered as a secondary relationship between two different beings, which are given the function of indicating one another by a third, or by an observer who notes a certain agreement between them. The symbolic is not merely an intrinsic propriety of beings in so far as a being, to attain fulfilment, constitutes the differentiation which is retained in the unity, and which is in agreement with the original originating unity and so is its expression. A being is also 'symbolic' in itself because the harmonious expression, which it retains while constituting it as the 'other', is the way in which it communicates itself to itself in knowledge and love. A being comes to itself by means of 'expression', in so far as it comes to itself at all. The expression, that is, the 'symbol'—as the word is now to be understood in the light of the foregoing considerations—is the way of knowledge of self, possession of self, in general.

This is the only starting-point from which one can arrive at a correct theory of the symbol in general, where the symbol is the reality in which *another* attains knowledge of a being. On strictly scholastic terms, knowledge of a being by another is not the process which only takes place in the knower, and hence depends only on his potency and actuality, being related to an 'object' which persists completely unaffected in its own proper reality. On the contrary, the knowability and the actual knowledge of a being (as object of knowledge) depend on the degree of actuality in the thing to be known itself: *ens est cognitum et cognoscibile, in quantum ipsum est actu.* But then it follows: if beings are of themselves symbolic, in so far as they realize themselves in a plurality, and possess themselves in this derivative agreement of the 'other' with its primordial origin, the same holds good for the knowledge of these beings by others. A being can be and is known, in so far as it is itself ontically (in itself) symbolic

---

starting-point (which is not capable of proof by purely philosophical arguments) is that there is a plurality even in the supreme Being, without detriment to his unity. Hence our considerations presuppose the Trinity. They do not prove it, but use the knowledge of it given in revelation as the starting-point of ontological theological considerations. This is a perfectly legitimate method.

because it is ontologically (for itself) symbolic. What then is the primordial meaning of symbol and symbolic, according to which each being is in itself and for itself symbolic, and hence (and to this extent) symbolic for another? It is this: as a being realizes itself in its own intrinsic 'otherness' (which is constitutive of its being), retentive of its intrinsic plurality (which is contained in its self-realization) as its derivative and hence congruous expression, it makes itself known. This derivative and congruous expression, constitutive of each being, is the symbol which comes in addition from the object of knowledge to the knower—in addition only, because already initially present in the depths of the grounds of each one's being. The being is known in this symbol, without which it cannot be known at all: thus it is symbol in the original (transcendental) sense of the word.

We must now confront the notion of symbol thus arrived at, with some well-known data of scholastic philosophy, so that it may be still more easily understood. It would call for too wide a sweep through the history of philosophy, if one were to try to illustrate what has been said by showing the whole extension of the concepts of *eidos* and *morphe* (in the *philosophia perennis* from the time of the Greeks to the classic age of scholastic philosophy). If we could follow these lines, it could be shown that the two extremes of this extension, the manifest, visible 'figure' on the one hand (*eidos* and *morphe* together), and the 'essence' which gives rise to the figure on the other hand, make up together the full sense of one concept. For how does the figure-forming essence of a being (material, to start with) constitute and perfect itself? It does so by really projecting its visible figure outside itself as its—symbol, its appearance, which allows it to be there, which brings it out to existence in the world: and in doing so, it retains it—'possessing itself in the other'. The essence is there for itself and for others precisely through its appearance—in the 'analogous' measure, of course, in which a being is there for itself and for others according to its own measure of being.

A deeper understanding of Thomist ontology is then possible. For it is clear that St Thomas[10] recognizes the most diverse forms of the 'self-realization' of a being, which cannot be subsumed under the denomination of transitive efficient causality. The notion of *causa formalis* must be mentioned at once in this context. The 'form' gives itself away from itself by imparting itself to the material cause. It does not work on it

[10] For the following, see K. Rahner, *Geist in Welt*[2] (Munich 1957).

subsequently and 'from outside', by bringing about in it something different from itself and alien to its essence. The 'effect' is the 'cause' itself, in so far as the cause itself is the reality, the 'act' of the material cause, which is becoming its own 'potency'. But when the formal cause is such, it is not simply such as it must be considered to be previous to its actual formal causality. For there are, according to St Thomas, 'forms' which are not exhausted in their formal causality, because they are not completely 'poured out' on their matter; their primordiality is still 'reserved'. Hence not every form realizes its being by emptying itself fully and giving itself as act away to the other that consumes it (the '*materia prima*'). The difference between form and its actual formal causality need not be merely mental, even though this difference cannot be thought of in the same way as that between a substance conceived of as static (having already come to be from its formal causes) and its accidental 'second' act. The giving of the form by the formal cause, the '*formatio actualis*' of the potency by the (substantial) form, 'brings about' that which is formed, the actual thing (where it does not matter to us here what forms this process takes, once we distinguish between the dimension of substance and the formally quantitative being in time and space). This external manifestation of the substantial form or cause is indeed, according to the basic doctrines of scholasticism just alluded to, different from the form as such. But it still manifests this basic form in this very difference: it is a symbol which is created by that which is symbolized as its own self-realization. In this differentiated 'symbol' that which is symbolized is present, the form itself (creating the 'ontological-symbolic' difference between symbolic reality and symbolic representation), since it beings about the 'other' which it forms, in as much as it imparts to it the reality which the form itself has.

But apart from the concept of formal causality, there are other concepts of Thomist ontology which belong to the sphere of the self-realization which is a self-proclamation and hence—in the broadest but original sense—constitutive of a symbol. Here the concept of 'resultance' should be noted. St Thomas does not merely think of a finite being as a reality simply complete, constituted by God in its essence and faculties. He does not merely see it as a passive and static reality, which then sets a number of accidental acts, of an immanent or transitive nature, which emanate indeed from the substance by efficient causality and to this extent 'determine' it, but leave it untouched in its inner nature. He also recognizes an inner self-realization of the total essence itself (dependent of course on the creative activity of God), prior to its accidental 'second' acts: a self-realization which objectively and conceptually, according to St Thomas, cannot be simply reduced to formal and material causality, as this is usually understood in the traditional philosophy of the schools—and can still less be subsumed under the categories of the ordinary (second) 'activity'. Thus St Thomas recognizes, for instance, a 'resultance', an 'out-flowing' of the faculties from the substance. Thus for him the essence as a whole builds itself up—for the faculties belong to the totality of the essence, in spite of their being accidents; the substantial kernel emanates into its faculties and only thus attains its own possibilities; it finds itself—since it must be spiritual etc. by projecting from itself the 'otherness' of its faculties, which according to St Thomas is really distinct from the substance.

It does not follow at once from the fact that the 'other' results within the unity of the same being, for the achievement of the essence, that we have in it an intrinsic and connatural symbol as a moment of the self-realization of the being in question, or at any rate, we shall not pursue the thought further now. It is enough to have proved, from the theory of the emanation and 'resultance' of a faculty, a power, an accident, that the starting-point for our proffered theory of the symbol is perfectly Thomist. We shall only pursue this line of thought in one direction. According to St Thomas, we must also suppose the process of 'resultance' in the formation of a given quantity as such (with spatially limited dimensions) and as vehicle of other qualitative proprieties in a material being. When the substantial 'form'—'pouring itself out'—gives itself to *materia prima* (which is the ontological basis of spatiality, though itself without any determinate dimensions), the determinate quantity is brought about in this communication, really distinct from the substance (composed of *forma substantialis* and *materia prima*) and from the reality which comes from it. This quantity, which today we would call the given, concrete spatio-temporality, or spatio-temporal figure, with its further given qualitative determinations (which are however based on this spatio-temporality), is, according to St Thomas, to be definitely taken as the 'species',[11] the outward form, aspect and figure, which the basic substance

[11] The theologian is most familiar with the word from its use in the theology of the Eucharist, where this terminology has also become part of the vocabulary of the magisterium (*Denz.* 626, 676, 698, 876, 884, etc.).

provides for itself, to fulfil itself, to 'express' itself and to manifest itself thus. The 'species' of the material thing is undoubtedly the symbol—brought about by the essence, retained with the efficient cause in a differentiated unity, constituting the necessary 'communication' of the self-realization—in which the material being possesses itself and presents itself to view, in the varying forms proper to its being. In the case of the species of material things, we have in St Thomas—on this definite level of being and with the presuppositions which it entails—all the elements which we have worked out for the original concept of symbol in a more general ontology of multiple beings; the formation of the symbol as a self-realization of the thing symbolized itself; the fact that the symbol belongs intrinsically to what is expressed; self-realization by means of the constitution of this expression springing from the essence. There is another doctrine in scholasticism which can also be adduced to confirm the concept of symbol given above, of which we shall speak more fully in another context: it is the doctrine which holds that the soul is the 'form' of the body, the body being the expression of the basic spiritual reality of man.

To sum up and propound once more the results arrived at up to this, we may invert the first assertion which we put forward as the fundamental principle of an ontology of the symbol, by affirming as a *second assertion*: 2. The symbol strictly speaking (symbolic reality) is the self-realization of a being in the other, which is constitutive of its essence.

Where there is such a self-realization in the other—as the necessary mode of the fulfilment of its own essence—we have a symbol of the being in question. One might ask for whom does this self-realization in the other express the being and make it present, and who possesses the being in such a symbol—the being in question itself or another; one might ask in what (essentially different) degrees and in what ways this self-realization in the symbol and this presence are realized, in a self-discovery which is really knowledge and love or in a way relatively deficient compared to this. But these are secondary questions which, in comparison with these two first principles, enquire into distinctions which are secondary in relation to this general ontology of the symbol. They arise because the concept of a being is 'analogous', that it, it displays the *various* types of self-realization of each being, and being in itself, and hence also the concept and reality of the symbol are flexible. But because these are necessarily given with the general concept of beings and being—as the 'unveiled' figure of the most primordial 'truth' of being—the symbol shares this '*analogia entis*' with being which it symbolizes.

II. ON THE THEOLOGY OF SYMBOLIC REALITY

If what has been said up to this is correct, it is only to be expected that no theology can be complete without also being a theology of the symbol, of the appearance and the expression, of self-presence in that which has been constituted as the other. And in fact the whole of theology is incomprehensible if it is not essentially a theology of symbols, although in general very little attention is paid, systematically and expressly, to this basic characteristic. And again: since a simple listing of dogmatic assertions throughout the whole field of theology shows how much need it has of the concept of symbol and how much it uses it (no doubt in the most diverse acceptations and applications), the necessity of our general ontological considerations is confirmed once more from another direction.

We shall of course have to be content with a few indications. The attentive reader, especially if trained in theology, will not have failed to remark that the thought of the mystery of the *Trinity* was the constant background of the ontological considerations. The freedom of our method has already allowed us to appeal expressly to this mystery. We used it to show that a plurality in a being is not necessarily to be considered as a pointer to finiteness and imperfection, and that therefore a general ontology—which only speaks of beings strictly as such—may very properly start from the fact that each being bears within itself an intrinsic plurality, without detriment to its unity and perfection—which may eventually be supreme—precisely as the perfection of its unity. Hence an ontology confined to a particular field and likewise a theology may well ask what this means with regard to the symbolic nature of individual beings.

When we were working out the ontology of the symbol, we took no great pains to formulate it so that it would be immediately applicable to the theology of the Trinity in blameless orthodoxy. Even now we shall not try to establish expressly the convergence of this ontology and the theology of the Trinity (especially the theology of the Logos). It is enough for our purpose to point out very simply that the theology of the Logos is strictly a theology of the symbol, and indeed the supreme form of it, if we keep to the meaning of the word which we have already worked out, and do not give the term quite derivative meanings, such as the

ordinary language of popular speech attributes to it. The Logos is the
'word' of the Father, his perfect 'image', his 'imprint', his radiance, his
self-expression. Whatever answer is to be given to the question of how
binding the psychological theory of the Trinity, as put forward by
St Augustine, may be—whether the Father utters the eternal Word
because he knows himself or *in order to* know himself, two items at any
rate must be retained. One, the Word—as reality of the immanent
divine life—is 'generated' by the Father as the *image* and *expression* of the
Father. Two, this process is necessarily given with the divine act of self-
knowledge, and without it the absolute act of divine self-possession in
knowledge cannot exist. But if we retain these two elements, which are
traditional in theology—not to give them a higher qualification—then we
may and must say without misgivings: the Father is himself by the very
fact that he opposes to himself the image which is of the same essence as
himself, as the person who is other than himself; and so he possesses himself. But this means that the Logos is the 'symbol' of the Father, in the
very sense which we have given the word: the inward symbol which
remains distinct from what is symbolized, which is constituted by what is
symbolized, where what is symbolized expresses itself and possesses
itself. We omit the question of what this means—prior to a theology of
the Incarnation—for the understanding of the Father and his relation to
the world. If, following a theological tradition which began only since
St Augustine, one simply takes it for granted that *each* of the divine persons could set up, each for himself, his own hypostatic relationship to a
given reality in the world and so could 'appear', then the fact that within
the divinity the Logos is the image of the Father would give the Logos no
special character of symbol for the world, which would be due to him
alone on account of his relationship of origin to the Father. The Father
could also reveal himself and 'appear' without reference, so to speak, to
the Son. But if one does not make this pre-supposition with St Augustine,
which has no clear roots in the earlier tradition[12] and still less in Scripture,
one need have no difficulty in thinking that the Word's being symbol of
the Father has significance for God's action *ad extra*, in spite of such
action being common to all three persons.

It is because God 'must' 'express' himself inwardly that he can also
utter himself outwardly; the finite, created utterance *ad extra* is a con-

---

[12] Here the opposite opinion was practically unanimously held. Cf. e.g. M.
Schmaus, *Die psychologische Trinitätslehre des hl. Augustin* (Münster 1927) 20 ff.

tinuation of the immanent constitution of 'image and likeness'—a free continuation, because its object is finite—and takes place in fact 'through' the Logos (Jn 1: 3), in a sense which cannot be determined more closely here. But it is not our intention to go into this difficult subject here. But it has to be mentioned, even if only in passing, because we could hardly omit this link between a symbolic reality within and without the divine, since it has also been noted to some extent in tradition.

If a theology of symbolic realities is to be written, Christology, the doctrine of the incarnation of the Word, will obviously form the central chapter. And this chapter need almost be no more than an exegesis of the saying: 'He that sees me, sees the Father' (Jn 14:9). There is no need to dwell here on the fact that the Logos is image, likeness, reflexion, representation, and presence—filled with all the fullness of the Godhead. But if this is true, we can understand the statement: the incarnate word is the absolute symbol of God in the world, filled as nothing else can be with what is symbolized. He is not merely the presence and revelation of what God is in himself. He is also the expressive presence of what—or rather, who—God wished to be, in free grace, to the world, in such a way that this divine attitude, once so expressed, can never be reversed, but is and remains final and unsurpassable.

But there are some comments to be made on the generally accepted dogmatic teaching which is here presupposed. They have not the same degree of certainty in theology, but they seem necessary if we are to have a proper understanding of the Incarnation in a theology of the symbol. If we simply say: the Logos took on a human nature, considering this defined doctrine of faith as the *adequate* expression of what is meant by the dogma of the incarnation (though such a description of the hypostatic union makes no such claim), the full sense of the symbolic reality, which the humanity of the Logos represents with regard to the Logos, is given no clear expression. For if the humanity which is assumed is considered only as that well-known reality which we know in ourselves, and which is only very generally 'image and likeness' of God; and if this humanity is supposed only to subsist in a static, ontic sense, that is, as 'borne' and 'taken on' by the Logos: then the humanity has no doubt the function of a signal or a uniform with regard to the Logos, but not in full truth the function of such a symbol as we have developed above. The Logos would make himself audible and perceptible through a reality which was of itself alien to him, had intrinsically and essentially nothing to do with him, and could have been chosen at random from a whole series of such realities. No matter how close we consider the union between the speaker and his means of communication—the union is in fact hypostatic—it would not change the fact that the sign and that which is signified are really disparate, and that the sign could therefore only be an arbitrary one. Or we could put it more exactly: the assumed humanity would be an organ of speech substantially united to him who is to be made audible: but it would not be this speech itself. It itself would only tell something about—itself; it could only tell about the Word in so far as the Word used it to form words and direct actions which would divulge something about the word by their meaning and their marvellous quality. It is not surprising that a theology with these unavowed, unconscious but effective presuppositions should in the concrete make Jesus the revelation of the Father and his inward life only through his doctrine but not through what he *is* in his human nature. In such a position, the most that could come in question would be a revelation by means of his (virtuous) actions.

To continue on these lines, and to give greater clarity to the inexhaustible content of the truth of faith which expresses the incarnation, one could take up here the Thomistic doctrine, that the humanity of Christ exists by the existence of the Logos. But when putting forward this thesis, one should be clear that this existence of the Word is again not to be thought of as the reality which—merely because of its being infinite—could bestow existence on any thinkable 'essence', as if it could offer any essence a ground of existence which in itself was indifferent to this essence rather than that or to which manner of existent being arose thereby. The being of the Logos—considered of course *as* that which is received by procession from the Father—must be thought of as exteriorizing itself, so that without detriment to its immutability in itself and of itself, it becomes *itself* in truth the existence of a created reality—which must in all truth and reality be predicated of the being of the Logos, because it *is* so. But then, starting from these Thomistic principles, we arrive at considerations and insights which show how truly and radically the humanity of Christ is really the 'appearance' of the Logos itself, its symbolic reality in the pre-eminent sense, not something in itself alien to the Logos and its reality, which is only taken up from outside like an instrument to make its own music but not strictly speaking to reveal anything of him who uses it. However, these considerations have already been put forward in an earlier chapter on the mystery of the incarnation.

We showed there that the humanity of Christ is not to be considered as something in which God dresses up and masquerades—a mere signal of which he makes use, so that something audible can be uttered about the Logos by means of this signal. The humanity is the self-disclosure of the Logos itself, so that when God, expressing himself, exteriorizes himself, that very thing appears which we call the humanity of the Logos. Thus anthropology itself is finally based on something more than the doctrine of the possibilities open to an infinite Creator—who would not however really betray *himself* when he created. Its ultimate source is the doctrine about God himself, in so far as it depicts that which 'appears' when in his self-exteriorization he goes out of himself into that which is other than he. However, we must refer to the earlier chapter for these considerations.

It follows from what has been said that the Logos, as Son of the Father, is truly, in his humanity as such, the revelatory symbol in which the Father enunciates himself, in this Son, to the world—revelatory, because the symbol renders present what is revealed. But in saying this, we are really only at the beginning of a theology of the symbol, in the light of the incarnation, not at the end. For in view of this truth, we should have to consider that the natural depth of the symbolic reality of all things—which is of itself restricted to the world or has a merely natural transcendence towards God—has now in ontological reality received an infinite extension by the fact that this reality has become also a determination of the Logos himself or of his milieu. Every God-given reality, where it has not been degraded to a purely human tool and to merely utilitarian purposes, states much more than itself: each in its own way is an echo and indication of all reality. If the individual reality, by making the all present, also speaks of God—ultimately by its transcendental reference to him as the efficient, exemplary and final cause—this transcendence is made radical, even though only in a way accessible to faith, by the fact that in Christ this reality no longer refers to God merely as its cause: it points to God as to him to whom this reality belongs as his substantial determination or as his own proper environment. All things are held together by the incarnate Word in whom they exist (Col 1.17), and hence all things possess, even in their quality of symbol, an unfathomable depth, which faith alone can sound. It would be well to explain all these abstract statements in detail, by applying them to individual realities—water, bread, hand, eye, sleep, hunger and countless other affairs of man and of the world which surrounds him, bears him up and is referred to him—if one wished to know exactly what theology of symbolic reality is based on the truth that the Logos, as Word of the Father, expresses the Father in the 'abbreviation' of his human nature and constitutes the symbol which communicates him to the world.

When we say that the Church is the persisting presence of the incarnate Word in space and time, we imply at once that it continues the symbolic function of the Logos in the world. To understand this statement correctly, we must consider two points. One, where a reality which is to be proclaimed in symbol, is a completely human one, and so has its social and existential (freely-chosen) aspect, the fact that the symbol is of a social and hence juridically determined nature is no proof that the symbol is merely in the nature of arbitrary sign and representation, and not a reality symbolic in itself. Where a free decision is to be proclaimed by the symbol and to be made in it, the juridical composition and the free establishment is precisely what is demanded by the very nature of a symbolic reality in this case and what is to be expected. A *non*-existential reality cannot express itself in this free and juridically constituted way, where the symbol is likewise a symbolic reality which contains the reality of the thing symbolized itself, because it has realized itself by passing over into the 'otherness' of the symbol. This would be contrary to the nature of the non-existential reality. But exactly the opposite is true when it is a matter of something which has been freely constituted by God himself and which has a social structure. When such a reality renders itself present in a freely constituted symbolism formed on social and juridical lines, the process is merely what its essence demands and is no objection to the presence of a symbolic reality.[13] But the Church, even as a reality tributary

[13] A profane example: when two spouses say their Yes before the legitimate authority (ecclesiastical or civil), this external, freely spoken word, which is to be uttered with certain formalities, is the symbolic reality. It is not a subsequent and extrinsic sign, which merely refers from outside to the 'thing' (the inward consent). The consent is given in the audible expression, so much so, that the intended effect (the permanent marriage bond) cannot be realized without this audible expression. The expression and the thing expressed really are related here like body and soul. They form an inner unity, where both elements are interdependent, though each in its own way. Still, this symbol, under which the thing symbolized is realized and made present, is something freely and juridically constituted. Hence whether a *'signum'* (*arbitraruim*) is a symbolic reality or the merely extrinsic representational symbol of a reality, cannot be decided by the mere fact that it is 'arbitrary'. This characteristic can actually be demanded by the nature of the thing symbolized, without detriment to the reality of the symbolism.

to the Spirit, is a free creation of the redemptive act of Christ and is a social entity. When therefore it is constituted along juridically established lines, the result does not contradict the fact that it is the symbolic reality of the presence of Christ, of his definitive work of salvation in the world and so of the redemption. Secondly, according to the Church's own teaching, especially as voiced by Leo XIII and Pius XII, the Church is not merely a social and juridical entity. The grace of salvation, the Holy Spirit himself, is of its essence. But this is to affirm that this symbol of the grace of God really contains what it signifies; that it is the primary sacrament[14] of the grace of God, which does not merely designate but really possesses what was brought definitively into the world by Christ: the irrevocable, eschatological grace of God which conquers triumphantly the guilt of man. The Church as indefectible, as Church of infallible truth and as Church of the sacraments, as *opus operatum* and as indestructibly holy as a whole, even in the subjective grace of men—by which it is not merely object but even motive of faith—really constitutes the full symbol of the fact that Christ has remained there as triumphant mercy.

The teaching *on the sacraments* is the classic place in which a theology of the symbol is put forward in general in Catholic theology. The sacraments make concrete and actual, for the life of the individual, the symbolic reality of the Church as the primary sacrament and therefore constitute at once, in keeping with the nature of this Church a symbolic reality. Thus the sacraments are expressly described in theology as 'sacred signs' of God's grace that is as, 'symbols', an expression which occurs expressly in this context.[15] The basic axioms of sacramental theology are well known: *Sacramenta efficiunt quod significant et significant quod efficiunt*. If these axioms are taken seriously, they point to that mutually supporting relationship which in our notion of the symbol intervenes between it and what is symbolized. Hence too in recent times theological efforts have been multiplied[16] which try to explain the causality of the sacraments in

[14] Cf. O. Semmelroth, *Die Kirche als Ursakrament* (Frankfurt 1953). The Church is of course the 'primary' sacrament in relation to the single sacraments, not to Christ. Cf. K. Rahner, *The Church and the Sacraments. Quaestiones Disputatae* 9 (London & New York 1963).

[15] Cf. e.g. *CIC Decret. Gratiani* III *de consecratione* II, c. *Sacrificium* 32 (ed. Friedberg I, 1324).

[16] Cf. esp. H. Schillebeeckx, *De sacramentale Heilseconomie* (Antwerp 1952); 'Sakramente als Organe der Gottbegegnung', in *Fragen der Theologie heute* (Einsiedeln 1957) 379–401. L. Monden, 'Symbooloorzakelijkheid als eigen Causaliteit van het Sacrament', *Bijdr.* 13 (1952) 277–285.

terms of the symbol. Theologians try to show that the function of cause and the function of sign in the sacraments are not linked merely *de facto* by an extrinsic decree of God, but that they have an intrinsic connexion by virtue of the nature of things—here, their symbolic character, rightly understood. *As* God's work of grace on man is accomplished (incarnates itself), it enters the spatio-temporal historicity of man as sacrament, and *as* it does so, it becomes active with regard to man, it constitutes itself. For as soon as one sees the sacraments as the action of *God* on man—even though it takes place through someone who acts as 'minister' by divine mandate and gives body to the action done to man and so renders it concretely present and active—then the question no longer arises as to how the sacramental sign 'works on'[17] God, and it is no longer possible to ask whether this sign produces grace by 'physical' or 'moral' causality. For at no stage can the sign be seen apart from what is signified, since it in understood *a priori* as a symbolic reality, which the signified itself brings about in order to be really present itself. But we can on the other hand see that the sacrament is precisely 'cause' of grace, *in so far as* it is its 'sign' and that the grace—seen as coming from God—is the cause of the sign, bringing it about and so alone making itself present. So the old axioms receive their very pregnant sense; *sacramenta gratiam efficiunt, quatenus eam significant*—where this *significatio* is always to be understood in the strict sense as a symbolic reality. So too: *sacramenta significant gratiam, quia eam efficiunt.* In a word, the grace of God constitutes itself actively present in the sacraments by creating their expression, their historical tangibility in space and time, which is its own symbol. That the juridically established structure of the sacraments does not run counter to this view of the sacraments as symbolic realities has already been explained equivalently, when the same objection was eliminated in the question of the Church as symbolic reality of the grace of God.

Further indications of the prevalent structure of Christian reality as a unity of reality and its symbolic reality must be omitted here. They can only be presented adequately when the bodily reality of man, and so his acts in the dimensions of space and time, history and society, are conceived

---

[17] Where, for reasons that are good in themselves, one rejects a 'physical causality' (of instrumental type), one soon finds oneself embarrassed. In the ordinary notion of the relationship between sign and grace, the sign almost necessarily becomes a '*titulus juris*' to grace with regard to *God*: it becomes a sort of 'causality' of the sacramental action directed towards God.

of as symbolic realities embodying his person and its primordial decisions. This would be the real starting-point for reaching an understanding of the historically attainable life of the Church as symbolic embodiment of the Spirit of God and of the inner history of the dialogue between God's free love and human freedom. The result of this would be to show that no adequate treatise can be written '*De Gratia*', unless it contributes to the theology of the symbol in the Christian history of salvation.

We call attention only in passing to the theology of the *sacred image* in Christianity.[18] An exact investigation into the history of this theology would no doubt have to call attention to a two-fold concept of image which is presented by tradition. One is more Aristotelian, and treats the image as an outward sign of a reality distinct from the image, a merely pedagogical indication provided for man as a being who knows through the senses. The other is more Platonic, and in this concept the image participates in the reality of the exemplar—brings about the real presence of the exemplar which dwells in the image. The ultimate reason why theological explanation of the image can vary so widely is the principle which we have already adduced; that there are in fact 'symbols', images, which are of the nature which is ascribed to sacred images in a more strongly Platonist theology. The only question is whether sacred images in the strict sense—statues and pictures—may be explained without more ado in terms of the symbol of the primordial type which we have discussed; or whether such images belong to the class of derivative and secondary symbols, which of course exist, as a result of relatively arbitrary arrangements and conventions. The question is further complicated by the fact that the images which portray the incarnate Logos and his saints— in contrast to God the Father, the 'invisible', and to some extent the angels—depict the human body, of which we shall have to say later that it is the natural symbol of man. It is not surprising therefore that ancient theology and that of the Byzantine Church should also have made this distinction between God the Father or the Trinity and the incarnate Logos when justifying the use of images, and did not consider everything as equally capable of being portrayed. However, we cannot go into this here. This set of questions was recalled only to indicate that a theology

[18] For the literature on the distinction which is only outlined here, cf. A. Grillmeier, *Der Logos am Kreuz* (Munich 1956) and *LTK* II², 458–460, 461–467 and note 3 above.

of symbols could find in the Greek theology of images support and confirmation for its more general considerations.

It might be thought that *eschatology* would be the part of theology
which treated of the final disappearance of the sign and hence of the
symbol, in favour of a naked immediacy of God with regard to the
creature—'face to face'. But this would once more be a position—this
time with regard to eschatology—in which the symbol is considered as an
extrinsic and accidental intermediary, something really outside the reality
transmitted through it, so that strictly speaking the thing could be attained
even without the symbol. But this presupposition is false, and it is still
false with regard to eschatology. For the true and proper symbol, being
an intrinsic moment of the thing itself has a function of mediation which
is not at all opposed in reality to the immediacy of what is meant by it,
but is a mediation to immediacy, if one may so formulate the actual facts
of the matter. In the end, of course, many signs and symbols will cease to
be; the institutional Church, the sacraments in the usual sense, the whole
historical succession of manifestations through which God continually
imparts himself to man, while he still travels far from the immediacy of
God's face, among images and likenesses. But the humanity of Christ will
have eternal significance for the immediacy of the *visio beata*.[19] The
incarnation of the Logos may well be considered as the indispensable
presupposition for strictly supernatural grace and glory,[20] so that the
gracious freedom of God with regard to these two realities does indeed
remain, but remains a freedom. And the dependence of the self-communication of God to the created spirit in glory with regard to the
incarnation does not indicate a merely moral relationship, arising from
the fact that the incarnate Logos once 'merited' this glory for us in time.
The relationship is a real and permanent ontological one. If we accept this
proposition (which cannot be propounded more fully now), it implies
that what has been affirmed of the symbolic function of the incarnate
Logos as Logos *and* man, also holds good for the perfected existence
of man, for his *eschata*. Eschatology also teaches us about the symbolic
reality which conveys to us the immediacy of God at the end; the Word
which became flesh.

[19] Cf. K. Rahner, 'The eternal significance of the humanity of Jesus for our relationship with God' in *Theological Investigations* III (London & Baltimore, 1967);
J. Alfaro, 'Cristo Revelador del Padre', *Greg.* 39 (1958) 222–270.

[20] This statement cannot of course be demonstrated here. We ask the reader simply
to accept it as at least a possible theological proposition.

We sum up the result of this second stage of our considerations in some affirmations:

3. The principle that the concept of symbol—in the sense defined in nos. 1 and 2—is an essential key-concept in all theological treatises, without which it is impossible to have a correct understanding of the subject-matter of the various treatises in themselves and in relation to other treatises.

4. The principle that God's salvific action on man, from its first foundations to its completion, always takes place in such a way that God himself is the reality of salvation,[21] because it is given to man and grasped by him[22] in the symbol, which does not represent an absent and merely promised reality but exhibits this reality as something present, by means of the symbol formed by it.

III. THE BODY AS SYMBOL OF MAN[23]

This preliminary draft and outline sketch of a possible theology of the symbol in general is still to be completed by some considerations on the body as the symbolic reality of man, in keeping with the general theme of

[21] Here we need not dwell on the fact that all mysteries of salvation in the really strict sense, and hence salvation itself, always consist of a self-communication of God by a type of quasi-formal causality, in contrast to the efficient causality whereby God creates *ex nihilo sui et subjecti* something distinct from himself. So in the hypostatic union, in uncreated grace (which in alone grace attains its true being, though sanctifying grace also implies in its concept a 'created' grace: cf. K. Rahner, *Schriften zur Theologie I*[3] [Einsiedeln 1958] 347–375: 'Zur scholastischen Begrifflichkeit der ungeschaffenen Gnade'. English translation, 'Some Implications of the scholastic concept of Uncreated Grace' in *Theological Investigations* I (London & Baltimore, Md. 1961) 319–346), and in the quasi-formal causality which the divine essence exerts in the *visio beata* on the spirit of man (as *quasi-species impressa*).

[22] The free acceptance by the spirit of man is also a *totally* human act, which is therefore also a bodily one and hence also takes place in the symbol; and so the act is also historical and social and hence also 'ecclesial'.

[23] Some bibliographical references from the most recent literature on the subject: L. Klages, *Grundlegung der Wissenschaft vom Ausdruck* (Leipzig [5]1936). Ph. Lersch, *Gesicht und Seele* (Munich 1932). A Gehlen, *Der Mensch. Seine Natur u.s. Stellung in d. Welt* (Bonn [4]1950). H. Plessner, *Lachen und Weinen. Eine Untersuchung nach den Grenzen menschlichen Verhaltens* (Sammlung Dalp 54, Berne [2]1950). A. Wenzl, *Das Leib-Seele-Problem im Lichte der neueren Theorien der physischen und seelischen Wirklichkeit* (Munich 1933). M. Picard, *Das Menschengesicht* (Munich [3]1929); *Grenzen der menschlichen Physionomie* (Zurich–Leipzig 1937). V. Poucel, *Mystique de la terre*, vol. 1, *Plaidoyer pour le corps* (Le Puy 1937). J. Bernhart, J. Schröteler, H. Muckermann,

which the theology of the symbol forms part. It is not the intention of this essay to investigate the relationship between the heart of the God-man and his love. This question concerns directly the meaning of the word 'heart' in devotion to the Sacred Heart, and the dogmatic enquiry into the object of this devotion. Hence it lies outside the scope of this essay. But in a general theology of the symbol which is meant to be a preparation for a theology of devotion to the heart of Jesus, we may be allowed to say something more explicit about the theology of the body as symbol of man. These considerations will bring us automatically to the threshold of the real theology of devotion to the heart of Jesus. This third part of our considerations takes up a subject which is a relatively minor part of the subject-matter already treated, and which has been touched on already, at least implicitly. But the attention given to this special subject is demanded or at least justified by the general theme of the book.

That the body can and may be considered as the symbol, that is, as the symbolic reality of man, follows at once from the Thomist doctrine that the soul is the substantial form of the body. When we do not take just any scholastic doctrine on the relationship of soul and body—all scholastics affirm, along with the Council of Vienna, that the soul is 'form'—but the strictly Thomist one, then the above affirmation is clear. For if we ascribe to the body an actual being, a positive content, which is *prior* to the reality of the soul, it would be impossible to see why *this* bodily entity should be still the expression and so the symbol of the soul. At best, we could call 'expression' what the soul, by means of its 'in-

---

J. Ternus, *Vom Wert des Leibes in Antike, Christentum und Anthropologie* (Salzburg 1936). K. Rahner, *Hörer des Wortes* (Munich 1941) 175–189; the same, *Geist in Welt* (Munich ²1957); the same, *Theological Investigations* II (London & Baltimore, Md. 1963), 265–281, and III (London & Baltimore, Md. 1967) 'Priest and Prophet' sections 1 & 2, and ' "Behold this heart": Preliminaries'. B. Welte, *Die Leiblichkeit des Menschen als Hinweis auf das christliche Heil*: Beuroner Hochschulwoche 1948 (Freiburg 1949) 77–109. M. Reding, 'Person, Individuum und Leiblichkeit', *Tüb. Th. Quartalschrift* 129 (1949) 195–203. W. Brugger, 'Die Verleiblichung des Wollens', *Schol.* 25 (1950) 248–253. G. Trapp, '*Humanae animae competit uniri corpori* (*S.Th.* I, q. 51, a 1c). Uberlegungen zu einer Philosophie des menschlichen Ausdrucks' *Schol.* 27 (1952) 382–399. L. Binswanger, *Grundformen und Erkenntnis des menschlichen Daseins* (Zürich ²1952). G. Siewerth, *Der Mensch und sein Leib* (Einsiedeln 1953). W. Stählin, *Vom Sinn des Leibes* (Stuttgart ³1953). *Anima* 9 (1954) 97–142, special number on the body. C. Tresmontant, *Biblisches Denken und hellenische Überlieferung* (Düsseldorf 1956) 62–77. J. B. Metz, 'Zur Metaphysik der menschlichen Leiblichkeit', *Arzt und Christ* 4 (1958) 78–84.

formation', makes of this prior entity which perseveres in its previous reality. At the very most, something *in* the body could be symbol of the soul, but not the body as such and as a whole. But man, strictly speaking, according to the clear doctrine of Thomism, is not composed of a soul and a body, but of a soul and *materia prima*. And this matter is of itself the strictly potential substratum of the substantial self-realization of the '*anima*' (which is its 'in-formation' in the metaphysical sense), which by imparting itself thus gives its reality to the passive possibility of *materia prima*, so that anything that is act (and reality) in this potentiality is precisely the soul. It follows at once that what we call body is nothing else than the actuality of the soul itself in the 'other' of *materia prima*, the 'otherness' produced by the soul itself, and hence its expression and symbol in the very sense which we have given to the term symbolic reality. This is not the place to defend this Thomist concept, which alone can guarantee the strict unity of man and the real humanness of his body, against the empirical objections which seem to prove that the material reality of the body has a greater degree of independence and a proper reality less tributary to the soul. But the '*forma corporis*' is polyvalent with regard to the accidental determinations of the body. Hence *which* precise possibilities *of its own* the soul realizes may well depend on the prior determinations of the concrete matter, precisely when all the determinations of the actual body are constituted by the soul. Once this is understood, one will see no insuperable objection in the ordinary difficulties brought up against the doctrine of the '*anima unica forma corporis*'. Hence we may formulate in our theory of symbols:

5. The principle that the body is the symbol of the soul, in as much as it is formed as the self-realization of the soul, though it is not adequately this, and the soul renders itself present and makes its 'appearance' in the body which is distinct from it.

A genuinely Thomist natural philosophy would however have to complete this strictly axiomatic statement by adding an essential complement, which is important in our particular context. We could formulate this addition as the sixth principle of our set of themes: in this unity of symbol and thing symbolized, constituted by soul and body, the individual parts of the body are more than mere pieces put together quantitatively to form the whole body; they are rather parts in so special a way that they also comprise in themselves the whole, though this is not true in the same strict way of each of the individual parts.

This supplementary statement must be explained to some extent. To make its understanding easier, there are several points which may be made. It is well known that in every human expression, mimetic, phonetic etc. in nature, the whole man is somehow present and expressing himself, though the expressive form is confined to start with to one portion of the body. Medical science which is concerned with the whole man, even when it does not try precisely to be 'psychosomatic', knows that it is never merely a particular organ that is sick, but always the whole man, so that the condition of the whole man is manifested in an organically localized illness, just as it is also to some extent determined by the illness. This is so true, that in psychogenic illnesses of the body, the most diverse illnesses of different organs can substitute vicariously for one another. It has always been more or less clearly known that the axiom: the part is only understandable in the whole, and the whole is in each part, was true above all of the human body. The axiom is represented even in Scripture, I Cor 12.12–26. In the light of this immediate experience, the scholastic doctrine, that the soul is fully present in each part of the body, being simple, comes to have a fuller and deeper meaning. It is not just that the simple substantial principle of a quantitatively extended entity must inevitably be as a whole in every part of this entity. The assertion also means that this substantial 'presence' of the soul implies that it determines and informs each part *as* part of the *whole*. And this once more cannot merely mean that the part is ordained, as regards its physiological function, to the service of the whole. It also implies that in a mysterious concentration of the symbolic function of the body, each part bears once more within itself the symbolic force and function of the whole, by contributing its part to the whole of the symbol.

But this propriety of each part of the body must be placed squarely in the perspective of its ontological origin: it must be seen as coming from the originating principle of the body and its parts in their unity and arrangement, that is, from the soul. And this 'soul' once more must not be understood—quite unscholastically—as a fragmentary portion of the whole man. It is the one originating source of the whole man, which explicitates itself in what we know as 'powers', faculties and acts of the soul (understood now empirically in the concrete), and which expresses itself in what we call the body of man (understood as animated by the soul). And this prior ontological unity of the whole man also appears in each part of the body; as the unity unfolds, it projects its proper manifestation, its symbol, into the part in question and thus possesses itself there as a whole, though not totally. This symbolic relationship of the part of the body to the original whole, from which the part derives, may vary in intensity in different parts of the body, but it can never be entirely absent wherever a given part is substantially informed by the soul. No doubt a material reality is either informed by the spiritual soul or it is not: from the purely abstract viewpoint, the actuation is '*in indivisibili*'. Yet differences clearly exist in the various 'parts' (organs, etc.) of the body with regard to their power of expression, their degree of belonging to the soul, their openness to the soul. We may therefore say that the organs privileged in this respect are those which according to the data of empirical observation are of irreplaceable value for the survival and perfection of the whole. It is a moot point whether biological and physiological necessity corresponds to symbolic function in like degree in the various parts, and the question is probably to be answered in the negative. But a proper answer would call for very difficult researches and considerations, involving questions of historical evolutionary descent, which cannot be undertaken here. But if we are right in what we said about the presence of the whole in the part and therefore about the symbolic function of the part, then we are also justified in saying that a word used to designate part of the human body (head, heart, breast, hand) in a symbolic sense, does not signify only the part as such, that is, as a quantitative, material piece of the whole body: it always signifies the one whole, composed of the symbol-generating origin and the material piece of reality which, as portion of the whole, single and symbolic body, bears within it under a certain aspect the symbolic function of the whole body.[24]

All discussion of the object and meaning of devotion to the heart of Jesus should take place in the perspective of a theology of symbolic reality. Such a theology has not yet been written, and the foregoing considerations do not replace it. Their only aim was to show—and this has perhaps been achieved in spite of their brevity and other defects— that such a theology of Christian symbolism could and should be written, because reality in general and above all, Christian reality is essentially and

---

[24] That is why we have tried to define the whole matter in hand in an analysis of the nature of the 'primary word'. Cf. K. Rahner, *Theological Investigations* III (London & Baltimore, Md. 1967); *Mission and Grace* III (London & New York 1966) 193–210.

from its origin a reality to whose self-constitution the 'symbol' necessarily belongs. There may be still a long way to go from such an insight
to the full understanding of the devotion to the heart of Jesus. But it
would be a way which would lead to a deeper understanding of this
devotion.

We refer in conclusion to one more point, which may help to show
how directly the ideas here put forward are connected with a theology of
devotion to the heart of Jesus, no matter how much is still to be done in
detail for the exploitation of the general theology of the symbol.

A large number of present-day theologians determine the object of
devotion to the heart of Jesus as follows. They presuppose 'a broader but
proper sense of the word heart' in general, and then take it that the word
designates 'the whole subject of the inner life' (including in fact the
bodily heart), the *cor ethicum*, the *principium fontale et subjectivum vitae
interioris moralis* (so Lempl, Noldin, Donat, Lercher, Solano, etc.).
Hence these theologians often reject the idea that the bodily heart of
Christ is revered in so far as it is the 'symbol' of the love of Christ (as
Nilles, Franzelin, Billot, Pesch, Galtier, Pohle-Gierens, Scheeben, etc.,
put it, in contrast to the other concept of heart). This older view—
whether it means that the bodily heart is revered because it is the symbol
of the love of Christ, or that the love of Christ is adored 'under' the
symbol of the heart of Christ—involves, according to Solano, etc., a
division of the single object of the devotion to the heart of Jesus, as it is
found in fact in the practice of piety and as it is expressed in the teachings
of the magisterium. The unity of the object is said to be saved only by
over-subtle explanations.

Hence the first-named group of theologians reject more or less definitely
the expression, that the heart is the symbol of the love of Christ. So for
instance Solano, who does so most clearly.[25] But then this view is confronted with a difficulty; even the most recent pronouncements of the
magisterium have no difficulty in speaking of the heart as the 'symbol'
(so *'Haurietis aquas'*). Hence Solano is forced to explain; *'Encyclica
"Haurietis aquas" terminologiam "Symboli" quidem conservat, nec tamen
putamus hoc magisterii documentum subtiliorem hanc questionem voluisse
tangere, quae et solum modum concipiendi spectat et a recentissimis auctoribus
diversimode iudicatur'* ('The Encyclical retains the term "symbol", but we

[25] Cf. Patres S. J. . . . in Hispania Professores, *Sacrae Theologiae Summa* III
(Madrid ³1956) 224f. (n. 542f.); 237 (n. 566).

do not think this document of the magisterium wished to deal with the more subtle question involved here, which has to do only with the manner in which it is understood and which is solved in different ways by modern authors'). There is no great objection, from the point of view of the formal principles of interpreting documents of the magisterium, to this way of solving the difficulty in Solano's position, which is supported by serious arguments, by the texts of the ecclesiastical devotion to the heart of Jesus, and by recent authors. But it is a pity that one should feel bound to come into conflict, apparently at least, with the terminology of the Encyclical, for the sake of this good position. In reality, the apparent contradiction arises only from the fact that Lercher, Solano etc. consider only the concept of symbol where the symbol and the thing symbolized are only extrinsically ordained to one another. But if one presupposes the concept of symbol as it has been developed in these pages, and applies it to the (bodily) heart of Jesus, it follows at once that one can accept the position of Lercher, Solano, etc., and still have no difficulty in speaking of the 'heart' as a symbol, as the Encyclical does. In a real theology of the symbol, based on the fundamental truths of Christianity, a symbol is not something separate from the symbolized (or different, but really or mentally united with the symbolized by a mere process of addition), which indicates the object but does not contain it. On the contrary, the symbol is the reality, constituted by the thing symbolized as an inner moment of moment of itself, which reveals and proclaims the thing symbolized, and is itself full of the thing symbolized, being its concrete form of existence. If this concept of symbol is presupposed, then 'heart' means exactly what the authors in question mean by their broader but still proper concept; the inner centre of the person, which realizes itself and expresses itself in the bodily existence. And one can still describe the bodily heart as symbol of the whole (since it is an inner element of this whole) and hence retain the terminology of the Encyclical. When understood in a sense which it does not impose but still leaves free, it is quite adequate to the matter it deals with.

We note on the other hand that in medieval tradition and in St Margaret Mary, 'heart' is used spontaneously in the broad sense; it does not designate simply the 'bodily heart', nor does it designate simply the 'inwardness' of Christ in the metaphorical sense. It is used as a 'primordial word' of religious speech, and signifies from the start the unity of both— a unity which has not to be created subsequently, as when an object is linked to a sign exterior to it as its symbolic representation. The unity is more original than the distinction, because the symbol is a distinct and yet intrinsic moment of the reality as it manifests itself. But then this older terminology is perfectly justified by the ontological and theological considerations which we have put forward. And this is the only way by which devotion to the heart of Jesus can escape the otherwise fatal question, as to why one cannot revere the love of Christ, to which one has after all immediate access, without making a special effort to think expressly of the 'bodily heart'. Reality and its appearance in the flesh are for ever one in Christianity, inconfused and inseparable. The reality of the divine self-communication creates for itself its immediacy by constituting itself present in the symbol, which does not divide as it mediates but unites immediately, because the true symbol is united with the thing symbolized, since the latter constitutes the former as its own self-realization. This basic structure of all Christianity, which a theology of the symbol should investigate, is found once more in the devotion to the heart of Jesus, and is its perpetual justification.

10

THE WORD AND THE EUCHARIST

THIS investigation is entitled 'The Word and the Eucharist', meaning the question which is usually discussed under the more general heading of 'Word and Sacrament', and it is an invitation to treat the general question in the perspective of the sacrament of the altar. But the wider question and its solution cannot be simply taken as known. And the problems in question have only been given notable place in Catholic theology quite recently, while a unanimous answer is still lacking. It seems then that we should first treat the general question and then institute the more particular enquiry about the relationship between the word of God and the central sacrament of the Church. This gives us the headings for the two parts of our investigation.

I. THE WORD AND THE SACRAMENT IN GENERAL

When we discuss the relationship between these two things, the word in question is of course the word of God, as it appears in the preaching of the Church. The word of God is thus displayed at once as a word which is also the word of man, on the lips of men who are charged by the Church to deliver this word to men. But the Church, though preaching by divine command, is always likewise the hearer—even in those to whom the word has been entrusted for preaching—and hence the believer. Thus the word of God always comes as the word that is *heard* and *believed*, the word that is preached and attested because believed. Thus it is always praise of God directed to God, who gave this word to the Church to be at once heard and preached by the Church.

When the word is thus understood as the word of God on the lips of the Church, the Church which believes and praises, preaches and has authority, the question arises at once of how the word stands with regard to the sacraments in the Church. The reasons are both intrinsic to the case and conditioned by the situation. First, the intrinsic reasons. As soon as one asks oneself what this word of God in the Church precisely is, how it works, how God speaks in it, whom it addresses, what it should accomplish in the hearer, what speakers and hearers it presupposes and constitutes, a number of affirmations must be made—on the basis of Scripture and by the nature of the case—which, as we shall see later, have an astonishing similarity, to say no more, with the affirmations generally used to describe the sacraments. And this is the real reason for enquiring into the relationship of word and sacrament. They are so like each other that one cannot but ask what is the reason for their similarity and what is the possibility of making a distinction between them in spite of, or indeed because of their similarity and its cause. Otherwise there can be no real theological understanding of the matters in question. Then there is another reason. Word and sacrament constitute the Church. Or to put it more exactly: the power to preach the word of God by the authority of God and of his Christ, and the power to administer the sacraments to men are the two basic powers of the Church which are constitutive of its essence. We need not here go into the well-known controversy as to whether two or three basic *'potestates'* are to be distinguished in the Church: the *potestas ordinis* and *iurisdictionis*, or the power of teaching, governing and sanctifying. In any case, the power of the sacrament and the word characterize fundamentally the nature of the Church. But these two powers cannot simply exist side by side, without relation to each other, if they constitute the one Church as the one presence of the one salvation in the one Christ. Thus ecclesiology itself poses the question of the relationship of word and sacrament. And finally, the question is suggested by the teaching on the sacraments. We are accustomed to consider the 'word' as a constitutive and indeed the formal, that is to say, decisive element of the sacramental sign. If we are not to remain on the surface of things, we cannot treat this word, which occurs in the middle of the sacramental action itself, as of no particular import: it must be the word addressed to us by the authority of God himself, the word which Christ himself speaks in us and through us, the word which is active and effective of what it signifies because it is his word, the word which renders present what it proclaims. Here again it is impossible to avoid the question as to how this word is actually related to the authoritative word of Christ which is heard elsewhere in the Church.

In view of all this, it is really astonishing that we Catholics provide no space, no systematic place for a theology of the word in the average theology of our schools, in the Latin manuals, etc. We speak in fundamental theology or apologetics of the magisterium of the Church, of the powers which the Church received from Christ as it was made teacher of revelation. But this section of fundamental theology proceeds to speak directly only of the Church. The word of God is discussed only *in obliquo*. But even here the word is always restricted silently, and hence all the more effectively, to a matter of doctrines. It is the word which *teaches* something, the true and binding word 'about' something, the word which makes a statement about something. It is not treated as the word in which the reality itself draws nigh and announces itself and constitutes itself present. Thus the treatise on the magisterium of the Church cannot be considered as fully equivalent to a treatise '*De Verbo divino*'. Even less is said of set purpose in the treatise on the sacraments in general, about the relation between word and sacrament. Thus a theme which appears to be highly relevant has remained to a great extent unnoticed in the Catholic theology of the last few hundred years.

The present situation of Catholic theology seems however to be changing all this. There are many reasons for the new approach, which can only be briefly signalled here. Present-day preaching is in such straits that it feels the need of a theology of preaching and not merely of counsels of a psychological and pedagogical type bearing on rhetoric and homiletics. But a theology of preaching cannot but force us to take up a theology of the annunciation of the word of God. Biblical theology has ceased to regard itself as the mere transmitter of proof-texts for the theses laid down by the theology of the schools. As it listens more attentively to Scripture itself, it can no longer overlook the fact that the Old Testament and above all the New have more to say about the living, efficacious, mighty and creative word of God than the standard theses of the theology of the schools has grown accustomed to say about it. It is significant that in the index to Denzinger, for instance, there is no section on 'The Word of God': the section '*De Revelatione*' is too much concerned *a priori* with doctrine to be considered an equivalent. We note here the same phenomenon which may also be observed in fundamental theology: in contrast to present-day Protestant *and* Catholic biblical theology, revelation is always taken in the theology of the schools as a purely doctrinal revelation couched in statements, not as a revelatory action and event, in which God acts creatively to bestow grace upon men, uttering his word in it and for it, as in inner moment of this action on man—or in which, to put it biblically, the action is the word, because God's word must produce what it says.

So too the present-day discussion on grace is leaving aside a too material concept of grace to stress its personal element—primarily understood as the uncreated self-communication of God—and is thus finding an approach to the word of God and a more comprehensive understanding of it, regarding it as the means whereby a person discloses himself and freely imparts himself to another. Further, as the theology of the Greek Fathers comes into its own, the incarnation itself is being regarded as a moment of the redemption, and not merely as the act whereby someone is placed in a position where he can be redeemer, if he wills and dedicates himself to the task by a completely new act, so to speak. Thus the advent of the incarnate Logos of the Father is being almost inevitably seen as the most radical case of a salvific, creative word of God in general, which calls for a theology of the word of God as a soteriological entity in general. This would be even clearer, if the incarnation of the Logos were not regarded as the incarnation of just any one of the three divine persons, so that any other of them could just as well have become man, but as the incarnation of the Word precisely and exactly *as* such, since on account of his inner-trinitarian propriety it is precisely he who becomes man and who alone can do so.

The closer communication which exists once more today between Catholic and Protestant theologians also forces us to re-consider a theology of the word. Catholic theology, no more than the magisterium, has never been able to accept the formula, that the fellowship of Protestant Christians constitutes the Church of the word while we Catholics are the Church of the sacraments. Among the Protestants of the centuries since the Enlightenment, preaching (thanks to a genuinely Protestant impulse) was almost everything, and the sacraments almost just something like an appendix to the preaching of the pure doctrine, a relic explicable as no more than a traditional survival. And for all practical purposes, Catholics mostly regarded all preaching merely as the unavoidable preparation for the sacraments (and Christian life), while the sacraments were taken to be totally different from the word, since of course they contained no 'teaching' 'about something'. But Protestant theology is now beginning to take the sacraments seriously again, and to see their essential and irreplaceable significance for Christian existence. And we Catholics are reflecting more expressly on the fact that we are the Church of the word of God, which does not merely mean that the Church is God's class-room where Christians are taught how to behave if they are in fact to receive the sacraments and lead decent lives.

What is desired therefore is a theology of the word in which its essence as word of God in the Church is clearly brought out. All we shall be concerned with here is to note the characteristics of the word which are of immediate significance for the intrinsic relationship of word and sacrament. Even in this restricted field, it is obvious that we cannot really develop the theology of the word here and establish it from theological sources. We shall only try to draw up a list of theses in which at least the most important points are stated, and then indicate where perhaps the theological foundation for the theses in question may be found.

1. The word of God is uttered by the Church, where it is preserved inviolate in its entirety, and necessarily so, in its character of the word of *God*. This statement should be clear. To deny it would be to deny the essence of the Church, in which and through which (and not passing by it) Christ makes his message contemporary to all ages as the word of God, the Church through which he is present to us in his own mission.

2. This word of God in the Church is an inner moment of God's salvific action on man. Salvation is indeed the work of God, but this work of God is not totally identifiable with the word of God which comes in human words, in so far as it comes in human words. For God's salvific action on man is not merely a forensic imputation of the justice of Christ. And it is not merely the announcement of a purely future act of God. Nor is it constituted merely by man's faith, however this is to be further interpreted. It is a true, real, creative action of God in grace, which renews man interiorly by making him participate in the divine nature—all of which, being the condition of possibility of a salutary action on the part of man, is prior, at least logically, to such *action* of man. But this act whereby man is created anew by God through his prevenient gift, cannot take place, in the case of a man actively exercising his personal freedom, without man's personally participating in this new creation in faith, hope and love: indeed, man's act is an intrinsic moment of the whole process. This follows at once from the fact that not only the grace of divinization, but even the *acceptance* of this gift must according to all theological sources be characterized as grace. Hence the acceptance of the divine gift of justification is itself part of the gift, in so far as this

grace works as efficacious grace to bring about the act of acceptance in its entity and works as elevating grace to bring it about in its quality. It follows that the free, personal consent must be brought about as such by God, that is, as a spiritual, personal act, as an act which knows itself as an act of acceptance. But this prevenient grace of God, which constitutes man's act in its reality and bestows on it its quality, is to be qualified as enlightenment and inspiration according to the theological sources. Hence it is by definition 'word', that is, spiritual self-communication of God to the creature, especially as this grace is not this or that created reality, but the real self-communication of God in 'uncreated' grace and— at least according to Thomistic doctrine—every entitatively supernatural grace creates a conscious condition of consciousness in man by means of its supernatural formal object, which cannot be brought about by any purely natural object. But this inward self-communication of God, 'verbal' though it is in itself, cannot alone be adequate for the normal and fully developed act of its acceptance. Of itself it would remain to a certain extent merely a transcendental, unobjectivated knowledge of this gracious act of God on man, which could not be brought into the region of reflective consciousness. That might be enough, under certain circumstances, for a salutary act (even as an act of faith with regard to a 'revelation'), a point we shall not deal with here: but this inner word of grace alone cannot make it possible for man to have a developed, objectivated, fully conscious understanding of himself as the believing recipient of the divine self-communication. For if the verbal communication of God was already complete in the inner word of grace, in the 'illumination' by interior grace alone, then man would always and essentially accomplish his salvation only in the non-reflective, unobjectivated transcendence of his being, while the dimension of worldly objects and categories remained outside the scope of salutary acts, and man would be claimed by God only in the 'fine point' of his soul, in his secret profundities, but not in the whole width of his being with all its dimensions. Or if not, man would already be absolutely certain of his state of grace and ultimately of the *visio beatifica*: because he could develop merely from the depths of his conscious grace the whole content of this blessing, since the adequate presentation of the inner divinization to consciousness is by definition '*visio beatifica*'. Further, if things were so man would not be claimed by the event of salvation in his social dimension. But if man is essentially and primordially a being in a community, even in the dimension of the individual salutary decision, then knowledge of his grace cannot be adequately given by his inner experience of grace alone: it must also come to him from without, though not exclusively, from the world, from the community, from the history of salvation which is a social event historically transmitted. But this means that the proclamation of the word of God, that is, the word in so far as it is conveyed by the *historical*, external salvific act of God as an intrinsic moment of this act and by the community of believers, belongs necessarily to the inner moments of God's salvific *action* on man.

3. As an inner moment of this salvific action of God, the word shares in the special character of the salvific action of God in Christ (and the Church). To understand this statement, we must recall the essential connexion between the inner word of grace and the external, historical, social ('ecclesiastical') word of revelation. Both are essentially connected and are still ordained to one another, even where there is (perhaps) in fact a separation between the two of them in a given individual destiny—a point which cannot be dealt with here. The external, historical word expounds the inner one, brings it to the light of consciousness in the categories of human understanding, compels man definitely to take a decision with regard to the inner word, transposes the inner grace of man into the dimension of the community and renders it present there, makes possible the insertion of grace into the external, historical field of human life. And on the other hand: it is only the inner grace, as light of faith and inward connaturality with God, that makes it possible for man to hear the external, historical word of God strictly *as* the word of God, without subjecting it to the *a priori* of his own human spirit and thereby debasing it. In a word, for the full normal accomplishment of the personal self-disclosure of God to the personally actualized man, the inner word of grace and the external historical word come together, as the mutually complementary moments of the one word of God to man. From which it follows that this one word is in itself an action of God on man in grace, an element of his revelation in acts. Hence it participates inevitably in the character of the salvific action of God on man in Christ. Assertions about God's salvific action on man are of their nature assertions about the word of God—understood as two-fold in the unity of the inner and the outward word. On this basis, the next thesis can be understood as the development of the thesis just put forward.

4. This word of God (as inner moment of the salvific action of God on

man and so with it and because of it) is the salutary word which brings with it what it affirms. It is itself therefore salvific event, which, in its outward, historical and social aspect, displays what happens in it and under it, and brings about what it displays. It renders the grace of God present.

To prevent the reader rejecting the thesis at once, on the ground that it is exactly the definition of a sacrament, we must anticipate our next thesis to some extent. There it will be said that the actual effectiveness of the word of God is essentially variable, and hence the nature of the word of God in the thesis just stated is defined according to its most intensive realization as it well may be, without denying or obscuring the fact that this realization can take place at a very low potential—which is the usual basis on which Catholic theology considers the word of God in the Church. But it will also be said that the full and adequate realization of this definition of the word of God will prove to be what we call sacraments in Catholic theology. For the moment then let us proceed to outline and explain our justification of this definition of the word of God in the Church as the presence of the act of God's salvation of men in the Church. Taking for granted the proof to be given later, that the proposed definition of the word of God in general will not do detriment to the nature, particularities and special position of the sacraments, the word of God itself will here be explained as the word which displays itself effectively, as the presence of the action of God on man.

First however an explanation of the logic of the matter. Two things can exist side by side, each being by its essence a completely different entity. And the nature in each case can be to some extent statistically fixed and unchangeable, so that it exists in the way it is and must be according to its essence, or it cannot exist at all. But an essence may also be intrinsically changeable; the same essence (being, for instance, life, spirit, dignity, beauty and so on) can be realized in ways which not only differ specifically, but are only analogously alike. In this case it is perfectly justifiable and methodically unobjectionable—though perhaps not always strictly called for—to describe the thing in question in terms of the supreme term of the analogy, its highest form of realization (if this is accessible and known), and to take the other, secondary attributions as *deficient* manners of the realization of the thing in question (supposing, of course, one can explain how and why such deficient realizations of the essence came about). This is to be borne in mind in what follows.

We have now to prove that the word of God, in its full, original sense, is not to be taken as a set of doctrinal propositions 'about something': it is not just the intellectual description of something which exists and is available completely independently of this doctrinal instruction. It is a revelatory, actualizing word, in which and under which alone the thing designated is present, in a reciprocal relationship of such a kind that the word is formed by the thing which thus comes, and the thing comes by making itself thus audible. Proof of this may be offered in very different ways.

The first and decisive proof would be that the sacred scripture of the Old and New Testament understands the concept of 'the word' in this way. It seems to me possible to affirm that present-day biblical theology teaches this thesis expressly, though it does not seem to trouble itself much about the question of how the thesis can be reconciled with the doctrine of the magisterium on the sacraments. The word of God —on the lips of the preaching Church as elsewhere—is not '*didache*', (teaching), from beginning to end, but proclamation in which the arrival of the thing proclaimed itself takes place. It is the mighty, creative *dabar* (word), of God to man, the way in which the reality which is being proclaimed discloses itself, and thereby and thus becomes present to us, coming forth itself from its divine concealment and coming where *we* are for the very first time. Detailed proof of this may be omitted, since this view is that of Catholic biblical theology at the present day, to say nothing of Protestants.

But even if the dogmatic theologian does not find the biblical theology of the exegetes entirely convincing, he has data of his own, in a form readily available even in the theology of the schools, which can explain this thesis of the revelatory efficacity of the word of God. Every dogmatic theologian is actually familiar with the matter in question, even though in other terms, at least when he starts with the hearing of the word in faith. We all say that the message of faith, the proclamation of the word of God, is directed to believing ears, and is only fully intelligible there. But such hearing in faith can only take place in the connaturality with the word of God which comes through grace. This grace of hearing in faith and love and of responding in a fully human way is not just any aid which is given to produce finally a merely human act: it is the acceptance of justification in the self-communication of God which takes place by virtue of the *reality* here present by its being proclaimed and accepted. Hence at least the message heard in faith is for every dogmatic theologian not just the hearing of a statement about something, but the reception of the reality itself about which the audible statement is made—the reality which causes its communication to be heard and lovingly believed. But since the message of faith is preached by God's authority and command, to summons man imperatively and demand from him, in the name of God, a faith which he can only have by God's grace, the message is in itself a clear assurance from God that he is offering the possibility of faith and hence the reality of what is believed, which he desires to give as truly as he offers it. For if it is true that God never refuses the grace for a salutary act, where he demands the salutary act as the moral duty of man, it is also dogmatically certain that where the moral obligation of faith arises from the preaching of the faith, and in so far as it arises, grace too is offered, which is the reality of what is preached. Thus the word of God, as preached and imperative, is the coming of what is preached, as the possibility of the acceptance of the reality itself which is preached. We need not dwell on the fact that in this preaching it is never a matter of just individual truths of a historic nature on their own. All the individual truths are uttered and held as elements of the one announcement in which God proclaims his own self-communication to the world and to each individual in Christ Jesus. And thus of course the last foolish objection is excluded, which says that everything that is preached does not itself become reality in the hearer as he hears the word which discloses it. For the one, actual, permanent reality of salvation which implies the individual elements is in fact uttered: offered in the word, it is really present and accepted in the hearing of faith and love, and in it everything historical and purely objective belonging to it which is a moment of this real salvation; anything else is actualized only in so far as it is the presupposition and historical condition of this reality.

With this we must end the very summary outline of the possible proofs of this thesis. It is in itself very obvious. However, in Catholic theology it is mostly dealt with under other headings and in other perspectives, and hence at first sight the thesis may appear strange and unusual. Let us take just one example to clarify the matter. A sinner hears the authoritative word of the Church calling him to repentance. Can we say that if he hears and accepts this word of God through the Church in faith and love, the event of God's offer of the grace of repentance infallibly takes place in him—though of course there is no absolute certainty about the *de facto* fulfilment of these conditions, any more than there is about the necessary dispositions for the sacraments? Can we say that then there is infallibly a repentance which on account of the universal salvific will of God is not just the subjective attitude of the man on the human plane, but God's action on him, which consists of the fact that in the communication of sanctifying grace, which is fundamentally God himself, God himself is accepted as he who confers salvation? This can and must be affirmed. It is basically no more than a simple truth of our faith. But this means that in this efficacious preaching of the word of God, that which is preached takes on the character of an event. It means that the grace of God is not merely spoken of, but takes place as an event in this utterance. The word which speaks of grace and grace itself must then always be distinguished as moments of a total process, because they do not simply coincide, any more than the efficacious sacramental sign is simply identical with the grace which it signifies and produces. But this does not change the fact that word and reality, in contrast to ordinary human speech, are essentially related to one another and form a unity. The word of preaching is the efficacious proclamation which brings about what it speaks of, the grace announced: it is truly word of life, creative word of God.

5. To avoid misunderstandings, however, we must at once add another thesis: this word, which is in the nature of an event and an exhibition, takes place in the Church in essentially varying degrees of concentration and intensity. The concept of word of God in the Church which we have arrived at is analogous: it is capable of and subject to inner changes. This is something with which we are all familiar, if we consider this word with regard to its summons to *belief*. From *this* point of view we are all perfectly familiar with the intrinsic changeableness of the concept. We all affirm that all words of truth in the Church have not the same binding force. They have not all the same absolute character. There are words of truth in the Church which demand from man the absolute assent of his faith and hence are also absolutely linked with the reality of the matter attested. But there are also words in the Church which certainly mean to make a statement, impart truth, present realities to men's minds, but still do not claim and guarantee this ultimately indissoluble bond with the thing intended. They claim our assent in certain circumstances, and rightly so, because without them the truths affirmed absolutely would not be assimilable in the actual exercise of the knowledge of truth. But they are assertions where the Church does not actualize and exercise fully and

entirely its character as the definitive eschatological presence and dis-
closure of truth—does not pledge its official teaching infallibility, as we
say. We are used to giving norms for distinguishing between one word
of truth and another, precisely because we rightly see the two in the *one*
perspective. They are not simply disparate attestations of the truth. They
are analogous modifications of the one word of truth, which in the first
case attains a full and radical realization of its essence, but in the second
appears to some extent in a provisional, secondary, subsidiary and
deficient guise, in which it serves, makes possible, prepares for and pro-
tects the first truth in question. Thus as regards the word of God in the
Church, we are quite familiar with the analogous nature of this concept,
which lends the essence of the word an inner mutability. But we must say
the same of the word of God as the revelatory presence of that which is
announced in it. The coming and presence of God in his word in the
Church as he proclaims himself is not always simply the same. There are
degrees. And we know these degrees, since we say for instance that one
has the grace of infused faith and another has also the grace of infused
charity and so justification itself. By speaking in this way, we make
distinctions, though in other words, between the degrees of God's self-
communication to men, or of the existential acceptance of this self-
communication by men. And these are in fact degrees of how the word of
God makes the reality present. The reality in question always strives for
a single, all-embracing goal: which is that God should bestow himself
totally on man, in man's total acceptance, through and in love which
justifies, of this self-surrendering love of God. But this single and absolute
goal of grace is only reached by stages in finite man who is involved in
history and so attains only by a gradual process the single totality of his
life. (The coming of justification is a historical process, which post-
Trindentine theology was correct in considering a matter of phases, unlike
the medieval doctrine which saw it more statically—though our present-
day theology is now in great danger of reducing the whole process to a
mere temporal succession of disparate single acts, which would be to
atomize the process.) And the same historicity and phased activity is also
to be predicated of the word of God. It can realize its essence only in a
historical process, it is not always and at every moment fully its whole
self: it grows, it *becomes* what it is and must be, it can have its deficient,
provisional and preparatory phases and moments. It is not possible here to
depict the causes and types of the inner changes in the being of the word

of God in the Church and in the process of Christian existence, to measure
so to speak the extent of possible variation in the forms taken by the word
of God. Various elements contribute to determine the actual degree of
concentration and intensity of the word of God in each case, and hence
that of the coming of what is preached and the certainty of this efficacious
presence alike. Since it is essentially a matter of the word uttered in the
dialogue between God–Christ in the Church on the one hand, and the
human hearer on the other, both sides share in these moments: the difference in the content of the utterance; the consequent difference in its
importance; the varying degrees of commitment on the side of the Church;
the essential difference of the existential import of the situation on the side
of the hearers, where this word is uttered as God's word and redemptive
answer to the given situation; the difference in the ecclesiological importance of this dialogue between the Church (as bearer of the word of
Christ and abiding presence of his word of grace in the world) and man
as member of this Church, a difference on which again depend in part the
varying degrees of commitment of the Church in the proclamation of this
word; the difference in the concrete recipients of the word—as for instance
when the Church as a whole or an individual in his most intimate and
unique quest of salvation is addressed, or again, when neither is in question, but something provisional and intermediate, through which the
word inevitably becomes something like pure teaching; these and other
elements, which would have to be worked out, make for the inner varia-
bility of the one essence of the word of God in the Church.

In the light of the foregoing, it might perhaps be possible to work out
a fundamental analysis of the meaning of the many different expressions
used in Scripture to designate the word of God. They all point to the one
essence of this word, but signify this essence in its inner changes: to
speak prophetically, to teach, to exhort, to instruct, to edify, to console,
to persuade, to announce, to transmit, to recall, to utter the (sacramental)
word of life, to judge, to give testimony, etc. But we cannot go into this
here. We turn at once to the supreme and most intensive realization of the
essence of the word, the sacramental word. Hence our next thesis is as
follows:

6. The supreme realization of the efficacious word of God, as the coming
of the salvific action of God in the radical commitment of the Church
(that is, as the Church's own, full actualization), in the situations decisive
for the individual's salvation, is the sacrament and only the sacrament.

Before we try to explain this thesis and indicate its justification to some
extent, some preliminary remarks are called for. To begin with: an
authoritative and effective word, which brings about something real (as
for instance in worldly matters, the official promulgation of a law, the
last will and testament, etc.), is by nature completely dependent on its
being couched in the form ordained by the ultimate author of its
efficacious character. If something of a doctrinal nature is to be imparted
which is independent of the means of communication, the validity of the
communication need only depend on the fact that the matter is correctly
expressed and proposed intelligibly to the hearer. More is obviously
demanded in the case of a 'practical', operative word which not merely
affirms something but constitutes it. And this overplus can be determined,
not merely by the nature of things, but also by the positive institution of
the speaker from whom the constitutive force of the word is derived.
Further: we are accustomed when speaking of the sacraments to distinguish between the word and the element, or in hylomorphic terms,
between matter and form. But this distinction, correct though it be in
itself, ought not obscure the fact that both elements, the word and the
sacramental action, participate in the symbolic character of the sacrament
and hence in its quality of being *word*. The sacramental action too has the
character of a word. It designates something, it expresses something, it
reveals something that is of itself hidden. To put it briefly, it too is a
word. Hence it is not at all surprising that the distinction between matter
and form, action and word, can be applied only very artificially in some
sacraments. In the sacraments of penance and marriage there are only
words. The sacramental sign consists solely of these words, which is not
contrary to the nature of the sacrament, because its nature is to be an
efficacious sign, an expressivity which produces and presents what is
rendered perceptible. Thus it is perfectly legitimate and objectively
perfectly justifiable to subsume the whole sacrament under the concept
of the efficacious *word*. In some sacraments this efficacious word must be
pronounced in a form which includes the element of the ritual action.
This is due to the positive decree of him who institutes the efficacious
word. One can of course ask what are the intrinsic reasons why in these
cases, by the will of Christ, the significant word should have this still
more bodily form. These reasons must surely be important and easy to
find and will ultimately stem from the incarnational character of Christian
salvation as a whole. But this does not change the fact that basically a

sacrament is and remains an efficacious *word*. For signs and words, from the metaphysical and theological point of view, are of exactly the same nature: especially as in all the sacraments we have signs which, in so far as they are sacramental, always go back to a positive institution of Christ. In this sense they are not simply an intrinsic echo of the thing which is rendered audible. They are all freely created signs, in the same sense that 'words' are, which are not merely signs of the thing, but likewise always signs of the free personal self-disclosure of a person, in contrast to things, which have always automatically made themselves known and cannot be closed in on themselves. In other words: since grace is the free personal self-communication of God, its divulgation is always free and personal and hence essentially word. Thus the whole sign of grace, no matter what form it takes, must partake of the character of the *word*.

In the relationship of matter and form in the sacraments, we must not overlook the following: it is not true and it cannot be true that the material element in the sacrament (water, ablution, etc.) is decisive. The ultimate reason for this is easily seen. One could formulate it as the following thesis: in the case of strictly supernatural realities (which ultimately consist of the gratuitous, personal and radical self-communication of God in his own trinitarian glory), a purely natural thing in the nature of an *object* can never function as a sign in such a way that the supernatural reality could be attained through it alone. Whenever a reality of the world is to be sign, indication and historical presence of a strictly supernatural reality, it can be so only when the spiritual, transcendental ('subjective') openness and orientation of man, pointing beyond the finite to God himself, becomes an intrinsically constitutive element of this sign. But this implies that supernatural reality can display itself only through the medium of the human *word*, as long as it cannot present itself in its own proper reality, which is basically in the immediate vision of God. For a more exact proof of this thesis I may perhaps be allowed to refer readers to the discussion in my book 'Hörer des Wortes' (Hearers of the Word). In any case, it is all to be found ultimately in the first Vatican Council, session 3, chapter 2, where it is taught that a divine revelation in *words*, in contrast to the natural revelation through created things, is absolutely *necessary*, if man is ordained to a *supernatural* end. Man can therefore be informed of this end only by the word, not by means of natural objects. It follows that in the manifestation of grace which is called the sacrament, the word is necessarily and inevitably the decisive element: an objective element in the nature of a thing only enters this manifestation of the supernatural in so far as it is absorbed into this utterance in the word.

Hence there can be no objection, at least on principle, to the effort to determine the nature of the sacraments from their quality of 'word'. The only question is whether such an effort can succeed in delimiting, 'defining' their essence in contradistinction to other words in the Church. The effort is made in the thesis here put forward.

But before we try to explain the thesis itself, we must consider briefly some efforts which show a certain similarity to our own, because these definitions too start from the insight gained by biblical theology into the character of event and efficacity belonging to the word of God in the Church: and thus they are faced with the problem which is otherwise not felt very keenly in Catholic theology—how the sacraments are to be distinguished from the word of God elsewhere, since God's word after all is absolutely efficacious of itself. The difficulty which all these efforts have to meet, and ours too, is the doctrine of the Council of Trent. Omitting all reflexions on the theology of the word, which is rather surprising, in view of the Protestant doctrine, the Council declares that the sacraments (and eventually, the desire for them) are the source of the grace of justification, and hence are absolutely necessary (*necessitate medii*), where this doctrine, taken in the strict sense, is no doubt to be understood rather *sensu exclusivo* than merely *sensu positivo*. (Cf. e.g. Denzinger 843a: all true justice begins, grows and is restored through the sacraments.)

It is true that according to the mind of the Council, apart from the question of the efficaciousness of the word of God in general as a salvific event, its statement about the exclusiveness of the sacraments is to be taken *cum grano salis*. For the Council mentions for instance a growth in grace which can be merited apart from the sacraments, which is a growth in the grace of justification. The Council mentions actual graces which precede sacramental justification. And when it says that under certain circumstances the sacrament can be replaced by the desire for it, it certainly does not—as St Thomas would—affirm that the sacrament works by anticipation. It ascribes this justifying effect to the subjective faith and love of man himself, making the desire only an implicit condition, as all theologians unhesitatingly affirm since Trent. In this they follow Scotus, and show perhaps too little hesitation and too little sense of the problem, but in any case they do not come into conflict with Trent. However where this 'non-sacramental' justification takes place, even though including the desire of the sacrament, faith remains the root and foundation, as the Council itself says. And as faith comes from hearing the word of God, the Council and its doctrine provide at least a start for a theology of the word of God, where it is itself a salvific event and not merely an instruction about the possibility of such a grace acting upon man.

Nonetheless, the question still remains from the Council of Trent, as to how a theology of the intrinsically efficacious word can be reconciled with the doctrine of the sacraments as the efficacious signs and words of grace. The efforts of recent theology to solve the question, which we barely indicate here, must not be considered false in what they positively affirm. But to my mind they are not quite adequate. Wilms, for instance, distinguished word and sacrament as one would infallible *truth* and *operation* of grace. But this is precisely to renounce once more the biblical notion of the efficacious word. Others say that the word apart from the sacraments produces its effect *ex opere operantis*, while the word in the sacraments does so *ex opere operato*; others say that the former produces only actual grace, while the latter confers sanctifying grace, or that the former arouses the disposition, while the latter gives grace to the man so disposed, the former proclaims the coming of grace, the latter effectively gives it. Such distinctions are to be found for instance in Victor Warnach, Hänsli, Betz and others. We are not at all, as we have said, interested in rejecting the positive elements contained in these positions. All we think we should do is to make some remarks which will show how problematic these distinctions are.

It has already been said that justification can take place in a salutary action even outside the sacraments—through the necessary intervention of the word of God—and that in such cases the *votum sacramenti*, the desire, is the condition but not the cause of it, according to the general opinion of theologians. This alone makes it impossible to ascribe to the word of God outside the sacraments merely actual grace, to the exclusion of sanctifying grace. The interpretation of the relationship between word and sacrament thus criticized may perhaps be further defended by saying that 'non-sacramental' justification always tends by its whole nature towards a tangible sacramental realization of this justification and only finds its true completion therein: but this, while correct and of decisive importance, is already to go beyond the principles of the theory in question.

Further, it must not be thought that the distinction between *opus operatum* and *opus operantis* can be presupposed as something quite obvious and perfectly clear in such efforts to solve the problem. For the meaning of *opus operatum* is not at all very clear. If one simply says that *opus operatum* is the operation which produces grace in virtue of Christ, without merit on the part of the agent of this operation or on the part of the subject on whom it is performed: then we must recall that all grace comes by the power of Christ, and that there are non-sacramental occasions on which grace is given without any merit, as is the case with every prevenient actual grace. And here it should be noted that it would be quite wrong to say that because each sacrament confers a specific grace, the effect of the sacrament is only habitual grace, as if actual grace could not be an effect of the sacrament as such. It must also be noted that according to the ordinary doctrine of theologians, there can very well be an *opus operatum* which is not at once a sacrament. Thus the notion of *opus operatum* alone is not of itself adequate to demarcate a sacrament in contrast to anything else. Or at any rate, some further criterion must be invoked when such a distinction is made. If the infallibility of the effect is stressed in the notion of *opus operatum*, we have to point out first, that this infallible effect, in spite of being ascribed to the sacrament 'taken on its own', is in fact, according to the Council of Trent, bound up with a condition in *actu secundo*: the (varying) dispositions of the recipient. And this readily intelligible fact is not altered because the condition is not precisely the cause of the effect in question, but merely the condition necessary for it. Further, there are still other cases where, by the free disposition of God, grace is infallibily connected with some action which still remains a mere pre-condition, to the exclusion of merit, as for instance purely petitionary prayer as such for something which makes certainly and unconditionally for supernatural salvation and the glory of God. Such prayer is certain of its effect, according to the express promise of Jesus, whose words it is not our business to modify. Why is this not an *opus operatum*? After all, it is a word to which infallible efficacity is acribed by Christ's promise; and a sacramental sign, the prayer at extreme unction, for instance, can take the form and the formal sense of a petition to God. It may be suggested that we must take all these elements together—primarily therefore the absence of merit, the infallibility of effect, relation to sanctifying grace—to have the concept of *opus operatum*. But the question still remains as to whether these characteristics cannot also be found united outside the sacraments, and above all, as to how this combination is to be given a unified basis so that finally the real essence of an *opus operatum* and hence of a sacrament—when the other conditions are fulfilled—may be understood. However, these remarks must now suffice as critical notes on the present-day attempts to solve the question of the demarcation, as between the efficacious word of God in the Church in general, and the efficacious word of God which we have precisely in the sacraments. We now come to the explanation and the outline proof of the thesis proper.

In its positive sense it really hardly needs to be proved. The sacramental word is so unquestionably the supreme form of the efficacious word of God that the tendency in Catholic theology is rather to make it the only efficacious word. The word in the sacrament—along with the ritual action as an element of the whole speaking sign—is clearly efficacious, effects what it signifies, is uttered by the authority of Christ, is the word which undoubtedly represents the supreme exercise of the authority of the Church and hence also its supreme moment of self-realization, brings about the decisive thing in the history of the individual's salvation, first and second justification. Hence this word is certainly the event in which God imparts himself in his own reality and majesty as eternal salvation as he justifies and sanctifies man. It is certain that no higher form of God's efficacious word is conceivable. Thus the only question about the thesis here proposed is whether the sacraments can be clearly and sufficiently distinguished from other forms of God's efficacious word, and whether the nature of a sacrament can be sufficiently clarified under this aspect. Some further remarks are called for on these questions.

First, an indirect answer may be given: anything that can be said of a sign may also be said under the heading of 'word'. If Catholic theology usually uses the notion of sign to determine the nature of a sacrament and mark it off from other things, the same process should also be possible when dealing with the 'word'. The only question is what specific notes must be attached to the generic concept of 'sign' or 'word' so as to reduce this genus to the species 'sacrament' and so determine the essence of the sacrament. That these features include the mission of Christ, authority from him, the fact that the word is uttered and the sign performed in his name is an obvious truth which sets no problems. In the classic definition of the sacraments the generic concept 'sign' is specified by the addition of the difference: (*signum*) *efficax gratiae—ex opere operato*. The same formal process of logic could also be applied to the concept 'word' and the sacrament could be defined: the word of Christ on the lips of the Church, which confers grace *ex opere operato*. But even when we prescind from the fact that this traditional definition of a sacrament already raises difficulties, quite apart from the considerations which we have put forward, new problems arise from what we have said under thesis 4, which make the definition of a sacrament harder to deal with. We can no longer maintain that the conferring of grace can be ascribed only to the sacramental word in the strictest sense, since we are bound to ascribe such efficacity—even though in varying degrees—to *every* word which God utters, even when he does so through the Church. And hence we cannot take the concept of 'opus operatum' to be so obvious and so clear in itself that we can use it at once as the *differentia specifica* in our definition. Nonetheless, it is still possible to affirm: if, starting from our basic principle—the concept of the *efficacious* word of God in the Church, which is variable in its efficacity— we succeed in giving a description or demarcation or definition of the concept 'opus operatum' and insert this 'definition' in the required definition of a sacrament, instead of the mere phrase 'opus operatum', we have certainly arrived at what we sought. The definition would then be traditional, because it only expresses more exactly what is asserted in the standard definition, by giving the words sign and *opus operatum* a clearer sense. And such a definition will likewise be found capable of distinguishing the sacramental word from other forms of the efficacious word, because it describes the special form of its efficacity, which belongs only to the sacramental word, in such a way that this description coincides with that of the *opus operatum*. This is precisely what we have sought to do in the statement put forward above. Let us look at it in detail.

In the statement in question we indicated two features which when taken together constitute, to our mind, the objective content of the concept *opus operatum* in its unity: the word as the fullest actualization of the Church in its absolute commitment, and the word spoken in the decisive situations of human salvation.

To understand why these two features when taken together cover in fact the concept of the *opus operatum* and indeed determine it more exactly than is usual, we must reflect on the nature of the Church as the primary sacrament. Unfortunately, this can be done here only extremely briefly. The Church, in its concrete reality, is the permanent sign of the fact that God does not merely *offer* the grace of his self-communication but that in the triumphant efficacity of his grace—efficacious in formal pre-definition with regard to mankind as a whole and the Church—he also powerfully brings about the acceptance of this offer. Grace is not merely in the world; it is not merely there as an offer: since Christ and through Christ it is also in fact triumphantly there. It is not just that the world *can* be saved if it wills, it *is* in fact saved, as a whole, because God brings it about in Christ that the world does will to be saved. It is the redeemed, not just the redeemable world. In and through the eschatological triumph of grace the destiny of the world as a whole is already decided. The history of salvation is not yet closed for the individual as such and the knowledge of his future, but as a whole the history of salvation is already decided positively. And of this eschatological situation of the history of salvation, as already basically decided in the positive sense, the Church, as historically visible, is the sign, the historically audible word which proclaims this victory and in which this victory constitutes itself present in the world. And the Church is such in her unfailing truth and her inexhaustible saving powers, as well as in the unconquerable subjective holiness of her members as a whole. Both elements are there, and not by an arbitrary disposition of God, though such a two-fold disposition did not exist, for instance, in the Old Testament: they are there because with and through Christ the kingdom of God is there in the world, really and invincibly, and the Church is the abiding presence of this very Christ; they are there in the incarnational reality of the Church, as the historical sign and word of this victory which is already definitive. Since the Church is the presence of Christ in the world, as the eschatologically definitive salvation and the definitively triumphant grace of God, the Church visible, its historical tangibility, its character of being the word proclaiming salvation, is definitive and eschatological. But this means that the reality of the Church has the character of a sign, definitively and inviolably, finally and for ever. The pre-Christian, Old Testament, and other non-Christian manifestations of God's salvific dealings with men in the realities of accessible history could be rendered ineffective by men's disbelief, their refusal to hear—as is still possible today with regard to individual words of God to individual men. More than that, they could void themselves, lose their character of efficacious promise of God's salvation; they could be abolished and hence always existed as the crisis of a history of salvation that was still undeclared, merely provisional and the shadow of reality. They were never valid except in so far as they went beyond themselves to point on to the future: they were the coming, not the presence, of the grace of God.

The Church is of itself the final, irrevocable, eschatologically permanent word of salvation to the world. In it God has of himself uttered permanently his word of grace to the world, his last irrevocable word, which is no longer open to change in the dialogue of a history still running its course. And thereby he has declared that this is his last and efficacious word, not the word that judges and rejects. And hence the Church is the primary sacrament, and the treatise '*De sacramentis in genere*' is a treatise on the genus, the origin and root of the sacraments, and this is the Church. (This could give us, incidentally, a new and broader basis for discussing the old question, so difficult historically, of the institution of all the sacraments by Christ himself: he instituted the sacraments, which are not attested by any express texts of Scripture, by instituting the Church; and he instituted the sacraments which were explicitly instituted, *as* moments in the institution of the Church, as is perfectly clear from all the three sacraments in question.) And now the concept of *opus operatum* may be envisaged in its real origin. This concept cannot be defined simply by saying, in formal juridical terms of a decretal theology, that such a process is efficacious of itself and without merit on the part of the subject of the process. For there are other processes, as we have already said, of which the same may be said. But the *opus operatum* is to be taken as the supreme degree of the Church's actuality, as the act of its self-*realization*—and as such, much more proper to its nature as a society than if the *opus operatum* was something static and substance-like, less dependent on an act being done. It follows at once that such an act participates in the nature of the Church, as described when we said that it was the final, unvoidable and instrinsically definitive sign of God's absolute self-bestowal on the world in his triumphant grace. And precisely the same may be said of the basic acts of the Church. Where it actualizes itself in an ultimate commitment of its being towards an individual, becoming for him the aforesaid merciful word of God in the concrete critical situation of his salvation, hence the final efficacious word, no longer provisional and conditional in a dialectical dialogue: this is precisely what we should describe as an *opus operatum*. The *opus operatum* is the eschatologically unconditional word of God to man, which is no longer in the balance and in danger of being abrogated by a new and different word in the history of salvation. The *opus operatum* is the eschatologically efficacious word of God, as the absolute self-realization of the Church, according to its essence as the primary sacrament.

Though this is a self-realization of the Church in its primordial sacramental nature, by means of an absolute engagement, as the definitive manifestation of God's grace in history, it is by the nature of things subject to certain conditions, some of which are intrinsic, others dependent like the Church itself on the free decree of Christ. It depends on intrinsic conditions: because this absolute self-realization of the Church with regard to the truth of the word which constitutes this self-realization, is clearly only possible where it is a matter of the whole Church's being committed to this truth. And where it is a matter of the efficacity of a word which of its nature is mostly or always directed to the individual, such an absolute commitment is only possible where the individual is envisaged in situations decisive for his salvation, and not in cases which represent insignificant factors compared with the totality of the Christian existence of the individual. (It is the same as in moral theology: a radical *subjective* decision is only possible with regard to '*materia* objective *gravis*'.) This does not mean of course that we are now enabled to deduce the seven sacraments purely *a priori*. It can be demonstrated that the group of seven is not purely arbitrary, that it is not just as easy to imagine that there could be substantially more or fewer sacraments. Such positivism in theology would already be suspect from its inevitable *consequence*: that it would call for proof in each sacrament of strict, verbal, explicit institution by Christ. And this is not only historically impossible, it must be rejected as historically improbable. But this again does not mean that it must be possible to deduce the sacraments *a priori*, individually and as to their fixed number. Nor do we mean this, when we say that each sacrament is an act of the absolute self-realization of the Church in an absolute commitment. The Church itself in its concrete reality is the free institution of Christ—with regard to the time and place of its origin, and hence with regard to many other things which do not simply stem from its essential nature of being the presence of Christ as eschatological salvation in the world. And thus its nature, in its actual concrete realization, cannot be wholly and definitely deduced from its basic, abstract concept. We may and must be simply prepared to accept *a priori* the basic acts which the Church recognizes as corresponding to its essence individually and exactly and retains as such in its understanding of itself. Our definition of a sacrament may not be objected to on the grounds that other such absolute acts of self-realization are thinkable, or that some sacraments cannot be so easily identified as such acts. By the nature of things, there must be a certain margin of freedom in marking the frontier between the absolute and the non-absolute acts of self-realization, we have to register *a posteriori* what is outside the boundary, when dealing with particular questions when marking this frontier. It is nonetheless clear that initiation (in its two-fold character of baptism and confirmation) and reconciliation (of the sinner, with the holy Church and with God) are such basic acts, both for the Church itself and in the history of the salvation of the individual as such in and in face of the Church. If in *these* cases the Church could not realize itself absolutely as the primary sign of the eschatological grace which is historically tangible in it, then it could never do so and it would not be that sign. If man exists essentially in society, if therefore his social nature is of significance for salvation, and if for the Church itself this society is of significance, both on account of its fruitfulness and on account of the marriage partners: then marriage is an essential moment in the life of the Church, which becomes manifest in an essential way in the marriage of its members. It is decisively represented by marriage, and it appears there as itself, in a historically tangible manifestation which attests the Church. Hence marriage must partake of the absolute character of sign which belongs to the Church, that is, it must be a sacrament. Whether this consideration is of itself stringent or not is a matter of indifference. In the course of its history, basing itself on biblical data, the Church has recognized marriage as a sacrament. And it did so, because marriage represents the love which unites Christ and the Church, and such a sign cannot be an empty one in the New Testament. It recognized therefore marriage as a sacrament, because it has a symbolic relationship to the Church itself, and therefore because the Church finds itself once more in marriage. And thus our basic observation on marriage is proved correct, and again, the correctness of the observation is confirmed, even if it were not simply stringent as the individual theologian's private considerations, outside the self-understanding of the Church. That the installation of an office-bearer in the Church can and must be thought of as a radical situation in the Christian existence of the individual—in so far as he appears, so to speak, on the side of Christ as opposed to the Church—as well as in the self-realization of the Church, in so far as it gives itself this leadership, seems obvious enough. And so too is the sacramental character of this action, in virtue of our fundamental principle. As we shall speak of the Eucharist in particular in the second part of this study, there remains only the anointing of the sick. Without weakening its true sacramental character, one may find it possible to take it—like confirmation in relation to baptism—as a development of the comprehensive sacrament of the forgiveness of sins in the Church with regard to its sinful members. There is much to be said for this point of view, and it means that there need be no particular difficulty in deducing this sacrament from our basic principle. Since the sinful member of the Church has sinned against the essence of the Church as a *holy* society and hence as witness to the sanctifying grace of God in the world, every time the Church absolves him from his sin, it realizes its own essence in fundamental fashion. For the Church is the presence of God's grace of pardon. If then the anointing of the sick, in view above all of the epistle of James, chapter 5, is taken as a sacrament of the forgiveness of sins, in a particularly urgent situation to be sure—how close to one another the two sacraments were felt to be is still palpable in Origen—its sacramental quality is relatively easy to deduce from our basic principle (in so far as such a thing, as has been said, may be readily demanded). If however one is determined to keep the sacraments of penance and extreme unction clearly apart, then one must stress the fact that a decisive situation exists, for the individual and for the Church, wherever the imminent danger of death places a member of the Church in the decisive crisis. It is at least very probable that here the word of grace on the lips of the Church must have an absolute seriousness. These considerations should suffice to understand the anointing of the sick in the perspective of our basic principle.

Granted this principle, namely that the sacraments are basic acts of the self-realization of the Church with regard to individuals at decisive situations of their lives, we can understand the character of these processes as *opus operatum*, and likewise, because the Church is instituted by Christ as the primary, permanent sign of his triumphant eschatological grace in the world, their sacramental character. Thus our description of the sacraments as efficacious words of God is justified, once it is supposed that it can be satisfactorily shown that other processes in the Church, which are not sacramental, do not also fulfil this definition and hence prove it to be false or insufficient. As regards this last requirement, we saw that all other acts in which the Church realizes its being as the permanence of the (basically) efficacious grace of God's word in the world, are insufficient. Either they are not directed to the individual in this decisive way, or they do not find him in a situation decisive for salvation, or at least not in a specifically new one—the result being that such processes need not be taken as real sacraments, since they need be no more than concomitant, introductory or complementary aspects of a sacramental process. Or again, they are not processes which signify precisely grace as such, or they cannot be considered as the Church's absolute commitment, as the radical self-realization of the Church in its character of primary sacrament. We cannot be asked to prove that it is absolutely *impossible* that further sacramental processes should exist. Hence it is enough to maintain, for the rest of the proof, that no one can name a process in the Church outside the seven sacraments which fulfils clearly and definitely all the conditions of a sacrament named in our definition. If one lists the processes found in fact in the Church—which we may be excused from doing here—one will always find that some or at least one of the above conditions and criteria are lacking. Our definition can therefore be taken as correct until proof of the contrary.

The considerations which we have put forward are of course no more than cursory indications. We should above all have proved more clearly, fully and definitely that our view of the essence of the Church as the eschatological sign of salvation leads to a basic understanding of the *opus operatum* which is an improvement on the usual one—though it does in fact contain, on the basis of our principle, all that is indicated elsewhere as characteristic of the *opus operatum*. But this cannot be undertaken now.

But before ending this first part of our considerations, there is perhaps one task which should be performed more explicitly. This would be to show, as is indeed yet to be done in this discussion of the sacraments, what was in fact the starting-point of our considerations. It remains to be shown that the efficacious word of God does exist in the Church outside the sacraments, and that this word does not first become efficacious and does not only appear as the presence of God's grace in the Church, when it becomes sacramental in the strictest sense. We must make at least some observations on this question. Every word of God on the lips of the Church, which precedes, accompanies and follows the sacramental word of the Church, must always and everywhere be considered as ordained to this sacramental word. For God does not say all sorts of things to men, and his words are not a miscellany of disconnected subjects. In the last resort he utters only one thing, which is himself as eternal salvation in the Spirit of the incarnate Logos of God. And hence the diverse words have all an intrinsic connexion and derive their sense and value from this one concentration of meaning, which comes to a climax in the sacramental word. And hence so far as it is within the whole, each word of God in the Church takes on, in keeping with its significance within the whole, the character—analogously and in a lower degree—of the one whole word of God. As we indicated at the start, there exists between the sacramental word of God in the Church and the other words of the Church's preaching, the same relationship as between the process of sacramental justification and the non-sacramental. There is one sacramental process of justification, and it is necessary to salvation. But the Church and the theologians have never maintained, at least not since the early middle ages, that there could be no non-sacramental justification, because otherwise the value and necessity of sacramental justification would disappear. It cannot be said that from the point of view of history of dogma and systematic theology the question of the relationship between these two 'ways' of justifications has been solved wholly satisfactorily. But the basic lines of a solution are clear enough, and they are the same as in our own question of the relationship between the sacramental and non-sacramental word of efficacious power in the Church. We must not start by taking the two things as independent and disparate juxtaposed realities: they are phases and moments of the same process. The one, complete, efficacious word of God's salvation has its history and therefore its phases; each phase shares the being of the whole, the *whole* reality is truly present and effective in each phase. But this does not make the succeeding phase superfluous and meaningless. On the contrary, it is what really demands it, because it is only in the fully-formed, historical and tangible whole, that is, in the sacrament, that the essentially-envisaged whole, the decisive moment, reaches its full 'manifestation'—a manifestation which is of the essence of the thing in an incarnational structure of salvation. A process as a whole, since it pervades all phases and yet is only fully present in the whole, can display a sort of shift in the phases: in the 'reviviscence' of a sacrament which has been unworthily but validly received, we have the historically tangible event of salvation *before* grace; in justification preceding the sacrament, the situation is reversed—because the thing essentially envisaged is already there, before its historical sacramental manifestation has been fully expressed, when it is called sacrament. This second case is so normal, starting in Scripture with the case of Cornelius and going on into the sacramental theology of St Thomas, without prejudice to the necessity and meaningfulness of the sacrament, that St Thomas even held that it formed a binding rule. And yet St Thomas never doubted for a moment the sense and necessity of the sacrament. But all grace has an incarnational structure. All acceptance of the grace is an acceptance in faith, in hearing, of the word of God, which is uttered interiorly or externally or in both ways. Hence all phases of such a salvific process have basically the same structure. They are phases of the self-realization and historical self-presentation of the one and the same essence of the one efficacious word of God, which, where and only where it attains under God and Christ its unambiguous, historical and ecclesiological presence, its embodiment and eschatological absoluteness, is called sacrament. But because the word reaches its supreme degree of actualization in the sacrament, while always aiming at this degree, it is inchoate everywhere in this quality of efficacious word. It can have a lesser degree of efficacity, because its content is too specialized, or because it is existentially addressed to a man only under a particular aspect, or because it is from the start only the setting and accompaniment of the sacramental word—and so on.

The following point must finally be noted, if our thesis is to be understood correctly. If the thesis is correct, then it is clear from the start that the sacramental word and the word uttered in the preaching of the Church are similar and dissimilar in *all* elements which characterize the word of God. Hence in what we have said up to this, we do not claim to have analysed, noted and distinguished all the elements of the word of God which can possibly be thought of and which are theologically important for our special question: the word as statement and as event, the word as part of a dialogue, the word as eschatological word, the word as participation in the incarnation and the redemption on the Cross, the word as anamnesis, as prediction, as affirmation and as promise, as call and answer at once, as interior and exterior word etc. In these and other aspects the non-sacramental and the sacramental word both agree and differ. And since we have not analysed these various aspects in detail, the theory which we have proposed is only a formal draft of a solution, it does not really state the full contents of the solution. The agreement and disagreement touching each of these moments of the sacramental and non-sacramental word would have to be precisely considered, before it could be said that the proposed theory had been to some extent properly developed. Thus it is not against what is positively implied in the results of O. Semmelroth's work, for instance, on our problem. He maintains that the strictly sacramental word is more closely connected with the answering word of mankind in Christ on the cross (since the sacraments are specially related to the work of the cross, while the cross is not only the event of the word of God to man, but also man's answer to God in the dialogue: mankind, summed up in Christ, accepted God's offer of himself in the incarnation). The non-sacramental word in the preaching of the Church is said to be a continuation of the coming of the Logos of God into the world, as the offer of God to mankind. The distinction is undoubtedly correct. But it seems to me to be only one of the many distinctions between the two forms and phases of the one word of God. And it also seems to me that in this theory the non-sacramental word, in spite of the stress laid on its efficacity, is seen too much as doctrinal (even though the element of event is included). Hence the theory seems to overlook to some extent the fact that we find in the Church, in the real preaching of repentance for instance, a non-sacramental word, in the nature of doctrine and in the nature of event, which refers men to the event of the cross and hence does not derive entirely from the incarnation.

II. WORD AND EUCHARIST

We shall now try to apply these general considerations to the sacrament of the Eucharist.

It should be clear at once that all that has been said hitherto comes here to an unsurpassable climax. The Eucharist is 'word': because here the incarnate Logos of God is himself present in his substance; because here the absolute proclamation of the whole mystery of salvation takes place: there is the anamnesis, in which the event of God's giving himself to the world and the acceptance of this gift on the cross of the Son becomes actually present among us, sacramentally, in the space and time we live in; and there is the anticipation, sacramentally, of final salvation in the *pignus futurae gloriae*, because here the *death* of Christ and his *coming* are exhibited and proclaimed; and because here we have the supreme self-realization of the Church. For here the Church realizes itself in an absolute commitment which not merely regards the individual: the Church itself, as the community of salvation, actuates itself supremely in the sacrifice and meal of the Eucharist. There is no need to develop this further here. But if all this is true, then the Eucharist is not only the supreme case of those acts of self-realization of the Church which are called sacraments, it is the real origin of all other sacraments—which again are so much the self-realization of the Church that all other words and actions of the Church have essentially the functioning of serving these acts of self-realization, and are only really justified and intelligible in the light of the sacraments. And then we can say that the Eucharist is simply the word of God in the Church which supports and conveys all other words, which forms the centre whence all the reality of the Church derives its meaning. The Eucharist is the word of the Church absolutely. As the Council of Trent says, it renders present not merely the grace of Christ but the source of grace itself; it is what the Council had chiefly and most intensively in mind when it anathematized those who taught that all the sacraments of the Church were of equal dignity. It is the word through which the triumphant and divinely-accepted act of redemption is present as an actual reality. It is the word which when uttered and heard in faith, alone gives full reality to what the Church is: the presence of Christ and his redemption in the world. All other words, sacramental and non-sacramental, must therefore be considered merely as exposition and application, preliminaries and echoes of this word, which makes the crucified and risen Lord and his whole work of salvation present in the Church. All the teaching of the Church merely points to this event, which is present and permanent in the word of this sacrament. All the words of the other sacraments merely distribute and bring down to concrete situations the reality and the presence which is here in its totality. All words of command, exhortation and correction can aim only at one thing: that man should come there, and come with a mind to believe and accept in love what is here present in sacred solemnity: the gift of God to man in him who gave himself up for us. It is indeed possible, and perhaps only too often a reality, that man's acceptance of the incarnate and crucified Logos, with the ultimate decisiveness which brings salvation, takes place *outside* the Eucharistic celebration. But even here it takes place by virtue of the event which constantly procures for itself in the Eucharist a new manifestation and presence in the midst of the Church, and imparts itself invisibly to all by becoming sacramentally visible here.

But here in fact the temptation might arise, to see in the Eucharist the strongest 'No' to all that has been said up to this. It could perhaps be urged that the Catholic piety of the West has implicitly felt the difficulty since the end of the tenth century. While in Protestant piety the Church is the sacred place where the word of God is efficaciously preached, in

Catholic piety, more or less since the time of Berengarius, the Church is the place where the sacrament is mutely and apparently wordlessly present, as the silent presence of the Lord. And so this very sacrament brings up once more the old question as to whether there are, as Thomas à Kempis says, simply *two* tables in the Church, one for Scripture and one for the bread of life; and whether it remains an open question, how these two tables, which seem to be so different, are ultimately related to one another; and whether there is really a choice between being the Church of the word or the Church of the sacrament.

But it can be seen at once that these questions are based on misinterpretations and stunted versions of Catholic doctrine. The Eucharist is in all truth the sacrament of the word absolutely, the absolute case of the word anywhere. To understand this properly, we must bear in mind that according to the Council of Trent, Christ is present by virtue of the *panis vinique benedictio* (Denzinger 874), the consecration (Denzinger 876). No doubt the Council of Trent does not emphasize very expressly the *permanent* importance of the word pronounced over the bread and wine, as a constitutive element of the visibility or historical perceptibility under which Christ is present. But its importance is recognized in so far as the Council emphasizes expressly (apart from the places noted above) that the body and blood of Christ are present '*vi verborum*' (Denzinger 876; 1921). And it also appears from the fact that the Augustinian definition of a sacrament is acknowledged without any difficulty as applying also to the Eucharist (Denzinger 876), while this definition expressly names the word as an element of the sacramental symbol. Further, the Council of Florence says expressly in the *Decretum pro Armenis: forma huius sacramenti sunt verba salvatoris, quibus hoc confecit sacramentum*—'the form of this sacrament is the words of the Saviour by which he instituted this sacrament'. Here it must be emphasized from the scholastic point of view that the '*forma*' is not primarily the *efficient* cause of the sacrament, but a permanently constitutive element of the sacramental sign itself. The words of consecration are not the means whereby the sacrament came to be '*in fieri*', to continue to exist apart from these words. They are an element of that by which the sacrament exists and abides. It is only because they permanently refer back to the words of consecration that the species of bread and wine constitute the sign which indicates and contains the presence of Christ. If we say that Christ is present under the species, we can also say that Christ is only present through the permanent validity of the anamnesis, the words of consecration pronounced over the bread and wine. The species would not really be sacramental species if they were not being constantly determined by the words of consecration, the words of explanation, which are pronounced over them. We must avoid taking too materialistic a view in this matter. A sign is by nature a properly human reality; it can therefore be constituted not merely of material entities—and this is true also of the sacraments—but also by specifically human realities, such as the permanent validity of a statement. These are not ideas put forward just to suit this particular thesis. They are good ancient scholastic tradition. Compare for instance Ch. Pesch: *num verba sint forma constitutiva huius sacramenti. Species eucharistiae per se non significant quod continent, i.e. Christum, nisi in quantum ad hanc significationem determinatae sunt per verba. Neque enim intelligimus has species esse consecratas et significare Christum, nisi in quantum scimus circa eas prolata esse verba. Unde relatio signi est in speciebus, ut sunt determinatae verbis et hoc sufficit ut verba dicantur in genere signi constituere hoc sacramentum* (Praelectiones, VI, n. 785) ('Are the words the constitutive form of this sacrament? The Eucharistic species do not signify what they contain, Christ, except in so far as they are given this signification by the words. We do not know that the species are consecrated and signify Christ except in so far as we know that the words have been pronounced about them. Thus the species contain the relation of sign, in so far as they are determined by the words. With this it can be said that the words, being in the nature of a sign, constitute this sacrament'). Pesch then cites Suarez (Disp. 42, sect. 7) and de Lugo (Disp. 1, sect. 4 and 5). We can therefore say that the eucharist too as a sacrament is in the nature of a sign. The explanatory words of Christ are not merely the efficient cause of this sign, but an intrinsic constitutive element of it. If the sacrament of the altar, in consequence of its character as food, is a permanent sacrament, then it must also be permanent *in genere signi*—with all the constitutive elements which go to make up the sign. But if the explanatory words are a constitutive element, they must also be considered permanent, even though they are ended as a sound. There is no difficulty here. A word in its *human* reality is not completely dependent on and just merely co-existent to its sound in the physical world. A word of love, a promise, a threat still exist after their audible expression has passed away. And thus the words of consecration remain as an element of the sacramental sign even 'after' the actual moment of consecration, which was the reason for their being uttered, but not for their being permanently in existence. And so the Eucharist, even as a permanent sacrament which is 'reserved' in its special place, is constituted by the explanatory words of the Lord on the lips of the Church. The Eucharist is and remains the presence of the Lord through and under the efficacious word, which has two components: the purely material one, indeterminate in itself and needing to be determined, of the physical species of bread and wine, and the more spiritual one, formal, determinative, clear, clarifying and declaratory, that of the explanatory words of the Lord. And both are needed—both having the character of a sign and hence of a word—to form the one sign in this sacrament, through which he that is signified is present.

We may even go a step further. The word of God in this final, definitive age of Christ is the triumphant word which—freely, of course—is heard because God has so uttered it in the power of his grace that it is really heard. For the Church is the community of believers to the end, and as a whole it is also subjectively holy, and hence truly believing. In this reciprocal relationship of efficacious word of God and the effective hearing of the word effected by God himself, both realities are ordained to each other in such a way that one may safely say: if one did not exist, the other could not exist either, that is, be what it is. In other words, the word of the sacrament of the altar, which means the presence of the Lord, is supported by the faith of the Church, which hears this word and so really confers on it its true reality, that of the powerfully triumphant word—just as on the other hand the faith of the Church in the Lord present in the Eucharist is supported entirely by his word, under which he is present. We are not speaking of course of the faith of the individual as the individual. The presence of the Lord is independent of this. The Reformation doctrine which maintained that the act of faith alone constituted the presence of the Lord was false and heretical as applied to the individual; but it can have a good Catholic sense when said of the Church as a whole. If it were not, by the triumphant grace of God, always the believing Church, it would not be the word which it is, triumphant, eschatological and efficacious, nor would it then be the word which is the triumphant eschatological presence of the Lord. It must always be remembered that the Church is not just the resultant sum of its fallible and possibly unbelieving individuals, but the efficaciously predestined community of those embraced by the grace of God, without whom the Church would not be what it is—

though it is likewise not just this. We have therefore a perfect right to say that the Lord is present in the absolute word of the Church, heard and believed in the Church, the word which proclaims the death of the Lord till he comes again: and in and with him his redemption is present, as something granted to mankind absolutely and definitively, though the individual as such must still work out his salvation in fear and trembling.

The efficacious word of the Mass, being the proclamation of the death of Christ, is the primary kerygma. And every other efficacious word becomes so in the Church because it participates in this kerygma in such a way that the whole force of this primary kerygma can already be embodied in the participation, and for this very reason this mere participation is intrinsically ordained to be absorbed into the Eucharistic kerygma, to find there its full manifestation. It could be said that we find the same relationship existing between the objective word and the sacrament as Catholic theology has always seen to intervene between the actual reception of a sacrament, of the Eucharist in particular, and the desire or *votum* of a sacrament. In the desire of the sacrament, the whole power and reality of grace can already be there: one need only recall for instance the doctrine of Trent on spiritual communion, which is not make-believe and the mere longing for something not there, but the reception of the grace of the sacrament even without the sacramental sign. But the *votum* is precisely the *votum sacramenti*, and it is supported by the grace which provides itself with its most unambiguous eschatological presence in the history of salvation by means of the sacrament, and which is only fully itself when it has provided itself with its complete historical figure in the public life of the Church.

If we are correct in the way we have determined the relationship of the Eucharist and the other sacraments to the word, there can be no question of dividing up and distributing the effects of the two entities as between word and sacrament. Grace is always there in the form of the word: grace is present always and everywhere from beginning to end, from the first word of preaching to the sacrament inclusively, in the form of the word. And this one word of grace and this one grace in the word has its own proper stages as the word of God, as the word accepted existentially in faith, as the word of the Church. And where this word attains its absolute climax, as the incarnational and eschatological word of God, and absolute self-expression of the Church as a whole and as directed to the individual, the word of the Eucharist is heard.

I I

THE PRESENCE OF CHRIST IN THE
SACRAMENT OF THE LORD'S SUPPER

THE theme to be treated is the presence of Christ in the sacrament of the Lord's Supper according to Catholic faith in contrast to Lutheran Protestant faith.[1] The theme seems to me to be very difficult. Not merely because I am not an expert on this subject. Not merely because the question touches a central mystery where the lack of personal commitment would endanger or render impossible the understanding of what is taught and professed, while personal commitment makes it more difficult for us to understand one another. The particular reason which makes this theme seem very difficult for me is quite different, and I should like to state it at the very beginning, even at the risk of making my—our—position more difficult with regard to our Protestant brothers. The reason is that it is not at all easy to say what we teach in this matter. This statement may seem surprising; it seems to be quite improbable in the light of the clear, sober and realistic language of the Council of Trent. Our forefathers and indeed the vast majority of present-day Catholic theologians would be puzzled if they heard this statement, especially as in contrast to other points of doctrine, the doctrine of the real presence of Christ in the sacrament did not cause the Council Fathers much difficulty at Trent. They merely repeated, as was in itself the right thing to do, what the Church had already been saying for many hundreds of years before them when such discussion arose, in the same explicit formulas. But it still seems to me difficult today, to say what we really profess and what we do not profess. Why that is so or at least why it appears so to me will appear later. But the fact that it is so—if it really is so—is a heavier burden for the Catholic than for the Protestant theologian. For past confessions of faith are normative for his faith—and his

[1] This section is the text of a lecture addressed to Catholic and Protestant theologians. No effort has been made to change the original style.

theology—in a much more absolute sense than they are for Protestant theologians. As long as he can distinguish clearly and articulately the simple language of the faith and creeds of his Church from further theological theories and opinions about the dogma of the Church, the task of the Catholic theologian is simple. But when it is not so easy to distinguish the explicit dogma in terms of what is binding on the Church from the theorems of theology, his task is harder, both in itself and in its controversial elements. It is not that he doubts in the least about the binding quality of the doctrine of the Church, but because he finds it heavy going to repeat it exactly. Anyone who doubts that this is possible must have the fixed opinion that all pronouncements of the magisterium must, because they are binding, possess the supreme degree of intelligibility of unvarying quality—which would still be something different from rational perspicuousness and intrinsic evidence. This is not true. A new age, a new historical situation, can make a doctrinal proposition seem clearer or more obscure *quoad nos*, by the simple fact that it puts it into a new context of knowledge—even if one felt sure of how it was understood earlier, even when one accepts it fully as valid for oneself, and even when one puts it into practice without difficulty in the exercise of the Christian life. This seems to me to be the case with the theme which is now in question. It seems to me therefore that there is nothing for me to do except to state clearly the nature of this difficulty, even though it is primarily a problem within Catholicism and makes our position more difficult in face of Protestant theologians. This is all rather obscure, but it will become clearer. In other words, I am concerned to say, right from the start, that I do not consider it the task and the duty of a Catholic theologian to act as if everything were perfectly clear, as if the firmness of his assent to the doctrine of his Church depended on his having the answer to all questions.

We divide our remarks into three sections:

1. Preliminary remarks.
2. The doctrine of the Council of Trent on the real presence of Christ in the Eucharist.
3. What remains obscure and open?

I. PRELIMINARY REMARKS

1. I must renounce any effort to give a survey of the history of the dogma of the real presence and of the development of the doctrine. In this context

the effort would only lead to facile simplifications. It is true that here as elsewhere it is important for the Catholic theologian to trace the historical way to the express formulation of the faith which the Church—his Church—professes. But the ultimate foundation of his assent to this faith is not the fact that he can prove historically the legitimacy of this historical way. Hence a purely descriptive method which merely registers opinions cannot at once be considered unjustifiable in a given context. This is all the more true, since the Catholic theologian cannot admit that a later certainty and a later clarity in Church dogma is illegitimate or subject to possible revision, simply because it did not always exist.

And we shall likewise omit discussion of certain themes, which are connected with our actual question but are still not identical with it: the question of the reservation and adoration of the Eucharist, the questions connected with the two-fold nature of the species, the question of reception *sub utraque specie*, the more precise questions about the presence of Christ in the sacrament which arise from the divisibility of the species— the breaking of the bread, the drinking from one chalice. The omission of the controverted question of the *sacrifice* of the Mass—and hence the question of the presence of the sacrifice of the *Cross* in the Eucharist—has been agreed on already.

2. Another preliminary remark is called for. It concerns a basic attitude to the theme, which results from certain theological *a prioris* in general.

(a) In the doctrine of the Eucharist, a Catholic cannot make the silent presupposition that a dogmatic assertion can only refer to something which lies as such beyond the region of human experience. In other words, an assertion cannot at once be rejected as a dogmatic assertion, as a truth of faith, simply because the objects within its scope are not really removed from human experience. The empty grave, for instance, is the object of an assertion of faith and not mythology, though the empty grave is in principle within the scope of non-religious assertions. Truths of faith cannot be so restricted, in principle at least, with regard to their objects, that the possibility of contact with profane knowledge can be excluded *a priori*, so that nothing can result from them for the region of the profane. I can never say, for instance, that the historical existence of Jesus is in principle of no importance for the Christ of faith. Hence for instance, if the Catholic doctrine of the Eucharist contains metaphysical implications, the Catholic theologian can never see in this the *a priori* proof that he has trespassed beyond the bounds of a truth of faith. Since

God in his act of salvation and revelation has *also* intended the reality in which we usually live, though not this alone, and since he intervenes in it and transforms it, a basic historical or metaphysical scepticism, an absolute discontinuity, postulated *a priori*, between truths of faith and other assertions is inacceptable. This general principle must be stressed as a preliminary to our particular question, since otherwise the impression might easily arise, unavowed perhaps but hence all the more forceful, that the Catholic dogmatic assertion about the real presence, on account of the 'realism' with which it speaks of a tangible reality, goes beyond the bounds of any possible dogmatic assertion—that it postulates a 'miracle'. This is the first point.

(b) On the other hand, we must also affirm the following: in view of the bearing of a truth of faith on salvation, and of the fact that it is directed to all men and that its real content must be understood at all times, it is *a priori* improbable—more we may not say—that a dogma can only be formulated and understood in dependence on a well-defined philosophical system. It is not clear, of course, in such a statement, what we are to understand by a philosophical system, where it begins and where it leaves off. It cannot be said that every concept which is not immediately traceable to the most primitive experience is at once so much of a philosophical product that there could be no question of it in a truth of faith, or that it could not be implicitly guaranteed as correct by a truth of faith. Catholic theology—I state this merely as a fact, without any polemical purpose—will never allow itself to appeal easily and quickly to what is paradoxical and not amenable to logic. But if that is so, if one is steadfast with regard to the mystery, and if one really tries to be guided by the facts, one cannot simply avoid all the rational consequences of the immediate truth of faith, or leave them aside as of no interest even for the defence of this truth. Nonetheless, it has proved true again and again—and most controversies *within* Catholic theology derive from this fact—that the truths of faith do not clearly imply any particular philosophical system, which would then be imposed as binding by the magisterium on account of this implication. Hence just as we Catholic theologians cannot practise *a priori* a non-metaphysical dogmatic theology, so too we need not expect *a priori* that dogmatic theology will provide us with any particular metaphysical system—an Aristotelian hylemorphism for instance in the present question. With this—I should almost like to say, unhappily—we have gained no clear and handy principle, which will enable us to steer a smooth course between a theology devoid of ontology and a theology transformed into a metaphysics: but at least we have been warned against both.

II. THE DOCTRINE OF THE COUNCIL OF TRENT ON THE REAL PRESENCE OF CHRIST IN THE EUCHARIST

We shall omit, as we have said, the presentation of the Catholic doctrine of the presence of Christ in the Eucharist, and simply present the doctrine itself according to the most express declarations of it in the Council of Trent. We may remark here that the history of the discussions of this point at the Council is not very enlightening and helpful. Hence this too we omit here.

1. The Council confesses the real presence of Christ in the sacrament.

(a) As regards the *presence* as such, the formulation varies. The Council speaks of a '*contineri*' (Denzinger 874), of a '*sacramentaliter praesens sua substantia nobis adesse*' (l.c.), of a '*suum corpus praebere*' (Denzinger 874; 876; 877), of an '*in Eucharistia esse*' (Denzinger 876), of a '*sub speciebus existere*' or '*contineri*' (Denzinger 876; 885), of an '*esse in sacramento*' (Denzinger 886) and '*in hostiis remanere*' (Denzinger 886).

This '*contineri sub specie illarum rerum sensibilium*' is characterized as a '*vere, realiter ac substantialiter contineri*' (Denzinger 874; 883) and contrasted with a '*tantummodo esse in sacramento ut in signo vel figura aut virtute*' (Denzinger 883).[2] This '*realis praesentia*' (Denzinger 874, title) is described as one which we '*vix verbis exprimere possumus*', but which is to be affirmed in faith; it is distinguished as a sacramental mode of existence from the '*modus existendi naturalis*' which belongs to the exalted Lord in heaven (Denzinger 874). For the fact of the real presence, the Council appeals to the words of Christ in the Synoptic gospels and in St Paul, which are supposed to show clearly that Jesus' words had their proper sense and not a figurative or metaphorical one, and hence that he really gave his Apostles his real body and blood. This is said to have been the constant doctrine of the Fathers and the unanimous interpretation of the Church. More precise general reflexions on the nature of this presence are not given.

---

[2] The encyclical *Humani generis* (*Denz.* 2318) condemns as erroneous the opinion by which '*realis Christi praesentia . . . ad quendam symbolismum reducatur, quatenus consecratae species non nisi signa efficacia sint spiritualis presentiae Christi eiusque intimae coniunctionis cum fidelibus membris in corpore Mystico*'.

(b) The whole Christ is present, and wholly present under each species: his body and blood *vi verborum* of the consecration, but the whole Christ with body and soul, humanity and divinity, because he is the man transformed and raised from the dead, who is no longer subject to the separation of body and soul in death, and because a separation of humanity and divinity is impossible on account of the hypostatic union (Denzinger 876). Hence the real presence is affirmed, without distinction, of 'Jesus Christ true God and man' (Denzinger 874), of his body and of his blood (Denzinger 874; 876), of the *totus et integer Christus* (Denzinger 876), of body and blood along with soul and divinity, of the 'whole Christ' (Denzinger 883; 885).

(c) Christ is present by reason of the *panis vinique benedictio* (Denzinger 874), the *consecratio* (Denzinger 876). The *permanent* significance of the word which is pronounced over the bread and wine, as a constitutive element of the visibility under which Christ is present, is not stressed very explicitly by the Council. But it is affirmed in so far as—apart from the words just quoted—the Council expressly emphasizes that it is '*vi verborum*' that the body and blood of Christ are present (Denzinger 876; 1921), while the whole Christ is there *concomitanter* (l.c.). It is also affirmed by the fact that the Augustinian definition of a sacrament is recognized unhesitatingly as applying to the Eucharist, since this definition states that the word is an element of the sacramental symbolism. And the *Decretum pro Armenis* of the Council of Florence (Denzinger 698; cf. 715) says expressly: *forma huius sacramenti sunt verba Salvatoris, quibus hoc confecit sacramentum*, where it must be emphasized, precisely from the scholastic point of view, that '*forma*' does not indicate primarily the efficient cause, but a permanent constitutive element of the sacramental sign. It is only by their being constantly referred back to the words of consecration that the species of bread and wine constitute the sign (*symbolism* in the Augustinian sense) which indicates and contains the presence of Christ.[3] The sign of the presence of Christ, the notification of the real presence, is therefore the one sign composed of the empirical

---

[3] Cf. Pesch VI no. 785: '*num verba sint forma constitutiva huius sacramenti; species eucharisticae per se non significant id quod continent, i.e. Christum, nisi in quantum ad hanc significationem determinatae sunt per verba. Neque enim intelligimus has species esse consecrates et significare Christum, nisi inquantum scimus circa eas prolata esse verba. Unde relatio signi est in speciebus, ut sunt determinatae verbis et hoc sufficit ut verba dicantur in genere signi constituere hoc sacramentum* (cf. Suarez, disp. 42 sect. 7; de Lugo, disp. 1 sect. 4.5).

perceptibility of bread and wine and of the word, which is pronounced over them in obedience to Jesus' command for the anamnesis, by ordained representatives of the Church, with the intention of performing the act which the Church is charged to do. (As regards the 'intention', cf. Denzinger 424; 672; 695; 854; 860; 1318; as regards the priest, Denzinger 424; 430; 574a; 715). Part of the constitution of the sign, under which alone Christ is present, is the relationship of the bread and wine to a meal, their character of nourishment. Clearly as the Council rejects the doctrine that Christ is only present *'in usu, dum sumitur'* (Denzinger 886; 876), it concedes just as readily that this sacrament was instituted by Christ *'ut sumatur'* (Denzinger 878). Bread and wine are anthropological realities and concepts, and as such they are essentially related to consumption, to *usus*. And they are only the sign of the real presence of Christ in so far as they have this relationship. But since the character of nourishment is prior to the consumption strictly as such—it is not constituted by the latter, but it renders the latter possible—and because Christ affirmed that what he gave was his body (Denzinger 876), before the Apostles ate of it, Christ is present before the actual *usus*. But this does not deny, but rather affirms, that the sign of the presence of Christ is the blessed food as such. The more clearly therefore the reverent adoration of Christ in the sacrament is referred back to the eating of the body of Christ, the more Eucharistic piety corresponds to the full truth and reality of the sacrament.

(d) Granted the suppositions made above, the real presence is there independently of the faith of the individual priest or communicant, so that even the sinner or the unbeliever receives the body of the Lord, though only sacramentally and not spiritually, that is, when the objectively real event of the reception of the body means judgment for him (Denzinger 881; 880). Hence the reception of the body, though of course it does not set up a reciprocal physical influence between the body of Christ and the communicant in the realm of experience as such (cf. Denzinger 546),[4] is characterized as 'sacramental and real',[5] and not merely as 'mentally spiritual' (*spiritualiter*) (Denzinger 890), though the Council

---

[4] The *'hoc est substantive et essentialiter, non autem quantitative vel qualitative vel localiter'* of the formula of union put forward by the Lutherans at Marburg could be subscribed to by Catholic theologians (cf. *Die Bekenntnisschriften der evangelisch-lutherischen Kirche*, published by the Deutschen Evangelischen Kirchenausschuss [Göttingen ²1952] 65, n.1).

[5] This corresponds to Luther's *'ore edi et bibi'* (*Solida Declaratio* VII, 32: Die *Bekenntnisschriften* . . . 982), to the *'naturale corpus'* (l.c. 33).

itself calls the sacrament a '*spiritualis animarum cibus*' (Denzinger 875), and it was recognized in the debates of the Council that the phrase '*manducatio spiritualis*' could have an orthodox sense (D.Th.C., V 1327).

(e) If we prescind for the moment from the question of '*in usu—ante usum*', it seems to me that with regard to the real presence in the sacrament itself, otherwise than with regard to transubstantiation, there is no essential difference between the Catholic and the Lutheran faith. For the Lutheran confession also teaches a real presence, by which Christ is 'truly, really, vitally' present in the sacrament; it uses '*vere et substantialiter*' to characterize this presence, it rejects the '*in figura*' (*figurate*) or the mere '*in virtute*' just as much as Trent. It further seems to me to be of decisive importance that the Lutheran confession, like the Council of Trent, appeals for this to the fact that this confession relies on the unambiguous words of Scripture, and on the faith as it is accepted in the whole Church.[6] It also rejects expressly the idea that *fides* brings about the real presence (*Solida Declaratio*, VII, 10, 121), it holds that even unworthy unbelievers really receive the body (l.c., 12, 123). It is the doctrine of the Sacramentarians and not of the Lutherans, that there is no essential difference between the *word* about the heavenly Christ and the *sacrament* of Christ present among us here (SD, VII, Introduction): '*edere corpus Christi*' and '*credere in Christum*' are not the same. Hence there is a real presence of an objective nature, which is prior to faith's reception, faith's appropriation of the sacramental happening. One could put it this way: the true body of Christ is not merely received '*vere et substantialiter*', but it is there and is given and *thus* received. '*Sentiunt et docent cum pane et vino vere et substantialiter adesse, exhiberi et sumi corpus et sanguinem Christi* (SD, VII, 14) (cf. also the '*vere porrigi etiam indignis*', contrasted with the '*vere sumere*', l.c., 16).[7] It seems to me incorrect to try to water down this consent (partial though it is) between Catholics and Lutherans by invoking a dissent which is supposed to go deeper, as for instance in the general notion of sacrament, the meaning of faith etc. For this consent is attached by both sides to something that precedes all theological back-

[6] *Apologia Confessionis Augustanae* 10 (*Die Bekenntnisschriften* . . . 247/48).

[7] We should also note what '*usus*' really means in the Lutheran vocabulary: the *whole* liturgical process, not the *sola manducatio quae ore fit* (*Solida Declaratio* VII, 85f.). Lutherans take it for granted that Christ must be adored in the Eucharist *in usu* (*Solida Declaratio* VII, 15, 126). The concept of *usus* in *Denz.* 876 seems to be narrower.

grounds and *a prioris* in all good theology: the word of Scripture and the consent of the Church and its tradition.

I find it therefore incorrect to interpret the real presence in Lutheran doctrine[8] in such a way that the body of Christ is said to be already present everywhere and at all times, on account of the permanent actuality of the sacrifice of the cross and/or the ubiquity of the body of Christ—so that all that remains to be done is to 'distribute the ever-present gifts'. No, even according to the Lutheran confessions, an event takes place: the body of Christ which is not always already present becomes present through the words of the anamnesis of the Lord's Supper. Lutherans and Catholics are at one in affirming that the coming to be of the presence is in the nature of an actual happening. Otherwise there would be no point in the Lutheran restriction of this presence to the '*usus*'. Nor in the linking of this presence to bread and wine. Nor in saying that the unbeliever eats the body—'eating and drinking with the mouth'. Luther teaches expressly in the large catechism for instance, that the word must take place or the element remains a mere element, but that the sacrament only becomes the body and blood of Christ when the word is spoken.[9] One may call the Catholic doctrine of transubstantiation a 'miraculous transformation' (of which more later), but it seems to me certain that to make the real presence of Christ the 'universal presence' of a 'love not bounded by space' is Calvinist at the very best: it is not Lutheran (against Prenter). There would have been no need in this position to appeal to the omnipotence of God and the marvellous nature of the happening, as Luther does (in the large catechism). Luther's effort to bring in the doctrine of the divine ubiquity to explain the real presence of the body of Christ is a theological after-thought, which should not be used as the invariable starting-point to explain and restrict the view which Luther wished to have maintained with regard to the sacrament, because the explanation should be brought into line with what is to be explained, and not vice versa. Hence the 'multiple presence at will' of Chemnitz ('*ubicumque velit*', SD 29, 78, 92) is a more correct (though restrictive) interpretation of Luther's doctrine than the absolutely universal presence of the human

[8] As in the latest essay by Regin Prenter: 'Das Augsburgische Bekenntnis und die römische Messopferlehre', *Kerygma und Dogma* I (1955) 42–58, esp. 55.

[9] The *Solida Declaratio* VII, 10, 121 is even clearer, as is the *Formula Concordiae VII Negativa* XI (*Die Bekenntnisschriften* . . . 1014, 802): the body of Christ is present, *ubi coena Domini celebratur*.

nature of Christ, as found in Brenz and the *Formula Concordiae* (803, ll. 11 and 18) and in the quotations from Luther in the SD, 81ff.

2. The Council confesses that the real presence of Christ in the sacrament comes about by transubstantiation.

(a) The meaning of this affirmation is expressed as follows (Denzinger 877): *conversio totius substantiae panis in substantiam corporis Christi* . . . *et totius substantiae vini in substantiam sanguinis eius quae conversio convenienter et proprie a sancta catholica Ecclesia transsubstantiatio est appellata.*[10] In the corresponding canon (Denzinger 884) this *conversio* is called *mirabilis et singularis,* and then further interpreted (the expression 'accident' from scholastic philosophy being avoided) by being said to take place '*manentibus dumtaxat speciebus panis et vini*'.[11] This is not the first time that the expression *transsubstantiatio* occurs in documents of the magisterium. Berengarius' confession of faith at the Roman Council of 1079 mentions a '*substantialiter converti*' (Denzinger 355), and the term *transsubstantiari* is used to describe the process by Pope Innocent III (Denzinger 416); *transsubstantiatio* is mentioned in the profession of faith drawn up by the Fourth Lateran Council (1215—*transsubstantiatis pane in corpus et vino in sanguinem,* Denzinger 430) and that of the Second Council of Lyons (1274, Denzinger 465—*quod in ipso sacramento panis vere transsubstantiatur in corpus et vinum in sanguinem Domini nostri Jesus Christi*).[12] The definition given in the Council of Trent is taken almost word for word from St Thomas, III, q. 75, a. 4.[13]

[10] The same definition in the Tridentine profession of faith (*Denz.* 997) and *Denz.* 1469 (Benedict XIV's profession of faith for the Orientals) and *Denz.* 1529 (against the synod of Pistoia).

[11] Elsewhere too the word '*species*' is always used: *sub specie illarum rerum sensibilium* (*Denz.* 874), *sub panis et vini specie* (876), *sub alterutra specie* . . . (876), *sub specie panis* (877), *sub unaquaque specie* (885). But the expression *vini accidentia* is already found in a brief of Innocent III (416) and later in the condemnation of Wycliff by the Council of Constance (582); *species panis et vini* however in the fourth Lateran Council (430) and in the *Decretum pro Armenis* (698). (All numbers refer to *Denz.*)

[12] Further texts *Denz.* 544: *transsubstantiatio;* 581 against the affirmation of Wycliff at Constance: *substantia panis* . . . *et substantia vini* . . . *remanent in sacramento altaris;* the same in *Denz.* 666; *Decretum pro Armenis* A.D. 1439, *Denz.* 698: *substantia panis in corpus Christi* . . . *convertuntur; Decretum pro Jacobitis* A.D. 1442, *Denz.* 715: *transsubstantiari; Denz.* 1529, against the Synod of Pistoia of A.D. 1794.

[13] Luther, however, is still wrong, when he ascribes the formation of the concept of transubstantiation to St Thomas (M. Luther, *Werke.* Kritische Gesamtausgabe VI, 456[36]). The expression comes from the theology of the 12th century (Magister Roland, about 1150; Stephen of Tournai, about 1160; Petrus Comestor 1160–1170).

The Encyclical *Humani Generis* states disapprovingly that some Catholic theologians had voiced the opinion that the doctrine rested on the out-moded concept of substance and needed to be corrected (*'transsubstantiationis doctrinam, utpote antiqua notione philosophica substantiae innixam'*, Denzinger 3018)—in the sense of a purely spiritual presence of Christ. Since the dogma of transubstantiation, even in its explicit formulation, has stood for centuries in the faith of the Church, the Church would have had to deny its own being, as it understood itself to be, if it gave up this doctrine. While the Council of Trent had had to struggle to find the correct expression for its faith in such matters as inherent righteousness, certainty of salvation and so on, it was otherwise with transubstantiation. There was no real debate about it at the Council. The Council regarded this doctrine as something definitive, on which there could be no going back.

(b) The Council finds proof of this doctrine[14] in the fact that Christ declares that what he offers (the Apostles) under the appearance of bread *is* his body. This means that if the words of consecration are to be taken in their strict and literal sense, and if they bring about the event of the presence of the body of Christ, then what Christ offers his Apostles is not bread, but his body. This statement, as it stands, must be accepted by all who refuse to give a vague, figurative meaning to the words of Christ. Hence we frequently find in the Lutheran confessions of faith the words *'panem esse corpus Christi'*—and not first and last *'porrecto pane simul adesse et vere exhiberi corpus Christi'*[15] or the like. But if what Christ gives

[14] Cf. J. A. de Aldama, *De S. Eucharistia*[2] (Madrid 1953) 294 no. 105; '*nota: argumentationem totam* (on transubstantiation) *fieri ex veritate verborum . . . sc. nisi admittatur transsubstantiatio, veritas verborum Christi salvari non potest.*' This argument is said to be certain, at least along with the declaration of the Church. And apparently (*ut videtur*) also independently of it. After the Council, the opposing view of Scotus(?), Durandus and the Nominalists (*DTC* V, 1305f.), namely that transubstantiation cannot be proved from the words of Christ, is said to be no longer tenable.

[15] Concordia of Wittenberg, 1536, no. 2 (*Die Bekenntnisschriften . . . 65*); Grosser Katechismus, *De sacramento altaris:* '*quomodo panis et vinum Christi corpus et sanguis esse possunt*'; this is the more original formula, compared to (*ibid.*): '*corpus et sanguinem . . . in et sub pane . . .*'. This is also recognized in the *Solida Declaratio* VII, 34/35 (*Die Bekenntnisschriften . . . 983*): the words '*sub pane, cum pane, in pane*' are to explain '*panem in coena esse corpus Christi*'. *The Schmalkaldian Articles* III, 6 (*Die Bekenntnisschriften . . . 450*): '*de sacramento altaris statuimus panem et vinum in coena esse verum corpus et sanguinem Christi*' (In the German text: *Vom Sakrament des Altars halten wir dass* [unter] *Brot und Wein im Abendmahl sei der wahrhaftige Leib*

his Apostles is his body, and if we must really and truly take it, without misgivings, that what our *experience* knows apart from our faith in the word of Christ is the same as before: then this two-fold premise, if it is not to be voided in one direction or the other, can be expressed by saying that what is given is really and truly the body of Christ, under the experimental reality (but only this!) of bread. If—borrowing an obvious terminology but not adopting its proper meaning—I call the proper, definitive and true reality of a concrete thing 'substance';[16] and if I see the 'species' (appearance, look, understood as an objective but partial and particularly prominent reality) as the way the reality presents itself to a particular standpoint, but not as it is criticized and disclosed in its relativity from the true and absolute point of view—in this case, the word of God; then it can be said that what is given is not the substance of the bread, but the substance of the body of Christ under the species of

---

und Blut Christi . . . [under the bread and wine is the true body and blood of Christ]' The 'under' is therefore an addition or correction in the manuscript: *Die Bekenntnisschriften* . . . XXIV; contemporaneous but secondary).

[16] Cf. F. Selvaggi, 'Il Concetto di sostanza nel Dogma Eucaristico in relazione alla fisica moderna', *Greg.* 30 (1949) 7–45. We read p. 13:

E' ovvio che nella definizione conciliare il termine sostanza deve essere preso in primo luogo in questo significato volgare, vago ancora ed indeterminato, secondo il quale la sostanza del pane è semplicemente il pane, ciò per cui il pane è realmente pane, ciò che si richiede per la verità della proposizione: questo è pane . . . Che la sostanza sia ens in se et per se subsistens, come rileveremo meglio in seguito, è una determinazione filosofica aggiunta al significato puramente volgare, e non richiesta dal senso della definizione . . .

He goes on to say (17) that there is no apodictic proof to be drawn from the definition, that the species is a *realtà oggetiva* and (really) distinct from the substance. This is said to be only the *interpretazione più naturale delle formule del Tridentino*, but not part of the dogma, merely the usual common doctrine of theologians. There is, he says, even less reason to count the other elements which Aristotle and St Thomas include under substance and accident (*ens in se subsistens* and *ens in alio*) as part of the dogma.

He says that modern science forbids us to speak as St Thomas did of a substantial form of bread which informs the mass of bread and gives it its substantial unity (42).

If, he says, we follow modern physics when speaking of physical change, and call it a change which can be described by a *definizione operativa*, that is, one that can be registered by a series of at least conceivable experiments, transubstantiation is evidently not a physical change (44). In this sense, the dogma of the Eucharist is outside the scope of physics and scientific criticism. The Councils of the Church never intended to define the scholastic theses of substance and accident. But the Church has made it sufficiently clear that it is fully in accord with this doctrine, which cannot be denied without temerity (44–45).

bread. If one also considers that the giving has the character of an event, that it includes or presupposes a happening, in other words, that it was not always true that this was the body of Christ, then one can and should express the matter as follows: what is offered to be eaten, the body of Christ under the species of bread, has come from the substance of bread by a change and transformation. One may call this a 'miraculous transformation' but still, transubstantiation is merely the exact form of the statement which is to be—logically—justified, and in which the Council sees the basis for the traditional doctrine of transubstantiation: that that which Christ gives his Apostles is his body, this and nothing else. If one said that what Christ gives his Apostles is bread and his body, understanding by bread, in a sort of positivist empiricism, the experimental reality strictly as such and nothing else, one would have said nothing contrary to Catholic dogma. At the most, one would not have covered it entirely. It is only when one says that the 'substance' of bread is there along with the substance of the body of Christ that one would be in formal contradiction to the Catholic dogma. But one would also have said something about which experience gives no information, and on which the words of Christ give no instruction, but rather say the contrary. For if what is given is *also simply* bread, hence bread from *every* aspect, hence the substance of bread—substance in the sense given above, which will be further developed, but not in the metaphysical sense of a given philosophical system—it would not be the body of Christ, but bread. And the bread could be called body only by the metonomy of taking the container for the contained, a metonomy unknown to tradition—and not suggested by the nature of things. But if one once accepts such a metonomy, a purely figurative and symbolic interpretation can no longer be excluded. The statement, of course, in the restricted sense first quoted above, would not be false, but it would say less than the Tridentine dogma. And one cannot say that one is rightly content with this modest formula, which simply couples extrinsically the word of Christ with the testimony of our limited, positivist experience. For this would mean that what is *given* is the body of Christ under the 'bread' in the merely empiricist sense. But then the question is inevitable: can this way of understanding bread in an empiricist and positivist sense be affirmed as absolutely as when we speak of bread in the language of everyday life, and mean bread which is also objectively and in itself nothing else but bread and is entirely bread? If the answer is yes, then the apparently modest statement of faith and positivist experience would be the equivalent of maintaining two substances; and every connexion between the appearance of bread and the body of Christ would be eliminated, though there must be one, if that which is given in the form of bread is to be truly the body of Christ. If one does not say (at least silently) that the substance of bread has ceased to be, then one speaks of bread (in the empiricist sense), in so far as it has absolutely nothing to do with the presence of the body of Christ. But it can no longer be said of such 'bread' that it is the body of Christ.

(c) Up to the present, we have merely been trying to explain the reasons given by the Council for transubstantiation. This effort has already involved us rather deeply in the explanation of this Catholic dogma and the delimitation of its meaning. We have not in fact been able to avoid a particular interpretation of the meaning and its demarcation, for which we ourselves must take responsibility and where it is not certain that al Catholic theologians will agree with me. Some further remarks are called for on the meaning and limits of the affirmation which speaks of transubstantiation, even though this must be on our own account and at our own risk, and even though it means anticipating to some extent the subject-matter of the third part of our investigation. If I go rather far afield, I can only ask to be excused. There is no other way of explaining what I mean.

First I should wish to make a conceptual distinction of a fundamental nature, which I shall make use of later. I should like to distinguish between a logical and an ontic explanation of a matter, and try to explain this distinction. The *logical* explanation of a statement about a given matter would be a statement which makes the statement to be explained clear, that is, more definite and unmistakable, by interpreting it on its own terms, that is, without appealing to matters distinct from the matter to be explained. The logical explanation—to put it crudely for the moment—explains by giving precisions, but does not affirm anything else in explanation of the matter in hand. Hence the conceptual tools used for the explanation can be deciphered in the matter itself and derived from it. This would still be the case if the *verbal* terminology used in the explanation were actually derived from somewhere else, provided that it were understood—implicitly or explicitly—that the terminology thus used was intended only in the sense, scope and implications which result from the matter to be explained itself. I suspect that we have in theology many such logical explanations of originally dogmatic statements. That it is sometimes, not always, so, may perhaps be indicated by the fact that the *more precise* declaration and interpretation of this declaration may vary widely among theologians, so much so, that one must ask oneself what is really held in common about the objective content of the dogma, when the further explanations differ so widely. I must forbear to give examples. But I may say in passing that the efforts of Catholic theologians to give an ontic explanation of the dogma of transubstantiation are profoundly different, and that this seems to me to indicate that the dogma of transubstantiation itself is a logical explanation of the words of Christ, not an ontic one, such as is attempted in the various free opinions put forward by Catholic theologians in the further explanation of transubstantiation. But more of this later. The *ontic* explanation of a statement about a given matter would be the explanation which asserts *something else* than the matter in question, but something which is capable of rendering it intelligible, and so preserving it from misunderstandings, by giving for instance indications of its cause, of the precise, concrete way in which it came about and so on. I have explained the darkness before my eyes ontically when I connect the statement, 'it grows dark before my eyes' with the switching off of the light or a physiological atrophy of the nerve of sight.

It should then be clear at once, that for the proper understanding of a logical explanation the retrospective reference to the assertion to be explained always remains necessary. For it is always a matter of the same content, and in the cases met with in theology, this is never accessible independently of the original formulations which are to be explained. Hence it seems to me that the ancient dogma of the Church about the hypostatic union of the two natures in the one person of the Word is an example of such a logical explanation of what is said in the Scriptures about Jesus Christ. One remarks in fact that when one tries to grasp the meaning of nature and hypostasis, in so far as they are really distinct from one another—which is the only way that these concepts are useful in the doctrine of the hypostatic union—one constantly has to have recourse to statements such as are made of Christ precisely in Scripture. The ontic explanation however (as the little example given above shows) is not confined to the matter to be explained but exists in its own right, because it in fact expresses another content. We cannot go into further particulars of the question here: but in spite of the constant retrospective reference in the logical explanation to the statement to be explained, a reference from which it derives its vitality and without which it perishes in empty verbalism and a conceptual rationalism without content, the logical explanation is of supreme importance. Everyone knows why basically, everyone uses this sort of explanation. Anyone who studies biblical theology for instance tries to say exactly what Scripture says, and yet cannot simply repeat the words of Scripture. The difference between Catholic and Protestant theology here seems to me to be only this—an essential one, to be sure—that for the Catholic theologian the logical explanation of the words of Scripture by the Church can become a definite truth of faith, while on principle for the Protestant theologian it remains—theology, which is always subject to revision in the opposite sense. We may remark in passing that though the logical explanation can become unchangeable dogma for us, our explanation still shows that a qualitative difference remains as regards Scripture. Both for its validity as binding in faith, and for its content and meaning, such a formula always remains bound to the word of Scripture (or primitive tradition), just as of course the word of Scripture only remains living and judging when it constantly finds its way into each changing historical situation through dogmatically binding explanations (of a logical type).

Presupposing this distinction, I should like to put forward the thesis that the dogma of transubstantiation (in so far as it is really strict *dogma*) is a logical and not an ontic explanation of the words of Christ taken literally. This of course must be properly understood. It does *not* imply that the statement about transubstantiation is not concerned with any objective reality as to its content. It does of course affirm a reality. It intends to say exactly what Christ says: that what he gives is his body and no longer bread, though bread had been there, because his declaration effectively changes the reality and produces what it affirms: the reality of the body of Christ instead of the substance of the bread. I call the doctrine of transubstantiation logical on account of its relationship to the words of Christ, which are to be explained and guarded against all misunderstandings that would weaken or deny their sense. By this I mean that the doctrine of transubstantiation tells me no more than do the words of Christ, when I take them seriously. The function of this doctrine is not to explain the real presence by accounting for *how* it takes place, so that the manner of its coming, understood in itself as *another* process, would explain how the real presence came to be. Transubstantiation, as a dogma, means more than just any sort of a real presence, but it does not affirm anything more than the real presence which is there when what is given is understood as the presence of the body of Christ. It is a way of formulating the truth that the body is present, and it is correct and significant so far as it explains and defends that truth. But it is not an explanation which reduces the truth to something else which could be grasped in its own distinct content. This thesis does not mean that the dogma so understood, and thus limited to its defined sense, has not further implications which in certain circumstances may also be made explicit in theological reflexion. The further explanation of the dogma of transubstantiation as given by theologians in books and class-room does in fact go beyond what is certainly defined in the dogma, and tries to turn the logical explanation of the words of Christ into an ontic one. This or that attempt may be, at least to some extent, the common doctrine of the schools. Possibly some element of such an attempt may be so strongly supported by stringent reasoning and the universal consent of theologians that it cannot be positively called in doubt without temerity (as we say). It may be that the Church rejects a particular effort in the line of a further ontic explanation of transubstantiation and the words of Christ which are given logical precisions thereby, as denying or endangering its dogma. But all such efforts of scholasticism in their various forms (reproduction, adduction, pure conversion and so on), presupposing the standard metaphysics of substance and accident accepted by this scholasticism—and which I for my part find quite correct—and other attempts of the same kind which are rather based on a Cartesian or a dynamic notion of material being, are explanations which are not to be identified with the dogma. This rests solely on the words of Christ, and implies only the possibility of what is implied in these words of Christ: it does not imply *other* matters which can only be known by presupposing a given philosophical system. Since it is not always easy to keep the two matters clearly apart, differences of opinion may occur among Catholic theologians as to what on the one hand is precisely and clearly implied in the dogma of transubstantiation (because implied in Christ's words) and therefore belongs to the dogma, and as to what on the other hand only belongs to the theological explanation of the doctrine in terms of a given philosophical conception. But that the two things must be distinguished on principle is undoubtedly accepted by all Catholic theologians. The dogma therefore, with regard to its sense *quoad nos*, is to some extent blurred round the edges: but this it shares with all human utterances, even those of Scripture. I can understand a text of Scripture quite well and accept it unconditionally, and still be in the dark as to whether this or that is implied in its meaning and hence affirmed along with the truth.

What is the *proof* that the doctrine of transubstantiation intends to be no more than a logical explanation, in our sense, of the words of Christ? It seems to me to be the fact that *on the one hand*, the Council declares that this doctrine is derived from the words of Christ.[17] Hence one can say that it can imply no more than what results from these words. This is not however a clear proof of the thesis put forward. It is possible *a priori* that a statement could be deduced from another, the content of which is not the same as the first. But if one notes *on the other hand* that apart from the meaning of the dogma so postulated and defined, the *further* theological explanation displays either merely verbal agreement or a lack of unity; and if one notes that the theologians state expressly, as a principle, that a distinction must be made between the content of the dogma as such, and its theological explanation with the help of certain metaphysical presuppositions: it all adds up to the correctness of the thesis.

If this thesis is presupposed, we can only repeat what we have already said about the meaning of the dogma of transubstantiation. How substance is to be understood dogmatically in the strict definition of the Council, what species (appearance, figure) means here, is to be derived from the statement itself which is to be explained. In an adequate and comprehensively valid statement of reality, therefore where God speaks or where man may rightly speak on his own behalf, substance is that which makes it objectively true that a certain thing pointed to and distributed is either really bread and bread alone, or is not bread, but the body of Christ. The species is the empirical appearances of a thing, as it presents itself to us, but not as criticized from a higher, more comprehensive, 'truer', standpoint. In this sense of the words we say: out of the substance of bread, while the mere species of bread remains, the substance of the body of Christ has come to be. The Catholic magisterium (in '*Humani Generis*') has recently rejected various efforts on the part of some Catholic theologians which looked for an easy solution, by interpreting away rationalistically the concepts of substance and species, giving a much too intelligible distinction between concrete reality and religious interpretation. The former became a parallel to accident, the latter to 'substance' and

---

[17] According to de Aldama, it is no longer possible to hold, with the nominalist theologians of the late middle ages, that transubstantiation can be arrived at except from the words of Christ.

transubstantiation was made very understandable, much too understandable. This will not do, because in the Catholic understanding of the faith, it is impossible to evaporate either the substance of bread or the substance of the body of Christ by idealizing them as some sort of realities only in the world of meaning and interpretation. Christ speaks in the dimensions in which he very concretely gives food to his Apostles, that food being his body. But even this most recent rejection of an incautious effort to interpret the doctrine of transubstantiation has in no way expanded the strictly defined dogma of the real presence of Christ and of transubstantiation. It still has the simple meaning which we have ascribed to it.

(d) Why the Lutheran confession of faith rejects transubstantiation while affirming the real presence I have not been able to see. In the Schmalkaldian Articles it is rejected as 'cunning sophistry'.[18] In the *Formula Concordiae* it is rejected as papistical, without any further reasons being given. In the *Solida Declaratio*[19] of the *Formula Concordiae* it is rejected only in a passing reference. But we may perhaps find here (983) an explanation of the negative attitude, because the Protestant doctrine of the union of bread and body is seen as an analogy to the doctrine of the two natures in Christ—though here it must be emphasized that the *Solida Declaratio* itself has to allow for the difference between a hypostatic and a sacramental union, and does so candidly. The third place where the *Solida Declaratio* speaks of the matter[20] likewise offers no further explanations. In the Confession of Augsburg and in the Apology the question is, as we know, evaded, and even the Refutation of the *Confessio Augustana* refers rather timidly to the fact that the doctrine of transubstantiation should be added to the teaching on the presence of the *Confessio Augustana*. No doubt there were several motives at work in the rejection. Some of the scholastic speculation with regard to transubstantiation may have been identified with the defined dogma, so that the dogma itself— especially from the point of view of a Protestant understanding of faith and theology—could have been taken to be 'cunning sophistry' and hence contested. One might also ask whether a more modern and positivist concept of reality did not play a part when it was maintained that the bread remained as it was before, hence that the substance of the bread remained. The rejection of the adoration offered to Christ in the sacrament outside the *usus* and the rejection of medieval devotion to the Eucharist may also have affected the issue, though there is no stringent

---

[18] *Die Bekenntnisschriften . . . 452.*   [19] *Ibid.,* 977, 983.   [20] *Ibid.* 1010.

logical connexion between the two matters. The appeal to Scripture (1 Cor 10.16; 11.28), where Paul calls the Eucharist 'bread' is probably a Scripture argument produced as an after-thought, because there is no reason why St Paul should not have called the Eucharist bread, either by reason of the species or by reason of its character as 'heavenly' food, whether there was transubstantiation or not. Perhaps the objection raised most recently by Prenter, that the Catholic doctrine involves a 'miraculous transformation', points after all in the right direction, to the ultimate source of all disagreement. I say what I mean in frankly polemical terms and hope to give offence to nobody: it is an effort to confine the action of God to the purely divine sphere; it does not intervene to change anything where the things of the world are—the bread, morals, the grave and so on. It remains somewhere beyond the experience of unbelief, which is quite true, but it also remains outside worldly reality itself; God's in his heaven; but nothing happens where the bread is. But then to my mind it would be more logical to say: Christ is present only in faith, indeed only through faith. It would then not be just an accident that on the whole the doctrine of Zwingli or Calvin has prevailed to a great extent with regard to the Lord's Supper. But this does not prevent us from being glad of the amount of agreement which exists between the Lutheran and the Catholic doctrine.

III. WHAT REMAINS OBSCURE AND OPEN?

I mean among us Catholics. And here I must be brief.

1. To begin with, the controversies in the schools about various Catholic efforts to express the dogma more exactly and give it an ontic explanation remain open and obscure. It is quite impossible even to list them briefly. But from various points of view, they are in themselves not unimportant. For their being tolerated in the Church, that is, the fact that the magisterium sees no threat to dogma in them, in spite of their mutual opposition, shows that one must really make a distinction in this question between theology and metaphysical ontic explanation on the one hand, and dogma and (logical) explanation on the other, so that really the most that is left open is where exactly to draw the line between the two. These scholastic controversies need a good cleaning, to rid them of the dust of the school-room, and little has been done in this matter. When properly understood and sincerely debated, they are concerned to a great extent

with matters which could be important for the understanding of the dogma itself. The adductionism of Bellarmine and the view defended for instance by de la Taille with reference to St Thomas, have as their foundation or as their consequence a very profound difference in the real nature of 'presence' in the real presence; the 'spatiality' of this presence is conceived very differently in each case. These questions could still be of interest to controversial theology in inter-denominational discussions. But first Catholic theologians must learn to see the theological importance of such ancient controversies between the schools in a new light.

2. A clearer line of demarcation must be drawn in our question between the dogma and the theological propositions. The difference is no doubt recognized as a matter of principle. But in actual practice, the explanation of the dogma becomes the theology of the schools, without much notice being taken of the change. I do not think that every manual of theology announces at once like Selvaggi when it comes to the notion of substance, that *'ens per se et in se subsistens'* goes beyond the popular notion as given in the definition of Trent. The effort at demarcation which we have made cannot claim to enjoy universal support, and still less, that it could not be better and clearer, even if one is convinced that an absolute delimitation, which is clearly made in conscious thought, is quite impossible, given the structure of human knowledge.

3. A more precise definition would also be very desirable for the concept *'substantia panis'*. Not only is it not quite clear what is the popular concept of substance, in contrast to a strictly systematic one in philosophy, but it is not quite clear what *'substantia panis'* means. Here we meet with obscurity, precisely when one keeps to the theology of the schools and does not take the popular notion of substance as described above, but follows a procedure, justifiable in itself and perhaps logically stringent, and thinks of it as the *'ens per se et in se'* of scholastic philosophy as most, if not all, Catholic theologians do. For then it must be said that the substance of bread, as envisaged by St Thomas and the Fathers of the Council—envisaged, not defined—does not exist. One may be convinced of the permanent validity of the metaphysical concept of substance, one may hold that this concept can be defended in a transcendental *a priori* methodology against all empiricism as a condition of possibility of any true affirmation. But still one can no longer maintain today that bread is *a* substance, as St Thomas and the Fathers of the Council obviously thought it was. One can only regard a morsel of bread as an agglomeration

of substances and we do not know in which elementary particles the notion of substance is verified, and in what particular fashion this concept can be imagined as verified in material beings, in view of the lack of sharp distinction between one particle and its surroundings, its 'field', etc. One could of course say that these questions made no difference to the dogma or to its ordinary metaphysical interpretation in the schools. One could say that if there is substance at all (and it is still certain that there is, even when the most modern physics is supposed, when this does not cease to be physics to become a mere positivism, not just methodologically but in objective content), and if there is an agglomeration of *substances* in bread (which may also be taken for granted), then there can be a transubstantiation of the substance of bread in the metaphysical sense (which goes beyond the necessary meaning of the dogma). It would be transubstantiation of the agglomeration of substances which we call bread, and hence theology would be justified in holding on to its ancient position, unaffected by the changes in modern science. We do not intend to challenge this answer. But one may perhaps doubt whether it is adequate.

First of all, it would be interesting to hear more precisely from the theologians who give this answer, what are the hermeneutical principles of conciliar interpretation which allow them to reach their *agglomeratum substantiarum* from the '*substantia panis*' of the Council. What is to prevent our saying that the Fathers of the Council thought of bread as *one* substance, and hence this is what they defined and hence this is what also exists? Is not this the procedure used in other cases where the assertions of a Council are interpreted? What then are the exact hermeneutic principles which must necessarily be deduced from such observation of the actual interpretation of conciliar statements? And then there is the question of the content: is the agglomeration in question, being an agglomeration of *substances*, of such a nature that one can say that the bread ceases to be when the substances in question cease to be? To put it another way: in our present-day understanding of the nature of bread (as manifested precisely in the doctrine of the agglomeration of substances), is not bread an accidental combination of elementary particles, of such a nature that it is precisely this accidental combination, under a typically anthropological aspect as such, which constitutes the nature of bread? Is *this nature* really gone, and has its disappearance become intelligible, when the substantiality of the elementary particles ceases? It is easy to understand that a man ceases to be a man when his substantiality ceases; but that something the precise essence of which is the accidental constellation of elementary substances ceases to exist, is less obvious. To put it again in another way: the being of bread appears to us today to be in the dimension which in scholastic terms would be called that of the *species* of empirical, anthropomorphic appearances; hence the being of bread does not appear to be affected at all when a change takes place in the metempirical dimension of the substantiality of the elementary particles. In my opinion, the explanation of the dogma in the logical sense, as given above, is completely unaffected by these questions. But the general scholastic theory of transubstantiation does not seem to escape all difficulties and questioning by its standard answer, which we anticipated above, to the difficulties raised against the scholastic notion of substance.

4. A further question is this: normally, scholastic works on dogma begin the treatise on the Eucharist with the real presence, and then come the sections on the sacrifice and the sacrament, in this order or the reverse. But in any case the section on the real presence is put at the start of the whole treatise *De Eucharistia* as the first and most fundamental part. This is explicable on formal and on apologetical and polemical grounds. But one must not try to dissemble the fact that this method has its disadvantages. It automatically puts the real presence in a perspective in which the local presence of Christ (to put it that way for once) is the main centre of interest and everything else is derived from this. I mean that we Catholic theologians have something to learn from the '*in usu*' doctrine of Protestant Christians, without denying the teaching of Trent. '*Institutum est . . . ut sumatur*' (Denzinger 878). To put it another way: the first truth of the Eucharistic doctrine is, 'This is my body', not, 'Here I am present'. The second statement is contained in the first, but does not exhaust its content and its point. Just like the Bible, the doctrine of transubstantiation should be a sort of barrier against taking the 'presence' as the first and fundamental concept in this treatise. It is not because Christ is present that we offer him as our sacrifice and receive him in communion, but the other way round. And hence one could ask oneself whether one could not formulate and clarify the basic statements on the Eucharist in such a way that while the real presence is clearly recognizable, the character of sacrifice and of food is primarily and comprehensively stated, and at the same time, the character of event which belongs to the process. This is not just idle hair-splitting. It has been said somewhat maliciously that the popular understanding of the Mass is that people

think of it merely as the consecration of the host in the morning for 'Benediction of the Blessed Sacrament' in the evening. This is an exaggeration which still contains a correct and important observation. Could we not find a more fundamental theological principle for the real presence, as we must call it, which would of itself bring out the true nature of this 'presence', namely that it is the presence of the sacrifice and the food? Does not a more comprehensive and unprejudiced biblical theology point perhaps in this direction? Could we not achieve in this way a clearer link between the real presence, and the Eucharistic adoration of the Lord implied therein, and the original reception, the '*usus*', which would make it possible to distinguish more exactly between the legitimate Eucharistic worship outside the Mass and certain unhappy developments? It cannot be denied that many late medieval or baroque forms of Eucharistic worship are in fact being pared down, with the official but discreet help of the Church.[21] What are the theological principles on which these moves are based?

5. The *history* of the dogma which we are dealing with has been comparatively well investigated. The patristic and medieval material is ready. Could not a new effort be made to see whether the somewhat lifeless account of the past, in which everything is brought down to the level of the conventional theology of today, could not be turned into a really vital quest for the truth? I do not mean that what has now become clear, what has since been 'defined', should become obscure again. But is there not more to be gained in the line of a profounder insight into the mystery of the Eucharist than we now possess explicitly, from a well-intentioned rekindling of the antagonism—not contradiction—between the transformism of St Ambrose and the very realistic symbolism of St Augustine? Is it for instance a clear and vital reality for our average popular piety that for all the reality of the presence, the reception of the body of Christ is only *res et sacramentum* for something that is in essential respects higher and more comprehensive, the union with Christ which takes place in grace and faith and love? That the real reception of the real body of Christ in the sacrament is only the sign and the means, and hence sacramental sign, for *this* unity, which is the decisive thing? This fact is in itself obvious to theologians. Is justice not done to it in ordinary piety,

---

[21] There are, for instance, the numerous 'expositions' during and outside Mass. And then again, there is a tendency for the Mass to absorb other forms of divine worship.

simply because it seems somewhat incidental and because piety always reduces theology to primitive concepts? Or is it not because theology speaks in such a way that this supremely important truth, so strongly emphasized by St Augustine, has been pushed somehow into the penumbra of theological consciousness and outside the range of piety, so that communion with the Christ who suffered and the proclamation of his death has become a friendly state visit accompanied by tokens of grace and favour, but which has nothing to do with the history of the death and resurrection or the eschatological future of the meal in the final kingdom of God?

ON THE DURATION OF THE PRESENCE OF
CHRIST AFTER COMMUNION

A SHORT essay which I wrote on thanksgiving after Mass[1] was greeted in a very friendly and grateful way. Many readers had the impression that an answer had been attempted to a question which is often put but not always well answered. Disagreement was expressed by some with regard to one point only in the essay. It was apropos of the statement: 'One should be careful to avoid the style of the old-fashioned instructions on holy communion and not to say that the reason for thanksgiving is that Jesus Christ is "still" really present in the communicant after communion' . . . 'all these assertions are false or at least not sufficiently well founded in theology'. We may therefore be allowed to make some remarks here in explanation and justification of this statement.

To begin with, it is quite understandable that in an essay concerned with a matter of the spiritual life this thorny theological question could not have been avoided. In pious books and religious instruction thanksgiving is often based on the continuing real presence of Christ after communion. The writer has a vivid memory since his childhood of the story of how a saint sent two acolytes with burning candles after a communicant who had left the Church immediately after communion. And those who think they must challenge the statement in question appeal to the fact that 'all' theologians hold the opinion which is here rejected as unproved or false. If then the reasons for thanksgiving are discussed at all, it is impossible to avoid opening up this dogmatic question, even though it looks rather strange in an essay on ascetics. For the precise question is this: how can the meaning and justification of thanksgiving be presented theologically in such a way that the reasons are really valid dogmatically

[1] Cf. K. Rahner, *Mission and Grace* I (London & New York 1966) 280–305.

and not just pious-sounding talk? This example, not very important in itself, shows finally how readily questions of the spiritual life can in certain circumstances bring up difficult questions of dogma and how it is not always possible, with the best will in the world, for ascetics and mystics to confine themselves only to the theses of dogmatic theology which have been defined by the magisterium or are otherwise beyond doubt.

In the comments made on the essay, it was surprising to find that the opponents of the thesis in question did not take the trouble to discuss the arguments which, as the writer thought, dealt at sufficient length with the reasons for the thesis. But in theology too it is incorrect to dismiss the unusual in favour of the cherished old opinions without giving any reasons.

It is not true that the appeal to the fact that practically all theologians (which we readily concede)[2] have been of the opposite view proves at once that their thesis is certain and that the contrary is temerarious. A common opinion of theologians—and there cannot be question of more than this in the present case, even when presented in the light most favourable to the adversaries—is only binding on an individual theologian when it is put forward by all theologians as *binding* or when they link it so closely to assured truths of faith that its denial would endanger these truths which are the basis for the opinion. There can be no question of this in the present case. For the theologians start from a principle which we do not deny or call in doubt, one on which on the contrary we are in entire agreement with them, and which is the only one to which they can and do appeal in this matter: the principle that the real presence of the body of Christ lasts as long as the Eucharistic species exists.[3] This is the principle from which they start. Their deductions are correct if and in so far as they can really be derived from this principle. But if the interpretation of the principle is so incautious and inexact that deductions are drawn which do not follow from an exact interpretation of the principle; and if it can be

---

[2] We may leave it an open question as to whether all of them really do. It seems that F. Hürth-P. M. Abellan think otherwise: *De sacramentis* (Rome 1947). They *distinguish* the ending of the presence by *consumptio* (*i.e. per modum cibi vel potus sumi*) and by *corruptio*; according to the common opinion, there can be only one reason, the *corruptio* in the physico-chemical sense.

[3] We may remark in passing that even this principle is given a prudent qualification by theologians, since the Council of Trent only defined the real presence before consumption, *Denz.* 886, 876; the principle is qualified by J. A. de Aldama for instance as merely '*sententia theologorum communis et certa*'.

shown that there are understandable but still incorrect reasons why this inexact interpretation of the basic principle should hold the field and lead to wrong conclusions: it will then be clear that a simple 'consequence', even if shared by many or all theologians for a long time, cannot claim to be accepted on dogmatic grounds.

The insufficiently exact interpretation of the common principle, which led to unproved or false conclusions, has to do with the concept and reality of the Eucharistic species. And the reason which makes this inexact interpretation understandable is the medieval concept of nature. Let us consider. The Council of Trent still speaks without misgivings of *the* substance of *bread* and wine. Every theologian now concedes, especially if he is explaining transubstantiation in the traditional sense against more modern attempts at explanation,[4] that in the case of the bread, in the individual species, we have not a single substance as in the case of the really primary particles of matter or other parts of nature such as man, beasts, etc., but an agglomeration of several substances. If one thinks out this difference in approach—which leaves the dogma as such certainly untouched—one sees at once that the older opinion had no occasion to, and could not, distinguish clearly and consciously between bread as an *anthropological* entity and bread as a physico-chemical body. Bread, though prepared by man, was considered without conscious reflection as a natural body such as occurs elsewhere and was interpreted as a single substance. One recognizes today that bread is a typically anthropological entity. Physically and chemically bread is no real substantial unity, but an accidental agglomeration of many combinations of atoms and molecules, united physically only by a very extrinsic, accidental and almost local concentration. Humanly speaking, however, and hence sacramentally, this formation is a unity, an intelligible unity, created by man, and possessing such unity only in relation to him, within the sphere of his life and action. Hence it is clear that the real presence of Christ only lasts as long as this *humanly* intelligible unity of 'bread' exists. No theologian can question this in principle. To make the point clear, let us consider for instance the following cases or possibilities. There is radio-active carbon in all wine. Transubstantiation is to be predicted of every particle of carbon with its *whole* reality as long as it is part of the consecrated 'wine', since it is part of the transubstantiated 'substance' of the wine. But this atom is sending

[4] Cf. my essay: *The presence of Christ in the sacrament of the Lord's Supper* in this volume pp. 287–311.

out a ceaseless stream of beta-particles, which somehow participate in the substantiality of the whole reality. But as soon as they leave the field of the 'wine', they no longer belong to the wine, and so no longer to the reality 'under' which Christ is really present. Or again, if one made a molecule of some substance radio-active, so that it remained in principle recognizable, and added it to the wine to be consecrated, this molecule—supposing it was not an absolutely foreign body with regard to wine, but for instance a molecule of alcohol—would also be consecrated and hence also transubstantiated. If this molecule, which is still recognizable, were removed from the field of the wine—it does not matter whether the procedure is possible or not, technically—Christ would no longer be present under it, though chemically and physically nothing had happened but an accidental change of locality in the molecule. This is so obvious, that it is now even possible and quite easy technically to separate such a tiny quantity of 'wine', by a purely quantitative division, that there can be no question of wine any longer in the ordinary sense of human language. The real presence of Christ then ceases under this tiny quantity, though it is chemically exactly the same as the larger quantity from which it was taken. The tiny quantity needs only to be so small, for instance, that it can no longer be seen. Hence St Thomas sees quite correctly (III, q. 77, a. 4) that a purely quantitative reduction of the species of wine can prevent one calling it wine any longer—though chemically it remains 'the same' as before for a long time—and thus the presence of Christ ceases. Hence St Thomas correctly denies (III, q. 77, a. 8c) that a small amount of consecrated wine still indicates the presence of Christ if it is mixed with a large amount of non-consecrated wine. 'This' concrete consecrated wine no longer exists as something separate and distinguishable from the human point of view, even though 'physically' and 'chemically' it exists in exactly the same way as before. On the other hand, leavened and un-leavened bread are considerably different from the purely chemical point of view, but from the ordinary human view-point, which is all that matters here, both are bread and hence *materia consecrabilis*. These cases and possibilities show that 'bread' is not a purely physical and chemical reality, but a sensible reality belonging essentially to the realm of man and hence having properties which cannot be comprised by chemical terms and hence can disappear—so that something ceases to be bread—even though in the field of physics and chemistry as such nothing 'essential' has been changed.

St Thomas was therefore quite correct (the example was referred to in the first essay) when he said that the presence of Christ ceases if the bread is ground down: dust is in fact not bread in the human sense of the term. St Thomas looked on such pulverization as a sort of substantial change even in the physical world, which it is not. But St Thomas recognized correctly that dust is not bread, even though in chemistry or physics it is still exactly the same as bread. Hence the presence of Christ also ceases. (This, incidentally, ought to be noted by priests with scruples, who are so over-anxious that they can never purify the paten well enough.) Hence the principle remains: only where the species of bread is present and remains present can we speak of the real presence of Christ. But this general principle must be made more precise. The species of bread, as a sensible reality, can also cease to be, without any essential physical and chemical change, that is, when bread ceases to be 'bread' from the merely human and not physical aspect. Chemists of the food industry could certainly produce something which was chemically and physiologically 'the same' as bread, but which could not be considered as *materia consecrabilis*. Even a larger amount of water or an extensive dehydration, without any 'essential' chemical change, could turn bread into something else, a sort of porridge for instance. It follows that what constitutes bread is not just properties, qualities and circumstances within the categories of today's physics and chemistry, but in addition, qualities that lie outside this field. And then once more it follows that something can cease to be bread if these other proprieties disappear.

The question then remains: can bread, once it is *eaten*, still be regarded as species in human estimation, that is, as bread? It should already be obvious that the question cannot be answered by demanding that bread must be chemically changed, in terms of organic chemistry, if it is to be regarded as something other than it was before. If such a change occurs, it is of course a sign that the bread is no longer there. But if there is no such change, that does not prove that in human estimation the bread is still there. Chemical change is a positive criterion, but by no means the only one. Hence at least one may not draw the conclusion: bread after being eaten remains 'the same' (chemically) in the stomach for some time, hence the presence of Christ continues. It was only because theologians were not accustomed to distinguish clearly enough between bread as a physico-chemical reality and bread as bread, that this over-hasty conclusion was drawn. We now assert on the contrary: bread once eaten is not a human reality, whose meaning is that of food, of being eaten. And from this we deduce that the presence of Christ no longer persists. It is to be noted in this view that not everything which can be taken into the stomach and there have a nourishing effect is, according to general human estimation, food in the sense in which it is to be understood here. Otherwise bread reduced to powder would still be bread, and a species introduced into the stomach by a tube would have to be called the reception of the Eucharist, which cannot be proved, to say the least, and is hard to reconcile with the prohibition of the Holy Office of 27th January, 1886, forbidding this practice. We can only call bread or food something which a normal man under normal circumstances is ready to eat by the normal process of eating. Here again it is not a matter of chemistry but of ordinary human usage, just as in the question of what wheat is *materia consecrabilis*, what matters is not the secrets of scientific botany and the theory of evolution but ordinary human language. And thus we can safely say that bread once eaten is no longer food, no longer bread, and hence no longer the sign of the presence of Christ. In the '*defectus circa missam occurrentes*' in the Roman missal, provision is specifically made (X, 14) for a vomited species not being eaten again, if it is nauseating. But can something which is not expected to be eaten, at least under certain circumstances, be regarded as 'food', as 'bread'? In practice under certain circumstances people follow a praiseworthy 'tutiorism' in sacramental matters which allows for the continuing presence of the body of Christ. But this is not an objection against our explanation of the question of principle.

The opposite view leads to awkward consequences, which show that the theory of the continuing presence has very frail support. First of all, it would leave one at the mercy of the experts in physiology and chemistry. It would be for them to judge how long the presence of Christ remains. But this is unacceptable. If it be said that the normal human view of the non-expert is quite competent to judge the matter of the presence of bread, we should have to answer: 'What standards does the ordinary man use to tell if something is bread or not?' If he says: 'It is chemically the same as it was before', he submits himself, whether knowingly and willingly or not, to the verdict of the scientists. If he says, 'That is what I am accustomed to eat as bread; that is the sort of thing I eat; that is my normal and natural food', he affirms implicitly that bread once eaten is no longer bread. This sort of thing is not eaten, because it has already been eaten and hence is not suitable for consumption. Further, this view leads, at least with psychological necessity, to the opinion, shared no doubt by great theologians, that the sacramental effect of the sacrament *ex opere operato* can still increase as long as the species is still in the stomach. As we already remarked in the first essay, this view cannot be proved; and it is incorrect, because it is the eating and not the presence of the species in man which is the sacramental sign. But in any case, if one maintains that food once eaten is still bread, and so Christ is still really present for some time in man, one should be able to indicate some way in which the process is *salutary*. Otherwise the assertion of the continued presence of the body of Christ in the stomach of the Christian would be quite pointless, since without such a salutary effect it would be merely a corporal, local presence, such as unbelievers and unbaptized can have—if they are near the tabernacle or have gone physically to communion. But if such a salutary effect were ascribed to the local presence so affirmed, it would be quite logical to wish to have the species so efficiently turned out that it remained as long as possible. And then the question would arise, which finally only the physiologist could answer, as to how long this beneficent presence is prolonged; and the duration of thanksgiving would have to be measured by the length of the resistance of the species in each case. In a word, once one has begun to think in the terms suggested by this theological hypothesis, one comes to strange conclusions, which can only be dealt with by common sense. And it would be better then to start with the simple truth that bread ceases to be bread by the very fact of its being consumed, which ends the real presence of Christ like any other circumstance that eliminates bread as a human species. This is the only thing which makes it understandable that it is precisely the *eating* of the body of the Lord, and not the fact of its having been eaten, the action of eating and not the process of digestion is the sacramental sign of grace. But this again is quite intelligible: only the human act as '*actus humanus*', not the physiological process as '*actus hominis*' is admissible as a sacramental sign, since only a human act can also be an act of acceptance of the grace offered under this act and be a confession of faith and a personal proclamation of the death of the Lord.

The resistance offered by a rather confused piety to these truths, which are really obvious, comes ultimately from the fact that a clear enough distinction is not made between the presence of Christ through his Spirit in the depths of man's being (in his 'heart'), and the bodily presence of

Christ in the sacramental sign and hence in the eating. This latter type of presence is not the higher and sublimer, the goal and reward of Christians, but the sign and the means of the permanent presence of Christ through the Spirit, which is indicated and increased by this sacramental sign. Christ really comes to us and stays with us through this sacrament. But this permanent presence, to which the reception of the body of Christ under the species leads, does not consist of the further presence of his body within the Christian for a few minutes longer. It is the continued and ever more profound presence of the Lord in the Spirit, in the truth, without which even his flesh profits nothing, as the Lord himself says. The climax of holy communion is this personal communication in the Spirit. And this event does not become greater and more magnificent if one maintains without any real proof that its *sign*, which is purely a means, still persists when the eating of the consecrated food is over and done with.

A piety which does not quite know what it is doing finds itself here in a strange confusion. It considers the moment of communion as the time when the Lord *begins* 'to be there', to hold audience so to speak, so that one can now start to talk to him in a way which even the justified Christian living in his grace could not do up till then, because the Lord was not 'there'. But again, this piety does not mark the departure of the Lord, who after all has to go away, if he is only 'there' for a time. It does not reflect on this. After some time, the pious Christian ends the audience so to speak of his own accord, without asking himself does this leave the Lord standing there, so to speak, or is the audience at an end because the Lord has departed once more. The theological theory which maintains that this presence only ceases after some time, when the species ceases to exist in the stomach, is a learned theory, which does not in fact occur in the normal life of piety. Otherwise one would have to ponder much more exactly on *when* the ending of this presence takes place, something to which the normal Christian obviously pays no heed. To put it another way: in the standard view, the coming of Jesus *and* his going should be equally remarkable events, to which the pious act of the communicant should be directed. But there is no question of this. But this shows that there is something which has not been thought out properly. Of itself, the matter is clear and simple—if the standard view is not presupposed. The sacramental sign brings about an increasing coming and going of the Lord in his Spirit and in his grace, by the eating of the true body of the Lord. This is the permanent fruit of the sacrament, which is *not* withdrawn by Christ's going away again. But this shows that a *continued* bodily presence, which is only ended after a certain time, contributes nothing to the meaning of the sacrament. For the simple reason, that it would then simply be withdrawn again. Of course, if communion is regarded as admission to an audience which would not be possible otherwise, and if thanksgiving after communion is explained on this basis, one will have to attribute decisive importance to the length of such an abiding presence after communion. But then one has abandoned the only view of this sacrament which can be verified dogmatically, that it means union with Christ through his (increasing) grace of the Spirit. If the bodily presence of Christ was the primary *effect* of the sacrament—in view of an audience—and not merely the sacramentally efficacious sign of the real effect, the pious Christian would inevitably have to attach supreme value to retaining the bodily presence of Christ as long as possible. Significantly, such is not his attitude. It was the task of the first essay to show that even so, thanksgiving after communion is right and necessary, as well as the adoration of the Lord in the sacrament. And thanksgiving is perfectly possible without our presupposing a prolongation of the real presence of the body of Christ after communion.

PART SIX

Eschatology

13

THE HERMENEUTICS OF ESCHATOLOGICAL ASSERTIONS[1]

To give a brief lecture on the dogmatic principles governing the hermeneutics of eschatological assertions in the Bible and in the preaching of the Church is to undertake a task which is clearly too great to be performed in such a short time. What we have to say will be judged more favourably, we hope, in the light of these circumstances.

The question here posed is important for theology in many regards. To begin with, it may be said that it has hardly ever been dealt with explicitly in Catholic theology. The question could not of course have ever been *totally* neglected. Eschatological assertions are constantly made in the preaching of the Christian faith and in theology; either they are taken from Scripture or a foundation for them is sought in Scripture. But (formally at least) they may not be absolutely identical with the eschatological sayings of Scripture or of the original apostolic tradition; they may be interpretations of these sources, which translate their words into another world of concepts, transpose them to make them fit into another picture of the universe. If so, the whole process, which has been going on as long as Christian preaching and theology existed, must have been guided by certain hermeneutic principles, used to some extent consciously in the execution of this task. And of course some sort of general hermeneutics always existed. But in the long run, neither the special hermeneutics applied unconsciously, nor the principles of hermeneutics in general, could be adequate to the task. And they do not render our present

---

[1] The text of this short essay is that of a lecture given by invitation before the Catholic faculty of theology at the University of Bonn, 13th January, 1960. It was not possible to change the text itself without giving the subject a completely new approach, which was out of the question at this stage. We have therefore tried to clear up certain misunderstandings and obscurities of the unavoidably brief text by adding a few notes. We may refer for a general survey of the whole subject to K. Rahner, 'Eschatologie', *LTK* III², 1094–1098.

effort superfluous, where we try to grasp consciously and formulate expressly some theological principles for the hermeneutics of special eschatology. It is possible for someone who has never studied the science of logic to think in fact more logically than the logician by profession. But this does not make reflex thought on logic superfluous. It is the same with an explicit hermeneutics of eschatological assertions in relation to a hermeneutics which remains implicit. The idea that such hermeneutics has been sufficiently catered for by hermeneutics in general rests on the false and primitive conception, that the eschata form a world like any other, so that knowledge of them—in spite of its being determined, like other knowledge, by the object itself—presents no particular problems apart from those of the knowledge of theological realities in general. But it cannot be said that an explicit and more or less specific hermeneutics for eschatological assertions is part of the normal study of Catholic theology. Dogmatic treatises on eschatology omit this question completely. With regard to their object, they are all still in the stage where philosophy was when it still looked on its task as a purely objective metaphysic of objects, without a theory and metaphysic of knowledge, that is, before the turn to the subjective at the beginning of modern times.

We need not delay on the proof that such a situation cannot be allowed to continue. The change in cosmology from ancient to modern times certainly presents a deep-seated problem for eschatological assertions. But the task thus imposed cannot be satisfactorily accomplished by taking eschatology as an objectivating treatise on the eschata, and then, when it makes individual assertions about particular eschatological realities, beginning to think out each particular assertion, asking how it is compatible with the views and opinions which are held today about the universe and its future. What is needed is a fundamental consideration of the type of knowledge possible in such assertions, a verdict on the nature and bearings of such assertions with regard to theology and profane knowledge. The whole controversy which arose with regard to the notion of 'demythizing' shows that there is a real problem here, the question namely of what is the meaning of eschatological assertions in general, what they are really concerned with, how far they are part of a truth of faith, how and on what basis such assertions in Scripture are to be interpreted. Here a question has undoubtedly been posed in Protestant theology, which Catholic theology is far from giving its due attention.

The correct method which would normally be called for by our task would be, at least to begin with, that of *biblical* theology. That is, we should ask what are the principles of hermeneutics suggested by Scripture itself, where it makes eschatological assertions. We should listen carefully to these assertions; we should compare the various sets of concepts, disparate at certain levels, which lie behind the assertions; we should enquire precisely into their real origin, their *Sitz im Leben* or social setting, which in this case would really be the absolutely primordial experience of revelation, compared with which all other eschatological assertions are derivative and explanatory[2]—and are meant to be so; we should meditate on and compare the various eschatologies which are to be found in Scripture itself; we should apply the principle of the *analogia fidei* to biblical eschatology; we should investigate historically various eschatological notions, images, motifs, etc.; and then it would be quite possible to take the guiding line of the biblical assertions on eschatology and deduce certain principles, which will be those by which Scripture itself demands to be interpreted in these passages. In the short time at our disposal, it should be obvious that we cannot take this way, if we are to reach any conclusions. We must therefore adopt the method, in itself more problematic,[3] of basic dogmatic considerations. In doing so, we must simply suppose that the results of this method would be confirmed by a hermeneutics derived directly from biblical data, or at least would not contradict such an *a posteriori* hermeneutics. But these preliminary remarks must suffice, even though they have neither described exactly the method to be pursued nor justified it *a priori*. We turn therefore immediately to the actual question.

[2] This does not of course mean (in so far as we are dealing with Scripture) conclusions and explanations which have no binding force. All we mean is that Scripture itself contains theology, that is, new conclusions are drawn from the first, primordial and irreducible truths of revelation, new connexions between them are noted, etc. These conclusions (being those of inspired Scripture and of the authentic bearers of revelation) are absolutely binding on us and are perfectly entitled to be called 'revealed'. But to see exactly the meaning of such derivative (though binding) assertions and their bearings, to know what is *not* intended in certain cases, to see what questions are left open, it can be very helpful, and indeed necessary, to note how these assertions themselves are arrived at, what they articulate and explain without meaning to go any further. The logical process of their derivation can explain and limit more precisely the actual content of their affirmation.

[3] This method is not of course 'problematic' because and in so far as it is dogmatic, in this case, 'systematic'—but because in this question it is hard to say in any particular case whether and how far such systematic considerations can lead to a result.

Thesis 1. The Christian understanding of the faith and its expression must contain an eschatology which really bears on the *future*, that which is still to come, in a very ordinary, empirical sense of the word time. An interpretation of the eschatological assertions of Scripture, which in the course of simply de-mythizing it would de-eschatologize it in such a way that all eschatological sayings of Scripture, explicit or implicit, only meant something that takes place here and now in the existence of the individual and in the decision he takes here and now, is theologically inacceptable. This first principle needs no long explanation. It cannot be doubted that the doctrinal preaching of the Church intends to make assertions about future events which are still to come in time. In this sense too it is 'prophetic'. And the Catholic theologian cannot doubt that such assertions are not merely the expression of the *present-day* sense of the faith in the Church, but that this present interpretation must be held definitely and absolutely as that of the permanent and unchangeable faith itself. A later interpretation which would de-eschatologize it is radically excluded according to the Catholic notion of faith and doctrine. It is sufficient to note this fact here, since we are dealing with the dogmatic principles of hermeneutics. But we may add that the self-understanding of Scripture itself, no matter how existentially interpreted, undoubtedly excludes such an elimination of eschatology. It is not merely contrary to the professed faith of the Church, it is also contrary to Scripture.

Thesis 2. The Christian understanding of the nature, life and personal being of God takes his 'omniscience' not merely as a metaphysical axiom, but as a strict truth of faith, and makes it include God's knowledge of future events. In so far as this knowledge embraces the realities of the world and mankind, there can be no denying or doubting, in metaphysics or theology, the fundamental 'abstract' possibility of the communication of such future events: they are known by God and they are human, and hence do not of themselves in principle go beyond the capacity of human understanding.[4] Thus there is a principle which dominates all that we are

---

[4] This condition is to be noted, since it is important for the following considerations. It is not enough to appeal to the omniscience of God in itself, to explain that God can reveal future events to man. It must also be possible to affirm that such communications are also possible with regard to man, that is, that they do not surpass his powers of understanding. It is not simply true that anyone can be told anything. Such a process may break down not merely because of the knowledge (or ignorance) of the speaker, but also because of the receptive capacity of the hearer. Hence it is at once clear that there are some types of knowledge, certain degrees of

going to say: the principle of open-mindedness which has to reckon with the fact, along with the first Vatican (Denzinger 1784; cf. '*Humani generis*', Denzinger 2317), that man, as partner of the living God who can reveal himself, may not restrict beforehand the scope of God's possible word. Man may use no *a priori* to set up his own bounds, beyond which God neither may nor can reveal anything still to come in the future.[5] Nothing of what we have to say may be considered as a law by which man controls what God may reveal to man about the future. In a Catholic explanation of the hermeneutics of eschatology it must also be remembered that prophecy, that is, the prediction of the future, has always been seen in Catholic tradition—under certain conditions[6] which need not be discussed

---

clearness and intensity of knowledge, with regard to future events, which are not accessible to man in his present situation (if this is not to be radically transformed by such revelation). The axiom, *quidquid recipitur, ad modum recipientis recipitur*, remains true here. The situation of the hearer forms an *a priori* law for the possibility of his hearing; the act of understanding, while it remains 'objective' and true, is also determined by the structure of the hearer, which is finite and conditioned. Not everyone therefore can hear everything. This is very true, and it is at the basis of the following considerations (Theses 3ff.), but here in Thesis 2 the first thing to note is that it still does not place any absolute limits on God's power of communicating in whatever way he wills such future events as have to do with man. Such events, precisely *because* they are human, cannot be simply beyond the powers of his understanding, though to say this is not to prejudge the nature of this understanding and its limitations.

[5] This is not of course to decide whether and to what extent such a communication implies, and brings about, a real and existential change in the human situation and the constitution of being, as its presupposition. A strictly supernatural revelation (supernatural as regards its object) presupposes for instance (in a really Thomist metaphysics of knowledge—one not spoiled by nominalism) that the reception of the supernatural revelation is also a subjectively supernatural act, that is, inspired by divine (indeed uncreated) grace. But since man, in face of God, cannot determine to what extent he can really be created anew by God (which is possible in spite of the permanence of his human nature, since this nature, while remaining human, is always *capax infiniti* [at least *in potentia oboedientiali*]): he cannot for his part determine *a priori* what he can hear from God and what he cannot. Hence the theses which follow do not lay down *a priori* laws as regards to what is possible in itself and in general; they provide a norm which is itself already based on what God has *de facto* instituted in the concrete order of his salvific action.

[6] With regard to future events, a genuine clairvoyance may be possible, without implying a miraculous divine revelation and prophecy strictly speaking, but which can be recognized by its peculiarities as a natural phenomenon. See e.g. K. Rahner, *Visions and Prophecies*, *Quaestiones Disputatae* 10 (London & New York 1963). It is to be noted that accounts of the future which *are* to be explained by parapsychology, and prophecies which are not really miraculous, do give the impression of *reportage*—fragmentary, to be sure, and arbitrarily selected and restricted.

here—as a divine prerogative, and, where it occurs, as a proof of God's action in fundamental theology (cf. for instance Denzinger 1790 (Vatican I); 2145 (Anti-modernist oath)). When therefore in what follows the import of eschatological assertions and their implications for the future are to some extent restricted, we are dealing with a restriction which follows in fact from the history of salvation and affects only ourselves: it is not an absolute metaphysical restriction of the knowledge of God or of his power of revelation which follows from the nature of God. There is no contradiction between an absolute, unconditional openness for any possible word of God, no matter how unexpected, no matter how incalculable, and the holding of concrete principles of interpretation, derived from the actual word of God, which deal with a given set of divine utterances. If one confined oneself to the principle that no restrictions or conditions could be imposed upon God, even with regard to his speaking of the future, it could very well happen that the sovereign freedom of God in eschatological discourse could in fact be restricted in the light of certain presuppositions, all the more fraught with dangerous consequences because unavowed. And such interpretation could restrict the admitted freedom of God's utterances, and our own absolute readiness to hear them, much more than if one offered principles for the interpretation of such utterances, derived from the word of God as actually spoken. Express principles, being matter of reflex thought, can be confronted again and again with the word of God and so subjected to criticism. It is the sort of thing which occurs in other places of theology also: whoever rejects *metaphysical* considerations and principles in theology, as being incompatible with the word of God and his sovereign dominion, does not in fact set himself free for the unchallenged lordship of the word of God, but becomes the slave of unspoken and hence more dangerous metaphysical prejudices. Let us suppose for instance that someone reads the eschatological assertions of Scripture like someone trying to reconstruct as exactly and vividly as possible some past event, by combining a set of fragmentary pieces of information into a sort of mosaic—more or less the usual procedure of our eschatologies, especially those of the more popular type—then he is unwittingly using a concept of man and his existential situation which is not only false, but certainly misses the real sense of the eschatological assertions of Scripture. This sort of reading of eschatological assertions as pre-views of future events de-eschatologizes man himself: it makes of him a being who in the here and now of his *present* existence is unaffected by the future, because the future is only what is yet to come from a distance, and no longer that which is at hand in its futurity. The eschatological message becomes a statement which does not touch us at all at the moment, because it refers unambiguously to a later time in the distant future and to nothing else. If we lack an *a priori* horizon of an explicit nature, we do not allow Scripture to say what it really wishes to say, without reading things into it beforehand, but we make its statement non-existential from the start. Hence, in spite of our acknowledging that God knows everything, including the future, and that he can enunciate *everything* if he pleases, we must try to define an *a priori* sphere for eschatological assertions, a framework within which they are to be understood.

Thesis 3. The sphere of eschatological assertions and hence of their hermeneutic is constituted by the dialectical unity of two limiting statements (of which the second is closely connected with our first thesis, but must none the less be repeated once more here).

(*a*) It is certain from Scripture that God has *not* revealed to man the day of the end.[7] This does not merely mean that physical time extends into a future where we cannot fix a date for the end and fulfilment. It is not just that we do not know exactly *when* the end comes; it is not just the moment of its arrival which is 'not yet exactly' revealed. The truth is that the end has for us a character of hiddenness which is essential and proper to it and effects all its elements. This is already implied by the Christian existentials of faith and hope: without this character of hiddenness in the fulfilment yet to come, faith and hope would not be what they are and must be if Christian. And again, if faith and hope are to exist, they demand that the future be essentially concealed. How then are we to reconcile the announcement of the *eschata* with their hidden character? It will not do to say that we know some things about them from revelation but not others. We cannot make a material division between what is revealed and what is hidden. It is precisely the *eschata* which have been announced that are hidden, and again, the announcement takes the hidden out of the region of what is merely unknown, absent and disregarded, but brings it into the region of what is present, *as* the hidden, unmistakable,

---

[7] Texts like Mk 13:32 belong in any case, even purely historically, to the basic elements of Jesus' teaching. Cf. also Rev. 1:7. We cannot of course here deal with the question of how this ignorance of the 'Day' is to be reconciled with the 'imminent expectation' and the naming of the signs by which the beginning of the end of the world is recognizable.

overwhelmingly menacing and irresistible. It is no longer a case of what the eye does not see the heart does not grieve for, but it still does not become something calculable and hence manageable, which ceases to be dangerous because we know 'what it is all about'. The revelation of the eschatological shows it precisely *as* a *mystery*. It is not possible to ask here what are the *a priori* conditions (of transcendence and freedom) which are to be supposed and may be supposed in man's spirit and existence, so that the hidden, precisely as such, does not disappear and become non-existent, but can be present as the unmistakable menace, *as* the un-expected, *as* the obvious which is the incomprehensible miracle. We cannot here consider more closely why the hidden can thus be present as the coming and the coming as the hidden, in God's word of revelation. We must be content to postulate here, as a hermeneutic principle and an objective truth, that it can only be true that we do not know the Day of the Lord, if God's revelation makes the future the unmistakable and the incomprehensible, the mystery of God permanently close, menacing and promising. More than ever, revelation is not the bringing of what was once unknown into the region of what is known, perspicuous and manage-able: it is the dawn and the approach of the mystery as such. It is absolutely essential for the eschatological to be hidden in its revelation. And this follows, as we have said, from Scripture itself. This already provides us with a very essential criterion for distinguishing genuine eschatological utterances, if not always by their form, at least by their content, from apocalyptic ones. It may therefore be said that wherever we have a pre-diction which presents its contents as the anticipated report of a spectator of the future event—a report of an event in human history which of itself excludes the character of *absolute* mystery and hence deprives the eschato-logical event of its hiddenness—then a false apocalyptic is at work, or a genuine eschatological assertion has been misunderstood as a piece of apocalyptic because of its apocalyptic style and form. We have therefore to investigate *how* it is possible that an assertion can bring the future into the present in such a way that it retains a very specific character of hidden-ness when it comes with threat or promise into our existence.

(b) The second element which constitutes and defines the sphere of eschatological assertions and hence their hermeneutic, is the essential historicity of man. If man is a being involved in history, which means more than a merely external temporal succession such as holds good for physical objects, he cannot understand himself in any given present moment without an aetiological retrospect towards a genuinely temporal past, an 'anamnesis', and without prospect of a genuinely temporal future. His self-understanding embraces beginning and end of his temporal history, both in the life of the individual man and of humanity.[8] Anamnesis and prognosis are among the necessary existentials of man. They may be present in the guise of indifferent forgetfulness, but they cannot be absent. Man possesses himself, disposes of himself, understands himself, in and by the anamnesis by which he retains his past and the prognosis by which he lays hold of what is to come. In eschatological thought, by virtue of the manifold strata of man's being, the future is present in various ways, corresponding to the plurality of man (in being, time, etc.). But if eschatological thought is concerned with *salvation*, and salvation is the fulfilment of the *whole* man and not just of some dimensions, then the thought of the fulfilment of certain elements, or better, the fulfilment of the one man under all aspects of his single, total and yet plural reality, cannot be absent. The prognosis must be concerned with the whole man according to all the necessary assertions which are implied in the plurality of his being and which cannot be reduced to one another. The reference to a real future yet to come, involving all the aspects of man's being, may be omitted; or it may be eliminated in favour of an existential actualism in the course of an ostensible 'de-mythization'; or it may be forgotten that man has a physical, spatio-temporal, bodily existence, even in matters of salvation and that the nature of man and of his one and total fulfilment must also be envisaged in the light of these things. But if so, man and his self-understanding have been really mythologized, because his linear direction in time towards what is still to come in time, and hence the dimension of his historicity, has been omitted. And since it is there that he works out his salvation with his God, his salvation would not take place where we really are. But if the presentness of man's being is his being referred to futurity, the future, remaining the future as such, is not just something spoken of in advance. It is an inner moment of man and of his actual being as it is present to him now. And so knowledge of the future, in so far as it is still to come, is an inner moment of the self-understanding of man in his present hour of existence—and *grows out of it*. Of this we must now speak at greater length.

[8] Cf. e.g. A. Darlapp, 'Anfang', *LTK* I² (Freiburg 1957) 525–529; 'Geschichtlichkeit', *ibid.* IV² (1960) 780–783 (with the literature indicated there); 'Anamnese', *ibid.* I², 483–486.

Thesis 4. If what has been said in 3a and 3b is correct, that is, if such real future is known and present, but as something hidden, we are to expect—under the reserves made in Thesis 1—that the content of this knowledge, no matter whence it comes, which is part of the present constitution of man, is the element of the future yet to come which is necessary to *present* existence. Knowledge of the future will be knowledge of the futurity of the present: eschatological knowledge is knowledge of the eschatological present. An eschatological assertion is not an additional, supplementary statement appended to an assertion about the present and the past of man but an inner moment of this self-understanding of man. Because man is, by and in being orientated to the future, he must know about his future. But in such a way, that this knowledge of the future can be a moment in his knowledge of the present. And only thus. This alone is sufficient to give the content of eschatological knowledge the character of hiddenness. If it were an account of the future anticipated and 'fore'-seen as it is in itself, then the future, as the fulfilment of what is *human*, could not really have the character of hiddenness and mystery. It could be marvellous, unexpected and amazing, just as if someone were to fore-tell that I should one day be emperor of China. But it could not be mysterious and hidden if it were described in terms of its own phenomena, created ones, even in the state of their fulfilment.[9] But if this knowledge is: 1. a moment in the self-understanding of the present of man, which self-understanding is a constitutive moment of the being of man as person and spirit; and 2. if this self-understanding essentially bears on freedom, risk and abandoning oneself to the uncontrollable:[10] then this known futurity necessarily shares the character of this existence, as something moving into the unforeseen.

[9] It might be objected that the future is hidden in any case, because the final state of fulfilment is very difficult to imagine, no matter how and whence knowledge of it is arrived at. But then we must answer that as the state of *our* fulfilment, a future fulfilment can only be grasped if it has an intrinsic relation to *our* nature as we know it now. Otherwise the fulfilment would remain alien and unintelligible. But if the intrinsic nature of the fulfilment is presupposed, and if its proper phenomena are supposed to be described on the basis of the future, it can no longer have the character of being hidden. If described in these terms, it must either be totally perspicuous and intelligible, or at least existentially (in this case, as a matter of faith) completely uninteresting for us at present.

[10] The chief reason why this is outside our control and prevision is the free disposition of the incalculable decree of God in his sovereign action, and not just the fact that man cannot foresee his own free action before it is done, and before it has exercised itself on its incalculable material in the world.

To expound a little further what we have said, we should have to say with regard to the content of such eschatological assertions that the future must be:

(a) something impenetrable and uncontrollable, since this alone leaves room for freedom—the true freedom of the creature, which must believe, hope, dare and trust, go out of itself, entrust and surrender itself to the uncontrollable.

(b) This future must be really there, that is, it must be looked forward to, something must be said of what is still to come. Existence must be really 'ex-sistent' in its regard—must step out of itself into the future in its reality and hiddenness; the future must be a real moment of the actual understanding of existence possessed by man. He may not think of himself as possessing himself merely by reason of his purely present state, or by reason of his own, calculated plans, to be fulfilled by his own power. All this must be kept permanently part of the acceptance of being disposed of by the incalculable, uncontrollable force of the future, a future which belongs to God and to him alone. All that can really be said about this future is that it can and must be the fulfilment of the whole man by the incomprehensible God, in the salvation hidden in Christ which is already given us. The formal concept of the finalizing fulfilment of the whole man —without which there can be no question of a real eschaton—is filled out, with regard to the individual, and with regard to humanity, the context in which alone salvation has meaning, by the Christian revelation of the eschata. But this only says that fulfilment is the perfection of the salvation already assigned and granted by God in faith to man and humanity in Jesus Christ.[11]

Thesis 5. If the thesis of 3(a) and 3(b) can be assumed, something may be

[11] We cannot of course attempt to prove here (though some indications on the matter will be given later on) that all eschatological assertions taught and held by the Christian faith can in fact be understood as developments of this one truth. But the end which brings the individual, man and the world in general to a close is precisely the completion of the beginning which came about with (the risen) Christ, and it is no more than this. This final consummation, as the end of all history, does not derive from another event which is still to come: the beginning, which is Christ, is the sole and adequate law of the end, and hence the fulfilment bears in all things the traits of this beginning. If this is understood, there will be no difficulty in accepting the statement made above. All one has to do is to test it by its opposite and ask oneself are there any obligatory truths of faith which are clear in content, and whose content cannot be reduced to this basic principle. If this can be rightly denied, the correctness of the basic principle is sufficiently demonstrated.

said about the source, the background of these eschatological assertions. We may at least presume that man's knowledge of the future still to come, even his revealed knowledge, is confined to such prospects as can be derived from the reading of his present eschatological experience. And thus we can understand that the progress of eschatological revelation in the pre-Christian and Christian revelation up to its climax in Christ is *identical* with the progress of the revelation of the actual history of salvation, that is, with God's actual action on man at any given moment. Thus the climax of eschatological revelation is necessarily what it actually is: that God has revealed to man his trinitarian self-disclosure and self-communication in the grace of the crucified and risen Lord, a revelation already actual, though still only in faith. Eschatology is therefore not a pre-view of events to come later—which was the basic view of false apocalyptic in contrast to genuine prophecy. It does not draw on future events, accessible because God is 'already' contemporary to them, in a metaphysical doctrine of the being and knowledge of God, and so can already speak of them. Eschatology is the view of the future which man needs for the spiritual decision of his freedom and his faith. It derives from the situation in the history of salvation brought about by the event of Christ, which is the aetiological source of knowledge. It looks forward to the definitive fulfilment of an existence already in an eschatological situation. It enables man to take the enlightened yet daring decision of faith where all is open but dark. And thus the Christian can accept his present as a moment of the realization of the possibility established in the beginning (which is ultimately Christ), a moment of the realization of the pre-established future which is already present and definitive in secret. And this future proves to be salvation, if it is accepted as the doing of God whose times and ways are incalculable, who alone disposes. For thus the scandal of actual redemption being actually contradicted (by a world in sin, the divisions of the peoples, the discrepancy between nature and man, lust, death, the lordship of powers and forces) is borne in patient hope, as participation in the triumphant and redeeming cross of Christ. Our present thesis does not deal with the contents of the eschatological assertions which have just been outlined, nor with their future exposition. The decisive point of the thesis is rather that the assertion or revelation concerned with the present situation of Christian existence is not completed by an *additional* and quite different communication about the future: the assertion in question is already this communication. The

Christian who accepts the revelation of Christ knows—in order to know Christ and *because* he knows him—that fulfilment is that of Christ, apart from which he really knows nothing about it. To put it another way: the Christian man knows of his future in as much as he knows of himself and his redemption in Christ through divine revelation. His knowledge of the *eschata* is not a supplementary piece of information added to dogmatic anthropology and Christology, but simply *their* transposition into the guise of the fulfilment. But such an anticipatory outline of one's own Christian existence in the light of its future fulfilment remains a strict revelation, because this interpretation which throws light on human existence is a revelation which takes place in the word of God. But it is precisely in what man hears from God as the disclosure of the truth of his existence that the revelation of the future takes place and vice versa. And both take place in the same measure and degree as this interpretation of man by God advances *in* the history of man, and hence unsurpassably in Jesus Christ, in whom God has given himself definitively and unsurpassably to man, as man's salvation. Christian anthropology and Christian eschatology are ultimately Christology, in the unity (where alone they are possible and comprehensible) of the different phases of the beginning, the present and the completed end. The mode of revelation, the source of the revelation of the future (the eschata) must be a forward-looking draft of existence orientated to the fulfilment of the end of time. Otherwise the object of revelation would be the future as directly seen and decreed in itself by God, described so to speak in a narrative which moves backwards from the future into our present. But then it would be impossible to explain what the essential, divinely guarded mystery of our open and unforeseeable future could be. And we could not explain how and why the future could remain, in fact and in principle, 'open' in such an account and not lose this essential character, when presented by the clairvoyance of such predictions. Nor could we explain why the account is clearly couched in imagery which is not derived from the phenomena of the future in itself, and does not claim in any way to be so. That the Scriptures have no such intention follows from the fact that these imaginative portrayals[12] of Scripture cannot be harmonized with one another, and

---

[12] The content of the assertions in the various eschatologies of Scripture, the meaning which they intend to convey and express, can of course be made consistent. But this is not true of the imagery as such by means of which the matter is described. There are many popular eschatologies of later Christian times which start with the

hence they cannot be meant as elements of the phenomena of the future reality itself. The *Sitz im Leben*, the setting of eschatological knowledge, the real original source of eschatological assertions is therefore the experience of God's salvific action *on ourselves* in Christ. It may be said in general that the event of revelation, the action of God on us in history, is the experience of his action on us in the grace of Christ. It is not merely and not primarily the communication of truths (even though this experience of God's action on us includes the *word* as an intrinsic element). And this is also true of the revelation of the eschata: they do not reach us in a discourse about the future still to come, but in an action, in which God has already really begun them in us. And so we can only speak of this beginning by describing it *as* a beginning which wills to fulfil itself and therefore brings with it the knowledge of this fulfilment (even though as something hidden).

If we hold fast to the principle that there is knowledge of the eschata only in the knowledge of the presence of salvation in Christ, we should be able to exclude in consequence *both* a false apocalyptic understanding of eschatology such as is found in certain sects and often colours Catholic theology of eschatology, *and* a totally existential 'de-mythizing' interpretation of such assertions. For we must not forget that man exists in real

---

silent presupposition that the eschatological images (coming on the 'clouds of heaven', the sound of trumpets, opening of graves, gathering in the valley of Jehosophat, being carried up in the air to meet Christ, the stars falling on the world, the general conflagration, etc.) are indications of the actual phenomena of the future eschata and hence the account given by a spectator of these future events. The phenomena are made to fit in with one another by the silent omission of part of the data or by ranging the events arbitrarily one after the other. We can see, however, from the tortuous nature of such misplaced harmonizations, and from the simplicity with which Scripture uses the most diverse imagery from very different sources, without much regard for the various assertions, that Scripture has no intention of describing the actual phenomena of the eschata themselves. (This does not necessarily mean that the sacred writers themselves distinguished very consciously and expressly the nature of their assertion from such ways of describing things.) But if biblical eschatology were an account derived from the future (instead of being a view of the future seen from and *by* the present), it would be impossible to understand why it does not describe things as they are experimentally and palpably 'in themselves'. If someone said that it was of course impossible, because we lack at present the necessary concepts and categories, he would be conceding, unwittingly or not, what we affirm. For all that can be and is in fact said of the eschata, on the presupposition now made, is precisely what can be said *by reason of* the presence of the eschaton which has already come, which is Christ.

time, which runs on to a future still really to come, and that he lives in a world which is not merely abstract existence but has many dimensions, all of which must attain salvation, including the non-existential, including the temporal one of profane succession. If we think of a concrete and not an abstract existence; if we recognize that the existential present of man is a concrete existence—embracing therefore all the dimensions of his being, including his involvement in the non-existential reality of the profane world; if one recognizes that salvation cannot be a determination of any one particular dimension of man, because that would be a really misleading mythologization: then it is possible to say even in Catholic theology that there can be no eschatological assertions which cannot be reduced to the assertion concerned with Christian existence as it now is. But a view based on such presuppositions would not be de-eschatologizing, but—to risk another neologism—de-apocalyptizing. This is necessary on principle, and also for the sake of a credible attestation of the Christian message today, to eliminate the many misunderstandings of biblical and ecclesiastical eschatology current on a popular level. It cannot be said that the task has been sufficiently explicitly envisaged and carried out in all circles of Catholic theology.

To sum up briefly what has been said, we may say that biblical eschatology must always be read as an assertion based on the revealed present and pointing towards the genuine future, but not as an assertion pointing back from an anticipated future into the present. To extrapolate from the present into the future is eschatology, to interpolate from the future into the present is apocalyptic. The eschatological assertion is part of man's nature and when it is concerned with the present as revealed by God's word, is Christian eschatology. The apocalyptic suggestion is either phantasy or gnosticism; it does not merely suppose, as Christians also must, that the future only exists in the inaccessible mystery of God as such, which remains within the light inaccessible; it also unwittingly supposes that the future already leads of itself a supra-temporal existence, of which history is only the projection on the screen of worthless time, and that time is not the real ground from which the eternal validity of man emerges, but a nothingness which is unmasked and really eliminated in this gnostic contact with the true reality, called apocalypsis.[13]

---

[13] This is not the place to examine at length the obvious objection, that Christian eschatology is preached above all by *Jesus*; that he possessed the beatific vision and infused knowledge; and that he therefore knew the eschata in such a way that he could

Thesis 6. This basic principle of the hermeneutics of eschatological assertions leads to further consequences, of which some are adduced here, to show somewhat more clearly the meaning and the bearings of this basic principle. The indications given do not follow any very exact systematic order.

(a) If eschatology, with regard to its content and certainty, derives from the assertion about the salvific action of God in his grace on actual man, and if its norm is to be sought in this assertion, it follows that the eschatology of salvation and of loss are not on the same plane. We may say at once, on the basis of our principle, that we cannot now avoid speaking of the two-fold end of history with regard to the individual and the whole of humanity. This eschatology tries to describe our situation in terms of its present intrinsic possibilities as they look to the future. It does no more than this. And the two possibilities must and truly do remain existentially open for man, who is a pilgrim, and makes, and can only make, his free decision in view of what is open and unforeseeable. It follows that true

---

speak of them as they are in themselves, and not merely as he knew them in the light of the present situation of salvation (even though it was an eschatological one). Suffice it to say that even if we concede the supposition without any nuances (though Jesus' knowledge, as here presupposed, may be so unique that it cannot be as readily translated into terms understandable by us as is commonly taken for granted), we may still simply deny that Jesus did in fact all that he *could* have done. (The basic necessity of such a distinction cannot indeed be denied by any theologian, once such knowledge on the part of Jesus is presupposed, when Mk 13:32 is considered. For then Jesus declares expressly that he says *less* than he knows and *can* say.) To put it another way: the actual eschatological preaching of Jesus is quite understandable as a prediction about the completion of what Jesus proclaims about himself and his mission in the present. For the content of Jesus' eschatology surpasses the eschatology of his times only in one point, which is however decisive and transforms all the rest: namely, that he himself in person is salvation and judgment, at the present moment, in a way that can never be surpassed. And hence he will be so also at the end, which however is described in terms of the usual contemporary eschatology. Jesus' prediction of the fall of Jerusalem is again a question which, being concerned with knowledge of events which are qualitatively *within* history and *within* the world, must be distinguished from the question of his knowledge of the absolute end of all things. Furthermore, it is quite possible to ask oneself whether the fall of Jerusalem, 'the State which was a Church', was not simply the logical conclusion, to Jesus' mind, from the rejection of his Messianic mission to this sacral and political institution. He could therefore have foretold its fall as such a logical consequence, especially as one must historically take into account the possibility that some of the formulations of this (genuine) prediction may have been influenced in the Synoptic tradition by the actual experience of its fulfilment.

eschatological discourse must exclude the presumptuous knowledge of a universal apocatastasis and of the certainty of the salvation of the individual *before* his death,[14] as well as certain knowledge of a damnation which has actually ensued.[15] But since eschatology is arrived at on the

[14] There is a problem here, of course, with regard to the mystical experience of 'confirmation in grace', such as is narrated in hagiography. We cannot of course go into the problem here, and we must confine ourselves to the following remarks. It must first be asked whether this mystical assurance of salvation really claims to be endowed with the *absoluta et infallibili certitudine* (*Denz*. 826), *cui non potest subesse falsum* (*Denz*. 802); or whether theologically speaking it is a 'certainty' (even though mystically transfigured) such as is always proper to Christian hope. It must further be asked whether 'death', as the decisive caesura in the history of salvation (and hence in knowledge of one's own present or future salvation) must always necessarily coincide with the moment of time when biological life ceases. When we think of those who are victims of total mental alienation but whose biological life continues, the usual identification becomes doubtful. If one may question the identification, our principle can be referred to the impossibility of knowledge of future salvation which precedes death as the caesura in the history of *salvation*. In this sense, the mystic in question may be regarded as dead so to speak as regards the history of salvation, and he may be conceded such absolute knowledge without detriment to the truth in question. If this solution seems too daring or forced, one can rest content with the first of the solutions indicated. Even the certainty of salvation claimed by mystics cannot invalidate the principle.

[15] The possible objections to this statement are of course well known. But the following position is undoubtedly tenable. Neither the doctrine of the Church in tradition and the extraordinary magisterium nor the teaching of Scripture compel us certainly to affirm definitely that at least some men are certainly damned, whether they can be named or must remain anonymous. On the contrary, all the eschatological assertions of Church and Scripture can be understood (without prejudice to any future judgment of the Church) as affirming that damnation is a genuine and inevitable possibility for the pilgrim. So too J. Loosen writes (*LTK* I², 711f.): 'We must *clearly* reckon with the fact that men *can* be lost. But revelation leaves us ignorant of whether some are *in fact* lost, and whether they are few or many.' Anyone who claims to know more and thinks that this makes the decision to be taken here and now more serious, makes the question existentially less serious. For he transfers it into the region of generalities. But it is really most serious and urgent when each one puts it to himself, when each one says of himself alone: '*I* can be lost'. But then he must say this in the context of Christian hope and affirm: '*I can* be lost, and I *hope* that I shall be saved'. And if this dualism which can never be eliminated or outgrown remains the most profound truth for each single individual, why should he know more about others, about others for whom we are to have as much hope as for ourselves, and whose destiny cannot really be more indifferent to us than our own? It would be wrong to appeal here to the fate of demons. For it would have to be proved that their situation with regard to salvation was the same as our own and that the difference in nature was unimportant in the matter—which is certainly impossible to prove. In saying this, we have not finished with the task of *detailed* exegesis, which

basis of *grace* now given, and since this grace, in Christ, is not merely the offer of the bare *possibility* of salutary acts, but must be acclaimed as triumphant, because rendered efficacious by God: the Church can and the Church must—in spite of pilgrim man's uncertainty of salvation—firmly proclaim that martyrs and some other men who have died in Christ have attained salvation. But it cannot allow itself a corresponding affirmation about the certain and actual damnation of other men. Thus Christian eschatology is not the *parallel* prolongation of a 'doctrine of the two ways' (which is rather Old Testament than Christian) to reach the two termini of these two ways. Its central affirmation is concerned only with the victorious grace of Christ which brings the world to its fulfilment, though couched indeed in terms which safeguard God's mystery with regard to individual men as still pilgrims and do not say whether the individual is included in this certain triumph of grace—or 'left out'. Hence on principle only *one* predestination will be spoken of in a Christian eschatology. And it contains only *one* theme which is there on its own behalf: the victory of grace in redemption consummated. Possible damnation can only be spoken of, but must be spoken of, in so far as, and only in so far as it is forbidden to man to take the sure triumph of grace in the world as providing him himself with already fixed and acquired points in his estimation of an existence which is still to be lived out in the boldness of freedom. Catholic theology has always rejected as heretical the doctrine of the double, antecedent and parallel predestination to glory *and* to damnation. It should consider that this also has consequences for the correct outline of an eschatology which does not really contain, except perhaps in books, two similar and equally well justified chapters on heaven and hell.

(b) All eschatological assertions have the *one* totality of man in mind, which cannot be neatly *divided* into two parts, body and soul.[16] All

---

must discuss various texts of the magisterium and of Scripture and show that the opinion here put forward is in accord with the texts in question. It is evidently impossible to do these studies here. But what has been said should indicate the guiding lines for detailed exegesis: in spite of all their concrete vividness, the eschatological assertions, taken as a whole and in the light of the *analogia fidei*, are meant to give a striking perspective of a possible future (not a backward reflexion from it), with which pilgrim man must clearly and inevitably reckon, in this age and situation where his decision must be made.

[16] Man consists of 'body and soul'. But in Thomist metaphysics, which are perfectly justifiable, one is bound to say that man consists of *materia prima*, and of

eschatological assertions merely repeat, transposing into terms of fulfilment, what dogmatic theology says about the one man in question. Hence
eschatology cannot but be marked by the same two-fold dualism which
is unavoidable in anthropological assertions about man who is always one.
It must be a universal and an individual eschatology, because man is
always both individual and member of society and neither can be completely absorbed in the other, nor can everything be said about man in
one statement alone. It must speak of man as personal spirit and as corporal
being and hence express his fulfilment as spirit-person and corporal being:
but the two assertions cannot be adequately reduced to one in which they
could be absorbed; and the two assertions cannot envisage objects which
are *adequately* distinct from one another. Eschatology is concerned with
the fulfilment of the individual as individual spirit-person which comes
with death as the end of the individual history. Eschatology is also concerned with the fulfilment of humanity in the resurrection of the flesh as
the end of the bodily history of the world. But in each case it is concerned
in a different way with the *whole* man. It cannot be read as two sets of
statements about two different things, each of which can simply be taken
separately. And yet the two sets of statements do not simply mean the
same thing, so that one set could be eliminated in favour of the other as
being for instance either too mythological or too philosophical. Since
this irreducible dualism in eschatological assertions, deriving from the
nature of man, is already palpable in Scripture, and could throw light on
the possibility, meaning and limits of a doctrine of an intermediate state
and hence on the precise meaning of 'purgatory'—which we cannot now

---

anima as *unica forma* and *actualitas* of this *materia prima*, so that 'body' already
implies the informing actuality of the 'soul' and hence is not another part of man
beside the soul. And body and soul, if the doctrine of *anima-forma-corporis* is really
understood and taken seriously, are two *meta*-physical principles of one single being,
and not two beings, each of which could be met with experimentally. However,
even if we prescind from all this, we must at any rate affirm that every *assertion* about
the body (as the reality of man) implies an assertion about the soul, and vice versa. I
asserts at least the transcendental relationship of each 'part' to the other, which
relationship cannot be understood unless its term is also understood. If these obvious
matters are not borne in mind in all anthropological assertions, 'body' and 'soul' are
taken to be two entities which are only subsequently combined in unity—a unity
which cannot then be really substantial; and though one may verbally profess the
philosophical and dogmatic doctrine of the soul as the form of the body, one has
really lost sight of it, though the soul is the form of the body by its inmost essence
and is so, in order *to be spirit*.

discuss more closely—it could therefore also be shown that the realities behind the concepts of the intermediate state and purgatory, and the ensuing development of dogma, must be regarded as quite legitimate and biblical.

(c) There is no point, on our principle, in creating a fundamental, absolute opposition and antagonism between an imminent and a distant expectation of the *parousia*. If the true and original source of eschato-logical assertions were an account of the future still to come as it is in itself, one should have to ask oneself why the length of actual time between Now and Then is not given more definitely, since the reporter of this pre-view must know how far off this future still remains. But if eschatology is the assertion about present salvation as it tends to the future fulfilment which is and must be essentially hidden, it must be essentially 'actualist' and hence an imminent expectation. But it must like-wise be a distant expectation, since it is the orientation of the present towards the incalculable future under the impact of the future salvation. All eschatological assertions must be seen in the light of this basic hermeneutic principle. If they are not really 'actualized' and existentialized as an imminent expectation properly understood, they will be regarded, unwittingly or not, as curious inside information about something really indifferent, something with which one has nothing to do since it only comes much later without affecting the present. If on the other hand they are so thoroughly existentialized and actualized that the whole future already takes place as and in the present, if the necessary process of actualization makes one lose sight of the genuinely temporal future which as such remains a dimension of man, then in fact man is mythologized, because the down-to-earth factor of time is denied him, a sober fact which is also part of his salvation. Thus we have gnosticism, because this know-ledge has let us into the secret and we already possess the ultimate and the real.

(d) Our basic thesis therefore is that it is *from* the present experience of salvation that the genuine future yet to come is known—as a preliminary outline helping us to understand properly the present. But this experience of salvation, the adequate source of eschatological assertions, is faith in the incarnation of the Logos, in the death and resurrection of Christ, as the historical events which are permanent, definitive and unsurpassable because God has communicated himself to the world in them wholly and therefore unsurpassably. It can therefore also be said that *Christ* himself is the hermeneutic principle of all eschatological assertions. Anything that cannot be read and understood as a Christological assertion is not a genuine eschatological assertion. It is soothsaying and apocalyptic, or a form of speech which misses and misunderstands the Christological element, because couched in a style and an imagery borrowed from other sources. It is therefore read in the light of the *terminus a quo* of its origin and not of the *terminus ad quem*, which is Christ, and the result can be either that these misunderstood texts are accepted as Christian truth or rejected as erroneous, so that the true sense of these texts is lost as well.

(e) There are certain formal principles of the theology of history which may be invoked here: 1. that history is directed towards a definitive end; 2. that it reveals an antagonism; 3. that the temporal, the historical, is always ambiguous; 4. that the forces at work grow radically stronger; 5. that the forces and epochs of the history of salvation and catastrophe are represented by concrete persons; 6. that sin is encompassed by the grace of God, etc.[17] With these principles in mind, we can derive from our experience of Christ all that can and may be said objectively in the Catholic theology of eschatology. We can say that time will have an end, that towards the end the antagonism between Christ and the world grows fiercer,[18] that history as a whole ends with the final victory of God in his grace, that this consummation of the world, in so far as it is the incalculable act of God's freedom, is called God's judgment, in so far as it is the fulfilment of the salvation already real, victorious and definitive in Christ, is called the return and the judgment of Christ. In so far as it is the fulfilment of the individual, who cannot be wholly absorbed and lost in his function as moment of the world, it is called the particular judgment. In so far as the world is not just the sum of its individuals, it is called the general judgment. In so far as it is the fulfilment of the resurrection of

---

[17] This enumeration of examples of such formal principles of the theology of history does not claim to be complete, or to offer the best and compulsory distinction between these principles. However, in the light of these principles, the subsequent statements in Catholic eschatology would undoubtedly be seen to be highly intelligible, and to derive from the material principle of this eschatology, which is Christ. Here it is to be noted that these formal principles are not to be taken merely as formalizing statements of the individual material utterances of eschatology. They can be perfectly well understood in the light of the history of salvation as realized up to the present, and in the light of its orientation towards the end, which it clearly displays.

[18] Cf. e.g. the article 'Antichrist' (R. Schnackenburg–K. Rahner–H. Tüchle) in *LTK* I², 634–638.

Christ, it is called the resurrection of the flesh and the transfiguration of the world.

Thesis 7. Our basic principle provides a fundamental criterion to distinguish between form and content in the eschatological assertions of Scripture and tradition. This does not mean that such a distinction could make a perfectly adequate and definite distinction between 'thing' and 'image'. This is impossible, if for no other reason than that no assertion about the thing is possible without some sort of image, and in this sense a 'myth'[19] can only be replaced by another, but not by language utterly devoid of images. And here of course one will not be so naïve as to think that the thing had once been thought of without images but that this lofty concept had then been clothed in 'imagery' for the sake of the weaker brethren. Thought is always image as well, because there is no concept without imagination. So too in St Thomas Aquinas, who maintains that there is no concept without a *conversio ad phantasma*, that is, a concept must be exteriorized and embodied in the imagination and the image, and hence too in 'picturesque' language. It is never then a matter of aiming at a language devoid of imagery and hence when dealing with eschatological assertions of trying to rid oneself of the picturesque diction to reach a sphere where the thing itself appears as it is in itself in its pure objectivity: there is no way of discarding the imagery, the indirect allusion, the mere convergence of diverse elements. But if several assertions, with their permanent element of imagery, are brought into relationship with each other—as can and should be done, in the light of our basic

[19] 'Myth' is to be understood here, of course, in a very broad sense—which is in fact objectively correct. It is an assertion about something (which may also be an event of the past or future) in which a set of concepts and imaginative elements are used, which cannot simply be derived from the thing in question, and are still necessary for the *conversio in phantasma*, without which, according to St Thomas, even the most abstract concepts are impossible. It might be objected against this definition of 'myth' that then every statement about something which could not be imagined in its proper phenomenal reality would also be a 'myth', though perhaps in an abbreviated and customary form, so that it was no longer consciously recognised as such. Or it could be said that this would be the case at least when the notion was not confined to static imaginative elements of expression, but also displayed movement and events. But then the objector should be asked whether there were convincing reasons which would prevent one from conceding this 'objection' as justified, without misgiving and embarrassment; and how he himself would give a clearer distinction between 'mythical' discourse and that which is not supposed to be such, if he bears in mind with St Thomas (and Kant) that there are no concepts without imagination, and hence that the richest concepts cannot exist without a correspondingly rich imaginative content.

principles, with dogmatic anthropology and Christology on the one hand, and eschatology on the other—the relationship between form and content in any given assertion will be fluid: the term of the analogy to which such an assertion points will be recognizable as the consciously ensuing difference between form and content, though it remains impossible to disentangle it completely. And hence the thing intended will be conceivable under a new form of expression, though formulated once more in a new type of imagery. We cannot say however with certainty that the new assertion, more abstract for instance or more immediately Christological or more formally anthropological, *adequately* renders the real content of the assertion which has been translated and interpreted. And so it must always remain connected with the ancient assertion, and every eschatology, no matter how modern, always remains a retrospective interpretation of the old, not a new and better assertion which replaces the old. But an approximate line can be drawn in this way between the form and content of an assertion, at least as regards the question as to whether something is to be so strictly attached to the *content* that a denial of it would have to be treated as contrary to the common faith held by the Church on the basis of Scripture, and so could and should be rejected as heretical. Where the line cannot be clearly drawn between content and mode of assertion in an eschatological assertion of Scripture or tradition, a minimizing interpretation can only be contested when it can be proved that such a restriction also meant in fact a restriction applied to the assertions which are at the base of eschatology, the assertions of Christology and dogmatic anthropology.

All that we have been able to say here amounts only to a thesis. A strict proof of the thesis has still to be given, and it should be in the following form. The dogmatic theologian must submit his sources and methods to a strict, critical examination and then ask himself what assertions are binding in eschatology. He must then see if and how he can reduce these assertions to a small number of basic assertions, of which it can be shown that his eschatology as a whole is the development and consequence. He could then ask whether it can be proved that these basic assertions are elements of his dogmatic Christology and anthropology, where the latter have merely been voiced in terms of the fulfilment of their content. If the answer is in the affirmative, then in view of the fact that the theologian, by virtue of his principles, has already comprised and applied the assertions of Scripture in his dogmatic eschatology, it may also be said that the eschatological assertions of Scripture are and intend to be (at least in what dogmatic principles establish as affirmed for certain) no more than such assertions of Christology and anthropology in terms of the fulfilment. But then this affirmation could once more be transposed into a basic *hermeneutic* principle which allows us to give the same meaning to biblical and dogmatic eschatology, where up to this it has not resulted clearly and unambiguously from the immediate meaning of the statements in question. Since this, the real proof of our thesis, cannot be worked out here, we may close with a rejoinder to those who are inclined to question the thesis here put forward. What are the clearly established dogmatic assertions which cannot be taken in this sense? I do not know of any.

14

THE LIFE OF THE DEAD

THE faith and the theology of the Catholic Church deal with the definitive state of human existence, attained and not ended by death, from a two-fold point of view, based on the limits which philosophy and revelation set one another. It is not easy therefore to present briefly the doctrine of faith and the theology which interprets it further, though not with the same binding force. This difficulty is reinforced today by the necessity of avoiding clearly and from the very start the impression that when we affirm that in death man does not perish but is transformed into a new manner of existence, we are not speaking of a rectilinear continuation of man's empirical reality beyond death. Of itself this idea provides a harmless, useful and almost unavoidable framework for the explanation of what is really signified, but it mostly creates today more difficulties than aids and so can lead people to reject the reality as well as the imaginative framework as impossible and incredible.

When therefore we speak of the dead who live, we must first say what is meant thereby, or rather, what is not meant. We do not mean that 'things go on' after death, as though we only changed horses, as Feuerbach puts it, and rode on. It is not a continuation of the peculiar distraction and vagueness of temporal existence, which is an openness always in need of new determinations and hence basically empty. No, in this regard death puts an end to the *whole* man. To think of time as simply lasting beyond the death of man and of the soul in this time, so that time is renewed instead of being absorbed into the definitive, is to cause oneself insuperable difficulties, with regard to the concept and the existential achievement of the Christian thought. But if one thinks that death is the end of everything, because man's time does not really go on, because what once began must sometime end, because finally time spinning itself out into infinity, the empty endless pursuit of the new which annuls the old, is really impossible and would be worse than hell: then one is the victim of the conceptual framework of our empirical time, just as much as if one considered that the soul 'went on'. In reality, it is *in* time, as its own mature fruit, that 'eternity' comes about. It does not come 'after' the time we experienced, in order to prolong time: it eliminates time by being released from the time that was for a while so that the definitive could come about in freedom. Eternity is not an immeasurably long-lasting mode of pure time, but a mode of the spirit and freedom which are fulfilled in time, and hence can only be comprehended in the light of a correct understanding of spirit and freedom. A time, such as that of the beasts for instance, which is not pregnant with these things, does not bring forth eternity. But when we try to think of man's spiritual and free existence as something definitive, we have to extract the notion from time, and we are almost forced to portray it as unending duration. To overcome this difficulty we must do what is done in modern physics and learn to think unimaginatively and to this extent perform a process of 'de-mythizing'. We must say: through death—not after it—*there is* (not: begins to take place) the achieved definitiveness of the freely matured existence of man. What has come to be is there as the hard-won and untrammelled validity of what was once temporal; it progressed as spirit and freedom, in order to be.

But how do we know that such things happen, arising from the evanescence of time, which we are and so bitterly experience? At this point of the question dogma and theology import into Catholic doctrine that two-fold unity of revelation and human knowledge to which we alluded in the beginning. To have anyone at all open to the message of the gospel, to 'get there' at all with the special nature of the Christian promise, the word of God in revelation summons man to a clearer and more decided act of the self-understanding which is found nearly everywhere in human history when man ascribes further life to the dead in any form whatsoever. But can we, of ourselves, echo today this conviction of the survival of personal existence in spite of biological death—calling it metaphysical knowledge or religious conviction or ethical postulate or what you will: the name does not matter for the moment? I am convinced that we can, if our mind is alert and our heart humble and wise, and if we accustom ourselves to seeing what the superficial and impatient cannot see—not that this blindness is a proof of the non-existence of what they cannot see.

To begin with: why are all those who love greatly, humble and good, as though radiant with the brightness of something inexhaustible and indestructible, to the heart of which they see in the great moments of their love? Why is a radical moral cynicism impossible to man where he has found what is truly his own? And compared to this authentic thing, must not cynicism be incorruptible truth and honesty, if the authentic can simply vanish in the void of nothingness? And if it be said: whoever thinks of such things in his authentic acts, in his great and unconditional acts, in his love, in the radical doing of his duty, has not understood the authentic, but missed it, the answer is: at such a moment, one cannot think of the authentic as perishing with time, because it is not temporal. For why should the authentic not be truly able to experience itself as it really is? Why does not the last loyalty capitulate before death? Why does true moral goodness not take fright at the apparent hopelessness and futility of all its efforts? Why does moral experience distinguish clearly between goods which are only beautiful because and as they pass away, and the good as such, where it would be blasphemy to fear satiety and hence to wish the good were transient? Is not this the great wisdom which we long for and revere: the tranquil brightness of that fearless peace, which can only reign in him who has nothing to fear? Does not he who really faces his end *calmly* show that he is more than time, which would have to *fear* its end if it were only time, because empty nothingness can never be the goal of action? And on the other hand, is it not this which is really deadly painful in death: that in its dark, inflexible ambiguity it seems to deprive us of *that* which had ripened in us to the experience of immortality? It is only because we have become immortal in our life that death with its menacing and impenetrable mask of destructivity is for us so deadly. A beast dies less of a death than we. These and similar experiences would be impossible if the reality which we experience were, of its nature and essence, something that perished, something that wished to be no more.

As in all questions of this type, personal attitude and decision goes hand in hand with metaphysical insight of an objective nature. This is not surprising, since the most profound, the most valid, the 'objective' truth *must* be the freest. Hence it is best in such questions to appeal at once to the spiritual experience where both are involved at once: metaphysical insight, which is not however a neutral lecturer on theories, but an act accomplished by man in the authenticity of his unique personal existence.

This happens in the moral decision. What takes place? The agent constitutes himself as having a valid end. In this decision the subject is immediately presented, in his being and his act, as something incommensurable with passing time. The subject's decision must of course have been strong and pure, if subsequent, articulate and hence thematic theorizing reflection is to grasp later what is constituted in the decision: the valid, which soars above time, as time falls away into what is no more. There are perhaps men who have never so acted, or who acted with insufficient alertness of spirit, and hence cannot follow us here. But where such a free act of lonely decision is done, in absolute obedience to the higher law or in radical love of another person, something eternal happens, and man becomes immediately aware of his validity as something born of time but taking place outside its mere onward flow.

There is no really thinkable sense in which this primordial, immediate presence of the eternal in the absolute value of moral decision can be called in doubt by saying that man only *thinks* that it is so. It is just as impossible as it is to doubt the absolute validity of the principle of contradiction by dismissing it as a merely subjective opinion or as valid merely in the precise moment in which it is affirmed, since it is affirmed in the very act of doubting its validity, as the very basis of the possibility of doubt itself. So too with the moral decision. If in the free moral decision the subject utters a No of doubt before the absoluteness of the moral law or the dignity of the person, the very fact that this negative decision is *absolute* constitutes once more the affirmation of what it doubts. Freedom is always absolute. It is the Yes that knows itself and risks all and wills to be for ever valid. Its self-affirmation as 'now and for ever valid' *is* spiritual reality, not just a questionable opinion about a supposition and a concept. It is the very reality by which all others are to be measured but which cannot itself be measured by the flow of physical time. To put it more concretely and also in terms of Scriptural thought; if one who had to live his moral existence before God and in the light of his absolute claim could flee into the radical void of the mere past and be submerged in its nothingness, he could really escape God and the absolute claim of his will: he could escape from what is present in moral decision as the unconditional and inescapable. The nothingness of the sheer past would be a rampart to protect the arbitrary choice against God. But the moral decision affirms precisely that it is just as impossible to be radically and destructively arbitrary as it is to deny the radical difference between good and evil in the act of decision—a difference which would cease to be absolute if it could be thought of as existing for the moment only and then no more. In the free act of absolute obedience and radical love, the act is willed *as* opposed to the mere momentariness of the present, and its supra-temporal truth can only be doubted from outside, not in the act itself. If the act were really no more than a moment of fleeting time, this fact would not be intelligible even as opinion and imagination, because even the imagined semblance needs some foundation, and time could not present the appearance of eternity, the semblance of eternity could not exist at all, if time did not live by eternity.

No, where man is 'self-collected', where he possesses himself and risks himself in freedom, he does not scatter a series of wasted moments, he gathers time in a validity which is ultimately incommensurable with the mere external experience of time. And this validity cannot be grasped in its genuine and primordial sense by the notion of *continued* duration: still less can it be swallowed up by the ending of what is merely temporal in us.

But if immortal man thus claims against time's mere dissolution that which is valid in his personal existence, it is only God's word of revelation which tells him clearly what is the actual concrete meaning of his being. It makes him experience his possible eternity for the first time, by revealing to him the *actuality* of eternity. The fulfilment revealed in the gospel message is manifold in content: eternity as the fruit of time means to come before *God* either to reach pure immediacy and closeness to him face to face in the absolute decision of love for him, or to be enveloped in the burning darkness of eternal god-lessness in the definitive closing of one's heart against him. Revelation, building on the grace of God and its power, presupposes that *every* man, no matter how his ordinary life appeared on earth, achieves so much spiritual and personal eternity in his life, that the possibility inherent in his spiritual substance is realized in fact as eternal life. Scripture knows of no life which is not worthy to be definitive, it does not recognize any life as superfluous. Since God knows each man by name, since *everyone* exists in time before the God who is judgment and salvation, *everyone* is a man of eternity, not just the enlightened spirits of human history. Further, the theology of St John makes it clear that the existence of eternity is seen as inserted in time, and that hence eternity grows out of time and is not just the after-thought of a reward appended to time. The *reality* of the blissful life of the dead is described in Scripture by innumerable images: as rest and peace, as a banquet and a state of glory, as being at home in the Father's house, as the kingdom of the eternal lordship of God, as the fellowship of all who have been perfected in bliss, as the inheriting of the glory of God, as day without night, as satisfaction without satiety. Throughout all these words of Scripture we sense the same thing: God is the absolute mystery. And hence the consummation, the absolute nearness to God, is itself an ineffable mystery to which we go and which the dead who have died in the Lord have found. There is not much we can say. But it is the mystery of unspeakable *bliss*. No wonder then that the sheer silence of bliss cannot be heard by our ears. And finally: revelation tells us that the *whole* of the unity of temporal man is given its definitiveness, so that it may also be called the resurrection of the flesh. And this doctrine of Scripture is not merely enunciated in words: it is experimentally seized in faith as a dawning reality in the resurrection of the Crucified.

In the Christian doctrine proposed by the Church of the 'immortality of the soul' and of the 'resurrection of the flesh' the whole man in his unity is always envisaged. This affirmation does not deny or call in doubt that there is a differentiation intrinsic to the definitive state of man which corresponds to the justifiable distinction of 'body' and 'soul' in his make-up. But if, as cannot be doubted, the 'resurrection of the flesh' in the creed of the Church means the definitive salvation of man as a whole, then the doctrine of the immortality of the soul, being a truth of faith and not just a philosophical tenet, is also concerned in fact with such a life, such a 'soul' as for instance Jesus placed in the hands of his Father as he died. Hence this assertion is also directed to the *whole* reality and meaning of man as he depends on the creative and life-giving power of God, *whereby* of course it refers also to what the philosopher as such may call soul in contrast to body, with a destiny which he may try to trace after death. It would indeed be the moment to ask the philosopher what right he has to follow the fate of an isolated element of the whole, and not rather investigate the destiny that would transfigure the one, whole man; though perhaps indeed the philosopher, for his own part, would not dare to call this unimaginable but hoped-for transformation of the whole, valid and permanent, the 'resurrection of the flesh', and would still be inclined to give the name of 'soul' to what has become definitively and permanently sensible in the whole, regarding it to some extent as an extract of corporeal being which has become definitive in death.

There is this further difference between what the *Catholic* faith has to say of the dead and the belief of most Protestant Christians. It maintains firmly in the doctrine of purgatory that death does indeed make definitive the freely matured basic attitude of man, which again is purely by the grace of God, since this finality is good. But it also maintains that the many dimensions of man do not all attain their perfection simultaneously and hence that there is a full ripening of the whole man 'after' death, as this basic decision penetrates the whole extent of his reality. Such a difference of phasing, which results from the plurality of man's structure, is in fact also to be seen in the contrast between the fulfilment of the individual in death and the universal consummation of the world, between the finality achieved by man in death and the clarification and perfection of this fulfilment which is still to come in the transfiguration of his bodily existence. Since it cannot be denied that there is an 'intermediate state' in the destiny of man between death and bodily fulfilment, unless one holds that what is saved is not what was to be saved, there can be no decisive objection to the notion that man reaches personal maturity in this 'intermediate state'.

There is no place in Catholic Christianity for intercourse with the dead as individuals, such as spiritualism aims at. This is not because the dead do not exist, not because they are really separated from us, not because their fidelity and love, made perfect before God, does not watch over us, not as if their existence were not truly embedded by death above all in the silent, secret ground of our own existence. But *we* are still creatures *in time*. And hence, unless God has wrought the miracle of a special revelation, as in the resurrection of the Lord, if the reality of the living dead as individuals were to be transposed into our concrete world, they could only appear as *we* are, not as *they* are. And in fact spiritualist seances display the spirit of the *earth-bound*, with their crude ideas and manias, not the tranquillity of an eternity filled by God. And it is always possible —as we are perhaps only beginning to suspect—that in such efforts at contact (where it is not simply a matter of objectivating our own dreams) there is a strange shift in the dimensions of time, where we do not meet *the* dead as they are *now* before God and in the definitive kernel of their being, but their as yet unredeemed and limited, confused and obscure past, which—still perhaps not totally accomplished—is then once more transposed into the categories of our own world. No, we meet the living dead, even when they are those who are loved by us, in faith, hope and love, that is, when we open our hearts to the silent calm of God himself, in which they live; not by calling them back to where we are, but by descending into the silent eternity of our own hearts, and through faith in the risen Lord, creating in time the eternity which they have brought forth for ever.

PART SEVEN

Christian Life

15

POETRY AND THE CHRISTIAN

ONE would have to be a poet to say anything significant on the subject of 'Poetry and the Christian'. For the poet, one may think, is certainly the first commissioned to speak on poetry. But one can console and encourage oneself when one begins to speak of this subject without being a poet, with the thought that the poet speaks to others, and hence to the non-poets, and hence that they too come of themselves into relationship to poetry and poets, and must know what poetry is about. And one can be consoled and encouraged by the truth that the believer, who is led by the Spirit of God, may judge all things, as the Apostle says. Theology as reflective faith cannot be completely alien to what fills the lofty hours of man and so must be gathered home to God as a whole, since the one seed sown by the one God must ripen in all the diverse fields of the world.

We should like however to bear in mind in the course of these considerations that the starting-point is a *theological* one. And we should also wish to remain conscious of our limitations as a layman in the field of poetry. Hence we do not start from where one should really begin, with poetry itself, but from theological reflection on man as he should be if he wishes to be a Christian. We simply ask therefore whether such a man—unwittingly or not—looks out for something which is afterwards seen to be poetry, and is there a preparation which he must undergo to be or become a Christian, which turns out to be a receptive capacity for the poetic word.

Before we begin, we must also note that we are not speaking of art in general, but only of the poetry of words, first of all because even this narrower field presents obscurities enough, and then because Christianity, as the religion of the word proclaimed, of faith which hears and of a sacred scripture, has a special intrinsic relationship to the *word* and hence cannot be without such a special relationship to the *poetic* word.

What does Christianity demand of a man, if it is to become a reality in him? When we try to answer this question, we do not mean that Christianity, that is, the grace of God, has just to wait for the presence of these requisites in man, can only investigate whether they are there or not. Certainly not. The grace of God creates these requisites for itself, it is the cause of their being accepted; it is the gift which is God himself, and it is the gift of accepting the gift which bestows itself. But the grace of God does not only start to work for the first time, when the word of the gospel reaches man through the official preaching. It precedes this word, it prepares the heart for this word by every experience of existence which takes place in the life of man. It is, in diverse ways of course, secretly and powerfully active in what we call human culture, because humanism itself, wherever it exists, wherever it still exists, revives, proves itself true and displays itself radiantly, would not exist at all, if the secret grace of God did not anticipate its own manifestation in the word of the gospel. And hence when we enquire into the humanist presuppositions of Christianity and its preaching, the question is again praise of the grace of Christ and is not to the prejudice of its might and guardian force.

The first requisite for man's hearing the word of the gospel without misunderstanding it is that his ears should be open for *the* word through which the silent mystery is present. More indeed is expressed in the word of the gospel than we grasp wordlessly, than we can also master without words. For in this word comes what is incomprehensible, the nameless, silent power that rules all but is itself unruled, the immense, the abyss in which we are rooted, the overbright darkness, by which all the brightness of each day is encompassed, in a word: the abiding mystery which we call God, the beginning who is still there when we end. Now, strictly speaking, every word that is really a word, and strictly speaking, only the *word* has the power of naming the nameless. No doubt, the word expresses, designates and distinguishes, demarcates, defines, compares, determines and arranges. But as it does this, he who has ears, he who can see (here all the senses of the spirit are at one) experiences something totally different: the silent, mystic presence of the nameless. For that which is named is conjured up by the word. And so it advances from the encompassing, quiet and silent source from which it arises and where it remains secure; that which is described and distinguished by the word, by the distinctive name, combines with the other as it is distinguished from it, in the unity which comprises the comparable and akin, and so points silently back to the one origin, loftier than both, which can indeed preserve both unity and distinction in one. The word puts individual things in order, and so always points to a fundamental background order which cannot itself be ordered but remains the perpetual *a priori* antecedent to all order. One can miss all this when one hears words. One can be deaf to the fact that the clear spiritual sound can only be heard when one has first listened to the silence beyond each distinct sound, the silence in which all possible sounds are still gathered up and at one with each other. One can disregard one's own comprehensive hearing, by allowing oneself to be enslaved by the individual things one hears. One can forget that the small, limited region of the determinative word lies within the vast, silent desert of the godhead. But it is this nameless being that words try to name when they speak of things that have a name; they try to conjure up the mystery when they indicate the intelligible, they try to summon up infinity when they describe and circumscribe the finite; they try to force man to allow himself to be gripped, as they grip and grasp. But man can be deaf to this eternal meaning of temporal words, and still grow proud of his stupid, unreceptive hardness of heart.

Hence words must be spoken to him, which are such that he recognizes that they are uttered by those whom he must take seriously, and that he sees that these words call upon him to decide whether he dismisses them as meaningless or strives to listen to them long enough in truth and love— till he understands that their whole meaning is to utter the unutterable to make the nameless mystery touch his heart gently, to make the unfathomable abyss the foundation of all that the foreground supports. Christianity needs such words; it needs practice in learning to hear such words. For all its words would be misunderstood, if they were not heard as words of the mystery, as the coming of the blessed, gripping, incomprehensibility of the holy. For they speak of God. And if God's incomprehensibility does not grip us in a word, if it does not draw us on into his superluminous darkness, if it does not call us out of the little house of our homely, close-hugged truths into the strangeness of the night that is our real home, we have misunderstood or failed to understand the words of Christianity. For they all speak of the unknown God, who only reveals himself to give himself as the abiding mystery, and to gather home to himself all that is outside himself and clear—home to him who is the incomprehensibility of silent love. Yes, he who would hear the message of Christianity must have ears for the word where the silent mystery makes itself unmistakably heard as the foundation of existence.

The second requisite for the hearing of the Christian message is the power to hear words which reach the *heart*, the centre of man. If God as the mystery wishes to enunciate himself in the words of Christian revelation, the word will aim at the *whole man*, because this God wishes to be the salvation of the whole man. The word seeks him out at his original unity, out of which the multiplicity of his existence grows and in which it remains comprised: the word seeks the *heart* of man. And hence the words of the gospel message are necessarily words of the heart: not sentimental, because that would not be heart to heart; not purely rational words of the intellect, since this can be understood merely as the faculty which grasps and masters the comprehensible, and not as the primordial faculty which allows itself to be gripped and overwhelmed by the incomprehensible mystery and is therefore called the heart for preference, if one is thinking of this primordial faculty of the inmost spirit of man. Thus, to be a Christian, one must be capable of hearing and understanding the primary words of the heart. And these are not merely concerned with man's scientific rationality and his dispassionate pseudo-objectivity. They are not just sign-posts for the biological will to live and the direction of the herd-instinct. They are so to speak sacral, even sacramental: they help to effect what they signify and penetrate creatively into the primordial centre of man. This capacity and readiness must be developed by practice, so that the primary words do not glance off the shell of preoccupations, are not choked in the indifference and cynical nihilism of man, are not drowned in chatter, but like a lance piercing mortally a crucified man and opening up the sources of the spirit, may strike the inmost depths of man, killing and bringing to life, transforming, judging and graciously favouring. We must learn how to listen under the severe discipline of the spirit and with a reverent heart which longs for the 'striking' word, the word that really strikes us and pierces the heart, so that mortally stricken and blissfully surprised, the heart may pour the libation of the muted mystery which it concealed, into the abyss of God's eternal mystery and so, being freed, find blessedness.

The third requisite for the proper hearing of the message of the gospel, which we choose to mention here out of many others, is the power of hearing the word which *unites*. Words distinguish. But the ultimate words which call to the all-pervading mystery and reach the heart, are words that unite. They call to the origin and gather all into the unifying centre of the heart. Hence they reconcile, they free the individual from the isolation of his loneliness, they make the whole present in each one; they speak of *one* death and we taste the death of all; they voice one joy and joy itself penetrates our heart; they tell of one man and we have learned to know all men. Even when they speak of the dire loneliness of a man uniquely isolated, they notify the hearer of his own isolating loneliness and point to the one sorrow of all and their one task, which is that they still have to seek the true unity of many divided hearts. Thus the authentic words unite. But one must be able to hear them, otherwise one cannot understand the message of Christianity either. For it speaks only of one thing, the mystery of love, which wishes to strike home to the heart of man as judgment and salvation: a love which is not a feeling but the true substance of all reality as it strives to manifest itself in all things. Only when one can hear the secret sound of unifying love in sundering words, has one ears to perceive truly the message of Christianity. Otherwise Christianity too is only a distraction beating on the ear with a thousand words that tire and stupefy the spirit, because it is asked to accept too much that fits in nowhere, which means death to the heart, because it ultimately loves only one thing, it can hear only one thing, the word of union which is God himself, who unites without dissociating.

The fourth and last requisite for the hearing of the message of the gospel which we shall mention here, is the capacity of recognizing the inexpressible mystery *in* the word which speaks of its bodily form, inseparable from the word but not confused with it: the power of becoming aware of the *incarnational* and incarnate incomprehensibility, of hearing the Word become flesh. And in fact, if we are Christians, and not just metaphysicians delving into the obscure grounds of being, we must remember that the eternal Word, where the obscure but personal unoriginated origin indicated by us as 'Father' in the godhead expresses himself absolutely and knows himself eternally, has become flesh and dwelt among us. The *Word*, where the unoriginated mystery is in possession of itself, the infinite Word which has none other beside it because it alone of itself says all things that can be said: this has become flesh, and without ceasing to be all has become this particular thing, without ceasing to be always and everywhere expresses itself 'here and now'. And therefore and since then and in this Word made flesh the word of man has become full of grace and truth. It is not just a sort of silently signalling finger, pointing away from what it delimits and illuminates into the infinite distance, where the incomprehensible dwells, silent and unapproachable: the incomprehensible itself, as grace and mercy, has entered the human word. In the region encompassed by the human word, infinity has built itself a tent, infinity itself is there in the finite. The word names and truly contains what it apparently only hints at by a silent signal, it brings on what it proclaims, it is the word which really only attains the full realization of its being in the sacramental word, where it really becomes what God's grace made it as he uttered his eternal Word itself in the flesh of the Lord.

And therefore the Christian must be open to the grace bestowed on the word in the Logos who became man. He must be schooled in the mystery of the Word which through the Word made flesh is the embodiment of the infinite mystery and no longer just a pointer pointing away from itself to the mystery. Deep down within the narrow earthly well of the human word the spring that flows for ever gushes forth, the flames of eternal love leap out of the burning bush of the human word. This propriety of the word, in its true and full reality, is already grace in the word, and the power of hearing such a word in its true sense is already grace of faith. But ever since the human word has existed as the embodiment of the Word of God which abides for ever, and ever since *this* Word has been heard in its permanent embodiment, there is a brightness and a secret promise in every word. In every word, the gracious incarnation of God's own abiding Word and so of God himself can take place, and all true hearers of the word are really listening to the inmost depths of every word, to know if it becomes suddenly the word of eternal love by the very fact that it expresses man and his world. If one is to grow ever more profoundly Christian, one must never cease to practise listening for this incarnational possibility in the human word. One must have the readiness and the capacity to find *permanently* the whole in the individual, one must have courage for what is clear and definite, in order to become aware of the inexpressible, one must bear and love the candour of what is close at hand, to be able to reach what is far away, but still not vague and without binding force.

What then is the word which the Christian must have the power, the practice and the grace to hear, if he is to be able to hear the Christian word of God's message? He must be able to hear the word through which the silent mystery is present, he must be able to perceive the word which touches the heart in its inmost depths, he must be initiated into the human grace of hearing the word which gathers and unites and the word which in the midst of its own finite clarity is the embodiment of the eternal mystery. But what do we call such a word? It is the word of poetry; this power to hear means that one has heard the poetic word and abandoned oneself to it in humble readiness, till the ears of the spirit were opened for it and it penetrated his heart. It may be that the poetic word, if it is to be—itself, must do more than fulfil the conditions which we have described as the proprieties of the word we sought. This may be so simply because we are perhaps obliged to ascribe our four characteristics to every word of Scripture—even though in very different degrees—and not every word of Scripture can be called a poetic word in the strict sense. However that may be, it can hardly be denied that these four characteristics belong essentially to the word which claims to be of poetic rank and dignity. And more we need not be able to say here. And so it is true that the capacity and the practice of perceiving the poetic word is a presupposition of hearing the word of God. No doubt grace also creates this presupposition for itself, and no doubt there are many men whose ear and heart are open for the seminal poetry of eternal existence only in the Christian message itself. But this does not alter the basic truth we have arrived at, that the poetic word and the poetic ear are so much part of man that if this essential power were really lost to the heart, man could no longer hear the word of God in the word of man. In its inmost essence, the poetic is a prerequisite for Christianity. It cannot be objected that there are enough true Christians who have no truck with the Muses. The artistic endowments of Christians can vary: not every Christian who can find the four aforesaid characteristics in large measure in the Christian word, is thereby a great poet. He need not even have much understanding of poetry.

All this is possible, because he may lack other faculties which the poet and those open to poetry possess. But if the poetic word evokes and presents the eternal mystery which is behind expressible reality and in its deepest depths, if it speaks of individual things in such a way that all is gathered and condensed in it, if it is a word which goes to the heart, or if, without being a poetic word, it conjures up the inexpressible in its utterance, if it fascinates and sets free, if it does not speak about something but creates in its utterance what it calls: can a man be fundamentally unreceptive to *this* word and still be a Christian? He is perhaps almost incapable of experiencing this poetic word except where it is more than mere human poetry, in which man speaks from his own heart of what he is, and in which as he speaks he hearkens to the murmur of the world. He can perhaps only hear the poetry of existence in the word in which it is uttered by God himself in his own words. But even then man hears and utters words in which the most secret essence of the poetic word still lives and works or is surpassed. In any case, poetry is one way of training oneself to hear the word of life, and again, when a man learns to hear truly the word of the gospel in the depths of his heart, as the word which God himself bestows, he begins to be a man who can no longer be totally unreceptive to every poetic word.

What does this mean for us today?

(a) Poetry is necessary. All that can be said of humanism in general holds good for poetry, as a work creatively produced and creatively received. In periods when humanism and poetry seem to be dying, buried under the achievements of technological skill and suffocated by the chatter of the masses, Christianity must defend human culture and the poetic word. They live and die together for the simple reason that humanism, which is also poetic, can never be separated from Christianity, though they are not the same thing. Humanism too lives by the grace of Christ, and the Christian thing contains the human as an essential element within its own being, though only part of it. If it is true that the message of the gospel will not perish till the end of time, then our faith is also true, that there will always be men whose hearts will be open to the inexpressible mystery which is love, become flesh in the word of man, which gathers and unites all. If such a word is promised perpetual struggle, amid dangers unrelenting in their terrors, but likewise abiding victory in victorious abiding to the end, then the poetic word is also promised ever new victories in endless struggle. The poetic word will never fail, because it grows out of the divine word which bears within it the inmost essence of the poetic word. We Christians must love and fight for the poetic word, because we must defend what is human, since God himself has assumed it into his eternal reality.

There is no way of deducing a formula from this essential propriety of Christianity, which will tell us exactly what the poetic element, which we can never renounce, must look like. Man undergoes the changes of history and so does his poetry. And no one need fear history less than the Christian, who must take history more seriously than any one else, since it bears his eternity in its bosom. And hence the Christian, when he acclaims the perpetuity of human culture and so of poetry, can never make his homage go only to the poetry of yesterday and the day before. He will wish the poet to say frankly what he finds in us, and to divine what the future brings, so that he may be the poet of his own new age, of *its* pain, of *its* happiness, of its tasks, its death and of eternal life. Here too there is only one way for us to be conservative if we are Christians. We must go to the Mass of life as we go to the Mass of the altar, and count the solemn memory of our origin and our past among the essential components of our existence—but in such a way, that we go therein to meet the unique future that calls us, knowing that God's future is our origin.

(b) One can of course be a good fellow and a good Christian in the common-place sense of the term and still be a miserable poet. But really great Christianity and really great poetry have an inner kinship. They are certainly not the same thing. Man's question and God's answer are not the same thing. But great poetry only exists where man radically faces what he is. In doing so, he may be entangled in guilt, perversity, hatred of self and diabolical pride, he may see himself as a sinner and identify himself with his sin. But even so, he is more exposed to the happy danger of meeting God, than the narrow-minded Philistine who always skirts cautiously the chasms of existence, to stay on the superficial level where one is never faced with doubts—nor with God. And hence the question of what is the proper educational reading for the immature is again an important matter to be discussed on its own merits. But the mature Christian will welcome all really great poetry openly and without embarrassment, reverently and with a love that is perhaps grieved and compassionate: because its subject is man, man redeemed or in need of redemption and capable of redemption, and so in any case it takes us beyond the two-legged creature which pre-occupies us only too often and too long in our everyday life, a creature somewhat cleverer than the beasts and therefore less certain of himself. The more deeply great poetry leads man into the abysses which are the foundation of his being, the more surely it forces him to face those dark and mysterious acts of human self-realization, which are shrouded in the fundamental ambiguity in which man cannot certainly say if he saved or lost. It is no accident, but in the nature of things, that great human poetry is obscure, and mostly dismisses us with our question unanswered, as to whether it was the mystery of grace or of perdition that was played out and described in it. And how else could it be? Poetry must speak of the concrete, it cannot take abstract principles and make them dance like puppets. But the individual and the concrete is a mystery which will only be unveiled by the judgment, which is God's and God's alone, but which the poet presents *as mystery*. Hence his poetry cannot be so simply and clearly edifying as some bad pedagogues would have it be, for the sake of their sheltered pupils. If we are not Manicheans, we know as Christians that really great guilt is terrible, because it is great and because it is guilt, but that it can only be great because some very great human qualities have found themselves and come to light in it—because evil as such is nothing. We recognize that God suffers sin to exist and be great and powerful in this world, and hence that it is not so easy to confine the great types of humanity to the saints. We Christians, as the Apostle says, cannot go out of the world, but must have fellowship with unbelievers and lechers (1 Cor 5.1–15), though not of course such as we have with our brothers in the faith. When then we come upon real poetry, and not the sort that parades empty unbelief and immorality under the pretext of writing poetry, it is not only not forbidden it is even imperative that we should take it seriously and carefully, even though it does not conform to the moral standards of Christianity, and we have not to pass judgment on 'those that are outside'. There is such a thing as anonymous Christianity. There are men who merely think that they are not Christians, but who are in the grace of God. And hence there is an anonymous humanism inspired by grace, which thinks that it is no more than human. We Christians can understand it, better than it does itself. When we affirm as a doctrine of faith that human morality even in the natural sphere needs the grace of God to be steadfast in its great task, we recognize as Christians that such humanism, wherever it displays its true visage and wherever it exists, even outside professed Christianity, is a gift of the grace of God and a tribute to the redemption, even though as yet it knows nothing of this. Why then should we not love it? To pass it by indifferently would be to despise the grace of God.

  (c) At one time writing and printing were laborious, time-consuming and costly. Writing and printing were confined to what was to some extent important. Today the book and the printed sheet are comparatively cheap compared to the rest of the cost of living. A thing unknown as late as the eighteenth century, there exists today not merely a copious literature to satisfy the needs of technology, science and society but a printed record of all the foolish and empty chatter which inevitably fills the daily round.

We have a literature which is no more than talk at the street-corners of everyday life, just printed gossip, mostly with illustrations. Our reactions to these productions should be just the proper behaviour of Christians with regard to the talk and chatter of everyday life. The Christian will distinguish the banalities of everyday life from the lofty and sacred utterance of poetry, and preserve this distinction of rank sensitively and strictly and try to educate others to this discernment of spirits. He will keep everyday life in its place, even when it is put down in print, and tolerate it within its proper bounds, because the Christian knows that ordinary life can and must go on. And he will fully recognize that the serenely gay, the redeemed, the frankly joyful, has its place in great poetry. He will not think that it only begins when guilt and distress, tragedy and dire torments come upon men. For the Christian can be *resolved* to recognize that an ultimate seriousness can be simple, relaxed, sweet and joyful, in the joyous seriousness of the children of God. He knows that the blessed freedom of heaven is really the only serious thing, much more serious than hell.

Poetry and the Christian. We have really said very little about this lofty theme. But if what we have said has achieved only one thing: if it has aroused or strengthened, in the Christian and especially in the Christian educator, a sense of responsibility for poetry and its meaning, we have done enough. How far the grace of God has gained mastery over us we cannot tell directly, because it is in itself invisible and intangible. Apart from having confident faith, there is practically only one thing that we can do here: it is to ask ourselves how far we have become men. One way, though not the only way, of knowing this is to see whether our ears are opened, to hear with love the word of poetry. And hence the question of how we stand with regard to poetry is a very serious and strictly Christian question, and one which merges in the question of man's salvation.

16

THEOLOGICAL REMARKS ON THE
PROBLEM OF LEISURE

THE theologian, in my opinion, can only ask questions about the subject of the five-day week which is discussed here. They are questions which he puts to the representatives of the other faculties, especially those of philosophy, sociology and medicine, questions which must be answered for him before he can form his own opinion as a theologian.

For the real point at issue is not at all clear, or not clear enough. At first sight it seems simple enough: five days work and two days recreation, which we can afford because even so we produce enough, and which we must allow ourselves, because our five-day effort is so severe that we need two days' relaxation to make up for it. The facts could be described and justified in this way, and it could be thought that with this the essential had been said.

But the issue is in fact much more obscure. And the theologian can only ask to have the issue put more clearly, because he himself is not competent to clarify it in his capacity as theologian. But he can at least say what are the points which do not seem to him to be particularly clear and what he wants to know to be able to consider the issue as a theologian, in the light of the word of God. It is only in this sense that I shall try to discuss the matter. And now let us face the obscurities of the issue. To begin with, has enough been done to clarify the concepts which are used in this question? It is a matter, as we have said above, of the correct proportions of work and recreation at the present time, as indicated by the conditions of our own day. But what is meant by work in this formulation? And if this concept needs to be clarified, the same would be true of recreation, because it is clearly to be understood in our context as a contrast to work. But in my opinion, there can be very different ways of looking at work, so that the problem of the correct distribution of 'work' and 'recreation' presents no clear concept. It is not at all clear what the process in question means, namely that one receives today as much money for five days of a given activity as one formerly received for six. It is not at all obvious that the process described in such neutral terms, a process which undoubtedly exists, can be described as a change in the proportions of work and recreation. What we mean by this will be clearer at once, when we ask ourselves what 'work' really means in the context in question.

I

Work and recreation were concepts comparatively easy to understand in primitive human relationships. The mere biological effort to stay alive demanded certain human activities, which occupied a considerable measure of time. This activity was called work. Because it lasted a considerable time, and used up much strength in the direct physiological sense of the term, this 'work' was followed by a time in which such work could not be done, because it was night time and because physical exhaustion forced man to a (relatively unambiguous) interruption of activity, to go to sleep and otherwise rest himself. This second period was called rest, recreation. The time not taken up by sleep was naturally filled with occupations and activities which formed a very clear and obvious contrast to work. When it was possible to sustain life without any particular effort, it followed at once, with an almost logical necessity, that no work had to be done or was done. But these primitive notions, which have of course been somewhat schematized here, are no longer ours. We give the name of work to a large number of occupations which do not serve, at least immediately, the sustentation of life biologically. A professor of pure mathematics 'works' according to our present estimation and is paid for his work. But our recreations on the other hand can be very strenuous activities. In our leisure time, when we are not 'working' we go in for mountain-climbing, for instance, which is much more strenuous than the rounds of a working postman, but we call mountaineering recreation and not work. We must clearly make distinctions in the notion of work which are blurred in popular speech. We must then note:[1]

---

[1] We omit the purely formal concept of work, in which only the 'transitive' character of work (or rather, of much work) is emphasized. Work does indeed often mean the activity of man which is applied to an external object and has a result which is in the nature of an object. But this formalistic concept is not practical here, because

1. The notion of work in *political economy*. A crude definition of this could be given by simply saying that work in this sense is every activity by which money is earned in the present-day order of society and economics. In this sense the artist works, and the pure scientist who has an official capacity. And the very same activity can be called work or recreation according to whether it is paid or not. A professor for instance of the local history of the Tyrol is paid for work which an inspector on a railway might do as a hobby and call a recreation for which he would like to have more leisure. A reconsideration of the relationship between work and recreation—understanding by recreation any activity for which one is not paid and which being economically unproductive for the agent has in general other positive values for him, as he would otherwise omit it— can pose a two-fold problem:

(a) If a man is, as we suppose, also occupied in activity during periods when he is not paid for it, *why* is he not paid? If this 'foolish' question is answered by saying: because in such periods he does nothing which is useful for the general economy, no real answer has been given to the question. There are many activities which are economically useless, that is, do not contribute either directly or indirectly to the production of consumer goods biologically necessary, and which are still paid for. A researcher in the field of Sumerian history is paid even in Russia, but he is not economically productive. One could force matters somewhat and try to see his activity as productive by saying that it is biologically and materially useful to play and do useless things for the sake of physio- logical recreation. But then one must admit that it is right to ask why it is not for all the activities that one pursues, but only for a given sector, obviously demarcated very arbitrarily, that one is rewarded with money which will enable one to acquire goods of economic value. Furthermore, payment is certainly made in modern society to reward people for not 'working': the non-working pensioner, who is still able to work but is paid by the state, is, strictly speaking, paid to give up taking part in work which serves the immediate production of goods, because a sufficiency of such goods can be produced without his participation. It would only

---

there are many leisure activities which are just as transitive. And again, there are many human activities which are so strenuous and well-directed that they can rightly claim the title of 'work', though they cannot be considered transitive, or can be said to be so only very artificially. Some people spend their leisure fussing about trifles, but others do real 'mental work'.

complicate the organization of production if he tried to participate. Such people are therefore given a share of these goods, on the condition that they do not share in the production. If we start therefore with the notion of work as used in political economy, that is, as paid activity, it is not clear how we are to undertake to make an intelligible distinction between work and recreation. Everything can be paid for and much is in fact paid for which under other circumstances is looked on as recreation and is not remunerated. Hence one could take the five-day week as a combination of payment for work and for renunciation of work, on the grounds that sufficient goods are produced even when one refrains from producing, so that in fact all claims are satisfied. One could even come to the conclusion that in our present social and economic system, everyone is really paid basically for his *whole* activity (composed of so-called work and so-called recreation). It would only be by reason of a technical manipulation of this payment that a rather arbitrarily chosen *section* of the whole activity is used as a norm for fixing the amount of this payment. In Germany and Russia, for instance, the state pays in fact for the whole of a student's studies, more or less. What is it that the student is at: work or recreation? And if his activity can only be subsumed with difficulty under one or other of these concepts, what is the student really doing, and how are work and recreation to be defined, when we suddenly find that it is impossible to distribute neatly the whole life and the whole activity of man between them?

(b) There is a second question which comes up in the purely economic view of work, if the notion is to be chemically pure, as it were, when taken as a basis for discussing the five-day week. Why should there be any curtailment of the time of activity for which one is paid, or which is used as the standard to determine one's share in the economic goods of society by means of money payments? Two answers to this question suggest themselves at once. (We leave aside the answer that shorter hours of work can be helpful in a crisis, especially if there is danger of an economic depression, since they facilitate the widest possible distribution of the whole volume of work available. We leave this answer aside, because shorter hours are not a very apt expedient in a crisis, and after all, economic problems as such can never be really solved by doing less work. We also omit the consideration that shorter hours may be regarded as a way of re-distributing national income; such consequences can be only secondary, and not the real aim and object of curtailment of working hours, since the desired result can, and if necessary should, be achieved otherwise.) The two really possible answers contain many questionable and obscure elements. It could be said that working hours must be shortened, because work is too strenuous today, because if prolonged to a greater extent (than in the five-day week) it is on the whole injurious to health. There may be a good deal of truth in this. But have the facts in question been proved? And what should be the nature of recreation if it is supposed that (always, on the whole) present-day work is so strenuous that if prolonged beyond forty-five hours a week it is harmful to health? Recreation would have to be taken in the form of the greatest possible cessation of activity, and hence in its most primitive sense. But that is not in fact what is meant, when the five-day week is demanded. The time is wanted for a very intensive activity, and not primarily and strictly for rest in the physiological sense. In contrast to the 'regenerative' function of leisure, which Marx still envisaged in view of the alienation induced by work, we hear today more and more of the 'suspensive' and 'compensatory' function of leisure, as it has already been designated.[2] One might try to evade this objection by saying that present-day work is primarily *felt* psychologically to be tiresome and repugnant, hence proves to be *psycho*-somatically unfavourable, and must therefore be relieved by a period which is found more agreeable in spite of the activity practised in it. But then the question arises as to whether present-day work *must* inevitably be felt so disagreeable. Could not this verdict on work as an unpleasant and tiresome burden be eliminated otherwise than by shortening the distasteful activity? And without such a reversal of attitude

[2] Cf. J. Habermas, 'Arbeit und Freizeit', in *Koncrete Vernunft, Festschrift für E. Rothacker* (Bonn 1958) 224: 'But today the average working hours are not so long, and, except in certain fields, they do not result in such bodily exhaustion, that leisure must be devoted primarily to the recruitment of physical strength in view of work. Instead of the regenerative function, we have today two other complementary functions of leisure which we call suspensive and compensatory. In one case, leisure is devoted to a type of work in which the alienation, abstractness and irrelevance connected with everyday work is suspended. This "work", so to speak, is meant to restore the freedom, the sense of reality and balanced achievement which is missing in daily work. One is not content with its defects, and tries not just to compensate for them, but to suspend them in the strict sense. Leisure promises a genuine fulfilment, which has nothing to do with substitutes for contentment. In the second case, leisure is devoted to something quite unlike work, which compensates for the psychic exhaustion and nervous strain which are the consequences of work. It really tries to fill a void and provide relaxation which have nothing to do with the beneficent tiredness which follows well-arranged work.'

towards the remunerated activity, would not even shorter hours still appear far too long?

One could also ask was it really true, that present-day work is more strenuous and tiresome than in earlier times, and a greater threat to health. This may perhaps be true in many regards, especially on account of the monotony, the extensive specialization of work at a conveyor-belt, and on account of the accelerated rhythm—real factors which certainly make work hard nowadays. But one could no doubt answer that manual work precisely has been made easier in many respects by the introduction of machinery and hence that it is not so easy to say whether the total amount of hard work involved is greater than it was hitherto. Thus the first answer to the question we have put is not sufficient on its own, and a *second* must be sought for which will be better or supplementary.

The second answer will be as follows. Even in previous times, men found the work which was generally paid for, to be hard and tiresome, and they always renounced it as soon as they could have without it the standard of living which they wanted or thought attainable at the moment. And since we can now produce the desired volume of material goods, thanks to technical improvements, by a less amount of tiresome activity (called work), it is quite understandable that we should not 'work' for a longer period and try to ensure, by means of a just regulation of working hours, that all should receive their fair share of this volume of goods which is sufficient for all. In a word: the cake today is big enough to go round even if shorter hours are worked. It would be pointless to prolong beyond what is necessary an activity which men always find tiresome.

But this answer too poses its problems. Is it true that the volume of goods foreseen as the result of shorter working hours is fully sufficient for everybody, if we look beyond a rather arbitrarily defined economic unit and think of the undernourished three-quarters of humanity? Can the free world and Christian Europe refuse to put this question, when the communist ideology is quite clearly determined to ask it? To put the matter figuratively in terms of the individual: can one say, I have planted enough potatoes when I have enough for myself, though my neighbour through no fault of his own has none and I could plant more if I wanted to work more, as I very well could? Could it not be our human and Christian duty, as well as one of enlightened self-interest, to develop the underdeveloped parts of the world, which is only possible when we do more work than is necessary to produce the volume of goods which we ourselves directly consume? Or can we still answer the question with a confident affirmative, if we ask for a universal five-day week on the grounds that even then we do not ourselves directly consume everything that we produce? And then there is another questionable element. Will all the people who live under an economy which has introduced the five-day week be content with the volume of national production limited in this way? Will the individual be contented with the share of the national product which has been allotted to him in view of his hours of work, or will all the individuals and so the people as a whole seek to increase the amount of goods by working outside official hours, because in fact they will only be contented by the amount of goods which can be produced by longer or the longest possible hours of work? In other words, will there not be a sort of 'black' work done in fact in the so-called leisure time? Will not these actual working hours bring down the value of the official working hours in the long run? Will not the monetary value of the official working hours tend to fall in the direction of the so-called minimum subsistence level? Is it really to be expected that men will in fact work shorter hours for a benefit in terms of money, when they are physically able to work more and this extra work is rewarded with economic benefits? One can doubt it, or at least that it will happen on a large scale. If it were to be realized on a large scale, two conditions would be necessary. Men must be able to earn so many material goods in their official hours of work that they already approximate closely to the upper limit of consumption and of material luxury that is physically possible. There are indeed cases where men renounce work which is physically possible, because even without this work they do acquire what they in fact want.[3]

---

[3] It must not be forgotten that for all practical purposes there was a five-day week in the middle ages. The Decretals of Gregory IX in 1234 already counted about 85 non-working days, including Sundays. From the thirteenth to the sixteenth century there were more than a hundred free days in some dioceses, not counting the holidays observed in particular places. Clearly, there was either no *wish* to increase the amount of economic goods by longer working hours, because people were content (on idealistic grounds) with the little that was produced. Or with the techniques, etc., then available, there was no *possibility* of increasing notably the volume of goods produced beyond the quantity which was in fact attained. Either or both of these factors together were responsible for the five-day week. But the example shows in any case, be it remarked in passing, that one must be cautious about saying that most people would not know what to do with so much free time. Even in times when it was harder to find things to do outside work, the five-day week was apparently found desirable.

Such people are not only found in Naples with its *dolce far niente*, but also under certain circumstances in America, where a less well-paid subordinate post is preferred to a very exacting executive post, though the latter is better paid because it is very strenuous. But one can doubt whether there are already many such cases or whether they will soon be very numerous. Most men feel that there is a very considerable difference between the amount of material goods that they would like to have and the amount they actually dispose of. The urge to do extra work will probably be felt for a very long time, where the possibility of such remunerative extra work exists. How and why should society suppress this possibility, when it limits the official working week to five days? If it cannot or will not do this, the five-day week will end up as the norm of the minimum wage for subsistence level. And the hobby of previous leisure hours will be transformed one way or the other into an economically useful supplementary job. Or—the second condition—men would have to be idealistic enough to use their leisure time to do things that are not economically profitable. They would have to be ascetical enough to abstain from economically rewarding work in their free time and devote themselves to values which, because they do not serve biological subsistence in any way, are not rewarded by money. But will very many men devote themselves to such values in the near future? Will very many men be capable of doing it in the near future, to an extent which will in fact occupy most of the longer leisure hours available to them? And if they were, or would be so in the future, could not all activities which did not immediately serve biological sustenance be left unpaid, even such as were rewarded before—poetry, art, science and so on? Could not such people be obliged to do economically useful work? After all, this would no longer take up so much time that they could not devote themselves to such higher values (in their leisure hours!)—in a society where other people were doing the like in their free time, also unpaid. We should then logically arrive at the communistic ideal, according to which everyone should perform real manual labour, that is, economically useful work, because in any case everyone has enough time for other things, and it is impossible to see why one should be paid for something for which another is not paid. Thus the problem of shorter working hours is not solved in terms of political economy by saying that the loss will be compensated for by more intensive work, by rationalization of methods of work and by more capital investment, by which the efficiency of work is improved. For the question remains as to whether men as a whole will be contented with the volume of production thus arrived at, even when they could increase the volume by possible extra work. And there is also the question as to whether more intensive work would not mean that the shorter working hours were only an apparent success, at least to some extent, in biological and human terms. Anyone who denies this, who maintains therefore that intensive work is biologically and humanly *easy* would have to explain why work which has become so easy needs to be shortened.

Thus the economic concept of work as paid activity leaves the theologian unclear about many things which he should know about the five-day week, if he is to judge this claim in the light of the eternal nature of man and of God's commandment.

2. A *medical* concept of work should be considered. In this sense, all activity which reduces the physiological capacity of man for action is work. The opposite notion, recreation, means all activity or interruption of activity which increases this physiological capacity for action. In this concept of work it does not matter whether an activity which represents work is economically useful or not, whether it is usually paid or not. Here then the question is whether the five-day week aims at lessening work understood in this sense, why it aims at this and whether it achieves this end. How problematic all this is, has really been pointed out already. We have already asked whether it is correct that such a reduction in working hours is medically necessary, on the grounds that it can be proved that the average job today is too strenuous and that the same amount of work as hitherto cannot be done without detriment to men's health. Is it correct that the too great strain imposed on present-day man by his work, supposing for the moment that it exists, would be relieved by a five-day week? Could not this objective be better attained by other means? By different methods of work, for instance, or by less broken-up periods of leave? Does the supposed strain imposed by present-day work really affect all the work which is to be shortened by the five-day week, or only certain classes of work? And if it only occurs in some, why are the same shorter hours claimed for all types of work? Or if modern man is really over-strained, does the supposed strain really ensue from the trade or profession he is paid for, and not in fact from other factors of modern life? Could it not come from the pace of life in general, the importunity of the amusement industries, the mismanagement of his life, the universal noisiness, the distance he has to travel to work, the disturbance of the

biological rhythm of his life by the inappropriate timing of his work (as in night work), a stronger feeling of insecurity and menace in his life, the loss of an absolute meaning for his existence? Would work be still found over-exacting medically if these other unfavourable factors of present-day life could be removed? And are not they the first things to be eliminated? If these harmful factors are not eliminated, as they cannot be for the moment, can they be compensated for by a reduction of working hours (which is not to be declared impossible without more ado, since such reciprocal compensation between favourable and harmful elements can very well exist in the biological sphere)? Or will shorter working hours really leave man all the more exposed to the harmful elements of modern civilization, since the working hours are perhaps the very time when he leads the most rational sort of existence from the biological point of view? Is there an optimum relationship between time and intensity of work and an optimum of production in a given time-unit which being of course different from each type of work, would have to be established separately in each case? Why is work now harder, as it is affirmed, than in earlier times? Is it perhaps that modern work makes more demands on the nerves and senses and is no longer so much a matter of mere muscle? Is the undue strain which present-day work is said to impose on the biological constitution of man fundamentally psycho-somatic in origin, that is, physiological in effect but psychic in cause, so that we should examine the personal attitude of man and modern society with regard to work, especially manual work? And if it were found to be so, at least in part, would the psychogenic damage to the biological factor in man be prevented by a mere shortening of the hours of work? Or should not other means be introduced to attain the desired effect, factors likewise psychogenic in nature? Another attitude to work? Other opportunities of success in work? Other possibilities of promotion? A different organization of leisure and not just its prolongation? A different social estimation of some types of work? A change in the environment? If the working hours are found to be so exhausting, why are so very few ready to purchase a reduction of working hours by taking less pay, though most workers avoid unhealthy work, even though it is better paid?

The medical concept of work poses questions which need to be answered by the other side, before the theologian can go beyond a few general principles and say something from his own point of view which may help with the problem of the five-day week.

3. The *anthropological*, human concept of work. This is harder to explain than the two previous concepts. There is still another aspect of work, which is not properly to be referred either to the economic usefulness of the product in terms of money or to the lessening of physiological capacity, and hence not to be referred either to the opposing concepts implicitly contained in these, unpaid activity and physiological recreation. We may approach the question this way. Let us prescind from the rhythm of the physiologically exacting effort of sustaining and protecting biological life and from the consequent interruption of this effort necessary for the recuperation of physiological strength. Is there still a sort of two-phase rhythm in human life, in a primordial, existential sense, to whose two components the words work and recreation could be ordained, and from which we could deduce the strict sense of the words, such as stems primordially from the nature of man? To understand this question, we must consider such notions as leisure, recreation,[4] play, liturgy, creative thinking, poetry and art and similar concepts. Such things cannot really be fitted smoothly into our earlier concepts of work linked with leisure and work linked with recuperation. Leisure can be physiologically very exacting, the actuation of human nature in play or liturgy can be very exhausting, and both can even be paid, at least in certain forms of society and political economy. We can even apply here the words of the Bible, that the labourer is worthy of his hire, though no one calls these acts of human self-realization work, or at least thinks of them as essentially characterized by their economic or physiological aspects, even though under these aspects they might be classified as work. But such activities cannot be essentially described as unpaid leisure or physiological recuperation simply because one is not ready to call them work. The decisive point in this context is as follows. What we call creative and recreational leisure (in our sense of time given up to 'the Muses') is only one side of the realization of human existence, which is opposed and complementary to another side, which we must designate in its primordial human sense as work. And here the notion of work too does not coincide with the meanings of the word we have met with previously. It points to that dimension of human nature where man, left to himself, is responsible for

[4] Leisure can mean 'free time for recreation' in the sense of recuperation of strength. In the following, it stands for free time given a meaningful content in the sense described in the text, including the time after 'work' which may give the feeling of relaxation. (Part of the original German note is concerned with distinction between two German words and is therefore not translated.—Tr.)

disposing of himself. The leisure of the Muse is free fall, the unplanned and unpredictable, confident surrender to the uncontrollable forces of existence, waiting for the irruption of the incalculable gift, the reception of grace, the aimless but meaningful hour. Man's existence must know such hours. But not only these. It must also contain plan and calculation, deed and performance, conquest and accomplishment, the effort to implement the project. Both must be there: leisure and—how else can we call it briefly and clearly?—work. But both mean primarily and primordially not two periods of time in human life, but simply moments in a man's self-realization which exist only in their relation with one another and are the primary constituents of human existence itself. Every human activity which involves the whole man in any way and to any degree is both work and leisure. It is freedom which is receptive, disposal which is disposed of, responsibility which surrenders itself, something done which is undergone, expression of the impression, action as reaction and vice versa. But since man's existence is truly temporal, since he attains his being in time, the dialectical moments of his plural, unified being explicitate themselves also in a temporal succession: each has its own proper and possibly distinct way of manifesting and exteriorizing itself. Hence, on the analogy of the receptive freedom which is its origin, we call the time when the Muse of leisure predominates in man's existence, free time or leisure, which when emptied of meaning appears as boredom in all its forms. And on the analogy of the self-determining freedom which is its origin, we call the time in which the working element of his nature and existence predominates, his work. Both are then primarily formal concepts, which have still to be filled out with their analogous content, because leisure and work can realize themselves, each in its own way, at all levels of human life and existence, provided that the whole man can really constitute and achieve himself on any such level, in any such region.

If the supra-temporal and transcendent reciprocal relationship between these two essential moments of man's being, leisure and work, is taken seriously, it is not surprising that leisure and work can and must be mingled in the most diverse ways and combinations in one and the same human activity. Sport, for instance, is a very peculiar mixture of leisure and work, when the whole man is active on the level of the physical.[5] In the dance and other similar forms of play, the element of leisure will

[5] Cf. H. Plessner, 'Die Funktion des Sports in der industriellen Gesellschaft', *Wissenschaft und Weltbild* 9 (1956) 262–274.

predominate on the same physical level. Pure science with no practical end in view can be predominantly work or leisure, according to whether positive plan and calculation or receptive inspiration is the major factor. These two primordial modes of human action, though they never appear separately, chemically pure, so to speak, manifest themselves differently in the successive stages of man's time. One period, as we have said, will appear predominantly as the time of unplanned, creative leisure, another as that of forward-looking, purposeful work. This distinction is valid not merely in the sphere of mental or indeed religious activity, nor is its application confined to the heroes of humanity. It holds good, with the necessary modifications, for all the acts of human existence, for the total experience of man, from his bodily activity to his religious act, though it is ultimately only possible—in spite of the analogy to human play seen in the animal's pleasure in the merely tentative exercise of its functions— because man is spirit, but precisely a spirit which can and must perform its bodily activities spiritually.[6] The possibility, however, that the element of leisure and the element of work may appear as either simultaneous or successive activities in human existence, is itself subject to the changes of history. According to man's historical situation, work and leisure will be more of a single act or appear as separate activities. And these historical differences can again vary widely. Some sort of recurrent rhythm of work and leisure always existed.[7] Play, pageantry, worship, etc. (as leisure activities) have always existed. But man's work, by virtue of its concrete nature, could of itself contain much that was in the nature of play and leisure, so that the need of setting apart separate times for the element of leisure was not felt as in the case of work more or less unadulterated. The

---

[6] K. Rahner, *Geist in Welt* (Munich [2]1957).

[7] Cf. J. Huizinga, *Homo ludens. Versuch einer Bestimmung des Spielelementes der Kulter* (Amsterdam 1939). G. Bally, *Vom Ursprung und den Grenzen der Freiheit. Eine Deutung des Spiels bei Mensch und Tier* (Basel 1945). H. Rahner, *Der spielende Mensch* (Einsiedeln 1952). D. Riesmann, 'Beobachtungen zum Wandel der Musse-gestaltung', *Perspektiven* 5 (1953). F. Klatt, *Die schöpferische Pause* (Vienna 1952). J. Pieper, *Musse und Kult* (Munich 1955); L. Rosenmayr, 'Die Freizeit in der modern-en Gesellschaft', *Wissenschaft und Weltbild* 8 (1955). M. Scheler, 'Arbeits- und Be-völkerungsprobleme' in *Schriften zur Soziologie und Weltanschauungslehre* II (Leipzig 1924). F. Giese. *Philosophie der Arbeit* (Halle 1932). Georges Friedmann, *Der Mensch in der mechanisierten Produktion* (Cologne 1952); *Die Zukunft der Arbeit* (Cologne 1953). V. Blücher, *Freizeit in der industrialisierten Gesellschaft* (Stuttgart 1956). J. Pieper, 'Arbeit, Freizeit, Musse' in *Weistum, Dichtung, Sakrament* (Munich 1954). H. Schelsky, *Die sozialen Folgen der Automatisierung* (Düsseldorf 1957).

collecting of fruits at a primitive stage of culture, hunting and even primitive war and primitive agriculture could contain so many elements of 'leisure' or could adopt them without interfering with 'work', that the desire and the need for separate times of leisurely activities could scarcely be felt. Work itself contained the unexpected and unplanned-for; it was always open to the novel intervention, it did not of itself prescribe a fixed rate of procedure. It could easily be adapted to men's moods, they could sing at it, talk to each other, sit more loosely to it by taking short rests or performing civic or religious rites and so on. Work has become essentially less leisurely today with the coming of technology. Not because it has become really more strenuous. To a great extent it is not more strenuous, at least if measured in terms of immediate changes in metabolism. But still, in the properly human sense of the word, it has to a great extent become mere 'work'. Its rhythm is imposed and directed by the physics of the machine, not by the psychology of man. To a great extent it is a fully planned work which allows of no surprises, which is carried out strictly according to rule. And since the rule is based on a far-reaching division of labour, it only claims very limited dimensions of man's existence, and it allows him an immediate experience of the full human meaning of his work—which is still there of course—only in a very restricted measure. (Mothers once knitted stockings for their children; a factory worker in America now makes stockings for strangers in Norway.) The disappearance of the leisure element from the mechanized and automated work of today makes it necessary that more time should be provided for leisure activities, whether or not modern work is physiologically very strenuous or leisure activity very refreshing. This then is the basic justification of the trend towards the shorter working week: the proportions of the elements of leisure and work in economically profitable work have been altered by mechanization. This does not deny that the shift is also medically disturbing and that shorter hours cannot also be claimed on these grounds. The imbalance of the human relationship between work and leisure brought about by the mechanization of work can be psychically disturbing and so be registered by somatic medicine also.

This analysis is not an attack on mechanization. But mechanization makes it necessary to organize a new equilibrium between the element of work and the element of leisure.[8]

[8] Cf. J. Bodamer, *Gesundheit und technische Welt* (Stuttgart 1955). F. Dessauer, *Streit um die Technik* (Frankfurt a. M. 1956). F. Pollock, *Automation* (Frankfurt 1956).

For, from the very start, these two moments of human activity were different. It was always necessary to aim at, and to restore continually, the proper balance of the two, both within the one activity and by means of a recurrent rhythm. And from what we have said it should also be clear that it is not just wrong, and something to be resisted at all times and in all circumstances, when after a five-day week people look for other work on Saturday. This work, even though it is economically productive and financially profitable to the worker, can still retain somehow the character of the voluntary, the hobby practised with pleasure, the improvised, the helping hand, the task that can be dropped at any time. And so it can very well fulfil the function of leisure in the life of the ordinary man, even though purely physiologically it may be to some extent strenuous. It can still be a time when man can find himself by means of his leisure, recollecting himself within his primordial freedom and in a confident surrender to the unforeseen.

II

The foregoing considerations have perhaps also provided us with a starting-point for the question of how the problem of the five-day week is to be seen in the perspective of human history as a whole, and what is its place in that history, which has itself too an intelligible rhythm. One could of course say that this problem is merely an element in the history of mankind once it has entered the mechanized age of the first and second industrial revolution—a problem that necessarily arises when mankind can use classic techniques, microphysical forces, automation and cybernetics to produce the necessary goods of the economy much more quickly than before. If the potential for a quicker production of such goods grows more quickly than the demand for these goods, even with an increase of population and higher standards of living, the time of activity allotted to these goods must necessarily be shortened and the time of work must be cut down. But there is more to it than this. Nothing has been said of the nature of technology, which has been introduced as the principle to explain everything in this answer. And it is not clear what this reduction in working hours means for man himself. Only the mechanism of the situation has been explained. And this only helps to explain the meaning of it for man, if we think that work is fundamentally something to be avoided as much as possible, so that every reduction of working hours is self-explanatory. We must therefore look further.

Man is a strange, paradoxical being. He is a spiritual subject which comes to itself in knowledge and freedom. It is not merely a function of a greater whole, one of the channels of a more comprehensive process. Man really acts and determines himself in an irreducible uniqueness: he is a doer and not just something done. And the self-same man forms a unity, which can never be completely resolved in reflexion, with a wider material and biological context, to which he belongs even with his subjectivity; and in this sense he is also a product of his environment, a function of a more comprehensive cosmic whole. He therefore possesses himself and at the same time belongs to others, he is free and yet only free within a limited field of prior possibilities, so that with regard to his resulting freedom it is impossible to say clearly and definitively what is a manifestation of his freedom as such and what is a consequence of the limiting factors in the field of his freedom. Man thinks and acts in terms of categories and in terms of transcendence at once, in an *a priori* synthesis which is always achieved but never fully analysable. His bodily nature is always determined to some degree by his spirit, and no spiritual activity can be found in him which is not also determined to some degree somatically. Being a free, personal spirit, he is never merely a function of society, and yet being a corporal being, he never has an individuality which is absolutely unrelated to society. He is always at home with himself, but he can never see himself except through the objectivations of his spirit: in the corporeal word, in the objectivated thought of his science and philosophy, in his artistic work. He is unique and irreplaceable, but can only find himself when he forgets himself in the love of another to whom he turns. One can try to eliminate the essential pluralism of man's one being either by reducing it to separate and contradictory elements, to the detriment of its unity; or one can treat the two moments as mere appearances of the one thing and try to reduce them to a material or spiritual monism. But then the great anthropological heresies arise, and man's misunderstood being is in immediate danger of self-destruction.

True as it is that this indestructible pluralism in man's one being is always essential to him and was always there wherever a man and not an animal existed, it is also true that this permanent and essential propriety of his being has and must have its history. For man is precisely the being whose acts do not merely proceed from his nature as a permanent invariable. Man is concerned with his own being as he knows and loves, he is dealing with himself: his own being is handed over to him. He cannot indeed really create or destroy, since he is a finite subject and hence finite freedom: he is a creature and in the act of eliminating himself he constitutes himself once more in his being. But that is why he is still dealing with himself, and the object of his free personal subjectivity is precisely this subject itself. And that is why these irreducible moments of his being which we have spoken of have their history in their mutual relationship. But since man throughout his history is spirit, and spirit becomes aware of itself, the history of these two moments is at least in part known and judged: it is a history wrought and reflected upon in freedom. The history of the finite spirit is thus the history of the subjectivity of man as it constantly becomes more aware of itself as its experience of being inexorably disposed of is constantly heightened. It is both: the growth of self-emancipating subjectivity, and the growth of the experience of man's being disposed of as a creature. For the greater his freedom (mental and physical) with regard to the objective world, the stronger can and should be his transcendental experience of his dependence on the absoluteness of God. And so too clearer reflexion on himself will become in like measure the experience of the bottomless and impenetrable strangeness of the subject itself—which is far from possessing itself fully and having itself completely at its own disposal, because it is strengthening its rule over things other than itself and emancipating itself from them. However, we cannot pursue here this aspect of the history in question. In our present context the other aspect is more important.

Man becomes more and more of a subject. He becomes more and more what he always was: he who disposes of himself and his world. He fulfils increasingly the word that stands at the beginning of Scripture, that he should subdue the earth, that is, everything he meets with as a free subject. As it presses in upon him and determines him, he gradually makes it the matter of his own active determination. In the course of history, man has taken his own bodily nature and his environment, and changed it from being a mere brute fact used as it was to sustain life, into material which he first moulds and then uses as he decides, so that his means of sustenance are the product of his subjectivity. In doing so, he remains of course not only dependent on God, being a constituted subjectivity in face of the absolute, but also on the existing world, being intrinsic to it and working on categories. But he modifies this dependence, in as much as his immediate environment is something which he has changed and made artificial in the positive sense of the term. And it is more and more true that even nature left in its natural state has been *deliberately* left so. It is essentially therefore just as artificial as the artefact which has been produced by the spiritual subjectivity of man. Now the aim of this transformation of the environment as it is pressed into service for the biological sustenance of life is not merely to maintain the subject in existence. It also aims, with increasingly more success, at relieving the subject of burdens: he needs to spend less and less of his subjective effort on the task of assuring his biological existence. The subject wishes to be the subject of its acts, that is, free. It is an intrinsic moment in the self-discovery of the subject that he should be freed from absorption in the sheer biological sustentation of existence. The reduction of the hours of work, in so far as work is understood only as an activity directed to sustaining life, is therefore an element of the growing subjectivity of man. For there are certain constants in his biological life—which is essentially less changeable than other elements in man, though it too is not an invariable—which condition and demand very precise means of sustenance and hence very precise activities. These are an element of man's bondage, from which his subjectivity gradually tries to free itself.

We can thus recognize that the shortening of the time of work is part of the history of man's self-discovery, in which the relationship between subjectivity and objective inclusion in a non-subjective whole is gradually and constantly being shifted in favour of the subject. But this does not answer the real question about the meaning of the reduction. For freedom is only explained when we know what man is set free for, what is the range and value of the possibilities opened up to man when he is released from the necessity of a given form of behaviour. The free space newly created cannot be filled up arbitrarily, since the arbitrary is irrational. If man were set free to live at his own sweet will, he would soon flee this freedom to return to a necessity which he finds understandable. And we do in fact see that when man is set free into a vacuum, so to speak, he does not know what to do with his freedom and escapes from it back into work again, as the one analgesic against empty boredom. And the economic utopianism of materialistic communism would be revealed as the illusory void which it is at the moment the longed-for freedom was achieved. No one would know how to use it. No one can, if he has decided that material things and economic goods are the only true reality. For then he cannot really wish that the material, biological and economic element should decrease to make way for an ever increasing measure of freedom, since that would be to want the real to yield to the unreal. The only reason why this is not yet apparent in communist systems is that there is still so much to be done in the line of political economy and because all the time available can be employed to serve the universal spread of communism and the orientation of the under-developed portions of mankind in this sense. The vacuum of its freedom has not yet been created. But what is the meaning of this freedom?

It can take two directions, as transpires from the nature of the process of emancipation itself. The possibility of working less while the need for economic goods for biological sustenance remains unchanged or even grows, is something that stems from the spirit. The spirit alone is inventive, it alone can create techniques, it alone can feel itself as a biologically defective being when compared to animals, and still as spirit master the world around it. But by creating techniques and so ridding itself of the necessity of working long hours for the sake of economic goods, the spirit is necessarily working for itself. It wishes to free itself, to 'come to itself', to act according to its real nature. This should not be taken to mean that the ideal of the spirit is abstract thought. Being human spirit, it is in its most primordial reality embodied spirit, which therefore realizes itself subjectively by creating objective, manifest cultural goods in time and space. But its object is to realize itself, which it does not, as such, in sustaining biological existence as such. But here too the spirit makes its contribution, because it is not just a being moved by instinct, which could afford to maintain biological life without spirit.

And biological sustenance itself is in the service of the personal spirit of man, since the spirit, living a biological life, can only realize itself with the help of biological elements. Since this is so, the personal spiritual element of man can also be activated in economically profitable work. Man as personal spirit does not first start to exist where tiresome, planned and economically profitable work leaves off—as Christianity always knew and emphasized against the low esteem for manual labour in antiquity and in liberalist circles. But the spirit only attains the proper heights and depths of its express self-realization in non-biological terms where it is no longer a mere means of sustaining biological life but where man exercises an activity which no longer has *any* immediate material usefulness. If man questioned the justifiability of all such acts and did his best to exclude them in favour of an exercise of the spirit ('technical intelligence') which was confined to technology and economics and avoided or tried to avoid anything 'useless', he would be denying that he was spirit and treating it as a mutation of the animal's instinct for biological self-preservation. The shortening of the time for economically profitable work is therefore the self-discovery of the spirit to fulfil itself in acts of no economic value. It is a moment of the emancipation of the spirit as it realizes itself as itself in a domain beyond that of economics and material things. This act of spiritual self-realization is still prior to the possible and justifiable distinction between (spiritual) work and leisure, which we have proposed above. For the spirit as such, and beyond the domain of the economically profitable, can realize itself purposefully and according to plan—in an activity which is not a leisure one, if you like. One could for instance work strenuously and methodically, according to an exact and purposeful plan, at excavating Hittite monuments. One would then be outside the domain of economic and biological tendencies, and therefore filling the free time gained by the reduction of working hours by that which gives sense to this emancipation. But one would still be 'working' in the sense of work as an activity distinct from leisure. If then we understand as 'spiritual work' a work of the spirit which has no economic ends, it may be affirmed that the real point of shorter hours is the spiritual work and the spiritual leisure of man; it is not really and primarily 'recreation' in the sense of recuperating biological and psychical strength; nor is it 'pleasure', even when this is understood merely as biological well-being, even in complicated and highly organized forms of the enjoyment of vitality. The leisure and working activities of man can of course take very different forms. It is far from being proved that what we now call science is the most essential form of the self-realization of the spirit. It is just as likely that it can take place outside the field of the 'speculative' in the modern sense. Love, fellowship, joy, the dance, music and art in general and many other things offer similar possibilities, for which man should be set free by a curtailment of working hours. Such spiritual activity in the line of work and of leisure can also of course take very different forms in various individuals, corresponding to their level of intelligence and culture—culture here being understood as human culture, not as intellectual learning. (Here begins the real problem of popular education, which is not solved by providing 'extension' or 'extra-mural' courses to popularize academic learning.) It is not within the scope of these considerations to develop and expound more precisely the content of such spiritual work and leisure (which may be successive or unified operations). We call attention in conclusion to one point only:

Spirit is essentially transcendent spirit, transcendence orientated to the mystery of absolute being. It is because it is transcendent in this way that it is spirit at all. If it emancipates itself by the provision of free time, it must also set itself free from the explicit development of the 'transcendental' as such. Otherwise it has not understood why and for what it has set itself free at all. But when the concrete transcendental is explicitated and articulated in knowledge and free decision—we have religion. And hence it must be affirmed—no matter how surprisingly pious and old-fashioned it may sound—that the liberation of man for his express spiritual existence as such is also liberation for a more intensive religious existence.[9] And here too we must affirm that whoever does not understand this, does not understand why and for what the spirit provides itself with free time apart from its time given to the service of biological sustentation and the production of material goods, and does not content itself with detaching itself from such service merely in the ultimate objectives of its action. One should not try to predict the future, because such prophecies are nearly always wrong. But without trying to foretell what men in fact will do, one may risk an assertion about what they are expected to do from the nature of things. It would be as follows. In earlier times it was taken for granted that men devoted to religious contemplation were allowed to share—by alms, foundations, etc.—in the benefits of the economy, even though they took little or no part in this production. In earlier times—and not only in Christianity—it was expected and considered right that the aged or certain classes should opt out of economic life to devote themselves to religious leisure. Under the new regimes of the future with their shorter hours of work, something of the sort can and must exist once more, under new forms and in greater measure. There should be men for whom society provides the possibility of a contemplative religious life, even though their contribution to the economy is slight. Why should this sort of thing be unthinkable except for scientific work and leisure, which is in fact now carried out with state backing without anyone's finding it objectionable? There is really no reason why a professor who is engaged on research into the latest species

[9] On the theology of work see: S. Weber, *Evangelium und Arbeit* (Freiburg 1921). P. Doncoeur, *L'Evangile du travail* (Paris 1940). M. D. Chenue, *Pour un théologie du travail* (Paris 1955). H. Rondet, *Die Theologie der Arbeit* (Würzburg 1956).

of ant should be subsidized by the state rather than a Carmelite nun who makes the adventure of mystical contemplation and love of God the content of her life. Here we may remark incidentally that this provides us with a starting-point for explaining why under certain circumstances the artist should be supported by the state, even if his creations would not gain him a living on the art market. In both cases —that of the contemplative religious and that of the artist—there remains the question, which we omit here, as to whether it is due and proper that the state itself should provide subsidies out of taxation or whether some other way of allowing them a share of the national income would be more fitting.

After this incidental remark, let us sum up the essential. Man as personal spirit strives by nature to free himself from the domination of the purely economic factors and biological self-preservation which is imposed by the constants of physical life. The time thus set free is a time for (spiritual) work and for leisure, both in their mutual co-penetration and unity and in the recurrent rhythm of successive periods in which the two possibilities of human, spiritual activity occur—an activity already freed from the search for the necessities of life. This activity—of a leisure and a working type—can be concerned with the categories of the human world: the provision and use of objective cultural goods and man's existence in the world in his encounters with his human environment. It can also be concerned with the transcendental—with religion and everything that is to be associated with it (metaphysics, art in so far as it bears on the ultimate mystery of being, etc.). It could happen that mankind achieves this emancipation much faster than the great majority of its members develop the capacity of filling this freedom with its true content. If one thinks of the under-developed regions and peoples, such misgivings are in themselves groundless. But the various portions of humanity develop at different speeds and it could happen that one portion gathers experiences for another—and should pay tuition fees. It may happen that mankind will in part create expedients, because it has not yet learnt how to use this freedom rationally. If one remembers that there have already been expedients which though fully non-productive in themselves were designed to conceal unemployment and to provide unemployment pay in an ostensibly satisfactory way, one will not find our supposition as absurd as it looks at first sight.

Such considerations show us what a fundamental problem it is, to disclose the sense of existence in such a way that man knows what to do when his growing mastery of the necessities of life makes it more and more possible for him to 'come to himself'. If in this self-discovery he finds things empty and meaningless he will take to flight. Either he will return to economically profitable work for its own sake (the flight of communism), or to keeping himself busy and merely distracted (the substitute with which the West makes do for the most part). How many sacrifices will it cost, how many false starts must be made, till man learns to 'do something with' the free time of freedom which he is beginning to win for himself, and for which the five-day week is only a symbol?

17

THE THEOLOGY OF POWER

THE 'theology of power' as the title of an essay can hardly mean anything except that we must try to consider the meaning which the concept of power takes on, when it is viewed in the light of the reality of God as known in Christian and Catholic teaching. Such a confrontation must be possible, if for no other reason than that we use the concept of power in the very first articles of the primitive Christian creed, when we call God the 'almighty'.

With this we have already mentioned something which is two-fold in its unity, and which brings us at once to the heart of the problem of human power. Power is clearly something which comes from God and testifies to him in the world, since a reality which we meet with in the world and which we call power is attributed to God himself, even though in a super-eminent sense. And at the same time, power is transferred into the region of those mysterious divine *powers* which are somehow reserved to God alone, can be understood only in terms of the godhead, and can never be autocratically and independently usurped. For we call God *the* mighty, the almighty he who alone is really mighty, and we remember that power ceases to be itself if it is fundamentally only partially powerful, half powerless and not able to claim to be alone all-powerful.

But before we proceed further, there are some preliminary remarks to be made about the ambiguity of the word power in our own experience in the world. The world and man are both multiple realities, each manifold in itself. For this reason alone power is not a univocal concept. To begin with, we understand power, very generally and vaguely, as a certain self-assertion and resistance proper to a given being and hence as its innate possibility of acting spontaneously, without the previous consent of another, to interfere with and change the actual constitution of that other. It follows at once that *all* beings, simply because they exist—in themselves and in contrast to others—inevitably have power in a certain sense and to a certain degree. And the nature of this power changes essentially according to the *specific nature* of the being in question, according to the *region* and dimension where there is this possibility of bringing about change, and according to the *means* used to bring about such a change in another or its ambit. Hence it is perfectly reasonable and correct to speak of the power of knowledge and of doctrine, of the faith, love, courage, prayer and so on. For each of these acts of man affect the situation of another previous to his giving his consent and change it at least in certain respects and to some degree—and so they exercise power. Indeed, the dimension amenable to such an act, and perhaps only accessible to such an act, can, under certain circumstances, be of a higher degree of being and of dignity than another. And then the act in question will be 'power' in a much sublimer sense and with much more real significance— within the degrees of analogy of the power of beings in general—than another possibility which can only act on a lower dimension of being and dignity in another man (or being). Hence the power of prayer, for instance, or of humility understood as the courage to do what is purely moral though apparently powerless, is on a higher degree of being, of a higher moral and ontological rank than for instance the power due to the possession of the atomic bomb—whether the so-called realist, who is only a short-sighted fool, admits it or not. This of course does not decide the question as to whether one could or should renounce the lower form of power, simply because he possesses the higher or acknowledges it.

When however in the following pages we speak of power, we mean, when treating of the proper subject of these considerations, only one very particular type of power, which is, so to speak, limited to a certain region. It is the power which could also be called *force*. It uses *physical* means— means which do not address themselves to the insight and freedom of the other—when it intervenes in the sphere of another, to act on it and change it without its previous consent. It is this type of power that we shall discuss. It presents us with the problem that is so oppressive today: that of physical force, which limits freedom, which disregards the decision of others to force facts into their existence—and for these reasons is often called brute force. We shall ask how it is to be judged in conscience, in the sight of God, what it really is and what it is for, whether it may exist or must exist, what are its limits, what are the dangers it brings with it, what are the ambiguities it entails. Let us insist once more: the power of which we *now* speak is not the only, the most noble or the mightiest force. Truth and love, acknowledged, affirmed and offered, are truly more real and nobler forces. They really do have of themselves the character of power— and not just because for instance they can be used and mis-used for ends concerned with the exercise of physical force. It could indeed be shown that those who are blind to this reality and efficacity of knowledge and love, who have no understanding of the genuine force of the offer of truth and love to the free will, who believe that this 'ideology' (as they will term it) is powerless against the physical and physiological, actually display themselves as worshippers of brute force and basically as hopelessly unrealistic men. But we cannot discuss *this* now, and we take up immediately the subject of the lowest form of power, physical force, as already defined, which often enough is popularly supposed to be the only form of power.

The *first* theological thesis which we must propose with regard to this type of power is the following. This sort of power ought never to have existed. In the actual order of salvation, as it is and as it was originally willed by God, it stems from sin. It is one of the forms in which guilt manifests itself. The justification of this statement, in the light of a Catholic and not merely Protestant understanding of man, can only be outlined here. Man of himself should be in a state of 'integrity'—free from concupiscence. What we mean is this. As we now know the constitution of man, he finds himself unable to integrate fully and clearly the whole reality of his existence, in all its dimensions, into the decision of his freedom. He experiences a dualism between what he wishes to be and what he really is. In his free decisions he never fully captures and masters himself. On the contrary, he is continually being affected by powers and forces from outside himself, which affect him *contrary* to his free decision and so make him 'suffer'. This experience of concupiscence and passibility is a form of manifestation of sin (though the expression 'manifestation of sin' is not to be confused with 'sin itself'). This is true also according to the Council of Trent, even though it attacks an interpretation given to concupiscence by the leaders of the Reformation, which describes this condition as being of itself not merely the consequence and manifestation of guilt but as itself sinful. It is only in such a condition of human existence, in the dimension of concupiscence and passibility, that physical force is meaningful and conceivable. It is merely an element of this condition, which Christianity considers the consequence of sin. In a world with the gift of 'integrity' freedom would absorb the whole being of man. There would be nothing that was not either a manifestation of this freedom or fully malleable for this freedom as its completely pliable and obedient material. In this world, where the free decision would hold good, an action upon another which by-passed his knowledge and his freedom and did not invoke them, would be a violation of this freedom as such, and hence irrational and immoral, and hence impossible: it would even cause the impassible to suffer. Of course, even in a paradisiacal order of things power would exist as a possibility of physical effectiveness, societies would be formed and hence there would be superiors and inferiors, direction and law. But all power would address itself to the free decision in an appeal to insight and love, and it *could* do so, because the decision would never be wanting. Hence it would not be physical force in the sense given above of the ability to intervene in the sphere of another, disregarding his will and the justice of such an intervention.

The consideration outlined above is not just a utopian denigration of power by a comparison with the unreal conditions of a paradise which no longer exists and which many will be tempted to see as merely the wishful thinking of man projected back into the past. The doctrine that concupiscence is the consequence of sin and the corresponding estimation and interpretation of power have a very important sense. For it follows that the Christian understanding of power is that though it will never be totally eliminated in this world, where there will always be sin and concupiscence, it is still something to be overcome, something that is or ought to be abolished and left behind (prescinding for the moment from the fact that in the general history of the world, according to the Christian theology of history, sin rather becomes more radical than harmless in the course of history). In the Christian view, concupiscence is not simply something permanently the same. It is not simply a constant which operates and dominates unchangeably as an existential in human existence. Stemming from a primordial historical event, it is itself a changing historical entity. It is gradually to be overcome, it is something to be fought against by means of spirit, love and grace. Though man's task is endless, though he fails at it again and again till victory is bestowed on him as grace in the coming of death and resurrection, man is a being who is to integrate his whole self more and more, including his material element, into the God-ward decision of his freedom under grace. This is true of the individual in the particular history of his life. It is also true of society in the general history of mankind. Any effort in this direction which succeeds even partially—insight, morals, public order, culture, humanism or whatever we may call it—is essentially an effort to suppress the use of physical force, to restrict the field in which it is justified. Anyone who thought that force was the surest and simplest way, who held it was the most real thing and basically the only reliable thing, who would make no attempt to abolish it and go beyond it, would be a secret heretic who had fallen away from the truth of Christianity, since he would refuse to admit that this force stems from sin and should therefore be conquered with it. Thus the concept of force is seen at once to contain a dangerous and ambiguous element. It is possible and even justified in a world of blindness and passion, where men are not free and not penetrated by divine truth: but it is only so, because it is itself also a manifestation and consequence of the sin to which it answers. It follows at once that if it is to be used at all (of which we shall speak later), it can only be *rightly* used by someone who is aware of its danger and ambiguity, who knows that it is in a way really using Beelzebub to drive out the demon, and that here the barrier to the sin of another can, by virtue of the origin of this type of power, only too easily and automatically become the concrete form of his own sinfulness. We shall have to say as we go on that this physical force is also a reality of God's creation, willed by him and not merely entrusted to man, but imposed as a duty on the representatives of God. But in any case, we may never forget the full truth about it to which Scripture and the Church testify. In the actual order of creation and salvation, force is the result of sin and hence its manifestation (though not necessarily sin itself), and a temptation to sin, just as much as sickness, non-integrated passion, death, error is not personally blameworthy. They are all real existentials in human existence, which are 'natural' indeed, but still should not be there, according to Christian doctrine. In spite of their being natural and apparently to be taken for granted, in spite of their seeming to derive merely from the bodily nature of man, they are powers which it is the duty of the Christian to overcome and which can be rendered totally impotent only by the gift of the eschatological grace of God. Hence if a Christian simply had no misgivings or reserves about force, he would be either foolishly naïve or he would betray himself as the guilty lover of this fallen world of sin. However, we can only say more about this matter when we have made our other assertion about power—an assertion without which we would not have the Catholic statement, which is the comprehensive one.

The second theological assertion is this: power, including physical force, is (although stemming from sin, manifesting it and tempting to it) is not itself sin but a gift of God, an expression of his power, an element of the reflexion of God in the world. We are speaking, be it noted, precisely of physical force here as well—of coercive force, the force of might which goes into action of its own accord, unasked, even against protest, which intervenes in the sphere of another to change it and at times (because it is basically the same thing) to restrict it—without having been filtered, as it were, through the free consent of the other. It is of this that we say—having to bear in mind of course the compatibility of this thesis with the first—that it is not sin but that it is of itself a gift bestowed by God and a charge imposed by God. It can of course be abused, it can of course do harm, such great harm indeed that God can only answer it with eternal damnation, since it is used sinfully and guiltily. But it has this in common with everything created, everything that is not God: that all is ambivalent, everything is subject to perversion and misuse, and hence too of course power. But just as creation as such is not sin, just as that which is not God is not sin by the very fact that it is not God, similarly it cannot be said of power that it is sin. Of itself it is good, good in the true but ambivalent sense in which something is good, which is not itself faith and love coming from the grace of God and hence not in itself capable of being perverted. But why should we affirm that power comes from God and is good, like the good things of creation which can be a gift and a charge from God, which can offer the possibility of serving him, and which it may even be our duty to use? To begin with, such power is one of the existentials of man's existence, which cannot be eliminated from the nature of man on earth. For the sphere which represents the sum of the given possibilities of the free self-realization of man is the place where freedom is exercised. And as the space of freedom, it is the *condition of possibility* of freedom. But it is a space shared in common by *many*. And hence this very exercise of freedom—being that of a creature, depending on pre-requisites, as the freedom of a material, inter-personal and communicative being—is at once a restriction of the space of another's freedom, essentially and inevitably. No one can act freely without impinging on the sphere of another's freedom without his previous consent— without doing 'violence' to him and using physical force, in a metaphysical but very real sense. The freedom of one, when exercised in the one sphere of existence and freedom which is common to all, is necessarily violence towards others. One need not always feel it to be so, and one does not feel it because one is accustomed to it. But that does not change the facts. The bodily nature of man and its supporting environment are always involved in his free decision, which is therefore a physical act. But he thereby impinges on the sphere of others, previous to their consent, because physical space is strictly common to all, and if there are any sections marked off in it, this is already due to free acts and mutual agreement. But such intervention in the sphere of others is the essence of physical force. Hence its exercise is unavoidable, and man could only renounce it totally and on principle by simply leaving this common space of freedom by death—and even the act of dying would again be an alteration of this space of existence and freedom which is common to others.

We can do no more here than pose the question, which our time does not allow us to answer properly: how then, in view of the transcendental necessity of force for the exercise of freedom, is a form of human existence at all thinkable in which things would be otherwise, since one's own freedom is exercised at the cost of the ambit of others' freedom? How is an order of existence without power and force at all conceivable, such as we started with in our first thesis—where it was the presupposition of the assertion that physical force is in the nature of a consequence, manifestation and temptation of sin? Whatever be the precise answer to this question (to which we shall return implicitly later), we must here repeat that this transcendental necessity of force, the condition of possibility of created freedom, is therefore to be described as natural and willed by God. It is not intrinsically sinful.

In other words, we have here the same truth in Catholic theology which is expressly stated in it with regard to suffering and death. We say that force would not have existed in the original, sinless order of things willed by God, and at the same time we declare that it is natural in itself, created by God. Natural does not of course here mean simply the same as the obvious and unquestionable. The natural which we are dealing with here can be problematical, dangerous and obscure, even calling forth protest and resistance from man. For man was really destined and remains destined to a higher form of existence, and as son of God, called to the freedom of the children of God, he is determined by the supernatural existential of the order of grace and must always long for an existence in an order of things where his self-determination from within in sheer freedom is all. Force is said to be 'natural' in this context because it is not in itself at once contradiction and sin against the will of the Creator, because it is only when measured against a higher reality and a transfigured existence that it seems that it should not be, and because, not being of itself sinful, it can have the ambivalence which enables it to be taken up and absorbed by a higher power, that of grace and faith, and so become a manifestation of this grace and faith and hence of salvation. It is imperative to understand this second thesis properly. When we say that power is in itself a good gift, a favour and hence a charge given by God, and that it remains so, even though it is only a 'natural' reality, qualitatively different from grace, justification and salvation, in faith and love: we do not thereby affirm that such a reality is an obviously intelligible one. Though it is accessible to reason in its nature and justification, and though it is inserted as part of the whole into the one, supernatural and comprehensive order of existence which alone is valid, it is not a reality which is totally perspicuous and without embarrassing difficulties. Though it is fundamentally intelligible 'in itself', the Christian and the non-Christian cannot in fact come to an understanding about this 'natural' reality, if the latter really shuts himself off from the light of faith and grace. For a reality, though it may be declared to remain the same, is in fact altered when it appears as part of a different general order of things. And on this comprehensive system of reference, within which alone the concrete nature of power can be adequately understood, the believer and the unbeliever (who is really and not merely supposedly so, even with regard to power) are not at one. The believer will regard this power as created by God, and hence as not immoral in itself. He will accept it and use it, almost as though it were a burden—as something which the Christian uses as though he did not use it, because it passes away with the figure of this world (1 Cor 7.31f.). He will likewise recognize it as something created by God as part of his way, and as a means to that supernatural self-communication of God in grace which is the one total goal of the spiritual creature and which must be striven after if even nature is to remain true to its being in the long run. All that needs to be said, therefore, is that what we naturally recognize as an unavoidable necessity in the living of human existence is regarded in Christian and Catholic theology as created by God and of itself not sinful. It is therefore something permissible, and indeed imperative, in the life of the justified. And this thesis is not excluded by our first. For in Catholic theology, something can be natural and created by God, even though non-activated in the higher order of man's original state of innocence, because its activities and functions were suspended and surpassed by the higher grace of integrity—and hence even though when it appears in our fallen state it is likewise a manifestation of the general, inherited situation of guilt.

Having established this theologically, we can proceed to evaluate power as a reality of experience, in the light of natural reason. Nor need we now fear that such considerations may arouse misgivings, as if they could turn out to be a presumptuous self-interpretation of man and his possible modes of existence, which under certain circumstances could not survive the judgment of God in revelation and faith, but would have to be rejected as the ratification and self-justification of man in an absolute, salvific sense. Power *exists*. And it rightly exists, because it is the condition of possibility of freedom. Power and freedom are mutually and dialectically interdependent. Freedom is of itself the higher, because it is characteristic of the spirit. Physical power is in itself the lower, because it is, even though inevitably, in itself a material thing and hence narrows the range of freedom. The rights of freedom, which as such, in their *formal* essence, demand that force be absent, and the rights of power are rights which exist together. They are not of the same rank, and hence when they clash, they are to be judged and applied according to their rank. But their diversity cannot be reduced to a single higher principle within human existence, any more than the ontic dualism in man whence they spring, the dualism of spirit and matter, of freedom and bondage to the necessary pre-requisites of this freedom, of individuality and the social reality of man which is rooted in the material. Just as this ontic pluralism is permanent and must always be taken into account, so too the pluralism of these two principles. They have an order of rank, but neither can really be deduced from the other—even though their transcendental unity is founded on the unity of man's being. They cannot be *objectively* 'absorbed' into a higher principle, of which they would be the application. The principle of the absolute renunciation of force would not therefore be a Christian principle. It would be a heresy which misunderstood the nature of man, his sinfulness and his existence as the interplay of persons in the *one* space of material being. An order of freedom would be misunderstood, if it were taken to be an order of things in which force was considered reprehensible on principle. A fundamental and universal renunciation of physical force of all kinds is not merely impracticable. It is also immoral, because it would mean renouncing the exercise of human freedom, which takes place in the material realm, and hence it would mean the self-destruction of the subject who is responsible to God. One cannot make it a principle to avoid the use of power and force, in order to preserve oneself from sin, on the grounds that they are essentially a defilement and inexorably and always lead to sin. The real question in a moral theology of freedom is this: in what way, and in what proportions in each concrete case, and with what perpetually revised safeguards, can the right of legitimate power to alter and restrict the freedom of the individual (and of his free fellowship) be reconciled with the higher right of freedom, and with the right of the individual to a real, concrete and permanent sphere of freedom? Since the sphere of individual freedom is a variable quantity, and since the tasks of the legitimate authorities, for the sake of which they hold power, are themselves subject to historical change, this reconciliation is not something that can be fixed and firm once and for all: it must be constantly searched for anew. And hence comes, at least in the worldly sphere, the inevitability of a struggle for power. In the order of things in which we live, there is a genuine and *materially* irreducible pluralism of representatives and rights—rights, that is of both the upholders of freedom and of the holders of power. These representatives have not merely the right, but at times even the moral duty, of insisting on their respective rights. But it is not to be expected, given the fallibility of man, that both parties will agree in theory on the definition of their rights, even though there is no subjective fault on either side. Thus a state of tension between both parties cannot always be avoided. There will be no objective norms, formal or material, and no higher personal instance with superior power (and right) to decide, which could avoid or exclude at once the cases of conflict which are at least subjectively present and cannot be solved on a theoretical basis. Christian morality, convinced of the incorrigible fallibility of man, recognizes that conflict cannot always and on principle be avoided. There will be cases where might decides the issue with (at least formal) moral right, because force is used by the holders of power, in good faith at least, for a morally justifiable end—even though the moral justification of the end is contested by others. There are therefore real cases, where the concrete right lies subjectively and in practice on the side of the stronger might—where, to put it the other way round, subjectively and in practice the stronger might is also right. This does not mean that it always does what is objectively right, or that it is not obliged to aim at the objective moral good in its goal—in so far at least as the wielder of power can grasp subjectively the objective rightness or wrongness of his goal and can fulfil his duty of being objectively informed before setting his subjective sights. But might can be right at times, in the sense that a ruler can have the right to use force to attain an end which to the best of his knowledge is objectively right—even if those who suffer from this use of force deny that the goal is good and hence hold that the use of force is immoral. Power, which on principle always had to wait on the consent of those affected by it, would not be power at all. An order of society which demanded such consent on principle would be a utopian caricature of democracy, an anarchy where might would be much more aggressively brutal; and such a society has never in fact existed.

When we affirm that in actual life conflict and struggle are not always avoidable, we have not of course decided in any way what forms of resistance are morally permissible in a given historical situation. Nor have we indicated what forms of force are immoral, even when used by the stronger party in a legitimate struggle for a goal held subjectively at least to be justifiable and desirable, though contested by others. Some forms of force may be disproportionate to the justifiable end in view. In this fallen and sinful world the use of force should be held back, restricted and humanized as much as possible. But there will always be a struggle, which will always be denounced as unjust and brutal by one side, because it is rooted in the nature of the present constitution of man's existence, since it is only by putting forth his strength that man is free and erring. To recognize this fact is not to give free rein to the brutality and moral irresponsibility of power and its wielders. On the contrary, if this situation is envisaged with the relentless realism of Christianity—from which all utopianism shies away—there is more hope that the immoral use of force can be less easily disguised under a pretence of moral justification. It is true here as elsewhere that the lie, which surely exists, never has more chances and more appeal than where people act as if it did not exist. The intransigent pacifist is a greater threat to peace than those who reckon with the existence of force and its inevitable exercise, and therefore treat it as something real and indestructible, something that can be only *asymptotically* moral, but hold that it is governed by the moral law and conjures up the danger of mortal guilt. I say only *asymptotically* moral for as long as men can err, even with the best will in the world, as long as there is no universal court of appeal in the world which can guarantee in all cases the objective justice of the end pursued by force, there will always be, even apart from the use of force for subjectively wrong ends, instances of force being used in good faith for objectively immoral ends. And thus even men acting in good faith will be acting objectively immorally. We must further consider that as human existence becomes more complicated in the course of its history, all human relationships will become more manifold, less perspicuous and at the same time, of greater consequence. The possibility of error, and at the same time, the necessity of far-reaching exercise of force will be greater. It is then possible to think that the asymptotic approximation of the use of force (even that which is subjectively good) to that which is also objectively just will probably not become closer, but rather inevitably less. And this in spite of the fact that historical 'evolution' always means the creation of objectivated moral ideals which did not exist previously in the affliction of man. All that has been said can really be found in the simple truth that might is a real, characteristic and natural creation of God. Since it is a creation of *God's*, it is not at once simply sinful and anti-god. Because it is a *characteristic* creation of God's, it cannot be suppressed while this world lasts, it cannot be eliminated. At most, it can change its forms and manifestations in a long process—a process in which might again has a history, since it enforces this process of change. Because it is a *natural* creation, it can be used for good ends and can be perverted to serve sinful ones.

Thus we can arrive at a third theological thesis on power. In the actual order of things, its exercise—at least on the whole—is not irrelevant to salvation: it is a process either of *salvation* or *perdition*. This is true in a very radical sense. Some preliminary remarks are necessary, before we explain the meaning of this thesis. We assume—even in this thesis—as absolutely unquestionable that might is to be regulated by the norms of the natural law, since it is part of the natural creation. We also assume that this natural law can of itself be known by man's natural reason, without recourse to the strict word of revelation in Christianity. Hence it should be possible to reach agreement about these norms even with those who do not take their stand on Christian revelation—without prejudice to the reserve which we have made with regard to the practical difficulties of sinful man in knowing the exact norms of natural morality without the help of revelation. Further, we prescind from the question controverted in Catholic theology, as to whether in the actual order of salvation there are in fact human acts which are merely in accordance with the natural moral law, without therefore being new sins, and also without implying at once strictly supernatural salutary acts of grace and faith. Let us simply suppose here—though it does not favour our subsequent considerations—that such purely natural good acts can and do exist, that they do not stem from grace and faith and are not therefore salutary acts but are done by men who keep the natural law of their being, in human freedom, by virtue of their natural moral insight. But even in this hypothesis we must note that according to Catholic theology, divine revelation and also the grace of Christ are morally necessary, if mankind as a whole is to have clear and certain knowledge of the natural moral law, without admixture of error, with regard to practical moral norms and not just with regard to the most general principles of morality. According to Catholic doctrine it is impossible to fulfil for long the natural moral law as a concrete whole, without the help of divine grace. This special divine help, without which the substance of the natural moral law cannot be kept *for long*, may be safely called grace of Christ, so that its acceptance—a point that we cannot now go into—also implies love. The act of fulfilling the natural law which is performed with such help must also be regarded as a salutary act strictly speaking. It represents an event in the actual Christian order of salvation. To avoid misunderstanding, we add that this affirmation can leave it a perfectly open question, as to whether this grace of Christ must be and is known consciously by man *as* such *grace*. The statement in question remains true even if we suppose that the grace of God in Christ often does its humanizing and salutary work of giving a supernatural finality to human action, even where man is not consciously aware of it in any objectivated and articulate way—where there is in fact a Christianity which remains as it were anonymous. But even with this reserve, it may be safely said in theology that the whole of the free action of man, in its substance, in its real and radical decisions and in the long run, is either a salutary act inspired by faith, or sin, even where it seems to be only a matter of natural morality. Let us assume this truth and apply it to the use of force.

Power is not *just any* element in human life. It is (taking the word in a broader sense than we do elsewhere, but still letting it include our narrower sense), along with sexuality, indeed even more than this, perhaps one of the most fundamental forces in our existence. And it is not just something of limited and localized importance in human life: it pervades the whole, it is not merely something which occurs from time to time. And for both reasons it is one of the acts, in a very special way, which man cannot properly perform in the present order of sin and of Christ, without the holy and elevating grace of Christ, without faith and love. It is one of the acts in which salvation or damnation is decisively achieved. This may all seem for the moment a rather abstract and formal deduction. But if we look even a little more closely at the matter in question, it is easy to see the gist of these abstract theological affirmations. What happens when might is exercised? Something concrete and individual is given reality, without the consent previous of another person, in the sphere of his being. But such a thing is essentially very terrifying. For the concrete, in spite of our meeting with it every day, is always both a marvel and a terror when it is brought about by us ourselves. It did not exist, and it cannot be reduced totally, in its concrete and imprescriptible individuality to necessary principles, to a perspicuous necessity. It does not exist of necessity, it need not have been. But once it is there, it can no longer be really cancelled, since the single process of historical events is irreversible. It is one of the beings that are, though it does not contain in itself the cause of its existence, which it derives only from the force exerted by the free agent. And this entity which asserts itself so obscurely, brought about by a free act of power, is now inserted into the existence of *another* where it expands, changes the whole sphere of his existence, imposes on him unasked-for laws of action and decision, unintelligible because (ultimately) with regard to their nature and their being rather than not being, there is no key to them except the will of the other—who is a stranger. The free agent who uses force spreads himself so to speak beyond himself, and there are really no limits to this expansion, because it takes place in the wholly universal and common and unlimited medium of the material principle. Everything that takes place here has an immense chain-reaction as its consequence, even if in the unity of general history the effects of one particular cause cannot be distinguished from those of others. May one do this sort of thing? Can man find it justification and consolation enough in this concrete decision, if he is told that he cannot do otherwise, that he is still affecting the destiny of others even if he refrains from acting, to avoid sharing responsibility and perhaps guilt? Is not something done here, which strictly belongs to God: to determine the field of freedom before it has given its verdict? There is this also for us to bear in mind as Christians. All freedom has an eternal validity and an eternal destiny. In this eternal result, all freedom, in spite of the initiative allowed it in Christian doctrine (contrary to many views such as are expressed for instance in the 'Jedermann' of Hofmannsthal) also receives its determination from the matter and the field upon which the free act works: these are not finally eliminated as the unimportant material which freedom took up incidentally and let drop again. It is therefore clear that power acts in combination with this eternal freedom and contributes to the eternal result of the freedom of another. He is for ever not just such as he willed to be, but also such as he became through me, the other. May one do such a thing? What an enormous task is imposed on man, simply by the fact that he has power to act on the freedom of man! What a temptation that must be! From the Christian point of view it is not enough to say, as an abstract idealism usually does, that even in chains man is still free. That may be true in a certain sense. But in chains one cannot do precisely *the* definitive free act which one would otherwise have done: under the brain-washing and the incalculable influence of propaganda, of the imperious spirit of the age, and all other forces, one cannot, even if one remains free, do precisely what one would have done if the field of freedom were wider and different. And the free acts done under such conditions are not merely sloughed off by the agent, because he remained free or because in his freedom he could not act otherwise. It is precisely because he acts as a free agent, because he was not simply not responsible for his acts, that he absorbs into himself these presuppositions of his freedom which another has brought about, and for this very reason the free person is marked for ever with the traits imposed on him by force. Under these conditions, what should have happened is clear. The wielder of power should have canvassed those who were at its mercy, he should have done his best for his part to eliminate the results of his power on others, he should have tried to replace them more and more by the inner law from which the other is approached. He should have considered his power a challenge to himself, to be overcome by the higher power of love, of knowledge, of the good and rational embodied in himself. It is only under these conditions that he can really dare to impose on others, as their eternal destiny (or a component of it), a contingent and accidental concrete element which the free use of his power has brought into being and inserted unasked as something definitive into the sphere of another's existence. It is only when he feels his power as something provisional, as a charge imposed on the mighty themselves, as the bitterness and humiliation of his reverence and love for the mystery of the *individuum ineffabile* in the person of the other, that he can use his power aright. But who can claim that he does so? Who can deny that he is a sinner? Who can maintain that in practice the mightier is always the wiser and the more loving? Who can maintain that what is well-meant is also good, simply because the intention is good (and who can be sure of this?). The exercise of power is thus only too often sinful, subjectively and objectively. It is used in order to rule, and not because one wishes to serve; it is used as a means of self-assertion and not as the sword of God with which one is entrusted. Rulers deceive themselves and believe that they are in the right because they are in power; they claim they have the better arguments because they have reduced the others to silence. They are tempted to claim their rights by force, where justice itself would have enforced their claims, if they themselves were more just: but it is simpler and easier the other way. They are tempted to look on the *de facto* possession of power as at once the divine legitimation of it, as though it were true that God was always on the side of the big battalions. One is tempted to regard the mighty as the sole repositories of truth and the genuine reality and its future, and finally as the viceroys of God, while those who have lost power are thought to have been deprived of the one way of making history—whereas in fact they are empowered and charged to prove that men believe in the superior power of truth and love, even where they seem to perish, conquered perhaps by might. Power is something to be gradually modified and absorbed by love, like concupiscence and all its consequences. It should be used to bring about its own abrogation, though this is only absolutely possible eschatologically. It should be the agent of its own elimination—which is possible in itself, since it is God's creation and not of itself sin, which alone cannot have in itself the power to conquer itself. But it becomes something that tries to maintain itself definitively, and the mighty becomes someone who tries to remain what he is, who refuses to recognize that it is only by overcoming himself perpetually that he can legitimate what he now is—and may 'still' remain, if he constantly conquers himself to make room for the coming of the pure and blessed freedom of all. Power becomes sin. And it can demonstrate better than anything else what is the true nature of sin: the desire to be like God, the 'no' to service, the installation of self-will and the finite as the absolute, power for power's sake, which is sin.

But this same power, which can be temptation to sin and embodiment of sin, and inevitably is so if it is not redeemed by real faith and true love, can also be a manifestation and a concrete embodiment of true salvation, something not merely neutral but truly Christian and salutary. Not merely in the sense that something done with the right attitude and intention can be called good by reason of this inner attitude. The exercise of power can have a closer relationship to Christian existence. For power can be used, so to speak, not *because* 'I' have it but *although* I have it. It can be used by him who wields it as something imposed upon him. It can be humiliating and exigent from the start. For wherever it is exercised, its consequences remain unforeseeable. To be effective it always needs powers and forces, instruments and helpers, which must have their own proper structure and nature if they are to be of use. And the more they are used, the more radically they are put to work, the more fully they follow their own laws and thwart the plans of the mighty that use them. The more the ruler goes out of himself to intervene in the world of others, the more he must entrust himself to entities which even if they are only his material, oppose to him their own proper and ultimately indestructible being: he must entrust himself to relationships which he cannot ultimately supervise. Never did the might of the mighty bring them solely and clearly what they *planned*. The leader was always the follower as well, and his mightiest and best-planned deed was at the same time also the most unforeseen, which recoiled upon the doer and became his undreamt-of destiny. The proud and foolish do not recognize the intrinsic limitations of their power, they do not note perhaps its inner self-destruction or they learn to know it only too late, when they meet it as the damnation which guilty power prepares for itself. But the wise man knows the intrinsic weakness of its might, he accepts it as it is given, he does not really grasp it himself because he knows that whoever seizes it roughly must be deceived and blinded by power. For then it makes men blind, because men drunk with power can no longer see what reality really is. And the reality which has been ignored takes a terrible revenge: it cannot be totally mastered by power, because power itself, to be mighty, needs servants which it cannot itself replace: men, truth, loyalty, kindness, the quiet humility of the laws of sub-human reality, etc. These servants of power can be misled and misused by it, but only really in that narrow marginal region where they themselves still retain their own nature when they oppose themselves to power. This marginal region is very limited and does not last very long, even though all the cruelty of human history finds room in it. He who is wise and loving knows this well. He does not fly from power if it puts itself in his hand, he may even try to seize it if he sees it is being misused by others and if he feels truly creative force stirring within him. But he knows the tragic nature of power, its limitations and shortsightedness. It cannot long remain the same, because even the exercise of power for its own sake must set itself a goal, or at least must pretend to have one which has value and dignity in its own right. And hence sooner or later, this lie must be taken seriously, the goal attains a validity of its own and deprives the mighty of his power or even transforms him.

Further, the man loving and wise who is also powerful, is always struck and humbled by the dignity of the free men with regard to whom he exercises his power. In face of the others, he is like the surgeon faced with the patient who is seemingly at his mercy, but who has more power over the surgeon than he over the sick man, even if he uses his knife unasked and with the severity of genuine love. He exercises his power conscious that what he does remains subject to the dialectic of history, never fully succeeds, is always somewhat thwarted, and is always intrinsically part of that life which bears death within itself and wills to bring it forth as the fruit of life, without which all life remains barren. Only he who uses power in this way redeems it and sanctifies it. Only he who strips it of its power, by accepting the weakness of the cross, futility and death as salvation: only he who is ready to fail, even when he fights bravely, confidently and remorselessly, struggling even for power—he alone does not sin when he exercises power. For to use it without faith is to misuse it. It may not be said, nor can it be proved, that such misuse is present at every moment of such use of power. But power only exists when it takes in a life and a *period* and takes solid form. And here the statement is true. But faith—as it applies to our question—means acceptance of death and futility as grace, promise and eternal life. And the opposite is also true: the exercise of power can be such faith. Not simply and not even principally because the world belongs to God the Father almighty, because it should be in his service with all its parts, because power too is created by him and can serve him. Such a theology, based only on the order of creation and the natural law, would in fact be blind to sin and would not have passed through the mystery of the death of Christ. It would not be a *theologia crucis* and hence would not be truly Christian. Such an exercise of power, transformed by faith in salvation out of the depths of futility, is therefore not hesitant, half-hearted or cowardly. On the contrary, it is free even in face of death and hence it can dare all for which it can be responsible to God. It can defy superior force, because it still accepts even ruin as victory.

There are very many nuances in the Christian understanding of power. It cannot simply refuse to recognize power, because it is a creation of God. But its attitude to it cannot simply be positive without more ado, because as it now is, it exists only in the fallen world of sin and darkness, as it did not exist in the beginning and as it will not be at the end. Thus this might itself has the character of endurance, impermanence, decay and transition which Christianity attributes to this aeon—where we live on the understanding that it has already been ended by the coming and eternal aeon of Christ. The Christian cannot simply accept power naïvely as merely an obvious existential of human existence. For it exists *either* as the embodiment of sin, egoism, rebellion against God and the worldly impatience of unbelief, which refuses to accept the promised glory simply as eschatological gift of the power of God, but uses its own might—and hence inevitably brutality and cruelty—to try to force that glory down into this aeon itself and bring it under its laws; *or* it exists as the effort of faith which knows that power is always unreliable and unrewarding, but accepts it obediently as a task from God, as long as he wills.

INDEX OF PERSONS

INDEX OF SUBJECTS